S0-DVC-829

Development economics

Modern economics
Series editor: David W. Pearce

Economics of the labour market D Bosworth and P Dawkins

Basic econometrics M S Common

Theory of the firm M A Crew

Monetary economics G Dennis

Development economics S Ghatak

The political economy of Marx M Howard and J King

Welfare economics P Jackson and D T Ulph

Social economics K Lee and P Mackie

The economics of public transport C A Nash

Environmental economics D W Pearce

Microeconomics R Rees and H Gravelle

Macroeconomics A J Westaway and T G Weyman-Jones

Mathematical economics J E Woods

Development economics

Subrata Ghatak

Longman
LONDON and NEW YORK

Longman Group Limited London

Associated companies, branches and representatives throughout the world

Published in the United States of America by Longman Inc., New York

First Published 1978

British Library Cataloguing in Publication Data

Ghatak, Subrata
Development economics. – (Modern economics).
1. Underdeveloped areas – Economic conditions
I. Title II. Series
330.9'172'4 HC59.7 78.40119

ISBN 0-582-44873-5
ISBN 0-582-44874-3 Pbk

Printed in Great Britain by Richard Clay (Chaucer Press) Ltd, Bungay, Suffolk

Contents

Preface ix

Acknowledgements xi

1. Introduction 1
- 1.1 Introduction 1
- 1.2 Characteristics of the LDCs 1
- 1.3 Types of markets in LDCs 9
- 1.4 Production conditions in LDCs 9
- 1.5 Growth and development 12
- 1.6 Economic theory and the LDCs 14
- Appendix: measurement of income inequality 14

2. Growth theories and their relevance to LDCs 17
- 2.1 Introduction 17
- 2.2 Classical scenario 17
- 2.3 The Keynesian theory and LDCs 19
- 2.4 The Harrod–Domar model and its applications 22
- 2.5 The Neo-classical theory and LDCs 24
- 2.6 Marx's theory and LDCs 28
- 2.7 The Kaldor–Mirrlees model 34
- 2.8 The Polak–Boissonneult (PB) model 37

3. Dual-economy models 40
- 3.1 Introduction 40
- 3.2 The 'surplus' of labour and its contribution to development 40
- 3.3 The Fei–Ranis (FR) model 44
- 3.4 The Jorgenson model 49

3.5 Some extensions of the dual-economy models: Dixit–Marglin model 52
3.6 The Kelly *et al.* model 52
3.7 Dual-economy models: a critique 53
Appendix 56

4. Allocation of resources: investment criteria 58
4.1 The need for investment criteria in LDCs 58
4.2 The capital-turnover criterion 59
4.3 The social-marginal productivity criterion 60
4.4 The maximization of the rate of creation of investible surplus (MRIS) principle 61
4.5 The reinvestible surplus (RS) criterion 62
4.6 Balanced and unbalanced growth 69
Appendix: the dichotomy between savings and output maximization and its solution 73

5. Domestic resources for development 75
5.1 Introduction 75
5.2 The nature of money markets in LDCs 75
5.3 Money and economic growth 76
5.4 Inflation and economic growth 78
5.5 Objectives of fiscal policy in the LDCs 84
5.6 Fiscal policy and growth 84
5.7 Deficit financing and the LDCs 89
5.8 The tax structure in the LDCs 90

6. Sectoral allocation of resources: agriculture 97
6.1 Introduction 97
6.2 The role of agriculture in economic development 97
6.3 The concept of 'marketed surplus' 99
6.4 The model to mobilise agricultural surplus 103
6.5 Acreage response to prices 107
6.6 Marketed surplus, size-holdings and output 107
6.7 Limitations of price policy and some alternatives 114
6.8 Conclusions 115

7. Development planning 116
7.1 Concept of economic planning 116
7.2 Types of planning 116
7.3 Economic models and economic planning 117
7.4 The case for and against planning 118
7.5 Development planning models 119

7.6 Application of the Harrod–Domar model in development planning: India's first five year plan 121
7.7 A two-sector HD model for planning: the Kenyan case 122
7.8 The Feldman–Mahalanobis (FM) sectoral planning and the Indian second five year plan 123
7.9 Macro-econometric models in development planning 125
7.10 Input–output (IO) analysis in development planning 128
7.11 Linear programming (LP) and development planning 132
7.12 Micro-planning: aims of cost-benefit analysis (CBA) 137
7.13 The Little and Mirrlees (LM) method of project evaluation in LDCs 142
7.14 The United Nations Industrial Development Organization (UNIDO) 1972 guidelines 146

8. Industrialization, protection and trade policies 150
8.1 Major reasons for industrialization in LDCs 150
8.2 The role of tariffs in economic development 151
8.3 The optimum tariff argument 151
8.4 The infant industry argument 154
8.5 Distortions in the factor markets 157
8.6 The balance of payments argument 158
8.7 The employment argument 158
8.8 'Nominal' and 'effective' rates of protection 159
8.9 The cost of protection 165
8.10 Economic growth and trade 168
8.11 Terms of trade between developed countries and LDCs 169
8.12 Export instability and economic growth in LDCs 171
8.13 The role of the United Nations Conference on Trade and Development (UNCTAD) and some trade policies to help the LDCs 173
8.14 Non-tariff barriers, generalized system of preferences (GSP) and trading blocks 176
8.15 Regional cooperation among LDCs 176
8.16 Conclusion 177
Appendix: indices of instability of exports 178

9. Foreign resources and economic development 181
9.1 Introduction 181
9.2 The concept of foreign resources (FR) 181
9.3 Criteria for distributing FR 182
9.4 Different types of FR: tied and untied; bilateral (BL) and multilateral (ML); project and programme 186
9.5 Foreign resources for projects or plans 187
9.6 Bilateral (BL) and multilateral (ML) financing 188

9.7 Dual-gap analysis and its evaluation 189
9.8 Private foreign investment and the transfer of technology (TOT) to LDCs 194
9.9 Special drawing rights (SDRs) and the 'link' 201

10. Population, poverty and income distribution, employment and migration 209
10.1 Population and economic development 209
10.2 Population explosion in the LDCs and the theory of demographic transition 211
10.3 Low-level equilibrium trap 212
10.4 Fertility and population growth in the LDCs 213
10.5 Poverty and income distribution 220
10.6 Income inequality 221
10.7 Absolute poverty 226
10.8 Redistribution with growth 228
10.9 The employment problem 230
10.10 The Todaro model 235
10.11 Employment policy
Appendix: the definition of a poverty line 237

References 240

Index 263

Preface

The economic development of the less developed countries (LDCs) presents many important and interesting problems to students and teachers of economics. These problems are many in number and diverse in nature; it is hoped that this book will provide an analytical framework to deal with some of these major problems. It is generally known that many issues related to the economic development of the LDCs are not purely economic. Political, social and cultural factors work alongside the economic factors when the economies of the LDCs go through a process of growth and structural change. However, the problems which are dealt with in this book are mainly economic and further reference has been made in some cases to broader and very diverse institutional issues which a "kindred spirit" may wish (rather hopefully) to explore. This explains the reason for adopting a framework of analytical economics for the discussion of most issues raised in this book.

Although some useful books on development economics are available at present, one major reason for writing this book is to strike a greater balance between the theory and the practice. Thus, whenever possible, the existing theories on growth and development are evaluated in terms of the economic realities of the LDCs. The other important aspect of this book is that an attempt has been made to quantify the available evidence with the use of basic statistical tools like regression analysis. Next, given the importance which is usually attached to planning in the LDCs, a comprehensive chapter on both *macro-* and *micro-planning* with special reference to the application of cost-benefit analysis to project appraisal has been added. The role of agriculture with special reference to the supply response of farmers, has been particularly emphasized. Protection, in theory and practice, has been critically discussed. Topics of current interest like the transfer of technology, the role of the multinational corporations and the new international economic order have received due attention. Also population problems, particularly the problems of controlling fertility, poverty, income distribution, rural–urban migration and employment have been analysed carefully. Thus, the chief aim of this book is to provide a comprehensive textbook based upon rigorous qualitative and quantitative analysis.

This book is aimed chiefly at third year undergraduates taking courses in the field of development economics. Some understanding of macro- and micro-economics, welfare economics, elementary mathematics and statistics is assumed, though care is taken to explain complicated and technical issues in simpler ways. It is hoped that this book will also provide a background reading for postgraduate courses in development economics.

The manuscript has been written mainly between 1976 and the summer of 1977 while I have been teaching development economics at Leicester University. I have received valuable and constructive comments from many people during the course of my writing. I am particularly indebted to Professor David Pearce for all his valuable comments and for his generous help and encouragement despite his very busy schedule. I am very grateful to my colleague, Leo Katzen, who has not only read the entire manuscript and made many valuable suggestions for the improvement of the book, but has also been kind enough to write jointly with me Chapter 10 on "Population, Poverty and Income Distribution, Employment and Migration"; my thanks are also due to Paul Hallwood who has kindly read the entire manuscript and offered many useful comments. Thanks are also due to Peter Ayre, Ian Bradley, Anita Ghatak, Martin Hoskins, Homi Katrak, Lionel Needleman, Howard Rees, Frances Stewart, and Kerry Turner for their useful comments on different chapters of this book. On a wider academic front, I have drawn material from the works of Adelman, Bhagwati, Chenery, Corden, Chakravarty, Hicks, Johnson, Kuznets, Lipton, Meier, Myrdal, Amartya, Sen, Streeten, Thirlwall and Todaro. I feel therefore, that it is only fair to acknowledge my debt to their writings. I would like to pay tribute to Jeanne Cretney for her skill and patience, and for providing me with the necessary secretarial assistance. Also Joan Cook, Dorothy Logsdon, Elaine Humphreys and Pat Greatorex who have been kind enough to type the manuscript. Aņna Cooknell and Janut Westerman have taken the trouble of drawing the diagrams. Mr. M. Ramady has also helped me in the preparation of the index. To all of them, I remain very thankful. I would also like to thank the editors of the *Oxford Bulletin of Economics and Statistics* for granting permission to reproduce material from articles of mine which were originally published in that Journal.

My wife Anita and my baby daughter Churni had to pay the inevitable price of being rather neglected during the last two years. I am happy to say that they have paid this price very willingly (though not always silently). As a tiny compensation, this book has been dedicated to them and to my elder brother, Debaprasun and his son, Souma.

For all errors in this book which unfortunately remain, I take full responsibility.

Acknowledgements

We are grateful to the following for permission to reproduce copyright material:

Addison-Wesley Publishing Co. Inc. for a figure from *Linear Programming* by George Hadley; Basil Blackwell and Mott Ltd., for figures from 'Marketed Surplus in Indian Agriculture: Theory and Practice' from *Oxford Bulletin of Economics and Statistics* Vol 37, (1975) by S. Ghatak and a summary of a novel *Choice of Techniques* plus figures by A. K. Sen; Cambridge University Press for an extract from 'The Development of a Dual Economy' by D. Jorjenson from *Economic Journal* (1961) and a table and equations from *Exports and Economic Growth of Developing Countries* by A. Maizels (1968); Cornell University Press for a table from *Agricultural Development and Economic Growth* edited by B. F. Johnston and H. M. Southworth; The Economic Record and the author, Professor J. G. Williamson for an equation from '*Personal Savings in Developing Nations*' in *Economic Record* (1968); Frank Cass and Co. Ltd., for a summary of 'Determinants of Use of Special Drawing Rights by Developing Nations' and equations by Danny M. Leipziger in *The Journal of Development Studies* Vol II (1975) and a summary of 'The Informal Link between SDR Allocation and Aid: A Note' by Graham Bird in *The Journal of Development Studies* Vol 12 (1976); George Allen and Unwin Publishers Ltd., for a summary of a model in *The Economic Theory of Fiscal Policy* by Alan Peacock and G. K. Shaw (1971); Harvard University Press for extracts from 'International Aid for Underdeveloped Countries' by Paul Rosenstein-Roden from *Review of Economics and Statistics* and a figure from 'The Pricing of Food in India' by M. Khusro in *Quarterly Journal of Economics* (1967); Heinemann Educational Books Ltd., and Basic Books Inc. for two summaries from *Project Appraisal and Planning for Developing Countries* by I. Little and J. Mirrless (1974); International Association for Research in Income and Wealth for a summary of 'Aspects of Poverty in Malaysia' by S. Anand in *The Review of Income and Wealth* Vol 23; International Labour Office for a summary of 'The Difference Models on Migration' from *International Migration in Developing Countries. A Review of Theory, Evidence, Methodology and Research Priorities* by Michael P. Todaro; International Monetary Fund for equations from 'Monetary Analysis of Incomes and Imports and its Statistical Application' by J. J. Polack and L. Boissoneault in *IMF Staff Papers* (1959–60); Richard D. Irwin Inc., for a diagram from *Development of the Labour Surplus Economy* by J. Fei and G. Ranis; the author, Baron N. Kaldor for a brief summary of 'A New Model of Economic Growth' by N. Kaldor and J. Mirrless in *Review of Economic Studies* and a brief summary of the equations in 'Alternative Theories and Distribution' by N. Kaldor from *Review of Economic Studies* (1955–56); Lexington Books for a summary of 'The Indices of Instability' from *Trade and Economic Development* by O. Knudsen and A. Parnes (1975); Macmillan Publishers Ltd., for a table 'Determinents of Fertility: a micro-economic model of choice' by Paul Schultz in *Population Factors in Economic Development* edited by A. J. Coale (1976); Macmillan Publishing Co. Inc. for a figure from *Economic Dynamics* 2nd Edition by W. J. Baumol; Oxford University Press for a summary and figures from 'Conflicts between Output and Employment Objectives in Developing Countries' by F. Stewart and P. Streeten from *Oxford Economic Papers*, a table from 'Industry and Trade in Developing Countries' by I. Little, T. Seitovsky and M. Scott (1970), a summary of 'Over-pricing in Chile' in *Intercountry Income Distribution and Transnational Enterprises* by C. Vaitsos (1974), tables from *Redistribution with Growth* by H. Cheveny et al (1974); Oxford University Press Eastern Africa for equations from *Development Planning* by M. Todaro (1971); Penguin Books Ltd., and the author, Professor W. Elkan for a figure from *An Introduction to Development Economics* (1976); Praeger Publishers and the author, Professor Biehl for a summary of 'The Measurement of Fiscal Performances in Developing Countries' in *Quantative Analysis in Public Finance* (1969) edited by Alan Peacock; Prentice-Hall Inc., for figures from *International Economics: Analysis and Issues* by Charles Staley (1970); Stanford University Press for equations from *Theories of Economic Growth and Development* by I. Adelman (1962); The Economic Record and the author, T. W. Swan for a figure from 'Economic Growth and Capital Accumulation' in *Economic Record* (1956); The John Hopkins University Press for a table from *Indirect Taxation* in *Developing Economies* by John Due (1970) and a table from *The Structure of Protection in Developing Countries* by Bela Balassa (1971); The Manchester School and the author, Professor W. A. Lewis for a summary of the Lewis model in 'Economic Development with Unlimited Supplies of Labour' from *Manchester School of Economic and Social Studies*; University of Bombay for a summary and equations from 'What Kind of Macro-econometric models for Developing Economics' by L. Klein in *Indian Economic Journal* Vol 13 (1965); The University of Chicago Press for a summary of 'Growth, Stability and Inflationary Finance' by Robert A. Mundell in *The Journal of Political Economy* Vol 73; University of Delhi for a diagram from 'Ration of Interchange between Agricultural and Manufactured Goods in Relation to Capital Formation in Underdeveloped Economics' by D. Narain in *Indian Economic Review*

(1957); United Nations Industrial Development Organisation for an equation from *Guidelines for Project Evaluation* by A. Sen, P. Dasgupta and S. Marglin (1972); University of Kent for equations from 'Reconciling the Conflict between Employment and Saving and Output in the choice of Techniques in Developing Countries' by A. P. Thirlwall; Weidenfeld and Nicolson Ltd., for figures from 'Saving and Foreign Exchange Constraints' by V. Joshi in *Unfashionable Economics* (1970); Yale University for a table 'Evidence on African Small-Holder Supply Elasticities' from 'Small-Holder Decision Making Tropical African Evidence' by G. K. Helliner in *Agriculture in Development Theory* edited by Lloyd Reynolds (1975).

We are unable to trace the copyright owner of an equation from *The Approach of Operational Research to Planning India* by P. C. Mahalanobis and a summary of 'Poverty: An Ordinal Approach to Measurement' by A. Sen and would appreciate any information which would enable us to do so.

To Churni, Anita, Debaprasun and Souma

1 Introduction

1.1 Introduction

The problems of the economic development of the poor countries of today's world is one of the most widely discussed topics of our time. Experts in various fields such as economics, politics, sociology, and engineering have held different views about the nature of underdevelopment and poverty, its causes and its remedies. It has now been fully recognized that the nature and causes of the "poverty of the nations" are very complex and the remedies are neither easy nor quick. The understanding of the problem of underdevelopment requires a good knowledge of certain basic characteristics of the less-developed countries (henceforward to be referred to as LDCs). The analysis of these characteristics will shed some light on the peculiar economic and social conditions of production, consumption and distribution of income and wealth in the LDCs, which will help us to draw some policy implications.

1.2 Characteristics of the LDCs

Low per capita *real income*

Low *per capita* real income is generally regarded as one of the main indicators of the socio-economic conditions of the LDCs. A comparison with the economically developed countries (DCs) is striking (see Table 1.1). It shows very clearly the difference between the DCs and the LDCs. If the *per capita* income of the USA and India are considered, it is clear that an average Indian earned about 2.13 per cent of the income of an average American in 1971. Most of the LDCs exhibit this very low ratio of income to population. It shows the relatively low level of national income in most LDCs, or a high level of population, or both. Low *per capita* real income is a reflection of low productivity, low saving and investment, backward technology and resources, while the level of population is determined by complex socio-economic factors. Hence, the importance of population in relation to national income in the LDCs can hardly be overemphasized and this is discussed in the next section.

Table 1.1 Some socio-economic indices of development for some selected countries

Third World countries	*Population, mid-1975 (m.)*	Per capita GNP, 1972 ($)	Per capita GNP growth-rate, 1965–72 (%)	*Life expectancy at birth, 1970–75 average (yrs)*	*Birth-rate per 1,000, 1970–75 average*	*Death-rate per 1,000, 1970–75 average*	*Infant mortality per 1,000 live births*	*Literacy (%)*	Per capita *energy consumption, 1971 (kg coal equiv)*	*Total exports f.o.b., 1973 ($ m.)*	*Total imports, c.i.f. ($ m.)*	*Aid flows, 1973 ($ m.)*	*International reserves, Jan. 1975 ($ m.)*
Afghanistan	19.3	80[a]	0.8[a]	40	49.2	23.8	182	8	27	90[bc]	181[bc]	57.4	74
Bangladesh	73.7	70	1.6	36	49.5	28.1	132	22[d]	n.a.	357	874	425	n.a.
Cameroon	6.4	200	3.8	41	40.4	22.0	137	10–15	97	353	334	61.5	98[e]
Ethiopia	28.0	80	1.2	38	49.4	25.8	181	5	32	240	215	64.3	278
India	613.2	110	1.4	50	39.9	15.7	139	28	186	2,958	3,236	771.4	1,508[h]
Kenya	13.3	170	4.1	50	48.7	16.0	135	20–25	171	461	615	95.9	205
Nepal	12.6	80	0.1	44	42.9	20.3	169	9	9	n.a.	n.a.	31.2	138[f]
Pakistan	70.6	130	1.7	50	47.4	16.5	132	16[d]	n.a.	961	270.9	981	380
Sierra Leone	3.0	190	1.8	44	44.7	20.7	136	10	109	132	158	14.1	48
Sri Lanka	14.0	110	2.0	68	28.6	6.4	45	70–80	163	388	421	52.9	74
Upper Volta	6.0	70	0.6	38	48.5	25.8	182	5–10	13	24[c]	63[c]	57.3	74[j]
Angola	6.4	390	5.5	38	47.3	24.5	203	10–15	157	728	529	8.9	n.a.
Brazil	109.7	530	5.6	61	37.1	8.8	94	61	500	6,199	6,999	63.3	5,531
Burma	31.2	90	1.0	50	39.5	15.8	126	60	68	128	102	70.9	162
Chile	10.3	800	2.2	63	27.9	9.2	71	84	1,516	1,231	941	39.7	221
China, People's Rep.	822.8	170[a]	2.6[a]	62	26.9	10.3	55	25[d]	561	n.a.	n.a.	—	n.a.
Colombia	25.9	400	2.4	61	40.6	8.8	76	73	638	1,084	876	133.3	412
Egypt	37.5	240[a]	0.6	52	37.8	14.0	103	30	282	1,119	905	73.0	603
Hong Kong	4.2	980	5.7	70	19.4	5.5	17	71	1,040	5,051	5,637	0.9	n.a.

Table 1.1 (continued)

Third World countries (continued)	*Population mid-1975 (m.)*	Per capita *GNP, 1972 ($)*	Per capita *GNP growth-rate, 1965–72 (%)*	*Life expectancy at birth, 1970–75 average (yrs)*	*Birth rate per 1,000, 1970–75 average*	*Death-rate per 1,000, 1970–75 average*	*Infant mortality per 1,000 live births*	*Literacy (%)*	Per capita *energy consumption, 1971 (kg coal equiv)*	*Total exports f.o.b., 1973 ($ m.)*	*Total imports, c.i.f. ($ m.)*	*Aid flows, 1973 ($ m.)*	*International reserves, Jan. 1975 ($ m.)*
Republic of Korea	33.9	310	8.5	61	28.7	8.8	60	71	860	3,220	4,219	279.0	10,561
Malaysia	12.1	430	2.9	59	38.7	9.9	75	43[d]	n.a.	2,950	2,402	42.7	n.a.
Mozambique	9.2	300	5.6	44	43.1	20.1	165	7	178	304[c]	478[c]	3.9	n.a.
Peru	15.3	520	1.1	56	41.0	11.9	110	61	621	1,047	863	73.8	551
Philippines	44.4	220	2.4	58	43.8	10.5	78	72	298	1,788	1,773	220.4	1,607
Singapore	2.2	1,300	10.3	70	21.2	5.2	20	75	851	3,605	5,063	25.7	1,392[q]
Taiwan	16.0	430	6.9	69	24.0	5.0	28	85	n.a.	4,378	3,797	20.5	1,191[l]
Thailand	42.1	220	4.2	58	43.4	10.8	65	68	296	1,584	2,057	60.5	1,905
Turkey	39.9	370	4.3	57	39.4	12.5	119	46	516	1,318	2,091	82.4	1,861[l]
Zaire	24.5	100[a]	3.9[a]	44	45.2	20.5	160	35–40	77	691[b]	787[b]	130.2	140[l]
OPEC* countries													
Algeria	16.8	430	3.5	53	48.7	15.4	128	25–30	492	1,802	2,338	108.3	14,797
Iran	32.9	490	7.2	51	45.3	15.6	139	23	895	6,914	3,370	3.3	8,513
Kuwait	1.1	4,090	1.3	67	47.1	5.3	44	47	7,888	3,789	1,042	3.2	1,654
Nigeria	62.9	130	5.4	41	49.3	22.7	180	25	59	3,358	1,874	72.8	5,981
Saudi Arabia	9.0	550[a]	6.8[a]	45	49.5	20.2	152	5–15	988	8,638	1,993	3.3	14,285[l]
Venezuela	12.2	1,240	1.1	65	36.1	7.1	50	76	2,518	4,727	2,813	8.3	6,191

Table 1.1 (continued)

Developed countries	*Population mid-1975 (m.)*	Per capita GNP, *1972 ($)*	Per capita *GNP growth-rate, 1965–72 (%)*	*Life expectancy at birth, 1970–75 average (yrs)*	*Birth-rate per 1,000, 1970–75 average*	*Death-rate per 1,000, 1970–75 average*	*Infant mortality per 1,000 live births*	*Literacy (%)*	Per capita *energy consumption, 1971 (kg coal equiv)*	*Total exports f.o.b., 1973 ($ m.)*	*Total imports, c.i.f. ($ m.)*	*Aid flows, 1973 ($ m.)*	*International reserves, Jan. 1975 ($ m.)*
Australia	13.8	2,980	3.1	72	21.0	8.1	17	98[d]	5,359	9,517	7,658	—	4,194
Canada	22.8	4,440	3.2	72	18.6	7.7	17	98	9,326	26,309	24,918	—	5,802
Czechoslovakia	14.8	2,180	4.5	69	17.0	11.2	21	100[d]	6,615	6,288[c]	6,137[cp]	—	n.a.
France	52.9	3,620	4.8	73	17.0	10.6	16	97[d]	3,928	36,659	37,727	—	9,007
Germany Fed. Rep.	61.9	3,390	4.1	71	12.0	12.1	20	99[d]	5,223	67,502	54,552	—	33,075
Japan	111.1	2,320	9.7	73	19.2	6.6	12	98[d]	3,267	36,982	38,347	—	13,509
Netherlands	13.6	2,840	4.3	74	16.8	8.7	12	98[d]	5,069	24,071	24,735	—	7,284
Sweden	8.3	4,480	2.5	73	14.2	10.5	10	99[d]	6,089	12,201	10,628	—	1,786
USSR	255.0	1,530	5.9	70	17.8	7.9	26	99[d]	4,535	21,463[c]	21,108[cp]	—	n.a.
United Kingdom	56.4	2,600	2.0	72	16.1	11.7	18	98–99[d]	5,507	30,535	38,847	—	7,021
United States	213.9	5,590	2.0	71	16.2	9.4	18	98[d]	11,244	71,339	73,575	—	16,262

* OPEC stands for Organization of Petroleum Exporting Countries

Source: Todaro, Michael (1977).

[a] Tentative estimate.

[b] 1972 figure.

[c] United Nations *Bulletin of Statistics*, Vol. 29 No. 1, Jan. 1975.

[d] US Agency for International Development. Bureau for Population and Humanitarian Assistance. *Population Program Assistance: Annual Report* FY 1973 Washington D.C., US Government Printing Office, 1973.

[e] Aug. 1974 figure.

[f] Oct. 1974 figure.

[g] Mar. 1974 figure.

[h] Nov. 1974 figure.

[i] Sept. 1974 figure.

[k] June 1971 figure.

[l] Mid-1973 figure.

[m] 1966 figure.

[n] 1971 figure.

[o] Dec. 1973 figure.

[p] F.o.b.

[q] June 1974 figure.

Population

Most LDCs generally experience a high population growth-rate, or where the population growth-rate is not very high *in comparison with other LDCs*, the size of the population may be very high (e.g. China and India). LDCs usually experience high birth-rates but the advancement of medical science has led to a significant reduction in the death-rates (except in some African countries). This has engendered a situation which as been generally termed as "population explosion". One of the main implications of such population explosion has been the growth of the proportion of people who live on the subsistence or "poverty line", defined as the line of minimum calorie intake to keep the body and soul together in the LDCs. Another aspect of population growth has been the growth of the proportion of unemployed people in the LDCs who tend to migrate, chiefly from the villages to the cities in search of a livelihood.

Unemployment, under-employment and disguised unemployment and low productivity

Large-scale unemployment is a common feature of most LDCs. Factors like the population pressure, the absence of job opportunities, either because of the low level of economic activity or because of the poor growth rate or both, the choice of techniques which are capital rather than labour intensive, education which is unrelated to economic needs, rigid wages set without much regard to the social opportunity cost of labour and lack of investment could all explain such unemployment problems. The phenomenon of under-employment noticed in many LDCs is a situation whereby the type of employment has not much relation to the qualification of the employees, wages are above the marginal productivity of labour and a large portion of labour-hours remain unused. Disguised unemployment is supposed to occur when the employment of an additional unit of labour does not add anything to production. The reason for employment could be, say, family consideration rather than profit maximization. Reliable information about actual unemployment in the LDCs is difficult to obtain, but most data suggest that the proportion of unemployment in the LDCs varies between 8 per cent and 35 per cent (Turnham, 1971). The unemployed and the underemployed together in the LDCs would probably be about 30 per cent of the total work force (Todaro, 1977). However, most data on labour utilization in the LDCs are rather weak, particularly in the rural areas. Both the quantity and quality of information are better for industrial employment which in most LDCs varies between 5 per cent and 25 per cent. Substantial difficulties are involved in the measurement of the actual level of underemployment and disguised unemployment in LDCs in the light of the production conditions and objective functions of these economies. Due to the nature of the agricultural production cycles, work is sometimes available for six months in a year when labour-shortage rather than labour-surplus may be observed, particularly during the sowing and harvesting seasons in agriculture. Such seasonalities must be accounted for in the estimation of unemployment. Also, if *family* income or output rather than profit maximization is regarded as the objective condition, then the comparison between the marginal product of labour and wages becomes less meaningful.

Labour in the LDCs is relatively abundant in relation to capital and the productivity of labour is usually low in most LDCs in comparison with such productivity in the DCs. Such low productivity is the outcome of the paucity of capital and other resources, backward technology, lack of proper education, training and skill, and poor health and nutrition.

Poverty

Evidence from the LDCs with regard to the level of poverty suggests that a very significant proportion of their populations earn a level of income which varies between $50 and $75 per annum in 1970 prices. This income is regarded as the minimum level for bare survival in the LDCs. It has been estimated that about 1.3 *billion* people, which accounts for about 35 per cent of the world's population, lived at "subsistence level" by the end of 1970. This figure is staggering and more recent evidence may well suggest that the present situation might have deteriorated further (Bardhan and Srinivasan, 1975). People who live on the poverty line in the LDCs usually reside in the rural areas. This raises the problem of income distribution not only among the rich and the poor countries but also within the LDCs themselves.

Income distribution

The pattern of income distribution within the LDCs shows considerable variation. In general, there is evidence to suggest that the pattern of income distribution tends to be more unequal in most LDCs in comparison with the DCs (Ahluwalia, 1974 in Chenery *et al.*, 1974). However, the hypothesis that the high rates of growth of income in the LDCs will always have an adverse effect on relative equality has been rejected on the basis of current evidence from the LDCs (Ahluwalia, 1974). But this evidence does not alter the proposition that many LDCs experience severe inequalities in income distribution though some suffer less than others. In any case, evidence from 44 LDCs suggests that, on average, only about 6 per cent of national income accrues to the poorest 20 per cent of the population, whereas 30 per cent to 56 per cent of national income is obtained by the highest 5–20 per cent of the population. In some LDCs, such inequalities are extreme. For instance, in Jamaica, the poorest 20 per cent of the population obtain only 2.2 per cent of national income, whereas the highest 20 per cent obtain about 62 per cent of such income. In Iraq, Gabon and Columbia, the share of the poorest 20 per cent and richest 20 per cent in national income is 2 per cent and 68 per cent, 2 per cent and 71 per cent, 2.2 per cent and 68.1 per cent respectively (Jarvis, 1973; see also Todaro, 1977). However, some of the LDCs like Taiwan (1964), South Korea (1970) and Sri Lanka (1969–70) show low inequality as measured by the Gini co-efficients which stood at 0.32, 0.36 and 0.37 respectively for these countries (Ahluwalia, 1974; see also Appendix to Chapter 1). It is important to note that the recent technological progress in agriculture in some LDCs – sometimes called the "Green Revolution" – has led to a substantial rise in farm income and profits among the richer section of the peasants who have easy access to the crucial inputs like fertilizers, irrigation facilities, better seeds, credit and marketing facilities, and this has simply heightened the problem of distribution of such gains more equally particularly among the poorer section of the rural population who depend mainly on agriculture for their livelihood. This has sometimes been regarded as the "second-generation" problem of green revolution which requires urgent attention in the LDCs for maintenance of both economic and socio-political stability.

Predominance of agriculture in the national economy

Agriculture usually dominates the economies of most LDCs. It generally accounts for 45–90 per cent of the total output and about 60–95 per cent of total employment. Clearly, the economic growth and development of these countries will be closely tied to the general development of agriculture. Unfortunately, many LDCs, in order to promote rapid economic growth, negelected agriculture and decided to promote industrialization as quickly as possible. The need for industrialization in the "basic" sectors of the LDCs is generally understood and recognized. What is less clearly understood in most LDCs is that a basic industry cannot be built without a basis. Such a basis is usually provided by a well-developed agricultural sector which would supply "wage-goods", food, raw materials, labour, market and foreign exchange for the development of both the industrial and the agricultural sector. This balanced growth between agriculture and industry received inadequate attention from the planners and policy makers of most LDCs with the result that most developments have accrued to the urban rather than the rural sector where the overwhelming majority of the total population live in the LDCs – a phenomenon which has been described as the "urban bias" (Lipton, 1968a). It is suggested that this "urban" rather than "rural" bias could explain why poor people stay poor in most LDCs. Resources are usually directed for the growth of "modern" industrial sectors and whatever the gains in real income that accrue to the economy are usually distributed within the modern sector while the poor, rural sector is driven into further impoverishment and deprivation of resources (Lipton, 1977). In 1970, the American agricultural labourer produced, on average, output worth $7.11, his counterpart in Africa and Asia produced output worth only 0.21 cents.

Agriculture in many LDCs is characterized by high pressure on land, use of very backward technology, low saving and investment and hence poor productivity. A large majority of the peasants live in abject poverty and the rate of literacy is also very poor. The land is usually scattered and fragmented and the distribution of land ownership is haphazard in most cases. The use of modern technology like better seeds and chemical fertilizers is largely unknown in many parts though there are pockets of agriculture where modern farming methods, particularly the use of better seeds and fertilizers have made some progress. However, the availability of adequate water supply remains an important bottleneck in the development of agriculture in many LDCs. It has been demonstrated that without adequate water supply, the adoption of modern farming methods, like the use of fertilizers, is likely to show signs of diminishing returns (Ishikawa, 1967). It seems reasonable to suggest that the future development strategy for many LDCs could involve a recasting of priorities and the development of the agricultural sector requires most serious consideration.

Foreign Trade

Foreign trade generally forms a rather small part of the national income in many LDCs. There are however some exceptions, for example Hong Kong, and Taiwan. The pattern of foreign trade for most LDCs is usually characterized by former colonial trade relationships. This means that just as the former colonies used to export the primary commodities and raw materials to the imperial countries at the centre and import from them the finished products, so today's LDCs are chiefly the net exporters of primary products and net importers of industrial goods. In a way, such a trading relationship is dictated by economic history since most LDCs of today were under the political domination of today's DCs. Also, the pattern of trade reflects the pattern of production and resource mobilization in the LDCs and DCs. Primary exports from the LDCs chiefly consist of agricultural goods (e.g. jute and tea from India, coffee from Brazil, tea from Sri Lanka, cocoa from Ghana). The income from such exports sometimes fluctuates quite sharply either because of demand or supply conditions or both. These goods are generally exported to only a few markets – a phenomenon which is regarded as "market or geographic concentration", where the export of a few goods is known as "commodity concentration". The fluctuation in export earning is related to the fluctuation in the production cycles of agricultural goods on the *supply* side. Also, the development of many synthetic products has largely reduced the *demand* for primary goods from the LDCs. Note that the demand for a primary product is not usually price and income dependent. This implies that although there has been significant increase in the income (both total and *per capita*) of the DC in the last hundred years, the demand for the primary product has increased less than proportionality and this has contributed to the decline in export earnings of the LDCs. Similarly, when prices of primary goods fell, the demand did not rise in equal proportion and again the export revenue of the LDCs was lost. There is some evidence to suggest that the ratio of export price to import price (the terms of trade) has secularly moved against the LDCs *vis-à-vis* the DCs (though not in all the periods) over the last century, but this has been debated (see Ch. 8). Fluctuations in foreign exchange earnings of the LDCs are also observed, though their causes and consequences are still very much open to discussion. However, the schemes for the stabilization in the export earnings of the LDCs have received major attention in the United Nations Conference on Trade and Development (UNCTAD) as well as in the present North-South Dialogue (1977) through the funding of a Commodity-Buffer-Stock Scheme.

1.3 Types of markets in LDCs

After discussing the major features of the LDCs, it is useful to look at the operation of the different forms of markets in the LDCs. In traditional economic theory, it is generally argued that given the free operation of the market forces, free competition will ensure the optimum or most efficient allocation of all the existing resources and the situation will be Pareto optimal, i.e. it will be impossible to increase the welfare of any one individual without reducing the welfare of others. However, in most LDCs the market or the "invisible hand" does not always operate very smoothly and indeed the instances of market "failures" are rather frequent. Thus, an analysis of the production conditions in different market forms in the LDCs is necessary to illustrate the point.

1.4 Production conditions in LDCs

Let us assume, in line with the standard economic theory, that total output produced within a country (Q) is given by land (L_a), labour (L), capital (K), and organization (R). More formally

$$Q = f(L_a, L, K, R).$$

Resource allocation will be optimal at the point where the marginal productivity of the different factors will be equal to the factor prices. Such an allocation would also be socially most efficient as long as there is no difference between the social and the private costs of production. Private profits in a competitive economy will be maximized by applying the standard rule of equating marginal cost of producing the goods to prices (which, under free competition, are also equal to marginal revenue), and if there is no difference between private profit and social benefit, social welfare will also be maximized. It is contended that this 'if' is a big 'if' because markets in most LDCs are neither free nor homogeneous and hence the application of the marginal principles to the LDCs will not achieve their objectives. The nature of this criticism can be understood more clearly if the different types of markets in the LDCs are discussed briefly.

Land

Land in most LDCs is one of the major inputs, if not the major input, of production. The pattern of land ownership in most LDCs suggests that a great proportion of cultivated land is held by a small minority of landowners, whereas a great majority of the peasants frequently hold a small proportion of such land. Given the predominance of agriculture in the economies of the LDCs, and the fact that land is usually the most important form of asset to be held particularly in the rural areas, the impact of haphazard distribution of land on income distribution can easily be realized. The system of land ownership is also very complicated and a distinction is generally made between: (1) owner-cultivators; (2) the share-croppers who provide, say, bullocks and ploughs for cultivation for some return from cultivation; (3) the tenants; and (4) the agricultural labourers who are usually hired and fired with the fluctuations of production cycles in agriculture. Obviously, the share-croppers, tenants and agricultural labourers should not have much incentive to work when the returns from labour are generally low and fixed and when they are not the legal landowners. Land is generally fragmented, differing in soil structure, fertility and productivity. Many cultivators who own big plots of land are usually absentee landlords who take little interest in investment in the land, pay low wages to the hired labourers and could easily become the agents of "exploitation". The legal records of title deeds to land are very difficult to obtain in most LDCs. In most cases, very backward techniques are used for production and returns from land are usually low. Although the peasants are not generally unresponsive to economic opportunities, the lack of better inputs could lower such returns. But even if the inputs are provided, these may be available only to a certain class of farmers without showing tangible benefits for the vast majority of the peasants. The land market is far from free.

Adverse weather conditions usually aggravate the dire poverty of the tenants and landless labourers, and some small peasants are forced to sell the land and go into debt. Under such circumstances, it is no surprise that the "Indian peasants are born in debt, live in debt and die in debt". All this could well imply the urgent necessity to introduce major institutional changes and land reform in many LDCs.

Labour market

Most LDCs experience high growth-rates of population which add to the flow of labour supply every year. The labour market is far from homogeneous. Lack of skilled labour is observed in many African and some Asian countries. The supply of labour tends to exceed its demand by a significant amount which results in unemployment – open, or disguised or underemployment. Labour is primarily engaged in agriculture and services. The mobility of labour between the different regions is not high. Wages tend to differ significantly between the industrial urban and the rural agricultural areas, and migration usually occurs in substantial numbers from the villages to the towns. The level of wages usually paid in the LDCs does not bear any close relationship to the marginal productivity of labour, particularly in the rural areas. In many cases such wages are administered either by custom or by legislation, rather than market determined. Lack of proper educational facilities, poor health and the standard of nutrition and paucity of both physical and social capital could account for the low productivity that is often observed in the labour market in most LDCs.

Capital Market

Capital market in the LDCs is often narrow and difficult to measure. Usually, buildings, machinery and equipment are treated as parts of capital. The definition of capital is always difficult and such a definition can only be broad in the context of the LDCs because even the provision of some consumer goods could increase the flow of future income. Thus, the provision of education, shelter, transport and health services could easily add to the flow of future income and could be regarded as important elements of social capital.

Capital is one of the most scarce and important inputs in the LDCs and as such most LDCs have given major emphasis to the role of capital formation for economic growth. Low income generates low saving, low investment, low productivity and low income and the "vicious" circle is complete. The market for capital is assuredly characterized by duality with the organized urban sector, using sophisticated means to borrow and lend capital whereas the unorganized rural sector remains outside the control of modern business practices. The money market is also characterized by "financial dualism" (Myint, 1971), where the organized sector uses the modern banking and financial methods of transaction, the unorganized rural money markets are generally dominated by the "unholy" trinity of the "landlords-cum-merchants-cum-moneylenders" who frequently, acting as monopolists and monopsonists, could be the agents of "exploitation". The flow of funds between the two sectors is rather limited.

The capital scarcity in the LDCs usually accounts for its limited use. The duality and the complex structure of the capital market suggests the difficulty that lies in its treatment as a homogeneous unit.

Organization

The lack of entrepreneurship is regarded as one of the major bottlenecks in the development of the LDCs. Where the entrepreneur class existed, governments did not provide sufficient incentives for its prosperity. Lack of proper education and managerial skill went hand-in-hand in most LDCs and even where the resources were available, proper organization for the mobilization of such resources was inadequate. Motivation, culture, attitude, resources, institutions and public policy all had varying roles to play in shaping the types of organization that most LDCs have today (Myrdal, 1968).

Commodity market

The commodity markets in most LDCs are also characterized by duality. This is so because in parts of such markets (e.g. in agriculture) barter, rather than monetary transactions take place. This makes the estimation of the value of the product quite difficult without the use of some "shadow" or imputed prices. There are other difficulties with regard to the weights which should be attached to the evaluation of non-traded outputs. With the expansion of money-income, barter forms of transactions are probably on the wane in many LDCs, though their presence still adds to the problems of proper evaluation of the products.

It is in the light of these complex features of the market in the LDCs that their "growth" and "development" should be judged – a distinction to which we now turn.

1.5 Growth and development

Is per capita *real income a valid index for measuring development of the LDCs?*

The terms "growth" and "development" are usually used to mean the same thing. A growth of the *per capita* income is supposed to contribute to a general rise in the standard of living of the people in general. But growth and development need not be the same. For instance, Kuwait's *per capita* real income may be the highest in the world and yet the standard of living of an "average" Kuwaiti may not be the same as that of an "average" American. In other words, *per capita* real income figures are derived by dividing the total real national income by the total population to obtain an average figure and these averages could be misleading. Thus, the distribution of income must be taken into account before something can be said about the general level of development. A country's GDP may grow at a very fast rate and yet only a small proportion of its population could be the beneficiaries of such growth, while the masses of its population may not experience any improvement in their standard of living. There may be growth but no development. Instances are not rare and these are cited in the chapter on income distribution (Ch. 10).

Second, a fast growth-rate in total output may indicate a healthy state of the economy, but if population growth-rate matches the output growth-rate, then *per capita* growth-rate is negligible. Here also growth without development is possible. The important variable which is hindering the "development" in this case is the growth of population.

Third, the use of *per capita* real income or consumption data, converted into the foreign exchange rate, may not always be an adequate index to measure the development in a world of floating exchange rates. Also, the expression of *per capita* real income in terms of official exchange rates may not be very meaningful if such rates remain highly overvalued – a frequently observed phenomenon in the LDCs.

Fourth, growth without development is supposed to be the feature of "dual" societies in the LDCs (Boeke, 1953). Such "dual" societies are characterized by contrasts between the very rich and the very poor, between the towns and villages, between different social classes and so on. *Prima facie*, it is not easy to argue that dualism is the cause or effect of underdevelopment. If dualism is interpreted as class distinction and inequalities in income distribution, then its presence could be observed even in many economically developed countries.

Finally, the quality of life is to be regarded as an important index of development. It is contended that such quality is not adequately reflected in the index of *per capita* income growth. A country (X) may have a lower *per capita* real income than the other (Y), but the quality of life enjoyed by the citizens of X may be better than that of Y. Here the problem is one of setting up a synthetic index to measure the "quality" of life. Several factors are involved in the measurement of such "quality". To mention only a few:

(*a*) education and literacy rates;
(*b*) life expectancy;
(*c*) the level of nutrition as measured by calorie supply per head or by some such index;
(*d*) consumption of energy per head;
(*e*) consumption of iron and steel per head;
(*f*) consumption of consumer durables *per capita*;
(*g*) the proportion of infant mortality per thousand of live population.

It is clear that some of the factors mentioned above should be measured in terms of "non-monetary" rather than monetary indicators. In fact, attempts have been made to compare the standards of living among different countries by using the non-monetary indicators. Here the aim was to test a significant statistical correlation between the non-monetary and agrregate national income indices in order to forecast the real consumption per head which is supposed to be a better indicator of quality of life (See Beckerman, 1966, for details). Some other non-monetary variables which are supposed to explain *per capita* consumption are: (1) stock of radios and telephones; (2) consumption of meat; (3) number of letters sent etc. (Duggar, 1968). The final forecasts are then compared with the national accounts data on private consumption coverted in official exchange rates. The results of the study by Beckerman show some major differences between monetary and non-monetary indicators of *per capita* consumption. The results also show that while the highest 10 per cent of world population accounted for 35.2 per cent of the world consumption, the poorest 10 per cent obtained only 1.6 per cent of global consumption. These results simply highlight the gulf between the rich and poor countries (Beckerman and Bacon in Streeten (ed.), 1970).

The "quality" of life could also be measured by looking at the social and political developments of different countries (Adelman and Morris, 1967). It is generally assumed by development economists that an increase in investment, industrialization, agricultural productivity and economic growth would be closely related to the rise in the extent of economic and political participation by the people. However, events in many LDCs tend to suggest that a fast rate of economic growth has been associated with greater inequality in income distribution and a decline in people's participation. Indeed, if the *per capita* real income growth rate is less than 3.5 per cent, the relative share of the poor sections tends to fall. After adjusting for population growth this calls for an income growth rate higher than 5.5 per cent which few LDCs have achieved so far. Also, higher growth rates are necessary but not sufficient condition for raising the share of the poor (Adelman, 1975). Hence, to achieve greater political and economic equality, the case for socio-political and institutional changes has been strongly advocated (Adelman and Morris, 1973). "Without new institutions and policies specifically designed to improve the lot of the poor, there is no realistic chance of social justice in the under-developed world of our time" (Adelman and Morris, 1973, p. 202). Very few, now, would dispute this statement. The lack of major structural and institutional changes could only enrich the "new elites" in the LDCs without developing the standard of living of the poor. If the economic differences between the rich and poor countries appear like *A Tale of Two Cities*, then such a tale could also be heard loudly even within many LDCs.

The above analysis suggests that the *per capita* real income growth-rate is not a very satisfactory measure of economic "development" and it needs to be supplemented by other indices such as *per capita* real consumption, monetary, non-monetary, demographic and socio-political variables, e.g. life expectancy, infant mortality, education, literacy, distribution of income among the different classes, the level and extent of people's participation in the government and the degree of decentralization of economic and political power. The construction of such a synthetic index is very much an important topic of future research. On the other hand, although the level and rate of *per capita* real income growth is an imperfect index, it is difficult to believe that significant development could take place without a rise in *per capita* real income. This reason probably accounts for the great importance that is usually attached to the nature and changes of the level of *per capita* real income to measure growth and development in the economic literature.

1.6 Economic theory and the LDCs

The description of the major characteristics of the LDCs and the nature of their market would raise doubts about the application of the growth theories and models to the peculiar conditions of the LDCs. In the next two chapters we shall examine to what extent these growth models, which were mainly formulated in the context of the DCs, are relevant for the LDCs and to what extent they could be modified to analyse the special problems of these countries. In Chapter 4 the strategies of resource allocation will be considered, while in Chapter 5 policies to mobilize domestic resources will be analyzed. In view of the special importance of agriculture, Chapter 6 will be devoted to the analysis of its problems and prospects. Given the problem of market failures, the case for and against planning will be examined from both macro and micro points of view with special reference to the techniques of planning in Chapter 7. The role of foreign trade and foreign resources will then be examined in Chapters 8 and 9, while in Chapter 10 the problems of population, unemployment, poverty and income distribution will be discussed.

Appendix

Measurement of income inequality

Several methods to estimate how inequality could be described are available. Here we shall briefly state the major ones.

1. The first method is to estimate the ratio of incomes obtained by, say, the bottom 3 per cent of the population to the top 10 per cent of the population. Such an index really shows the extent of inequality between the very rich and the very poor.

2. The other index which is frequently used to measure inequality is the "Lorenz curve" (called after the American statistician C. Lorenz who invented it in 1905) which shows associations between percentages of *income receivers* and percentages of income. In the diagram (Fig. A1.1), the vertical axis shows different percentages of income whereas the horizontal axis measures cumulative percentages of income receivers. The diagonal line OA shows the line of *exact equality* because at every point on it, the percentage of income *receivers* is equal to the percentage of income obtained. The Lorenz curve depicts the *actual* association between percentages of total income and percentages of income receivers. Notice that in the rather unlikely case where the Lorenz curve is identical with the line OA, there is no inequality. On the other hand, the further the Lorenz curve moves away from the line OA, the greater is the inequality. Note that if the Lorenz curve of a country X always lies outside that of country Y, then the inequality in distribution of income is larger in the country X in comparison with the country Y. But if they intersect each other, then it is hard to tell which country suffers from greater inequality without making subjective value judgements.

Fig. A1.1

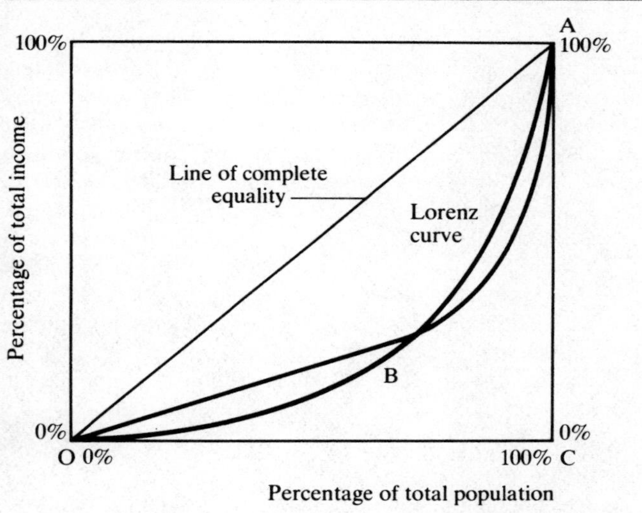

3. The most favoured index to measure inequality is the Gini-coefficient or G (called after Gini who invented it in 1912) which is the ratio of the area OAB to area OCA. Thus the Gini coefficient ranks according to the area between the Lorenz curve and the diagonal and it is a direct measure of income differences between every pair of incomes. Symbolically, if

y = income

m = average or mean income

n = number of persons

i = 1, 2, … n

then:

$\sum_{i=1}^{n} y_i = nm$ and the Gini coefficient (G)

$$G = (1/2\ n^2 m) \sum_{i=1}^{j} \sum_{j=2}^{n} /y_i - y_j$$

Where G = 0, everyone gets the same income; where

G = 1, only one person gets everything. Clearly for most countries, the actual value of G lies between 0 and 1. Note that G also shows the share of different groups of population in income. (For details and discussions of other methods, see Sen (1973); Atkinson (1970); and Pen (1971).)

2

Growth theories and their relevance to LDCs

2.1 Introduction

The development of the theories of economic growth – or what Marshall regarded as long-run equilibrium analysis – in the last thirty years has been remarkable. Such growth may partly be explained by the desire to analyse the problems and policies for economic development of many war-ravaged countries in the world after the Second World War and partly by the necessity to stimulate growth in many poor countries in Asia, Africa and Latin America. Sometimes, growth just happened and theorists decided to explain it. The idea of promoting growth is not new in the history of economic thought. Indeed, the classical economists envisaged a scenario to describe the process of economic growth. In this chapter we shall try to analyse the basic features of some of the major theories of economic growth and show their relevance to the problems of economic development of the LDCs. We shall start off with the discussion of the classical theory of growth.

2.2 Classical scenario

The theory of growth, as stated by the classical writers like Smith, Mill, Malthus and Ricardo can be described in a simple way. Given a certain amount of labour (and assuming, of course, the labour theory of value), at a certain level of production, wages will be paid to each worker according to the level of subsistence and any "surplus", i.e. the difference between total production and total consumption which is assumed to be equivalent to the total wage bill, will be accumulated by the capitalists. Such accumulation will increase the demand for labour and with a given population, wages will tend to rise. As the wage exceeds the level of subsistence, the population will increase according to the Malthusian theory of population. With a growth of population, the supply of labour will be encouraged and wages will again fall back to the level of subsistence. But as wages become equal to the subsistence level, a surplus will emerge again to encourage accumulation and demand for labour and the whole process will be repeated again in the next phase. The dynamics of growth ends as the law of diminishing returns sets in and wages eat up the whole of production leaving no surplus for accumulation, expansion and growth of population. The "magnificent dynamics" ends not with a bang but a whimper (Baumol, 1968). This is illustrated by Fig. 2.1.

Fig. 2.1

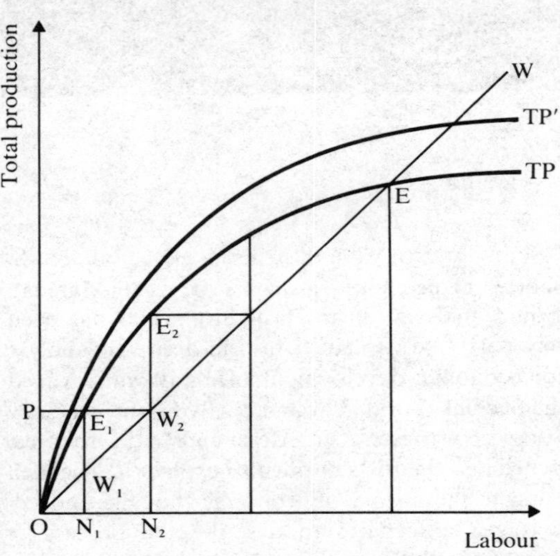

The vertical axis measures total production minus rent and the horizontal axis measures employment of labour. The line OW indicates the subsistence wage line. With ON_1 population, production is OP, wage per unit is N_1W_1 and surplus or profit is E_1W_1 when TP total production is the sum of wages and profits only. The emergence of a surplus engenders accumulation which leads to an increase in the demand for labour. Wages rise to E_1N_1 since the demand for labour rises with accumulation but population, and therefore labour supply, remains constant at ON_1. But once the wages are above the level of subsistence, i.e. $E_1N_1 > N_1W_1$, growth of population is stimulated to ON_2 – thanks to the Malthusian theory of population. Once the population is ON_2, a "surplus" emerges again, i.e. E_2W_2 as wages are driven back to the level of subsistence and the whole process is repeated until the economy reaches a point like E where the "stationary" state is attained. As wages are equal to production, there is no surplus or accumulation or expansion and the day of doom is reached. If technical progress is introduced (a shift of TP to TP′), then note that the day of doom is only postponed, but not eliminated.

The limitations of the classical model

1. It is important to note that the role of technical progress has been grossly underestimated in the model. The experience of the last two centuries has shown that the role of diminishing returns as the pointer to the day of doom has certainly diminished.

2. The "iron law of wages", which suggests that wages cannot be above or below the level of subsistence because of the Malthusian law of population, has been discredited as the sole explanation of wage determination with the growth and change of the industrial structure. For one thing, the "iron law of wages" is based only on supply whereas wages are determined both by demand and supply. For another, it does not take into account the role of trades unions in wage determination.

3. The Malthusian theory of population growth has been proved to be misleading in the light of the experience of economic growth of the economically advanced countries of today. The Malthusian argument that whenever wages are above the level of subsistence, people like to have more babies rather than bicycles, radios, televisions or cars seems to be invalid, both logically and empirically.

4. The classical model is too simple to account for all the complex factors which influence growth in the LDCs. For instance, labour is hardly a homogeneous input and nor is capital in the LDCs. Different types of labour and capital could affect growth differently. Accumulation need not be the sole objective function in peasant economies where people share and share alike. Also, attitudes, culture and traditional institutional values exert varying degrees of influence on growth.

2.3 The Keynesian theory and LDCs

It is interesting to note to what extent the Keynesian theory provides some answers to the problems of economic development of poor countries. It is significant to observe that in the classical theory money is a "veil" and has nothing to do with the determination of real factors like output and employment; money plays no role in the equilibrium analysis of value and distribution in the classical system whereas in the Keynesian model money tends to influence the equilibrium values of output and employment. Later, however, Patinkin tried to integrate value and monetary theory by introducing the real balance effect (Patinkin, 1968).

One of the main sources of conflict between the Keynesian and classical theories lies in the way the difference between demand for and supply of money should be corrected. In the classical theory, an increase in money supply will raise unwanted cash holding and, since a rational individual does not hold money for its own sake, excess money would be spent on goods and services, pushing the prices upwards, with a given level of output. The mechanism could be explained with the help of the quantity theory.

Let

$$MV = PT$$

where

M = quantity of money
V = velocity
P = price level
T = total transactions.

It is assumed that V and T are unlikely to change substantially, particularly in the short-run since V is mainly determined by tastes and T is largely given by the technology and the real resources. In such a situation, an expansion of M will have a direct and positive impact on prices. An increase or decrease in M will increase or decrease prices. The critics have, however, argued that if either V or T or both change with the change in M, then the direct relationship between M and P is unlikely to hold. To this, the "new monetarists" headed by Friedman point out that as long as the demand for money remains stable, an expansion of M would always lead to a rise in prices, though the effect may not be observed instantaneously. At a higher price the expansion of money supply would be consistent with ordinary transaction demand (=k) which is assumed to be a fixed proportion of income (=Y) or, M = kY.

In the Keynesian theory, an expansion of money supply will raise bond prices and reduce the interest rate, increase the level of investment and output and perhaps lead to a secondary effect on prices. Should there be excess capacity, the effect on prices of a rise in money supply would be even less. If we are concerned with an underemployment situation, prices should not be affected so long as the supply of output with respect to money supply is elastic. Thus the effect could well be on income, output and employment.

It is, however, difficult to see the application of Keynesian theory to the special features of an underdeveloped country. First, most LDCs have some form of "dualism" in their market structure (see Ch. 1). The money market particularly, tends to be affected by "financial dualism". The presence of the non-monetized sector also poses considerable problems as the use of monetary policies, e.g. changes in the Bank Rate and open market operations, is limited. Further, because of widespread illiteracy, people do not have sufficient knowledge about the financial assets which may be acquired. Nor do they have enough confidence in different forms of financial assets, so that investment is usually made in land or gold. Despite the presence of an organized and sophisticated money market, an unorganized money market, usually ruled by village money-lenders, merchants and traders, still predominates (Wai, 1957; Ghatak, 1976). Thus, people tend to spend more with expansion of money supply and this puts up prices in the classical fashion. This would be the case so long as the elasticity of output to the money supply is less than unity and, given the lags of response and the rigidities of the market structure, it looks as though the classical rather than the Keynesian theory would be valid for an underdeveloped country. Figure 2.2 attempts to explain this. It shows that if the money supply rises from OM_1 to OM_2, demand rises and output rises (as measured by OQ) from M_1T_1 to M_2T_2, given any excess

Fig. 2.2

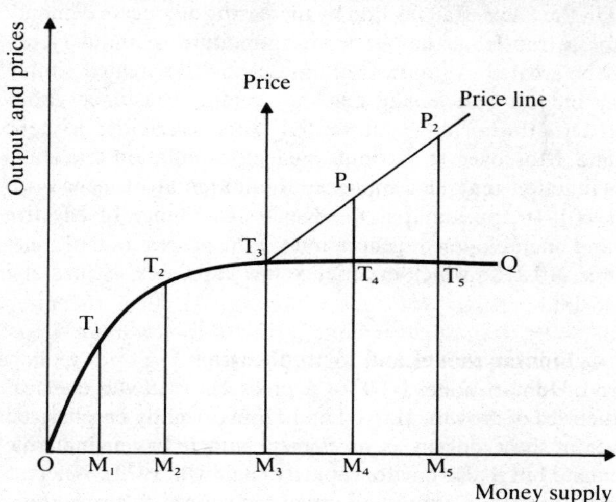

capacity or the availability of unused resources. Beyond T_3, output does not respond to increases in money supply. Thus, if money supply rises from OM_3 to OM_4, output will remain stationary if all the resources are used up, i.e. $M_3 T_3 = M_4 T_4$ but prices rise as measured by $P_1 T_4$. If money supply rises further to OM_5, prices rise to $P_2 T_5$. The classical model is valid beyond T_3 whereas the Keynesian model operates before T_3.

It has been argued sometimes that the problem of most LDCs is not always a lack of demand (indeed, with a low income, MPC, i.e. marginal propensity to consume, should be very high), but lack of savings and proper investment. Thus absence of an array of financial assets like bonds and securities as well as of financial institutions like banks (Gurley and Shaw, 1960) coupled with institutional and resource constraints plus population growth-rate may well induce one to approach the problem from the supply side (Lipton, 1969).

One of the major pillars of Keynesian economics is that income is generated by investment via the process of multiplier and hence so is consumption and *savings*. But in an LDC, given a very low elasticity of output, the Keynesian type multiplier has not much application because with a rise in investment, the money multiplier may operate but real income multiplier does not and hence prices tend to rise (Rao, 1952; Hasan, 1960). It has been argued that in LDCs there is no involuntary unemployment. Unemployment is usually disguised in the sense that although the marginal productivity of labour is zero or near zero and wages are higher than marginal productivity in underdeveloped agriculture, labour remains *employed* as the mode of production (use of *family* labour rather than *wage* labour) and objective function in traditional agriculture (income or output rather than profit maximization) are different in developed countries. The problems of unemployment can hardly be solved in the Keynesian fashion by increasing aggregate demand. Further, to allow for a transfer of labour from agriculture to industry, an industrial base must be created. An industrial base cannot be created simply by increasing *money* income and *money* demand. Again, consumer goods industries in many LDCs do not have substantial excess capacities to cope with increased demand. Moreover, redistributive effects of inflation and shifts in the consumption function may also influence the marginal propensity to consume (Hasan, 1960). It appears that the Keynesian theory of effective demand for income and unemployment generation via the process of multiplier loses much of its force in LDCs which experience low supply elasticities and structural rigidities.

2.4 The Harrod–Domar model and its application

In theory, the Harrod–Domar model (HD) is a cross between the classical and the Keynesian theories of growth. Harrod and Domar rightly emphasized that the prime mover of the economy is investment and it has a dual role to play. It creates demand but it also creates capacity (Baldwin, 1972). Whereas the Keynesians concentrated only upon the former, the classicists emphasized the latter. The variables chosen by HD are the broad aggregates, e.g. investment, capital and output. It is assumed that capital and labour are used in a *fixed* technical or behavioural relationship, and that output is related to the capital stock by the capital–output (c/o) ratio. The concept of c/o ratio has greatly dominated the present theories of growth and planning (for a good review see Myrdal, 1968) for LDCs and hence justifies some special attention.

Let Y be income or output, S = savings, and I = investment; and let $s = S/Y$, $v = I/\Delta Y$ investment/incremental output or the incremental capital/output ratio and $g = \Delta Y/Y$ (rate of growth of Y). Now, with fixed v, and given S = I in the equation, we have:

$$\Delta Y/Y = \frac{\Delta Y}{I}\frac{S}{Y} \quad \text{or } g = s/v \qquad [2.1]$$

Alternatively, in terms of a linear difference equation

$$\frac{Y_{t+1} - Y_t}{Y_t} = sb \qquad [2.2]$$

where b = output–capital ratio

$$\text{or} \quad Y_{t+1} = Y_t + sbY_t = (1 + sb)Y_t \qquad [2.3]$$

given that the proportional growth-rate of income equals the savings ratio times the output–capital ratio.

The solution to the difference equation is:

$$Y_t = Y_0(1 + sb)^t \qquad [2.4]$$

Although a solution to the model exists, the real problem that now emerges is related to stability. If we get away from the simple HD model where I is given by planned savings and where investment function based on expectations is absent, we can observe the problem even in the context of the Harrodian investment function of the accelerator type. The investment level is given by the expectations of additional demand and this investment via the multiplier generates effective demand. The real issues that Harrod confronted are:

(*a*) the conditions for realizing investors' expectations;
(*b*) the problems that emerge when the expectations are not realized.

In reality Harrod's model stands on a knife-edge because if investors expect more than the rate "warranted" by s/v (i.e. "equilibrium" or "warranted" rate of growth) then the actual growth-rate of demand will be greater than the anticipated rate leading to inflation as the expectation was too little. Conversely, if the expected rate of growth is lower than the warranted growth-rate, then the actual growth-rate will be less than the expected rate; it will mean that the investors expected too much rather than too little deflation. "The market thus seems to give a perverse signal to the investor and this is the source of Harrod's problem" (Sen, 1970). To maintain a steady state growth-rate, with labour requirements per unit of output being given, Y cannot indefinitely grow at a rate higher than n (= the growth rate of labour supply, fixed by non-economic forces); at a steady state thus $g = s/v = n$; but as s, v and n are determined independently, the steady state becomes a special case (Hahn and Matthews (1964) (i.e. HM) p. 6). Full employment steady state growth-rate stands on a "razor's edge".

Apart from the problem of instability, the HD model is based on a number of simplifying assumptions e.g. one-product (i.e. commodity composition of the total product is disregarded), fixed technological relationship between capital stock and income flows, constancy of savings ratio, absence of lags, vertical integration of the economy and no-problem about inter-industrial deliveries, absence of trade, no depreciation of capital and one-factor of production. But despite these restrictive assumptions (Chakravarty, 1959, pp. 39–40), the HD model has been used in many countries either as a rationale behind the planning exercises or as a part of forecasting mechanism (Myrdal, 1968).

The chief appeal of this model, perhaps lies in its simplicity. Given a target growth rate, g* and v, it is easy to find out the level of s that must be realized to attain g*. Again, if the sufficient level of s is not forthcoming to match a certain level of I to attain g* then the model states the required amount that should be borrowed from abroad. The model also predicts that given v, the higher the s, the higher is the g, or the lower the v with given s, the higher is g.

However, the application of the HD model is beset with numerous difficulties. We set out the major ones in the following:

1. The model is too aggregative and hence does not provide the basis for a detailed quantitative study, nor does it highlight the structural and regional problems.
2. The problem of estimation of capital is not easy in any country (Robinson, 1956) and is particularly difficult in LDCs.
3. The data available on most LDCs are such as to make the reliable estimate of capital–output ratios very difficult.
4. Labour along with capital is another input in the process of production. Even in a so-called labour surplus LDC, evidence suggests that such surplus is sometimes observed only seasonally (see Sen (1975) for a good discussion).
5. The assumption of a fixed coefficient of production may also be questioned just as it is equally possible to doubt the assumption about the absence of trade. However, the theoretical search for stability of the HD model continued and one way out was suggested by the neo-classical economists. In the following section, we shall examine the properties of the neo-classical model more closely.

2.5 The Neo-classical theory and LDCs

Basically the answer of neo-classical economists to the instability problem is to make the capital–output ratio flexible rather than fixed. It is assumed by the neo-classicists that the production function is "well-behaved", that there are constant returns to scale and no technical progress, and that capital is "malleable" (i.e. capital-stock can be adapted to more or less capital-intensive techniques of production; Solow, 1956, 1960; Swan, 1956; Hicks, 1965; Meade, 1961). Implicit within a "well-behaved" production function are the assumptions that capital and labour are perfectly substitutable and factors of production are paid according to the value of their marginal products. There is perfect foresight and flexibility of wages, prices and interest rates. It is generally argued that when the warranted growth-rate (g) is greater than natural rate $(n + m)$ and the economy tends to shoot through the full employment ceiling, labour becomes expensive in relation to capital. This would lead to the adoption of labour saving techniques. Thus the capital–output ratio will rise and s/v will fall until it is equal to $n + m$. On the other hand, if $s/v < n + m$, there would be an excess supply of labour which would reduce real wages in comparison with real interest rate inducing the use of more labour-intensive technology which would reduce v and increase s/v until $s/v = n + m$. The neo-classical model thus shows with the utmost simplicity that the Harrodian "knife-edge" problem is curable, i.e. steady state growth can be attained simply by varying the capital–output ratio. In fact equilibrium growth in a neo-classical model is consistent with the concept of dynamic disequilibrium, where output, capital stock, labour supply and investment will grow at a constant exponential rate or they do not change at all. It is the mythical "golden age" of Mrs Robinson (Robinson, 1956, p. 99). In a "golden age" economy one must have:

$$\overline{P} = \overline{P}_0 e^{qt} \quad [2.5]$$
$$\overline{K} = \overline{K}_0 e^{ht} \quad [2.6]$$
$$\overline{L} = \overline{L}_0 e^{nt} \quad [2.7]$$
$$\overline{I} = \overline{I}_0 e^{mt} \quad [2.8]$$

where P = production

K = capital

L = labour

I = investment

h, n, m = constant growth rates. (Bars over the symbols denote "golden age" equivalent growth margin.)
At full employment, investment must equal full employment savings and net investment should be equal to the change in capital stock.

$$I = \frac{dk}{dt} = sP \quad [2.9]$$

We have with

$$\overline{I}_0 e^{mt} = h\overline{K}_0 e^{ht} = s\overline{P}_0 e^{qt} \quad [2.10]$$

For all values of t the equation [2.10] can hold only when growth-rates of m, h and q are equal to one another. Also "golden age" growth-rate can take place with the rate of technical progress which should be capital-augmenting (for a simple proof, see Dernburg and Dernburg, 1969, pp. 129–130).

One major point to emphasize here is that "golden age" growth-rate is independent of the rate of saving (Swan, 1956) and this is different from the conclusion reached by HD. The reason is that a rise in the saving proportion will raise the growth of capital and output for a while but because of diminishing returns the original growth-rate will be restored. The marginal product of capital will fall if capital rises faster than labour and that will also account for the fall in the growth-rate of output. Two economies with the same growth-rate of population but different levels of s will have the *same rate* of growth (though *per capita* income levels could be different) because given $g = s/v$, whenever s rises, v also rises. Although this remarkable conclusion is partly based on capital-malleability assumption, notice that the non-malleability of capital does not preclude the steady-state solution because in the steady state the rate of profit is constant over time, and all machinery, independent of the time of its construction, will have the same labour intensity.

The neo-classical mechanism can also be explained in another way. Let us assume that output (Q) is produced by capital (K) and labour (L) and they stand in terms of the following relationship:

$$Q = K^{\alpha}L^{\beta} \quad [2.11]$$

In the type of production function given in [2.11] we assume constant returns to scale so that $\alpha + \beta = 1$. The increase in the stock of capital is the amount saved, sQ, where s is the saving/output or income ratio. The growth-rate of capital is sQ/K per annum (p.a.). Let q stand for the growth of output p.a. and n stand for the growth of labour. Given the equation [2.11] and after logarithmic differentiation, we derive the following equation to describe growth-rate of output:

$$q = \alpha sQ/K + \beta n \qquad [2.12]$$

All savings are invested through changes in the interest rate and excess capital is sQ/K per annum (p.a.). Let q stand for the growth of output p.a. interest rate (r) and the real wage rate (ω) equal to the marginal productivities of capital and labour respectively so that:

$$r = \alpha Q/K \qquad [2.13]$$

and $\omega = \beta Q/L$ [2.14]

In other words, the rate of profit is proportional to output–capital ratio and the wage rate is proportional to output per unit of labour. As α and β stand for output elasticities of capital and labour respectively, the relative share of profits and wages in the economy remains constant.

In Fig. 2.3 the linear growth-rate of capital sQ/K is taken as a function of Q/K by a line through the origin with a slope equal to a given ratio of

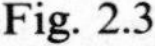
Fig. 2.3

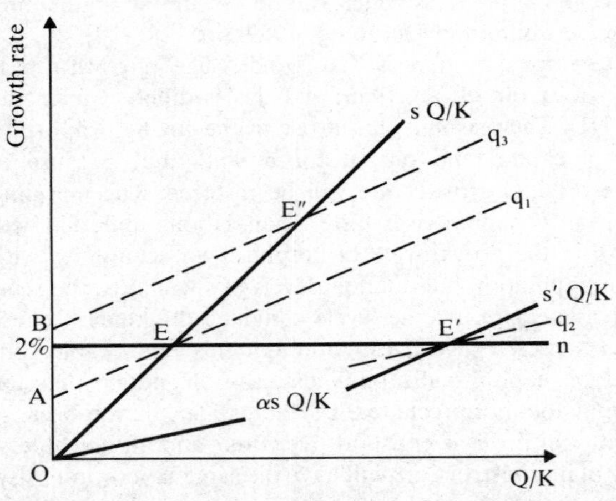

saving, say 20 per cent. This is regarded as the growth line of capital. The "contribution" of capital to output growth is given by αsQ/K in another line through the origin. The growth of labour supply is assumed as fixed (say 2 per cent).

The distance OA is βn (i.e. contribution of labour to output) growth.

Adding the two contributions of capital and labour we get growth of output q, since $\alpha + \beta = 1$. The three lines of growth must meet at a point like E where growth is, say, 2 per cent p.a. Output growth (q) lies between the growth lines of labour and capital and is divided in the proportion $\alpha : \beta$. Beyond E capital is growing faster than output and Q/K falls until E is reached and before E output is growing faster than capital and this leads to a rise of Q/K to a point like E. In short, equilibrium at a point like E is stable. In the Harrod–Domar model:

$$g = s/v$$

so that any rise in the saving ratio without any change in the capital–output ratio will lead to a rise in the growth-rate. But in the neo-classical theory capital–output ratio is no longer fixed and it could be raised, given a "well-behaved" production function. Here, if there is a rise in saving, capital–output ratio will rise by an equal proportion and that will leave the growth-*rate* unaltered. In terms of our diagram, let the saving ratio fall from 20 to 10 per cent. The point of equilibrium is now reached at E′ where the new output growth line (q_2) intersects n and s′Q/K. Note that the equilibrium rate of growth remains unchanged at 2 per cent which is given by the growth-rate of labour and the ratio of saving gives the output–capital ratio at which the equilibrium takes place. However, a rise in saving will raise the output per head and wage-rate though output–capital ratio and profit-rate will fall. But the growth-rate will remain the same.

So long as we have assumed away the role of technical progress, let us assume that technical progress is "neutral" (i.e. neither labour nor capital augmenting) and its contribution to output growth is k per cent p.a. above the contributions of capital and labour. This is given by the distance AB in the diagram. Output growth line is now given by q_3 and equilibrium is attained at E″. Note that at E″ both output–capital ratio and profit rate is higher in comparison with E. Also *per capita* output is not only higher at E″ in comparison with E but rising constantly (given by the distance between Q_3 and n. Its rate of rise is greater than m per cent (imparted by technical progress) because capital's contribution is also sustained by "technical progress at a higher level" (Swan, 1956, p. 337).

Application of the neo-classical theory to the LDCs

There are reasons which make the case for application of the neo-classical model to the developing countries very doubtful. For instance, it is difficult to accept the idea of a "well-behaved" production function in LDCs just as it is equally difficult to see the relevance of marginal productivity theory of distribution in peasant economies characterized largely by family farming rather than wage-labour. It is equally possible to argue that given the nature of market structure and financial mechanism in most LDCs, the neo-classical solution, i.e. equilibrium between r and the rate of profit would be difficult to achieve. Even when the equality can be achieved, it will be relevant only to the organized markets which are usually located in the urban sector without affecting much the partly monetized and unorganized rural sector. Further, land is generally excluded from the neo-classical production function. It is also difficult to define precisely the nature of capital in peasant economies apart from the problem of heterogeneity of capital and absence of an exact definition.

The major difficulties that arise in the application of the neo-classical model stem from analysis in terms of one-factor, capital, and the type of aggregation that has been highlighted. It is easy to comprehend some *ceteris paribus* assumptions but it is less easy to understand the existence of either a very well-behaved production function with indefinite substitution possibilities in peasant economies and the application of the principle of marginal productivity to dictate factor shares in such a way as to attain a profit rate which is commensurate with an interest rate at a steady state. In LDCs, rainfall variability alone would rule out any unique association between MP and income shares. In fact, one can get only a probability distribution of MPs and the greater the impact of future rainfall and the smaller the knowledge of that rainfall, the greater is the probability of obtaining a misleading result by applying the MP theory. Further, if the variance of rainfall is high, the risk premium will be high and the marginal value productivity equalization rule does not allow any trade-off between the variance and the expected value of profit. Moreover, factor-market imperfections and inter-farm differences in output from the same inputs would be high in less developed agriculture (Lipton, 1968b). Indeed, given fluctuations in weather and the subsistence living standards or below, the optimizing peasant needs "survival algorithms", not profit maximization. Thus, the logic of peasant economies renders the application of the MP rule difficult, partly because of the difference in the objective function and partly because of differences in institutions and social values.

There are other general criticisms of the neo-classical theory. For example, in the absence of any *specific* mechanism to bring about the equilibrium between investment and full employment saving, the balancing mechanism is supposed to be the interest rate (r) and an equilibrium rate of profit on investment which should be equal to r. But this conclusion must be qualified in the presence of risks and uncertainties. Again, monetary forces may determine a certain r which could lead to a choice of v inconsistent with a steady-state growth. Also, the steady-state profit rate may require real wages below subsistence level and hence the solution may not be feasible.

2.6 Marx's theory and LDCs

Marx rejected some principal features of the classical theory of economic growth and offered his own theory within a socio-historical framework in which economic forces play a major role. In Marxist theory, the law of diminishing returns has been discarded because Marx believed that the classical theory of stationary state was actually a creation of human actions rather than the end product of a natural, immutable law. For a similar reason, Marx also castigated the Malthusian theory of population.

Marx looked at economic development from a social and historical standpoint. Each stage of economic growth was regarded as the product of Hegelian dialectics of a game of contradictions where a thesis created its anti-thesis and the conflict between the two produced a synthesis. Marx also emphasized that with capitalism, *social relations of production* are much more important than exchange relations between goods. The *social* character of labour has been stressed in particular. Marx argued that labour productivity "is a gift, not of nature, but of history embracing thousands of centuries" (Marx, 1906, Vol. 1, p. 562). However, the Marxist concept of *relations of production* is rather vague. It has been interpreted as an "*organic* whole" characterized by the labour organization and skill, the standing of labour in society, the technological and scientific knowledge and its use in a certain environment (Bober, 1950). In the Marxist analysis, these "relations of production" determine the socio-cultural set-up of a society. Marx believed that capitalism would not end up in a quiet classical "stationary" state; rather, it would break up with a "bang" "when the expropriators are expropriated". Here, we shall only analyse the economic views in the Marxist theory, abstracting from social and institutional issues.

The Marxist model of economic growth depends on some major dynamic "laws". First, the law of capitalistic accumulation which says that the prime desire of the capitalists is to accumulate more and more capital.

Second, the law of falling tendency of the *rate* of profit which plays a crucial role in the breakdown of the capitalistic system. This law is illustrated below.

Third, the law of increasing concentration and centralization of capital which tells us that with the growth of capitalism, cut-throat competition among capitalists will lead to the annihilation of smaller firms by bigger ones which would lead to the growth of monopoly and concentration of economic power.

Fourth, the law of increasing "pauperization" which implies the growth of the misery of the working class with the advancement of capitalism, that would be reflected in wages being tied to the subsistence level coupled with the rise in the proportion of unemployed people or what Marx called the "industrial reserve army of labour", made possible by the substitution of capital for labour in the process of technical change.

The simultaneous working of these laws would generate contradictory forces which would eventually sharpen the class conflict between capitalists and workers or between "haves" and "have-nots". Capitalism would face a violent death in the final confrontation when the expropriators would be expropriated. Hence, Marx gave the clarion call: "Workers of the world, unite", as they have nothing to lose excepting their "chains".

The Marxist notion of the falling *tendency* of the *rate* of profit plays a crucial part in the whole process of change and can now be illustrated. According to Marx, the value of a commodity (w) is given by the sum of "constant capital" (c) or the plant and machinery *used up in production* plus the "variable capital" (q) or the wage bill plus the "surplus value" (s) or the value that labour produces in excess of necessary labour to produce a commodity. If the working day consists of 8 hours and only 4 hours are required to produce a commodity then for the remaining 4 hours the worker is producing a surplus value which is expropriated by capitalists (Sweezy, 1942). More formally,

$$w = c + q + s$$

and $s' = s/q$

where s' = rate of surplus value or the rate of "exploitation".

Thus, in the above example,

4 hours/4 hours = 100 per cent = s'

The rate of profit (p) in the Marxian analysis, is given by

$$p = \frac{s}{q + c}$$

or $$p = \frac{s/q}{1 + c/q}$$

Let $s/q = x$, i.e. the rate of exploitation and

$c/q = j$

or the "organic composition of capital". Then we have

$$p = \frac{x}{1 + j}$$

Now, it is clear that if x remains constant, p and j would be inversely correlated. A rise in j would take place as capitalism develops with continuous accumulation. Also, capitalists would substitute capital for labour whenever wages tended to rise above the subsistence level to maintain their rate of profit. The process would lead to higher unemployment among the working class and sharpen the polarization of forces. On the other hand, the crisis of capitalism would be reflected in the periodic fluctuations of growth and a falling tendency of the rate of profit. Such a falling tendency of the *rate* of profit would lead to cut-throat competition among the capitalists which, in its turn, would lead to monopoly. Eventually, the conflict between the 'immiserized proletarians' and the capitalists would toll the death knell of capitalism.

It is interesting to observe that the law of a tendency for the rate of profit to fall may not always be observed within an economic system. This could be easily demonstrated *within the Marxist model* (see Adelman, 1962). We have,

$$p = \frac{x}{1 + j}$$

Differentiating p with respect to time (t) we obtain,

$$\frac{dp}{dt} = \frac{1}{1+j}\frac{dx}{dt} - \frac{x}{(1+j)^2}\cdot\frac{dj}{dt}$$

or,
$$\frac{dp}{dt} = \frac{1}{1+j}\left\{\frac{dx}{dt} - p\frac{dj}{dt}\right\}$$

Note that the profit rate will *rise* if the rate of exploitation rises more rapidly than the organic composition of capital. Even if the rise in the organic composition of capital is higher than that of the rate of exploitation, whether or not profit will fall depends on the difference between dx/dt and the *product* of profit-rate and dj/dt. For profit-rate to *fall*, p dj/dt (which is negative), must be greater than dx/dt. But a *fixed* rate of exploitation and an increase in capital intensity may not go together because a rise in organic composition of capital would raise labour productivity which would either raise the rate of exploitation (which Marx assumes away) or a rise in real wages (which Marx rejected). Inevitably, the internal consistency of the Marxist model has been questioned (Sweezy, 1942; Adelman, 1962). Further, as it has been shown above very clearly, a rise in the organic composition of capital could *increase* the rate of profit with an increase of productivity and a change in technology. Under such circumstances, the intensity of competition among capitalists declines. Technical progress may be neutral or even labour-using (say, with the application of more and more seed and fertilizer in agriculture in LDCs). Thus the rise in the industrial reserve army of labour and a fall in the wage share in national income may not occur.

Other criticisms usually levelled at the Marxist model may also be mentioned briefly. It is contended that Marx's correlation between the growth of the average firm size and an increase in the degree of concentration need not always happen. However, the proportion of unemployment has increased in both DCs and LDCs in recent decades.

Empirically, wage share of national income in most DCs remained fairly constant for a long time and this phenomenon seems to have weakened the Marxist law of increasing pauperization (Kaldor, 1957). On the other hand, the Marxist prediction about the increasing concentration and centralization of capital is not rejected. However, the rise in the output–capital ratios in DCs probably reflects the growth of both accumulation and real wages, a phenomenon which Marx probably did not envisage within the strict framework of his analysis (Fellner, 1957).

Marx and the LDCs

On the problems of LDCs, Marx's analysis was rather thin. Marx paid some attention to Indian economic problems. The Indian society was regarded by Marx as an assembly of small self-contained "village systems" where people "agglomerated in small centres by the domestic union of agricultural and manufacturing pursuits". The socio-economic system of India stagnated because "these little communities (i.e. *village systems*) transformed a self-developing social state into never-changing natural destiny" (Marx, 1853). Marx thought that British rule in India would administer an (albeit rude) shock to the static India society, through the introduction of modern science and technology, which would break down the static society and usher in capitalism. However, the verdict of history has been somewhat different.

The quintessence of the Marxist theory of underdevelopment is well summarized by Adelman: "underdevelopment is the consequence of a particular adverse combination of initial conditions and structural parameters, which results in economic and social stagnation. Development can occur only as a result of an exogenous shock, the essential effect of which is to change the initial conditions in such a way that self-sustained growth takes place" (Adelman, 1962, p. 91).

Neo-Marxist theory of underdevelopment

The idea that the village system of LDCs could be changed by an exogenous shock has prompted some Marxist economists of today (whom we would call neo-Marxists) to use the Marxist model to analyse problems of LDCs (for a review of theoretical contributions to post-Marxian literature, see, for example, Bose, 1975). There are, of course, other sociological, political and historical reasons. Here, a very brief outline of the neo-Marxist theory of underdevelopment is stated.

Some neo-Marxists trace the origin of capitalism to the idea of mercantilists who believed in the principle of accumulation. Historically, the development of capitalism in Europe led to imperialism and colonialism which created a wealthy and strong centre (the imperial power) and a weak, poor periphery, which mainly consisted of colonies. The capitalistic and imperialistic development at the centre is supposed to have taken place through the exploitation of colonies at the periphery, and this is supposed to have been reflected in the movement of the ratio of export price or terms of trade against poor countries (Prebisch, 1964). Free trade became the convenient vehicle of "exploitation". Hence: "Underdevelopment, no less than development itself, is the product but also part of the motive power of capitalism" (Frank, 1975; also 1969; for an evaluation of the Prebisch thesis, see Ch. 8). The poor countries of today despite their political independence, have become *economically dependent* upon the developed metropolis because of their historical past reinforced by the "neo-colonial" ties of trade, aid and transfer of technology. As trading partners, the LDCs are dependent upon the DCs because the goods they usually produce (mainly primary commodities) are both price and income inelastic while the goods they want, they cannot produce themselves. It is argued that such a situation has led to "unequal exchange" between the centre and periphery (Emmanuel, 1972). The LDCs are further exploited and made more dependent upon the DCs with the growth of international capitalism and multinational corporations who in their global search for more profit can easily mop up "surplus" from LDCs (and DCs as well) as they can direct their investment from low-profit to high-profit areas quite easily (Radice, 1975).

Productivity is likely to remain low in those LDCs from whence the "surplus" or profit has been extracted and this could only perpetuate their poor economic conditions. The structural effects of such a system are seen in the prevention of the growth of indigenous enterprises, perpetuation of a small market which usually caters for "elitist" demand or the demand of the people who are included in the higher income groups in LDCs. Also, one finds the inadequate production of goods necessary for mass consumption, import of luxury goods which creates balance of payments problems and the choice of technology and products which are unsuitable for LDCs. Thus, the technology which is capital-intensive (often imported) usually creates more unemployment and poverty and accentuates the existing inequalities in income distribution. The indigenous "elite class" in collusion with international capitalism perpetuates the self-reproducing, static, neo-colonial structures of LDCs. This is, in a nutshell, the underdevelopment and dependency theory (UDT) in the neo-Marxist writings of today.

The empirical support of the neo-Marxist theory is usually derived from the experiences of the poor Asian and the Latin American countries in the last twenty-five years. It is argued that despite the modest growth of the real national income in these countries, both inflation and unemployment have soared. The increase in *per capita* real income has been slight, while in some cases it has actually fallen with poverty and inequality in income distribution increasing. This is regarded as partly the product of the UDT theory, partly of the so-called "socialistic" policies which consist of the manipulation of the Keynesian interventional policies rather than the restructuring of economies, say, on Chinese lines, and partly because of the unholy alliance of the international aid agencies, champions of state capitalism within the LDCs, who are against fundamental reforms and multinationals or the "fall guys".

Evaluation of the neo-Marxist theory of underdevelopment

Many of the hypotheses on the UDT, put forward by the neo-Marxist writers are not amenable to rigorous statistical analysis. Some of them will be dealt with in subsequent chapters. Suffice now to say that the debate on the movement of the terms of trade against LDCs remains inconclusive even today (see Ch. 8). Protection and import substitution have sometimes resulted in real income losses in LDCs and abdication of principles of free trade, over-valuation of currency and controls of trade have actually penalized exports and agriculture and rewarded industry and urban areas in LDCs (see Ch. 6 and Ch. 8). Ironically, "protection" has sometimes really meant the protection of the small sector of rich industrial monopoly capital at the expense of the vast agricultural sector where 70 to 90 per cent of people in LDCs live. However, the effects of multinationals on the economies of LDCs have been debated and the extent of "exploitation" is not always known (see Ch. 9). It is also difficult to accept the argument that the effects of the flow of foreign resources to LDCs have *always* been harmful. The argument about the choice of wrong technology or of product does not always clearly follow from the UDT theory as such a choice is not only exogenous but also endogenous.

In other words, even if multinationals wish to introduce from outside inappropriate techniques or products to LDCs, such an introduction or choice could not always be made without the internal support of recipient countries. At the theoretical level, it may be argued that the UDT defines the concept of development rather vaguely. It does not state clearly the ways to accomplish development; it is too much concerned with the analysis of how *underdevelopment* took place in the *past* rather than how *development* can be achieved in the *future*; it does not seek to estimate carefully the extent of exploitation. Naturally, statements like "Capitalism has created underdevelopment not simply because it has exploited the underdeveloped countries, but because it has not exploited them *enough*" (Kay, 1975 [authors italics]), become difficult to evaluate. Indeed, it has been argued rather pointedly, "Curiously enough, it is not clear that UDT provides any explanation of why more capital was not invested and accumulated in the Third World in the past, nor of why it should not now take advantage of cheap labour and soak up vast pools of unemployed people in the Third World today." (Leys, 1977, p. 96).

2.7 The Kaldor–Mirrlees model

Kaldor has discussed two models of economic growth (1957 and 1962). Here, we shall be mainly concerned with the one by Kaldor and Mirrlees (KM) in 1962. The crucial feature of the KM model is that the saving ratio can be made flexible to obtain a steady state economic growth. Unlike the neo-classical model, the capital–output ratio remains fixed. Note that KM discard the production function approach of the neo-classical theory and introduce a technical progress function. The neo-classical school has not specified any investment function; but in the KM model, an investment function is specified which depends upon a fixed pay-off period for investment per worker (1962). Both the assumptions regarding the full employment and perfect competition are dropped. Instead, KM start off with assumption that total income (Y) is equal to the sum of wages (W) and profits (P)

or $Y \equiv W + P$ [2.15]

Total savings (S) are assumed to be equal to savings out of wages (S_w) and profits (S_p)

or $S = S_w + S_p$ [2.16]

Note that $S = s_w W + s_p P$ [2.17]

and $S_w = s_w W$ [2.18]

$S_p = s_p P$ [2.19]

where s_w = propensity to save by wage earners

s_p = propensity to save by profit earners

S = total savings

Both s_w and s_p are assumed to be constants indicating the equality between marginal and average propensities.

Now $Y \equiv W + P$

and $S = s_w W + s_p P$

By substitution, we have

$$S = s_w(Y - P) + s_p P \quad [2.20]$$

$$S = (s_p - s_w)P + s_w Y \quad [2.21]$$

Since it is assumed that $I = S$ [2.22]

we have,

$$I = (s_p - s_w)P + s_w Y \quad [2.23]$$

Dividing both sides of the equation by Y, and rearranging, we obtain,

$$\frac{P}{Y} = \frac{1}{s_p - s_w} \cdot \frac{I}{Y} - \frac{s_w}{s_p - s_w} \quad [2.24]$$

Thus, the profit share of income is given by the share of investment to income. The stability of the model is given by

$$0 \leq s_w \leq s_p \leq 1$$

Notice that the flexibility of saving is achieved in the KM model by the assumption of different propensities to save by wage and profit earners. The specific value of savings necessary to obtain the solution would be given by income distribution between income classes. Given s_p and s_w, I/Y will determine P/Y. If it is assumed, *à la* the Keynesian parable of the widow's cruse, that $s_w = 0$, we then obtain

$$\frac{P}{Y} = \frac{1}{s_p} \cdot \frac{I}{Y} \quad [2.25]$$

Note that if the capital–output (K/Y) is fixed as in the HD model, we can write,

$$\frac{P}{Y} \cdot \frac{Y}{K} = \frac{1}{s_p} \cdot \frac{I}{Y} \cdot \frac{Y}{K}$$

or, $$\frac{P}{K} = \frac{1}{s_p} \cdot \frac{I}{K} \quad [2.26]$$

Since $P/K = V$, or the rate of profit earned on capital and,
$I/K = J$, or the rate of accumulation, we have,

$$V = \frac{1}{s_p} \cdot J$$

or $$s_p \cdot V = J \quad [2.27]$$

This conclusion betrays remarkable affinity to the Von Neumann case where Neumann puts $s_p = 1$. Thus, all profits are saved and in the equilibrium we obtain,

$$V = J\ (=n)$$

where n = the natural growth-rate which is assumed to be given. Thus the rate of growth is given by the rate of profit which is determined by the propensity to save of the profit-earners.

Kaldor's introduction of an "alternative" theory of distribution to analyse the problem of economic growth is interesting. However, several important criticisms have been levelled at the Kaldorian theory. First, Pasinetti mentions a "logical slip" in Kaldor's argument when he observes that although Kaldor has allowed the workers to save, he did not permit these savings to accumulate and generate income. In a more general theorem, Pasinetti has demonstrated that on a steady-state growth path, the profit rate depends only on the growth-rate and the propensity to save by the capitalists; it is independent of the propensity to save by the workers (see Pasinetti, 1962, for the proof). However, if it is assumed that capitalists as a class have been banished and capital is owned by the workers alone, then the relevant variables in the balanced growth path will be given by s_w and n (see, for details and proof, Samuelson and Modigliani, 1966; also, for a lucid analysis, Jones, 1975).

Second, Kaldor's assumption about the fixed propensities to save disregards the impact of life cycle on saving and work. Third, the assumption of a fixed *class* of income receivers is regarded as unrealistic (Samuelson and Modigliani, 1966).

Finally, Kaldor's model fails to exhibit an explicit *behavioural* mechanism which will ensure that the *actual* distribution of income would be such as to maintain the steady-state growth path.

Few empirical tests are available to know whether the Kaldorian theory could be applied to the LDCs. In one study that was conducted for the Indian economy, for the period 1948–58, no positive and statistically significant relationship was observed between profit share and investment share in income (Bharadwaj and Dave, 1973). However, due to the imperfection of data and rather small number of observations, more research is necessary to draw any firm conclusion. The present emphasis on the analysis of economic growth and income distribution by Chenery *et al.* (1974) in LDCs may lead to more theoretical and empirical research in this field.

Growth models for the "open" LDCs: An income or monetary analysis?

In growth models discussed so far, little attention has been paid to the impact of foreign trade on economic growth of the LDCs. One main reason for the lack of consideration of the role of trade in economic development of the LDCs is that trade usually forms a small part of the total income of these countries. On the other hand, there are quite a few exceptions. Further, at present it is difficult to see how the LDCs in general could be wholly immune to the ebb and flow of world trade. A general recession in the DCs is likely to affect most LDCs adversely because a fall in the level of income and aggregate demand in the DCs could also reduce the exports, output and employment in many LDCs. It is, however, true that LDCs who rely more on trade than others (more "open" or "dependent") are likely to be harder hit by a general recession in the DCs than others who are less "open". In any case, it is interesting to analyse the interrelationships between output, income, exports, imports and prices in the "open" LDCs and try to quantify the effects as far as possible. One attempt was made by Polak (1957) and Polak and Boissonneult (PB) (1959). In the next section, the PB model is discussed briefly.

2.8 The Polak–Boissonneult (PB) Model

The PB model is a simple way to analyse the effects of imports, exports and money supply within the circular flow economy. Once the imports, previous exports and credit creation of a country are known, the PB model could be used to find out the specific values of such imports, exports and credit creation that would be needed to reach target levels of income and reserves. The basic PB macro-model can be set out as follows:

$$Y_t = Y_{t-1} + \Delta MS_t \qquad [2.28]$$

where, Y = nominal national income
MS = quantity of money
t = income period in which money supply turns over once in income generating transactions.

Thus, t could be regarded as a fraction of a period given by the ratio of money to national income which would indicate the reciprocal of the average velocity of income. Thus the equation states that, given a stable income velocity, next year's income will be given by the sum of the present year's income and a change in the quantity of money. Alternatively, with a given income velocity, quantity of money will change from one year to the other by an amount equal to the change in income. Now the ΔMS_t is divided as follows:

$$\Delta MS_t = \Delta R_t + \Delta D_t \qquad [2.29]$$

where R_t = *net* foreign assets
D_t = *net* domestic assets

Next, we have a balance of payments equation:

$$\Delta R_t = X_t - M_t + C_t \qquad [2.30]$$

where X = exports
M = imports, and
C = net capital inflow.

The change in MS, and thus in Y can now be defined as,

$$\Delta MS_t = X_t + C_t + \Delta D_t - M_t \quad [2.31]$$

Let the exogenous variables be classified as Q_t, so that we have

$$Q_t = X_t + C_t + \Delta D_t \quad [2.32]$$

The equation for imports is given as

$$M_t = mY_t \quad [2.33]$$

By substituting the last three equations into [2.28] we have,

$$(1 + m)Y_t = Q_t + Y_{t-1} \quad [2.34]$$

Let the equation [2.34] be divided by (1 + m) and the elimination of the terms with Y in the right-hand side (RHS) of the equation [2.34] yields,

$$Y_t = \frac{Q_t}{1 + m} + \frac{Q_{t-1}}{(1 + m)^2} + \cdots \quad [2.35]$$

and the corresponding equation for imports is given by,

$$M_t = \frac{mQ_t}{1 + m} + \frac{mQ_{t-1}}{(1 + m)^2} + \cdots \quad [2.36]$$

The last two equations give income and imports in terms of Q_t, i.e. the exogenous variables.

For the sake of easy computation and to determine Y and M without first obtaining the value for exports, Q_t could also be defined as,

$$Q_t = \Delta MS_t + M_t \quad [2.37]$$

It is generally argued from the above presentation that since PB have tried to determine income via changes in the quantity of money, their approach is that of a monetarist (Schotta, 1966, Baker and Falero, 1971). Notice that in the PB model, income is sought to be determined by both money supply *and* the foreign exchange reserves so that such a model could provide simple policy guidelines to an LDC experiencing a foreign exchange bottleneck. The model is also useful to analyse the relationships between goods and financial flows. The advantage of the PB model is that it is simple and does not require too much information about a large number of variables and hence becomes suitable for application to the LDCs.

The critics of the "monetary" interpretation of the PB model have, however, contended that "far from being a version of the quantity theory, the Polak model is essentially Keynesian in its income determination characteristics" (Newlyn, 1969). The assumption of constant velocity in the PB model is rejected by Newlyn. "The constant velocity postulate is not a reflection of a propensity to hold money in relation to the level of income like that in the 'Cambridge k'. It is simply a reflection of structural factors" (Newlyn, 1969, p. 6). However, since the basic equation stated at the outset of the PB model requires that all income should be spent, it is important to retain the assumption of the constant income velocity. Nevertheless, the

PB model need not necessarily imply that a change in the equilibrium in cash balance would *lead* to income changes. Indeed, as Bolnick argues, if the first three equations are regarded as basic to the PB model, they could easily be given a Keynesian interpretation, while ΔD, X and C could be regarded as injections to the income flow. To maintain a constant velocity, it is conceivable that a change in income which leads to a change in the demand for money will have to be adjusted by changing the money supply (Bolnick, 1975). As Polak argues in his original article, an increase in the quantity of money "is determined by the increase in income . . . and the assumed ratio of money to income" (Polak, 1957, p. 23). Such an interpretation of the PB model would render it more Keynesian rather than classical. It seems that the PB model could be given both a monetarist and a Keynesian interpretation depending upon one's choice of the fundamental relationships among the crucial economic variables and direction of their causation. Note that Polak himself was partly responsible for the ambiguity that has been caused in the interpretation of his model. Thus, although in the first version of his model (1957) Polak suggests that the change in the quantity of money is given by the changes in income, in his second model (1959), Polak defines his equation [2.31] as a relationship that "yields an explanation of the change in money, and *thereby* of the change in income" (Polak, 1959, p. 351; for a clarification of such an ambiguity, see Prais, 1961; emphasis added is mine).

Empirical tests of the PB model

The empirical tests of the PB model carried out so far have been quite interesting. It is suggested that in Nigeria, changes in money supply have led to changes in expenditure which, in their turn, have led to changes in income and imports (Gray, 1963). The Mexican, as well as the Peruvian experiences suggest that both the monetary and the income mechanisms operate though the explanatory power of the monetary mechanism seems to be greater than that of the income or the Keynesian mechanism (Schotta, 1966; Baker and Falero, 1971). The Peruvian information also suggests that the role of foreign trade in explaining the changes in the net national product is less important than has been suggested in the literature. In both the monetary and the income mechanisms, government sector (measured by the size of public expenditure) has played a very important role (Baker and Falero, 1971).

Although it has been claimed that the monetary mechanism explains greater variation in income in comparison with the income mechanism, it should be mentioned that these results should be viewed with caution. For one thing, the explained variations of income by the two mechanisms by the statistical models employed for testing are not very large. Second, these models are rather simple and might easily have ignored more complicated relationships among the variables, given the economic structure of LDCs. This has been shown clearly in the values of the Durbin–Watson statistic in some of these models which signified the presence of auto-correlation or the impact of serially correlated variables which have been omitted from the model (Johnston, 1972). Further research is clearly needed in this field.

3

Dual-economy models

3.1 Introduction

The growth models which are examined in Chapter 2 are highly aggregated in the sense that no attempt has been made to distinguish between different sectors of the economy, e.g. agriculture and industry. However, since economies of LDCs are regarded as far less homogeneous than those of DCs, it is sometimes argued that the case of LDCs should be analysed in terms of "dual-economy" models. Unlike the DCs, the LDCs do not suffer from a labour supply constraint. The problem in LDCs is thus to transfer "surplus" labour from unproductive to productive employment to promote growth. Such a problem was first tackled by Lewis (1954).

3.2 The "surplus" of labour and its contribution to development

Lewis's model with "unlimited" supply of labour

Surplus labour – *à la* Lewis (1954) is defined as that part of the labour force that can be removed without reducing the total amount of output produced, even when the input of other factors remains constant. Lewis assumed a dual economy – a modern exchange sector and an indigenous subsistence economy. The capitalist sector uses reproducible capital and pays capitalists for the use thereof but the subsistence sector uses non-reproducible capital. Output per head is higher in the organized sector in comparison with the indigenous sector. Lewis argues that many poor countries such as India, Egypt and Jamaica have unlimited supplies of labour, but parts of Africa and Latin America may have a shortage of male labour. Unlimited supplies of labour exist in the subsistence sector since the supply of labour is greater than the demand for labour at the subsistence wage; i.e. the marginal product (MP) of labourers in the subsistence economy is negligible or zero, or at least below the subsistence wage.

This peculiar feature is regarded as disguised unemployment, implying that if some workers from the agricultural sector obtained alternative jobs, the rest (assuming they work harder and are willing to do so) could maintain, and in some cases increase, output. No unemployment benefit exists so the costs of maintaining the disguised unemployment/underemployed fall on the working population.

Surplus labour and the growth of the economy

Surplus labour can be used instead of capital in the creation of new industrial investment projects, or it can be channelled into nascent industries, which are labour intensive in their early stages. Such growth does not raise the value of the subsistence wage, because the supply of labour exceeds the demand at that wage, and rising production via improved labour techniques has the effect of lowering the capital coefficient.

Although labour is assumed to be in surplus, it is mainly unskilled. This inhibits growth (the same as land or capital scarcities) since the technical progress necessary for growth requires skilled labour. But should there be a labour surplus and a modest capital, this bottleneck can be broken through the provision of training and education facilities.

The utility of unlimited supplies of labour to growth objectives depends upon the amount of capital available at the same time. Should there be surplus labour, agriculture will derive no productive use from it, so a transfer to a non-agricultural sector will be of mutual benefit. It provides jobs to the agrarian population and reduces the burden of population from land. Industry now obtains its labour. Labour must be encouraged to move to increase productivity in agriculture. To start such a movement, the capitalist sector will have to pay a compensatory payment determined by the wage-rate which people can earn outside their present sector, plus a set of other factors which include the cost of living in the new sector and changes in the level of profits in the existing sector. The margin capitalists may have to pay as much as 30 per cent above the average subsistence wage (see Fig. 3.1).

Figure 3.1 represents the capitalist (or industrial) sector. The marginal revenue product of labour in the subsistence sector is shown by NR, OW is the industrial wage. Given the profit maximization assumption, employment of labour within the industrial sector is given by the point where marginal revenue product is equal to the rate of wages, i.e. OM.

Since the wages in the capitalist sector depend on the earnings of the subsistence sector, capitalists would like to keep down productivity/wages in the subsistence sector, so that the capitalist sector may expand at a fixed wage. In the capitalist sector labour is employed up to the point where its marginal product equals wage, since a capitalist employer would be reducing his surplus if he paid labour more than he received for what is produced. But this need not be true in subsistence agriculture as wages could be equal to average product or the levél of subsistence.

The total product of labour (ONPM in Fig. 3.1) is divided between the payments to labour in the form of wages, OWPM, and the capitalist surplus, NPW. The growth of the capitalist sector and the rate of labour absorption from the subsistence sector, depend on the use made of capitalist surplus.

Fig. 3.1

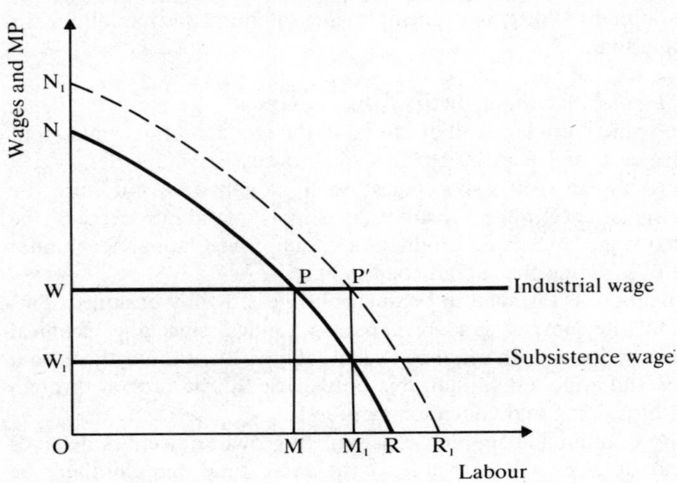

When the surplus is reinvested, the total product of labour will rise. The marginal product line shifts upwards to the right, say to N_1R_1. Assuming wages are constant, the industrial sector now provides more employment. Hence employment rises by MM_1. The amount of capitalist surplus goes up from WNP to WN_1P'. This amount can now be reinvested and the process will be repeated and all the surplus labour would eventually be exhausted.

When all the surplus labour in the subsistence sector has been attracted into the capitalist sector, wages in the subsistence sector will begin to rise, shifting the terms of trade in favour of agriculture, and causing wages in the capitalist sector to rise. Capital accumulation has caught up with the population and there is no longer scope for development from the initial source, i.e. unlimited supplies of labour. When all surplus labour is exhausted, the supply of labour to the industrial sector becomes less than perfectly elastic. It is now in the interests of producers in the subsistence sector to compete for labour as the agricultural sector has become fully commercialized. Note that it is the increase in the share of profits in the capitalist sector which ensures labour surplus is continuously utilized and eventually exhausted. Real wages will tend to rise along with increases in productivity and the economy will enter into a stage of self-sustaining growth.

Criticism of Lewis's model

Several criticisms are levelled at Lewis's theory of dual economic growth:

1. Economic development takes place via the absorption of labour from the subsistence sector where the opportunity costs of labour are very low. However, if there are positive opportunity costs, e.g. loss of crops in times of peak harvesting season, labour transfer will reduce agricultural output.

2. Absorption of surplus labour itself may end prematurely because competitors may alter wage rates and lower the share of profit (Mabro, 1967). It has been shown that rural–urban migration in the Egyptian economy was accompanied by an increase in wage rates of 15 per cent and a fall in profits of 12 per cent (Mabro, 1967). Wages in the industrial sector were forced up directly by unions, and indirectly through demands for increased wages in the subsistence sector, as payment for increased productivity. In fact, given the urban–rural wage differential in most poor countries, large-scale unemployment is now seen in both the urban and the rural sectors.

3. The Lewis model underestimates the full impact on the poor economy of a rapidly growing population, i.e. its effects on agricultural surplus, the capitalist profit share, wage rates and overall employment opportunities. Similarly, Lewis assumed that the rate of growth in manufacturing would be identical to that in agriculture, but if industrial development involves more intensive use of capital than labour, then the flow of labour from agriculture to industry will simply create more unemployment.

4. Lewis seems to have ignored the balanced growth between agriculture and industry. Given the linkages between agricultural growth and industrial expansion in poor countries, if a section of the profit made by the capitalists is not devoted to agricultural development, the process of industrialization would be jeopardized.

5. Possible leakages from the economy seem to have been ignored by Lewis. It is assumed boldly that a capitalist's marginal propensity to save is close to one, but a certain increase in consumption always accompanies an increase in profits, so the total increment of savings will be somewhat less than increments in profit.

Whether or not capitalist surplus is used constructively will depend on the consumption/saving patterns of the top 10 per cent of the population. But capitalists alone are not the only productive agents of the society. Small farmers producing cash crops in Egypt have shown themselves to be quite capable of saving the required capital. The world's largest cocoa industry in Ghana is entirely the creation of small enterprise capital formation (Elkan, 1973).

6. The transfer of unskilled workers from agriculture to industry is regarded as almost smooth and costless, but this does not occur in practice because industry requires different types of labour. The problem can be solved by investment in education and skill formation: but the process is neither smooth nor inexpensive.

Empirical tests of Lewis's model

1. Empirical evidence does not always provide much support for the Lewis model. Shultz (1964) in an empirical study of village India during the influenza epidemic of 1918–19 showed that agricultural output declined although his study does not prove "whether output would have declined had a comparable proportion of the agricultural population left for other occupations in response to economic incentive" (Sen, 1975, also 1967). Again disguised unemployment may be present in one region/sector of the economy but not in others. Further, empirically it is important to know not only whether the marginal productivity is equal to zero, but also the amount of surplus labour and the effect of its withdrawal on output (Sen, 1975, 1966).

2. Shultz did not distinguish between summer (*Kharif*) and winter (*Rabi*) seasons of agricultural production (Mehra, 1966). A study on India has shown that summer agricultural output (which followed the epidemic) did not actually fall. The fall in output observed by Schultz was mainly due to some random elements like weather conditions. However, the fact that the summer output did not fall even when there was a substantial reduction of labour tends to support the hypothesis of Lewis. In fact, an analysis of farm data (which is much more interesting than the results deduced from the aggregated data) reveals that while in some farms, marginal productivity (MP) of labour may be positive, in others it could be zero or statistically insignificant (Desai and Mazumdar, 1970).

3. Lewis did not pay full attention to the pattern of seasonality of labour demand in traditional agriculture. It has been established that labour demand varies considerably and such demand is at its peak during the sowing and harvesting seasons (Mehra, 1966). Thus, during some months of the year, the MP of labour could be much above zero.

4. The Lewis model was applied to the Egyptian economy (Mabro, 1967) and despite the proximity of Lewis's assumptions to the realities of the Egyptian situation during the period of study, the model failed (*a*) because Lewis seriously underestimated the rate of population growth and (*b*) because the choice of capital intensity in Egyptian industries did not show much labour-using bias and, as such, the level of unemployment did not show any tendency to register significant decline.

5. The validity of the Lewis model was again called into question when it was applied to Taiwan (Ho, 1972). It was observed that despite the impressive rate of growth of the economy of Taiwan, unemployment did not fall appreciably and this is explained again with reference to the choice of capital intensity in industries in Taiwan. This raised the important issue whether surplus labour is a necessary condition for growth.

3.3 The Fei–Ranis model

Among many points that have been made about the Lewis model, it has been emphasized that Lewis did not pay enough attention to the importance of agriculture in promoting industrial growth. Also it is argued that an increase in productivity (surplus of agriculture) should precede mobilization of labour. Indeed, Fei and Ranis (FR) observed the above mentioned points and tried to develop a dual economy model involving three stages of growth (1964).

The first stage of the FR model is very similar to that of Lewis. Disguised unemployment is supposed to exist as the elasticity of labour supply is infinity and the marginal product of labour is zero. In the second stage, it is shown that rising productivity in agriculture is the foundation for industrial growth necessary to sustain the third stage. In the second stage, it is argued that labour surplus may exist as average product (AP) which is higher than the marginal product (MP) and is not equal to subsistence level of wages (see Fig. 3.2); instead it is increasing. Note that the labour supply curve in Fig. 3.2(*a*) is perfectly elastic between S and T.

Fig. 3.2

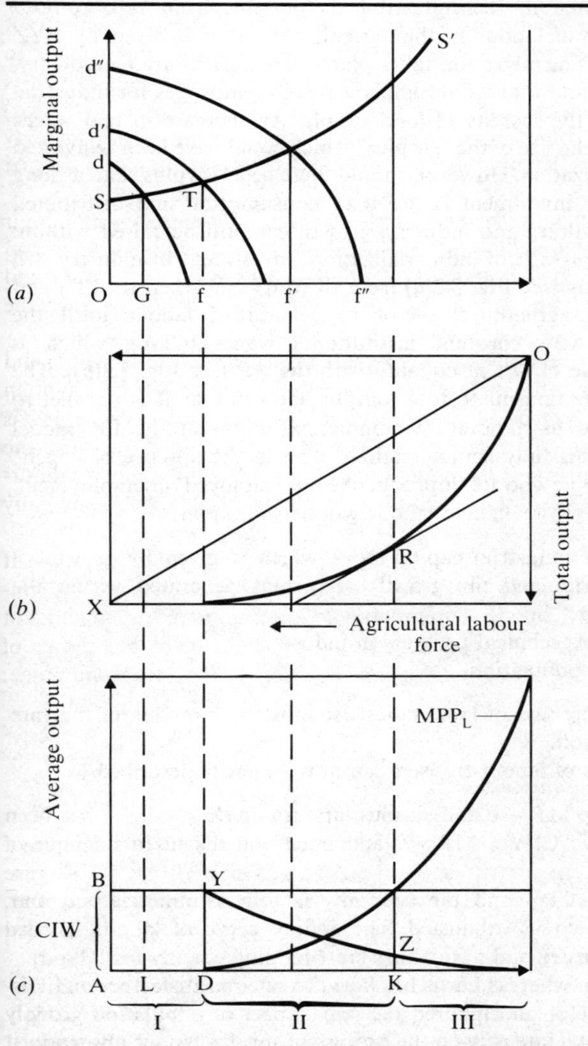

In phase (I), in terms of Fig. 3.2(*c*)

AL = MP = 0 and

AP = AB

Following the analysis of Lewis, FR argue that AD units of labour can be withdrawn from the agricultural sector without changing the agricultural output.

In Phase (II), AP > MP, but after AD it begins to rise (Fig. 3.2(*c*)). The growth of labour force in the industrial sector rises from zero to OG (Fig. 3.2(*a*)). The AP of labour in the agricultural sector is given by BYZ (Fig. 3.2(*c*)). After AD as migration takes place from agriculture to industry, MP > 0 but AP falls and that would imply a rise in real wages for industrial labourers because of the scarcity of food supply. An increase in real wages will reduce profit and the size of the "surplus" which could have been reinvested to promote industrialization. However, should there be a "surplus" and as long as it can be used for investment rather than consumption and distributed evenly between agriculture and industry, growth can still be raised without reducing the rate of growth of industrialization. Investment in industry will shift the MP outwards (see Fig. 3.2(*a*) from df to d'f' and then to d"f") and this will enable the agricultural sector to get rid of labour until the MP = real wages = AB = constant institutional wages (CIW), which is measured by the slope of OX at equality with the AP (see Fig. 3.2(*b*)). The MP = CIW where the tangent to total output line ORX at R is parallel to OX. This is regarded as a point of commercialization in the FR model because the economy is fully commercialized now in the absence of "open" or "disguised" (i.e. people who are unproductive but employed) unemployment. The amount and time to reallocate labour will depend upon:

(*a*) rate of growth of industrial capital stock which is given by growth of profits in industries and the growth of surplus generated within the agricultural sector;
(*b*) nature and bias of technical progress in industry;
(*c*) rate of growth of population.

It is important that the rate of labour transfer must be in excess of the rate of growth of population.

The three phases of labour transfer can now be easily described.

In Phase I: we have MP = 0 and surplus labour = AD.
In Phase II: we have CIW > MP > 0 and open and disguised unemployment = AK.
In Phase III: MP > CIW and the economy is fully commercialized and disguised unemployment is exhausted. The supply curve of labour is now steeper and both industry and agriculture start bidding equally for labour.

Thus, we find that whereas Lewis has failed to offer a satisfactory analysis of this subsistence sector and ignored the real impact of population growth and the choice of capital intensity on the process of surplus labour absorption,

FR emphasized that the agricultural sector must also grow in line with industrial growth if the mechanism that Lewis described was not to grind to a halt. Thus, three major points are highlighted in the FR model:

1. Growth of agriculture is as important as the growth of industry.
2. The growth of agricultural and industry should be balanced.
3. The rate of labour absorption must be higher than the rate of population growth to get out of the Malthusian nightmare.

FR argued that surplus can be extracted by the investment activities of the landlords and by the fiscal measures of the government. However, "leakages" could exist because of the costs of transferring labour (both private and social, like transport costs and building of schools and hospitals etc.), increased *per capita* consumption of agricultural output and the maintenance of a "permanent" gap between urban and rural wages. Note that productivity in agriculture may not rise even if higher *per capita* incomes were not consumed. This could happen if the supply curve of the labour is backward-bending, i.e. peasants reduce their work effort as their incomes rise.

It may, however, be pointed out that if *per capita* income rises, consumption patterns may change without an increase in food consumption. Further, the case of backward-bending supply curve of labour hardly has any empirical basis (Blake, 1962).

Evaluation of the FR model

Although the FR model is an improvement on the Lewis model in the sense described above, a number of criticisms have been levelled at it.

1. It is assumed in the FR model that MPL = 0 and the transfer of labour from agriculture would not reduce output in the agricultural sector in Phase I. But it has been shown (Berry and Soligo, 1968), that agricultural output in Phase I of FR model will not remain constant and may fall under different systems of land tenure (e.g. peasant proprietorship, share-cropping etc.) except under the following *three* cases:

(*a*) Leisure is an inferior good.
(*b*) There is leisure satiation.
(*c*) Leisure and food are perfect substitutes with a constant marginal rate of substitution for all real income levels.

If MPL > 0, leisure satiation is ruled out and if MPL = 0 complete substitution between leisure and food is not a sufficient condition for fixed output. The only sufficient condition is that leisure is an inferior good whatever the value of MPL may be (see Fig. 3.3). Let food be measured in the vertical axis and leisure along the horizontal axis. I_0, I_1 are the indifference curves between food and leisure of the agriculturist within the "potentially feasible" set of consumption points. OS is the subsistence level of food consumption without which labour in the agricultural sector will not live. OG is the maximum leisure and thus labour input is measured from right to left as the

Fig. 3.3

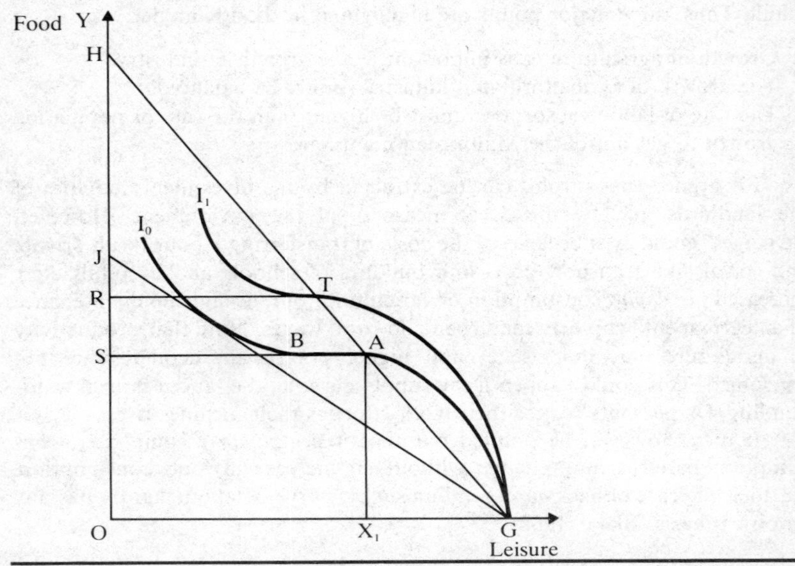

origin in this case is G. The falling slope of the transformation curve SAG implies that the agricultural worker is using up more leisure to the same units of land. The marginal rate of transformation between leisure and food is zero at a point like A. Note that at A, MPL = 0 and when the indifference curve is tangent at this point to the transformation curve, leisure satiation obtained as the marginal rate of substitution between food and leisure is zero. Let OS = subsistence level of income. When the wage-rate is given, the transformation curve is GH and its slope is the fixed wage-rate. Now, if one labourer is transferred from the agricultural sector and his land is distributed equally among the remaining labourers, SAG shifts to RTG. Note that at T, MPL = 0 and the same APL per hour as in A, given constant returns to scale. Let us assume that MPL = 0 where agriculturists are living at the subsistence level. In order to maintain the same level of output, when SAG shifts to RTG, the indifference curve going through T must be flat (see also Sen, 1966). But this would imply "leisure satiation" (as explained above), or leisure as a very inferior commodity (i.e. indifference curve going through A may not be absolutely flat, though the one which goes through T must be so). Leaving these conditions which Berry and Soligo consider as exceptional, total output would decline. *Per capita* output remains the same though, because otherwise consumption will be less than the level of subsistence, and labour input per head may either increase or decrease (see Berry and Soligo, 1968, for details of different types of cases).

2. It has been mentioned already that whether or not MPL = 0 is an empirical issue, given the seasonality in the food production in LDCs, it is more likely that the MPL would be greater than zero, particularly during the sowing and harvesting seasons. The Japanese data, even for the pre-First World War period, did not show the existence of an unlimited supply of labour (Jorgenson, 1966).
3. In the FR model, output is mainly determined by land and labour inputs, and the role of capital has been neglected. It has been shown that capital plays an important role in determining output, particularly when one considers the recent technological changes in agriculture in LDCs – sometimes called the "Green Revolution". (The literature on the "Green Revolution" is vast: see Brown, 1971; Byres, 1972 (who has listed 104 references); Frankel, 1971; Griffin, 1974, 1976).
4. FR ignored the role of foreign trade as they assumed a closed economy model. It is observed in the process of the economic development of Japan that she imported cheap farm products to improve her terms of trade. It may be pointed out that the relaxation of a closed economy assumption will soften the balanced growth constraint.
5. One of the major reasons to account for the sluggish expansion of the industrial sector in the LDCs could have been the very low productivity rises in subsistence agriculture. In such a situation, the rise in surplus from agriculture is much more an important determinant of non-agricultural employment than the reinvestment of surplus (Jorgenson, 1966). Indeed, this is the essence of the dual economy model as developed by Jorgenson (1961), who argues that for the improvement of the modern sector (i.e., non-agricultural) of the LDCs, it is imperative that the surplus must be generated and *it should persist*. We now turn to the discussion of the Jorgenson model in the next section.

3.4 The Jorgenson model

Jorgenson distinguishes between the modern (say industrial) and the backward (say agricultural) sector of the economy. Production in the backward sector is determined by land and labour and such production function is subject to diminishing returns. In the modern sector, output is given by labour and capital and the function is subject to constant returns to scale. It is assumed that the technical progress is neutral. Population growth is determined by *per capita* food supply and the net rate of reproduction (i.e. birth-rate minus the death-rate). Given these assumptions, Jorgenson argues that "surplus" in agriculture (food production net of consumption) releases labour to be employed in industry and the growth-rate of industrial employment is given by the growth of the surplus. After the initial investment, growth of accumulation is given by the growth of labour in the industrial sector and the terms of trade between the agricultural and the industrial sectors though industrial real wages could be more than agricultural real wages to allow for labour migration. The gap is proportional to industrial wages and is stable in the long run. This gap also determines the terms of trade between the two sectors and the investment rate in the modern sector. It is assumed that the economy is closed. The model can then be formally described as follows:

Let Y = agricultural production
L = total land available
P = total population

Let the production function be of the Cobb–Douglas type, i.e.

$$Y = e^{\alpha t} L^{\beta} P^{1-\beta} \quad [3.1]$$

where $e^{\alpha t}$ is the change in output due to technical progress. Since land is assumed to be fixed:

$$Y = e^{\alpha t} P^{1-\beta} \quad [3.2]$$

Now $y = Y/P = e^{\alpha t} P^{-\beta}$ [3.3]

where y = *per capita* agricultural output.

Differentiating with respect to time and dividing by y, we obtain:

$$\dot{y}/y = \alpha - \beta\, \dot{P}/P \quad [3.4]$$

Let $\dot{P}/P = \eta$

Then $\dot{y}/y = \alpha - \beta\eta$ [3.5]

or $\dot{y} = (\alpha - \beta\eta)\, y$ [3.6]

The general solution is then:

$$y(t) = e^{(\alpha - \beta\eta)t} y(0) \quad [3.7]$$

which specifies the situation where *per capita* income growth, $\alpha - \beta\eta > 0$, would be obtained for any positive level of output. In a backward economy, β (i.e. diminishing returns to labour in agriculture), is assumed to remain fixed. Hence, public policy should be used to alter either α (i.e. rate of technical progress) or η (i.e. the maximum growth rate of population), or both. An increase in output per head would be assumed as long as $\alpha > \eta$. Where $\alpha = \eta$, a "low-level equilibrium" is obtained.

In the industrial sector, the production function is given by:

$$Q = F(C, L, t) \quad [3.8]$$

where Q = total industrial output
C = capital
L = industrial labour
t = time, as technical progress is expected to be rapid in industries.

Let $Q = A(t) C^{\gamma} L^{1-\gamma}$ [3.9]

Let $\dot{A}/A = \lambda$

or $\dot{A} = A\lambda$ [3.10]

A little manipulation shows that:

$$\dot{q} = e^{\lambda t}C^{\gamma} \qquad [3.11]$$

where q = output per head.

Again differentiating with respect to time and dividing through by q:

$$\dot{q}/q = \lambda + \gamma \frac{\dot{C}}{C} \qquad [3.12]$$

To promote growth and to escape stationary equilibrium of a backward economy, it is necessary to accumulate capital. But to promote accumulation, it is imperative to extract positive agricultural surplus. Note that $\alpha - \beta\eta > 0$ is a necessary and sufficient condition for generating agricultural surplus and the generation of surplus is vital for industrialization. Jorgenson argues that the surplus should not only be extracted but it must persist to avoid any slipping back to the stationary state.

Note that Lewis and FR models predict a fall in capital–output ratio at a given rate (λ/β). Also given the assumption that capitalists save all of their income, Lewis and FR models predict rising growth rates of output and employment as capital grows over time. In the Jorgenson model, growth-rates of output and capital would be the same and employment in the modern sector will rise less rapidly than the rise in capital and output. (For a modification of Jorgenson's analysis, see Dixit, 1969; Kelly *et al.*, 1972.)

Evaluation of the Jorgenson model

Despite the elegance of the Jorgenson model, several criticisms of it can be made. First, Jorgenson ignores the role of capital in his agricultural production function. Empirical evidence does not always support this assumption (see, for example, the Japanese case, Nakamura, 1965; the Indian case, Shukla, 1965; and the Egyptian case, Hansen, 1968). Indeed, in some cases, capital has played a significant role in raising agricultural output. Second, although the production relations between the modern and the backward sectors are considered as different, no such difference in tastes (i.e. demand) is recognized. Also, most writers on dual economy including Jorgenson have ignored the "spatial" effects of structural change. Third, it has been shown that once the assumptions regarding taste and technology are altered, the predictions of the Jorgenson model (and indeed those of Lewis and FR models also) lose their generality (Kelly *et al.* 1972). Fourth, the neo-classical features of the Jorgenson model have their usual limitations. Fifth, although there may be some truth in the observations of Jorgenson (1966) and also of Schultz (1964), that the marginal productivity of labour in agriculture is unlikely to be zero, particularly in the sowing and harvesting seasons, the point is not important to find out the proper shadow price in a surplus labour economy. What is relevant to determine the shadow price is the difference between the "marginal productivity of the employed and the marginal productivity of the unemployed" (Marglin,

1976, p. 11) because "whenever a gap exists between a worker's marginal productivity and his opportunity cost, a labour surplus exists in the sense that is relevant for valuation of inputs and outputs. Shoe-shine boys, pedicab drivers and farmers are surplus if output would be increased by transferring men from these services and from agriculture to industry" (Marglin, 1976, p. 11).

3.5 Some extensions of the dual-economy models: Dixit–Marglin model

The dual-economy models have been extended to include dynamic behaviours. These models are fairly complex as they deal with dynamic optimization problems (see Dixit, 1968, Marglin, 1976). Here, we summarize their main features only.

In the models of Lewis and FR, the supply curve of labour is assumed as perfectly elastic at a given real wage rate (W) which is either fixed by the subsistence level or by institutional considerations. At full employment, APL < W, given the paucity of capital. Marglin (1976) has shown that in an economy with the features described by Lewis and FR, over a *finite* planning horizon, a dynamic optimal employment policy neither maximizes output nor surplus, but is in between, and the rule to pursue a dynamic investment policy is that demand price of investment should be greater than the marginal utility of consumption. Note that the rule in the neo-classical theory is that demand price of investment should be equal to marginal utility of consumption. However, as Dixit (1968) points out, in Marglin's analysis labour surplus and subsistence consumption persist and it is expected that the economy would attain full employment within a *given finite* time horizon. In Dixit's model, both consumption and full employment appear as constraints.

The optimal growth path for a subsistence economy consists of different phases. By the end of Phase I, enough capital accumulation takes place and APL > W, but unemployment is allowed to persist. In Phase II, full employment prevails but W = *per capita* consumption, i.e. investment is allowed to take place at the cost of consumption. As Phase II ends after a given time, *per capita* consumption is allowed to rise as the economy enters the neo-classical era. However, Dixit does not pay such attention either to the agricultural sector or to the terms of trade between agriculture and industry and marketed surplus. There are political and institutional constraints which can affect the solutions (Marglin, 1976).

3.6 The Kelly *et al.* model

In a *general* theory of growth in dual economies, Kelly *et al.* (1972) have tried to analyse the problems of transition and technological dualism in agricultural and industrial production, bias in technical progress, difference in consumption patterns and migration. The basic model consists of fourteen equations and fourteen variables. A useful feature of the model is the inclusion of demand analysis based on the work of Stone (1964) and Geary's (1951) linear expenditure system. The other interesting feature of the model is the analysis of demographic dualism. Simulation techniques are used to test the model mainly in the light of the experience of Meiji Japan (a Japanese Imperial Dynasty like the Moghuls).

In contradistinction to the Jorgenson model, Kelly *et al.* assume that both sectors use labour *and* capital. Given the parameter values and initial conditions, time paths of the endogenous variables are observed (e.g. declining labour share, fixed rate of technical progress, falling growth-rate of output, etc.). The choice of initial values is dictated by the experience of the writers in the Philippines and the simulation is carried out in the case of Meiji Japan. The writers claim that the model performed very well.

However, several questions remain unanswered. First, the exclusion of land in the agricultural production function is very surprising. Given the "satisfactory" performance of the model, it is implied that land is *not* a significant variable, affecting output. This is very surprising. The writers have ignored the role of foreign trade which is regarded by some as one of the major engines of growth. However, the authors' attempt to explore the sensitivity of the key variables to different parameters merit serious attention. It is of interest to note that shifts in demand parameters have significant effects on growth and structural change. In the disequilibrium model also, the sensitivity analysis of the relationship between economic change and demand is interesting.

But the analysis of the terms of trade is very sketchy. Despite these criticisms, it should be pointed out that the authors have adopted an interesting approach to analyse the problems of dual economies though the choice of a neo-classical framework of analysis and the experience of Meiji Japan to test the model must be viewed with caution.

3.7 Dual-economy models: a critique

The growth models considered in Chapter 2 are highly aggregative and some economists (Lewis, 1954; Fei and Ranis, 1961, 1964; Jorgenson, 1961, 1967; Dixit, 1968, 1971, 1974; Williamson *et al.* 1972) began to analyse the problems in terms of two sectors, viz., agriculture and industry. Briefly, the so-called traditional non-capitalist agricultural sector is supposed to be unresponsive to economic incentives and here the leisure preferences are imagined to be high; production for the market does not take place and producers apparently do not follow profit-maximizing rules: "disguised" or open unemployment is supposed to prevail throughout the rural sector and indeed the marginal productivity of labour is expected to be zero, and in some cases negative. (Nurkse, 1953). Income is equal to subsistence level (Leibenstein, 1957, p. 154) partly determined by physiological and partly by cultural levels (Lewis, 1954). Further, capital has no role to play in agricultural production (Jorgenson, 1967, p. 291). Two sectors are linked by the influx of surplus homogeneous labour from agriculture to industry. Nothing happens to the transfer of savings or capital and growth takes place when demand rises as a result of ploughing back of profits by the capitalists into reinvestment. The backward sector is eventually "modernized" with the transfer of all surplus labour from agriculture.

The extension of the Lewis model by Fei and Ranis (FR), (1964), also suffers from some limitations. First, no attempt is made by FR to account for stagnation. Second, no clear distinction is made between family based labour and wage based labour and nothing is said about the process of self-sustaining growth. The investment function is not specified and money, price, foreign exchange as well as terms of trade between agriculture and industry are ignored.

The dual-economy model of Jorgenson (1961, 1967) is based on familiar neo-classical lines but hardly helps us to accept it as a more sound theory or, better, in terms of its predictive capacity. For example, Jorgenson considers land and labour only in terms of their agricultural production function and ignores the role of scarce capital. Jorgenson assumes that a surplus arises when agricultural output per head is greater than the income level at which the population growth-rate is at its "physiological maximum". This is difficult to comprehend because a clear definition of physiological maximum is lacking and a surplus may exist even before the point at which income corresponding to this maximum is reached. Jorgenson, like Ranis and Fei, neglects the role of money and trade. No capital formation takes place in agriculture in Jorgenson's model; no attempt is made to analyse the problems of disguised unemployment in agriculture and it is boldly assumed that the industrial wage is equal to marginal productivity of labour. The shortcomings of the Jorgenson model, *vis-à-vis* the FR model, lie in the assumption of a "Malthusian response mechanism and a zero income elasticity of the demand for food" (Hayami *et al.*, 1971, pp. 22–23). Population growth in LDCs is not always determined by consumption per head. Also, the case for a zero income elasticity of the demand for food is not well supported in practice (NCAER, 1972). (For an extension of the Jorgenson model, see Ramanathan (1967), where some of the restrictive assumptions are relaxed.) In both the FR and Jorgenson models, it is implicitly assumed that the technical progress would be of a labour-augmenting type. This may not happen in practice (Krishna, 1975). The Lewis and FR models suffer from the additional weakness in laying the emphasis only on accumulation and not on technical progress. If growth in the Lewis–FR fashion means rise in income and if the marginal propensity to consume food is positive for any group of income recipients, then, with given output, food prices will rise which will raise wages and reduce profits and growth. Thus any type of accumulation increases industrial wages and at no phase is the supply of labour to industry infinitely elastic (Guha, 1969).

The earlier dual economy models failed to specify the precise relationship between two sectors (Dixit, 1968). It is contended that to take care of the interdependence between terms of trade and supply price of labour, a general equilibrium analysis may be necessary. Dixit (1968, 1971) implies that the important factors that affect the shadow price of labour are the degrees of sub-optimality of savings (the shadow price of savings in terms of consumption) as well as the price and income elasticities of the demand for food.

In general equilibrium analysis, if the interdependences are to be dealt with simultaneously, it becomes difficult to see how the results rest on the premises or whether the "tail is wagging the dog". Again, Dixit's assumption that the only activity which can be undertaken in the traditional sector is food production is not easy to accept. The traditional sector also enters into non-agricultural activities; market wages and the shadow price of labour could be different because of taxes which may be influenced by elasticity of marketed surplus. In any case, Dixit does not give much emphasis to the agricultural sector in his earlier model (1968). Thus, the closed economy models of the dual economy may be misleading (Newbery, 1974, p. 41) and the empirical estimation of a general equilibrium model is very difficult.

It seems that although the writers on the dual economy models adopted a useful approach to analyse the problems of LDCs, most of their work is devoid of any rigorous empirical analysis. An attempt has been made (Kelly *et al.*, 1972) to test a modified neo-classical dual-economy model with particular reference to Japan by using simulation techniques. It seems that the Japanese case is not very typical (Ishikawa, 1967) of LDCs. The other familiar neo-classical premises on which the model rests do not seem to be very appropriate. These include full employment, wage-labour and neglect of land as an input in the production function. The absence of foreign trade and lags in the economic system are also disturbing.

Although the dual economy models originated from the unnecessary neglect of agriculture the models themselves do not perform very well, not only because they are based on certain simple and sometimes incorrect assumptions but also because they fail in their predictive power. First, the division of the sectors into two completely independent compartments is dubious. Second, almost all the empirical evidence available at present, suggests that farmers in LDCs respond to price incentives in a way which is very similar to the response that one finds in developed countries (Bauer and Yamey, 1959, Behrman, 1968, Dean, P., 1966, Krishna, 1963, Ghatak, 1975). Third, it is doubtful whether disguised unemployment prevails throughout the year. Seasonal unemployment is easily observed in many poor countries, e.g. Algeria (Griffin, 1969). But employment in non-farm works is also observed in some countries (Griffin, 1969). Evidence also suggests that in some countries surplus labour could disappear at times of sowing and harvesting (Jorgenson, 1966, Schultz, 1964, Marglin, 1976). Fourth, wages could be higher than marginal products only when non-farming activities are wholly absent, no employment is offered outside the joint family farm and if no labour is hired (Berry and Soligo, 1968). But the experience of Latin America (Griffin, 1969), the case of migrant labour in Africa and the fact of hiring labour during sowing and harvesting seasons of main crops in India would not always support the zero marginal productivity theory. It is shown that all farms are not characterized by zero MP of labour. (Mathur, 1964). Fifth, the case of a backward-bending supply curve of labour (Boeke, 1953, p. 40; Higgins, 1968) in LDCs may also be debated.

If people live at subsistence level, it is only natural that they would seek to attain their survival algorithms and the trade-off between income and leisure would not be observed until a critical minimum income level is reached where the basic wants are satisfied. We shall elaborate this point in the next chapter. Sixth, the theory that only the capitalists in the urban sector can save, is questioned (Bergan, 1967). After investigating the saving behaviour in Pakistan and Bangladesh, Bergan concludes that, "rural areas . . . appear to have contributed at least three fourths of total savings of the country." Similarly, despite the fact that the Egyptian situation conformed well to some basic assumptions of the Lewis model, its application shows very poor predictive power partly because of the underestimation of population growth-rate, the nature of manufactures and the behaviour of capitalists (Mabro, 1967, pp. 341–377).

The predictions of the dualistic theories are threefold:

(1) aggregate *per capita* income should increase; (2) *per capita* rural income would remain fixed; (3) the rate of population growth would be the same as the growth-rate of agriculture. Facts from most LDCs show otherwise. In Africa (north of the Sahara), between 1960–67 *per capita* income fell by 0.3 per cent per year. *Per capita* rural income also fell in some parts of India (Bardhan, 1970a,b), in Spanish America (Griffin, 1969), and Pakistan (Bose, 1968). Between 1957 and 1966 the growth-rate of the population was greater than the growth-rate of food production in many countries (Griffin, 1969, p. 26). The models thus seem to be static and not historical. However, more research is necessary to draw firm conclusions about the utilities of the dual economy models.

Appendix

Within the Lewis and Fei–Ranis model, it is possible to demonstrate that the accumulation of surplus or profits by the capitalists need not always raise the level of employment in the industrial sector (see Fig. A3.1). The vertical axis measures the real wage and the marginal productivity of labour (MPL) and the horizontal axis measures the employment of labour. Initial equilibrium is reached at a point like E where the MPL = OW (real wage). Notice that the line WW′ is infinitely elastic because it is assumed that the supply of labour is unlimited at a subsistence level of wage or OW. The wage bill is given by OWEN and surplus or profits are equal to DWE. If the capitalist decides to choose capital-intensive (i.e. labour-*saving*) techniques of production, labour productivity rises as shown by the shift of the demand or the MPL curve of labour from DD to D_1D_1 but neither wages nor employment rises as the equilibrium is still attained at E. However, profits of the capitalists are greater after the introduction of labour-saving techniques and the area $WD_1E > WDE$. This may also be regarded as an illustration of growth without "development".

Fig. A3.1

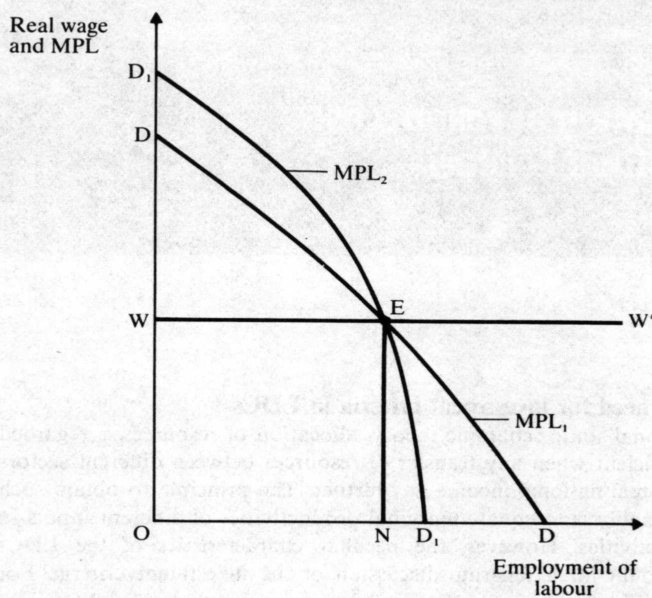
Real wage
and MPL
D₁
D
MPL₂
W
E
W′
MPL₁
O
N
D₁
D
Employment of
labour

4

Allocation of resources: investment criteria

4.1 The need for investment criteria in LDCs

In the traditional static economic theory, allocation of resources is regarded optimal or efficient when any transfer of resources between different sectors will not raise real national income any further. The principle to obtain such point of optimality is to equate marginal productivities of different inputs in alternative activities. However, the peculiar characteristics of the LDCs generally account for a separate discussion of the investment criteria. For example, the different markets (product, labour, money etc.,) in the LDCs are so imperfect that the market prices of resources, i.e. wages and interest, do not reflect their true social opportunity costs. Thus, market prices may give wrong "signals" for allocating resources and given the divergences between the marginal private net benefits (net of costs) and marginal social net benefits (net of costs), the use of marginal principles will result in misallocation of resources. Second, the LDCs may not be interested in the *static* principles of resource allocation.[1]* Given these principles, the LDCs may wish to maximize immediate rather than future output and consumption. But this may not lead to the attainment of a future optimal level. Third, it is normal in the application of the static principles that the existing distribution of income is assumed to be optimal and remains unaltered by the choice of development strategy. This is questionable if the choice of a strategy leads to maximum output but a more uneven distribution of income. That this can occur in practice has been shown in the process of "Green Revolution" in many LDCs. Fourth, the question of externalities in many sectors could well lead to the divergences between social and private costs.

Problems of investment criteria in LDCs are also related to macro and micro level decision-making processes. However, these processes could be, and sometimes are, interrelated. Thus, the planners may have to decide on the *sectorial* allocation of investments. Next, within the different sectors,

* See Notes at end of the Chapters.

given the resources decisions regarding the choice of *projects* should be made: finally, the project managers must also decide the *techniques* of production, given the relative prices of different inputs. Note that the choice of techniques could be easily influenced by the sectoral allocation of resources. Likewise, project allocation could be influenced by sectoral allocation. Again the choice of techniques may influence project allocation.

The debate among the different schools advocating different investment criteria has generally centered round the question of allocating scarce inputs in the LDCs (usually capital and sometimes foreign exchange) in the most efficient way to attain the best combination between present and future consumption, subject to the economic and social constraints. Since the arguments are different, and each has some merits and limits, we will proceed to discuss them in turn.

4.2 The capital–turnover criterion

The problems of investment strategies in most LDCs centre round the choice of values of the different variables of the Harrod–Domar growth model to maximize growth-rates. Assuming that S = saving–income ratio and C = capital–output ratio, the Harrod–Domar model states that g = S/C where g = rate of growth of output, (see Ch. 2). It is obvious from this equation that to raise the growth-rate, we are required either to raise S or to lower the value of "C". Given such policy options, Polak (1943) and Buchanan (1945) argued that given the scarcity of capital in LDCs the Harrodian "C" should be minimized. This is known as the capital–turnover criterion. The marginal capital–output ratio (i.e. the capital coefficient) shows the additional investment needed to obtain an additional unit of output. Usually, historical experience dictates the past values of the capital–output ratio though one can make allowance for failure. Total needs for capital can be obtained by the use of aggregate capital–output ratio and sectoral output ratios could be used to estimate the needs for capital in various sectors. According to Polak and Buchanan, those investment projects should be chosen which have a low "C", i.e. a high rate of capital–turnover.

The merits of this line of argument are as follows:

1. Given some capital scarcity in LDCs, the high capital–turnover criterion would lead to an efficient allocation of resources.
2. Since the rate of population growth and sometimes the size of population is very high, the supply of labour in most cases is greater than demand particularly in unskilled work. The choice of the capital–turnover criterion would lead to the adoption of labour-intensive techniques of production and this would help to alleviate the problem of unemployment.
3. Since many LDCs suffer from a balance of payments constraint because of their high demand to import modern technology from the developed countries, the use of capital turnover criterion will reduce such demand and ease the pressure on foreign exchange.

However, this theory is criticized on many grounds. To mention the major arguments:

(*a*) The use of this criterion ignores the externalities arising out of investments. Given the complementarities of different projects, a project which involves a higher capital–output ratio need not be assigned always a lower priority.
(*b*) The time element plays a crucial role because quick-yielding projects with a lower capital–output ratio in the short run do not necessarily have a lower ratio in the long run.
(*c*) In some projects, particularly within the agricultural sector in LDCs fixed capital may form a small proportion of total inputs of working capital, the fixed capital–output ratio may fluctuate substantially because of factors other than capital investment.
(*d*) The use of the capital–turnover criterion may go against the objective of maximizing the rate of economic growth if resources like skill and management are scarce.

4.3 The social marginal productivity (SMP) criterion

It has been contended mainly by Kahn (1951) and Chenery (1953) that in allocating investment, it is necessary to consider the total net contribution of the marginal unit of investment to national output (i.e. SMP) and not merely that portion of the contribution (or of its costs) which may accrue to the private investor. Efficient allocation consists of maximizing the value of national product and the principle to obtain this objective is to equate the SMP of capital in different uses. Note that where the social opportunity cost of labour is zero, there is no difference between the capital–turnover criterion and the SMP criterion. More formally the SMP criterion may be defined as follows:

$$\mathrm{SMP} = \frac{\mathrm{V}}{\mathrm{K}} - \frac{\mathrm{C}}{\mathrm{K}}$$

where V = Annual value of total output
C = Total annual cost of amortization
K = Total investment

To adjust for the total net effect on balance of payments (B), the above equation can be rewritten as:

$$\mathrm{SMP} = \frac{\mathrm{V}}{\mathrm{K}} - \frac{\mathrm{C}}{\mathrm{K}} + \frac{\mathrm{VB}}{\mathrm{K}}$$

where VB = Variations in income because of changes in one unit of balance of payments.

Like the capital–turnover criterion, the SMP principle also suffers from the following major criticisms.

1. The SMP principle ignores the multiplier effects on future income levels.
2. The SMP criterion does not make due allowance for the changes in the nature and quality of factors of production such as population and labour that may take place as a result of present investment.
3. In the labour-surplus economies where the opportunity cost of labour may be zero, the SMP criterion is open to the same criticisms which may be levelled against the capital–turnover criterion.

Until now we have been discussing the main strengths and weaknesses of the arguments which are advanced to the theory of maximizing current national income. We now turn to the discussion of the theory which aims at maximizing future rates of growth.

4.4 The maximization of the rate of creation of investible surplus (MRIS) principle

The MRIS criterion is chiefly advocated by Galenson and Leibenstein (1955). Their main objective is to maximize *per capita* real income at a future point of time. Galenson and Leibenstein emphasize the role of capital accumulation to achieve a higher rate of growth. Their main argument rests on the following premises. First, national income can be divided into two parts: wages and profits. Second, wage earners savings (or Sw = 0) but profit earners total income are available for investment. Third, one production function, which makes output per unit of labour a function of capital per unit of labour, prevails in the whole economy.

Given these assumptions, maximization of *per capita* real income at some future point of time would require an increase of capital per unit of labour at present. This implies the maximization of investment at each preceding period which in turn requires that profits share in national income should be maximized (or wages share be minimized). The implication is to choose those projects which involve higher capital intensity, i.e. where capital–labour ratio is highest. Allocation efficiency is achieved by distributing the available capital in different uses in such a way that "the marginal *per capita* re-investment quotient" of capital is equal in different projects.

Evaluation of the MRIS criterion

1. *Per capita* real income maximization at some future point of time has not been considered as a very realistic goal (Eckstein, 1957). It is argued that governments should be concerned with the welfare to be enjoyed at each period in future with the entire future growth of the system.
2. There is not enough evidence to assume that the propensity of the workers to save will be zero and that of the profit earners will be equal to one. Even if it is assumed that the only savers are profit earners, maximization of profit does not necessarily imply maximization of capital–labour ratio (Moses, 1957; Bator, 1957).
3. Maximum use of capital in some projects may well reduce the rate of profit particularly where we do not assume that production is the same function of capital for all sectors.

4. In labour-surplus economies as well as in LDCs characterized by large unemployment and underemployment, maximization of employment may well be a social and political objective (Brahmananda and Vakil, 1956). Realization of such an aim may well call for the use of capital–turnover rather than the use of the MRIS principle.
5. Many LDCs do not have markets large enough to support capital-intensive industry on an economic basis.
6. Unless a balance is struck between increases in production of capital goods and consumer goods, supply inelasticities in the production of consumer goods could lead to inflation.[2]

The capital-intensive industries in some LDCs have been set up by disregarding the doctrine of comparative cost advantages and by upholding the argument of protecting the infant industry. Sometimes, output of these protected industries is inferior in quality and their prices are higher in terms of world prices. When these industries are protected *sine die*, the benefits of obtaining a high reinvestment quotient in these industries must be offset by the high price paid by those industries which use their product and the consequent reduction in their reinvestment quotient. This argument is not without empirical foundation as has been shown in connection with the construction of a fertilizer plant near Paradeep in India (Sara, 1975).

However, all these criticisms do not necessarily invalidate one of the major points in the Galenson–Liebenstein thesis: the use of the SMP criterion may lead to a choice of projects and would imply a given income distribution which could affect savings rate. Eckstein (1957) argues that the use of fiscal policies may be necessary in such cases to obtain desired savings instead of banking upon planned investment based on reinvestment criterion. But given the limitations of the fiscal policy in raising savings Eckstein has proposed that projects with the highest marginal growth contribution (MGC) should be selected where MGC is given by the projects' direct contribution to consumption plus the present value of future consumption stream rendered possible by the growth of capital. However, the limitations of Eckstein's theory are obvious. For one thing, population is regarded as an exogenous variable; for another, income distribution is regarded as optimal throughout the analysis. However, Eckstein admits that where the government cannot achieve a satisfactory level of investment by fiscal means, those projects should be favoured which yield high rates of reinvestment. Next, if the time horizon is infinite, it is unreasonable to assume that the only critical factor in growth is capital at every period in the future. Moreover, the need to direct all reinvestments to a single project can also be questioned (Meier, 1976).

We shall now turn to the alternative criterion proposed by Sen and Dobb.

4.5 The reinvestible surplus (RS) criterion

The criterion suggested by Dobb (1960) and Sen (1968) is rather similar. For the sake of brevity, we shall have to consider only the proposed criterion as developed by Sen.

In the Sen model the economy is divided into two sectors: one is modern, the other is backward. The modern sector is again subdivided into two parts: one sector (A) is producing machinery with only labour; the other sector (B) is producing corn by using machinery and labour. In the backward sector corn (i.e. consumer good) is produced by labour alone. Labour productivity in the modern sector A is given by the capital intensity of the technology applied there where the capital intensity is given by the total number of man-years necessary in sector A to turn out enough machinery for one unit of labour in sector B. Sen assumes that wages in the modern sector are determined by the corn output produced by sector B. But since it takes some time to set up the modern sector, wages in the modern sector would have to be paid out of the "surplus" in the backward sector.

Sen, then distinguishes between the following aims: (1) Maximization of current output (i.e. corn); (2) rate of growth of output maximization; (3) maximization of undiscounted flow of output over a finite period of time. The choice of capital intensity will differ according to the nature of objective. Sen describes how a conflict can arise between the current output maximization principle and the criterion to maximize the rate of growth of output (see Fig. 4.1). Let the vertical axis measure output (corn) and the horizontal axis measure employment of labourers. In the south-east axis, the combination of labour and capital are measured. The curve OQ is the production function and OW is the given wage line which shows wages bills at various levels of

Fig. 4.1

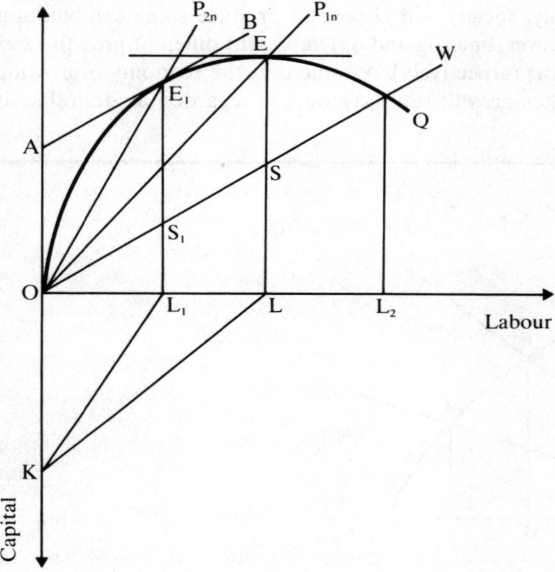

employment. At point E, we obtain maximum output (EL) and employment is OL which would work with OK amount of capital and the degree of capital intensity is given by the tangents of the angle OLK. Labour productivity is given by the tangent of the angle by P_{1n}OL. Note that at E, we find that the capital–turnover and the SMP criteria are satisfied. But if the objective is to maximize the reinvestible surplus to obtain a higher rate of growth, the point to choose is E_1, where AB is tangent to OQ and parallel to OW. Maximum surplus is shown by E_1S_1. It is easily observed that if the Galenson–Leibenstein criterion (i.e. MRIS) is followed, the point E_1 rather than E would be chosen, capital intensity would be higher at E_1 than at E (i.e. tangent of the angle OL_1K is greater than that of OLK) and labour productivity would also be higher (i.e. tangent of the angle P_{2n}OL is higher than that of P_{1n}OL). Note that given similar diagrams, it is also possible to show that maximization of current output may lead to the emergence of a negative surplus. However, maximization of output need not mean maximization of employment as can be shown by the difference between OL and OL_2. In fact, employment expansion beyond OL_2 leads to the emergence of negative "surplus" ("eating" the railways!).

The moral of the above exercise is to show clearly that there is a basic conflict between maximizing consumption at present (by using the capital–turnover or SMP criterion) or in future (by applying the MRIS criterion) (see Fig. 4.2). Let Pp′ be the production possibility frontier for a LDC. If all the resources are allocated to the production of investment goods, OP of capital goods would be produced; on the other hand, if all the resources are spent on the production of consumer goods, Op′ of consumer goods would be produced.[3] Obviously, society will choose to produce some combination of both the goods. However, lines og and og_1 represent different growth-rates (4 per cent and 6 per cent respectively). Assume that the economy is growing along og. But if a higher growth-rate (say og_1) is regarded as desirable, it

Fig. 4.2

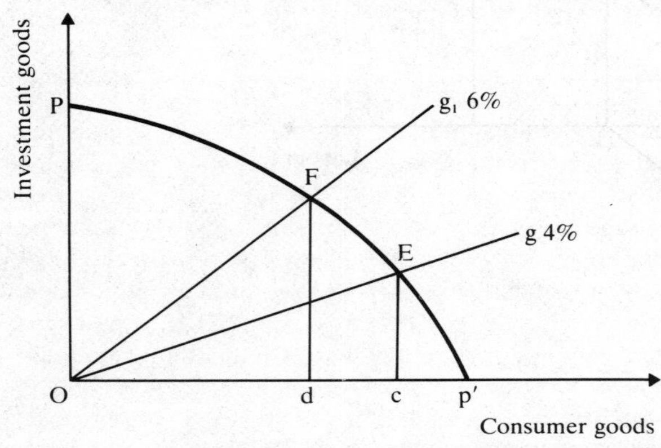

requires a cut of consumption goods by cd which would allow resources to be released for the production of more investment goods to take the economy to F and given a rise in the production of investment goods, growth-rate will be higher, i.e. 6 per cent instead of 4 per cent. But present consumption must be sacrificed to obtain the higher growth path, though, the choice of higher growth path at present will ensure higher consumption in the future as well.

As one of the solutions to the dilemma, Sen has proposed that since the choice of investment criterion depends upon the time horizon of output generation, the time preference and the social welfare function (assuming that such a function is available to the planners), the best way of looking at the problem would be to derive the alternative time-series of consumption obtained by following different criteria. The point can be shown clearly in Fig. 4.3. Let the vertical axis measure the output of consumer goods and the horizontal axis measure time. Output can be produced by either techniques K or L.

Fig. 4.3

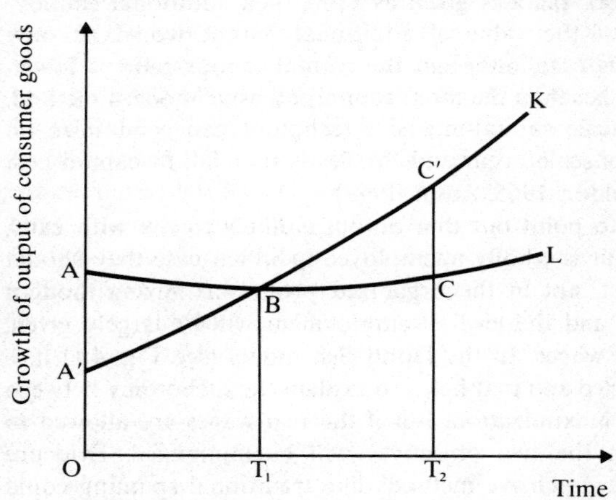

Technique K produces less output now than technique L but after B the rate of growth of output under technique K is such as to compensate for the initial loss of output by the year T_1. It is assumed that the area AA′B = BCC′. Although the use of technique L generates more output in the current period, it yields progressively less and less in future, given the slope of the curve AL. Now if the society is prepared to wait up to T_2 period (say for 30 years), consumption sacrificed at present could be made up by that time and after T_2, society would enjoy higher output and consumption by choosing technique K. But if the social welfare function is such that society values present output and consumption more than future output and consumption, then the society may well choose technique L.

Evaluation of the RS criterion

The choice between maximization of output and employment is more complex than the previous analysis would suggest. Output is a heterogeneous concept; so is employment (Stewart and Streeten, 1972). Since both output and employment change over time and since present output and employment may affect future levels, both intra- and inter-temporal weighting is very important. It is possible to state that generation of more output (with given capital and technology) will require more labour and to that extent the conflict between the objectives to maximize employment and output would be more apparent than real. However, the conflict between the two objectives would be more real if it is assumed that a new technology is chosen. The example given by Stewart and Streeten (1972) can easily be cited. Suppose £100,000 is the amount of money available for investment in a textile industry. Let the capital–output ratio be 2.5 if the advanced technology is used and if the capital cost per work place is given as £1,000, then additional output would be worth £40,000 and additional employment would be 100. But if a traditional hand-spinning technique is used, where the capital–output ratio is 5.0 and the cost per work place is given as £100, then additional employment would be 1,000 but the value of additional output would be only £20,000. Note that in this case, although the capital–labour ratio is lower, capital–output ratio is higher than the more capital-intensive modern method. This is because a large-scale capital-intensive technique can economize on capital since economies of scale occur and this leads to a fall in capital cost in relation to output (Kaldor, 1965, Amin, 1969).

It is also necessary to point out that output is likely to rise with extra employment (unless labour is wholly unemployed in which case they should not be employed, at least, not in the organized profit-maximizing modern sector, in the first place) and the level of employment will be largely given, *inter alia*, by the level of wages. In the Dobb–Sen model (see Fig. 4.1) it is assumed that wages are fixed and that helps to explain the dichotomy between employment and output maximization. But if the real wages are allowed to fall, the conflict between the two objectives will be minimized. Evidence suggests that more labour-intensive methods like traditional spinning could also save more capital per unit of output in comparison with modern factory methods (Bhalla, 1964). So long as indigenous materials could be used by the unemployed labour without involving a diversion of resources, an increase in employment will also lead to a rise in output. (See Appendix for a simple proof.)

It is usually assumed that higher consumption rather than saving will follow the use of labour rather than capital-intensive techniques of production and this will lower the growth-rate for the economy as a whole. A conflict then occurs between macro and micro concepts of efficiency (Meier, 1976). But such an argument rests on the following premises:

(*a*) wages are independent of the choice of techniques;
(*b*) all wages are consumed and all profits are saved;

(*c*) fiscal policy is inadequate to raise taxes to obtain the desired savings ratio and real wages are unlikely to be reduced even when inflation takes place in many LDCs.

Given these premises, the impact of the choice of increasing capital intensity on growth and employment within the neo-classical theory can easily be analysed using Fig. 4.4. The horizontal axis measures capital–labour ratio (C/L) and the vertical axis measures output per unit of labour (Q/L). The production

Fig. 4.4

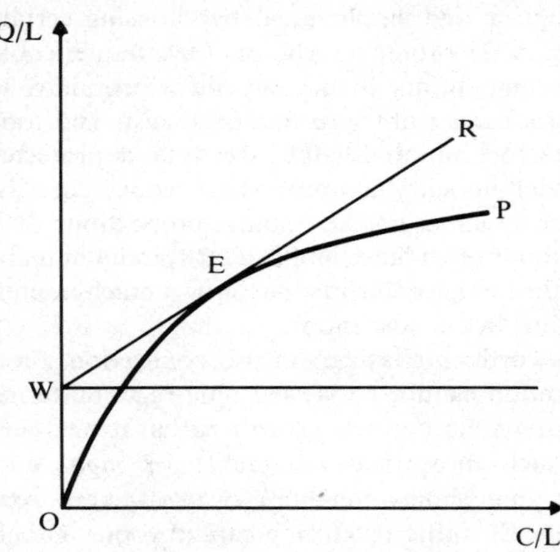

function is given by OP and it shows that for any output, present employment is maximized by using the most labour-intensive technology and this is reflected in a move towards the origin in the diagram. However, employment growth will be given by output growth at a given capital intensity (assuming away technical progress or even assuming *neutral* technical progress). Given the assumption (*b*) above, output and employment maximizing technologies will be determined by the level of wages. Let wages be OW and given the assumption (*a*), the rate of growth of the economy is shown by the slope of WR to the production function. The highest growth-rate is reached at E but this is not the point at which maximum employment is obtained since we have moved further from the point of origin. But if the technique of production to optimize the growth-rates of employment and output are the same, the conflict between them disappears. Note that the conflict will be aggravated if real wages rise.

Evidence suggests that wages are related to labour productivity, the scale of activity and the choice of technology and small enterprises which usually adopt more labour-intensive methods, (i.e. lower C/L) also offer lower level of wages (Dhar and Lydall, 1961, Shetty, 1963, Okita, 1964). Thus the choice of technique is not independent of the scale of operation and the level of wages. Also it is not wholly realistic to assume that all profits would be saved. A part of them may be frittered away in conspicuous consumption. Also, foreign and multinational enterprises repatriate some profits, interest and royalties which clearly reduces reinvestible funds. The implicit assumption in the Sen–Dobb model is that all profits would be saved because profits would accrue to the public sector and the means of production would be owned by the state. This may be questioned because most LDCs have mixed economies. Also, the inability of the government to raise savings by manipulating fiscal and wage policies is viewed with scepticism when the same government is able to sacrifice present consumption and employment by choosing certain techniques (Stewart and Streeten, 1972). Moreover, choice of techniques could be influenced by the degree of competition. In a competitive economy, to maintain or maximize profits, producers will try to minimize costs and look for optimum combination of factors of production, while in a protected economy, the producers are under no such compulsion to reduce costs by introducing technical progress or by choosing the optimal proportions. It is worth mentioning that despite labour abundance and capital scarcity in many LDCs, neither the domestic nor the foreign enterprise has shown much interest in taking advantage of the existing factor–cost ratios.

Some other points are also worth emphasizing in this connection. First, the problem of investment allocation cannot be viewed only in static terms. It is important to observe the dynamic optimal growth paths. It has been shown (Srinivasan, 1962) that such an optimal sustainable *per capita* consumption growth path exists for an economy consisting of two sectors – one sector producing consumer goods; the other producing capital goods. Others have also tried to analyse the theoretical properties of such growth paths (Findlay, 1966, Dixit, 1968, Bose, 1968, Uzawa, 1962).

Second, the choice of optimum technology is a rather complex issue. Different sectors may require different intensities which would be optimal; e.g. an optimal technology for agriculture may require the use of labour-intensive technology whereas such an optimality may be reached in choosing a capital-intensive method in generating power and electricity. Thus *micro* concepts of optimality should not be confused with the macro objective of maximizing output growth-rate by utilizing all the inputs which could be obtained. To achieve overall *consistency* in resource allocation, investment planning or programming is necessary. The use of input–output tables and programming models would be quite useful in such cases.

Third, different technologies embody different types of externalities which are not usually considered within a static analysis. Such externalities could arise because of the economies of scale in industries. Due regard to the externalities in a dynamic analysis may well influence the choice of techniques. Finally, the pattern of income distribution would be different with different technologies. A labour-intensive (say, a seed-fertilizer revolution in the agriculture of LDCs which could be labour-using) technology could raise total and per acre output, but because of higher employment and higher marginal propensity of agriculturalists to consume, saving–income ratio may fall leading to a fall in the growth-rate. It is, of course, assumed that higher savings and investment, rather than higher consumption leads to a higher rate of growth. Mirrlees (1975), on the other hand, has argued that growth can be increased by increased consumption. This line of argument is not new altogether as it has been shown before (Leibenstein, 1957) that an increase in consumption in LDCs will mean better nutrition, greater efficiency and higher productivity of labourers in LDCs. The empirical tests of such models have hardly been carried out either to accept or to reject such theories.

Empirical evidence suggests that choice of techniques does exist in many LDCs in manufacturing, metal working and textile industries (Bhalla, 1975). Similarly, cost of production and thus the choice of technique is influenced not only by prices but also by the scale of production. Also, relative factor–price differences between rural and urban areas in an LDC may influence the choice (Stewart, 1975). Again, substitution possibilities between different types of labour, between labour and working capital as well as the choice of products, can affect the final choice of technology.

4.6 Balanced and unbalanced growth

A lively debate has taken place between the advocates of balanced and unbalanced growth as strategies for economic development in the fifties and the sixties though after numerous qualifications of both versions, the merit of the initial debate and distinction has been considerably diminished. It now appears that both schools of thought have considerable grounds in common and the division between them is more apparent than real. Here we shall first analyse the arguments of the proponents of the balanced growth (BG) and this will be followed by the analysis of the theory of unbalanced growth (UBG). In conclusion it will be argued that the two theories instead of being substitutes are really complementary to one another.

As one of the main champions of BG, it was Rosenstein–Rodan (1943) who was first to point out the need to achieve growth by a "big-push" in East and South-East Europe. His arguments mainly rest on the desirability of surmounting the indivisibilities in both demand and supply. The emergence of the external economies from the use of "lumpy" social capital helps to remove the indivisibilities on the supply side. The bottlenecks on the demand side imposed by the narrow size of the markets could be removed if a number of industries could be set up simultaneously, each catering for the other. In Fig. 4.5 it is shown that given the demand and average cost curves D_1, D_2, and C_1, C_2 respectively for two industries, a clear loss is indicated. But the establishment of the industries simultaneously helps to shift the demand curve to D'_1 and D'_2 and with given cost curves both of them would be viable. A "big-push" or massive investment in many projects will enable the economy to remove the difference between social and private marginal product and the industries themselves, once set up, would be viable as they would not experience either supply or demand constraints. Nurkse (1953) has spoken about the case for balanced growth mainly on grounds of demand

Fig. 4.5

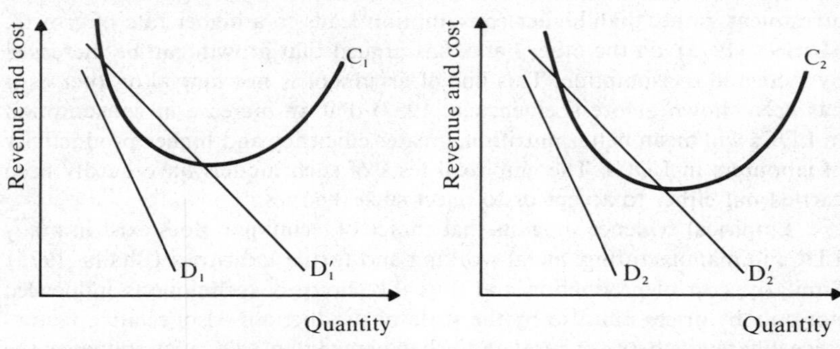

creation since it is assumed that the LDCs would not be able to raise their exports substantially. Lewis (1955) has argued for BG mainly because he wanted to avoid excess capacities and wastes. He has pointed out the need to maintain the terms of trade constant between different sectors so that the growth of any sector need not be adversely affected by an adverse movement of the terms of trade against it. The other point that Lewis has emphasized is that the relative rates of growth of each sector will be given by the income elasticities of the demand for their goods. Such a policy would overcome the bottlenecks that might emerge in the process of growth. Here Lewis has emphasized the vertical nature of production of the supply side while Rosenstein–Rodan and Nurkse have emphasized the horizontal interdependence of consumption (Mathur, 1966).

The arguments against balanced growth (BG)

Several arguments have been advanced against BG doctrine. Thus, Fleming (1955) has pointed out that if most industries expand at the same time, then assuming fixity of supply of factors and their full employment, inflation would take place. However, it may be mentioned that supply of factors may not remain fixed over time and in many countries, labour is hardly fully employed and BG need not lead to inflation (Nath, 1962).

Bauer and Yamey (1957) have also criticized the doctrine of BG on the grounds that it unrealistically assumed that the supply of food is elastic. But if BG means a balanced development of both industry and agriculture then the criticism will lose its strength. Bauer and Yamey have also argued that "any industry which is able to compete in the export market would be established independently of the schemes of balanced industrialization". But this argument will be weakened if the external economies of production, which would emerge by setting up many industries to increase the competitiveness of the export industries, are taken into account. (Nath, 1962).

Other criticisms of the BG theory are advanced by Hirschman (1958) and Streeten (1959) but these points of view could best be analysed in the context of the theory of unbalanced growth.

An evaluation of unbalanced growth (UBG) theory

The case for unbalanced growth according to its champions, rests primarily on the necessity to economize on the use of resources. For example, it is argued that since most LDCs experience a shortage of entrepreneurs, it is very difficult for them to attain a balanced growth (Bauer and Yamey, 1957; Kindleberger, 1958) and as such growth should be unbalanced because it helps the LDCs to economize "genuine decision-making" (Hirschman, 1958, p. 63). Next it is argued that growth should take place through shortages and excesses as it is assumed that every challenge would generate its own response. This is very much like the operation of the Say's Law in reverse: that demand creates its own supply. In fact, Streeten (1959) argued that technical progress in economic history has taken place mostly as an answer to the bottlenecks generated in the path of economic progress. Next, it is said that the case for UBG rests on the strong positive correlation between growth-rates of industrial output and that of its productivity (Scitovsky, 1959, Streeten, 1959). Assuming that such a correlation is present, *a priori*, such an event does not necessarily destroy the case for BG, nor does it support the case for UBG. It has also been argued that BG would require planning and most LDCs do not have either the required skill or the necessary reliable and adequate information to formulate such plans. Moreover, planning may involve huge costs in real (e.g. lengthy decision-making processes, "red tapeism", favouritism) and monetary terms (e.g. the financial costs of setting up the whole planning department plus its operational costs). Further, given the scarcity of resources in LDCs, all wastes or external diseconomies should be minimized as far as possible. Thus, development via the creation of excess capacities in social capital in comparison with the output produced by the direct productive activities is regarded as wasteful and the balance between the growth of output and social capital is regarded as irrelevant as it reduces induced investment (Hirschman, 1958). Hirschman has obviously considered the growth path via "shortages" (i.e. where output from direct productive activities is rising faster than social capital) as more efficient as it is likely to achieve greater induced investment.

The need to minimize external diseconomies is evident in LDCs. But Hirschman's analysis does not provide a convincing case for maximizing induced investment. It is known, as in Italy, that the creation of social capital is not enough to promote growth. Nor is it equally certain that induced private investment would be forthcoming, particularly in the creation of social capital whenever there are shortages (Thirlwall, 1974). It is much more difficult to say, with empirical evidence, that the choice of UBG path is "efficient" or optimal in terms of resource use. The strength of the UBG theory rests on the implicit assumption of supply elasticities for many LDCs but this is not a very realistic assumption. Next, the lack of balance between demand and supply could easily lead to inflation, with all its undesirable consequences (e.g. devaluation and its unfavourable impact on balance of payments when the marginal propensity to import is high, the price and income elasticities of demand for the exportables are low and the regressive effects on income distribution). Again, following the UBG theory, if resources are concentrated on the production of only a few commodities, the effects may not always be desirable. For example, from the standpoint of balance of payments, there is always the danger of putting "all the eggs in one basket" and thereby suffering due to the lack of trade diversification. Finally, although it is possible to cite forward (percentage of output used as inputs in other activities) and backward (percentages of output bought from other sectors) linkages in the manufacturing sector of the LDCs, such linkages are few between industry and agriculture in many poor countries.[4]

A reconciliation between BG and UBG theories

The above discussion shows that the two theories cover a lot of common ground and if several qualifications of the different arguments of these two schools are taken into consideration, it is possible to suggest that the two theories, instead of being substitutes, are really complementary to one another. This is clearly reflected in the statement of Streeten (1959):

". . . *choose projects which,* (*i*) *while advancing some sectors, concentrating the pressure or unbalance on groups and sectors whose response to a challenge is likely to be strongest;* (*ii*) *while creating bottlenecks also break them;* (*iii*) *while providing products and services for industry, agriculture and consumers, also induce new developments to take place in other directions, directly and indirectly related to them;* (*iv*) *while providing a new product or service require consequential investment in other lines.*"

Again, to reap the benefits of externalities, it may be necessary to undertake large investments and this approach need not be inconsistent with the idea of concentrating resources in a few sectors. If unbalanced growth is defined not so much in terms of shortages as in terms of concentration on certain activities, according to comparative advantage or the existence of increasing returns, balanced and unbalanced growth can be complementary strategies (Thirlwall, 1974). Similarly, the economies mainly dominated by private enterprises also recognize the need to strike a balance between present and future demand and supply and use planning and programming tools to obtain such balance. Although the concept of planning is normally associated with the doctrine of balanced growth, such a concept by itself need not mean total state control and ownership as planning may involve licensing the issue of directives and offer of subsidies to private enterprises. Historically, although economic development followed an uneven path, the need to obtain balanced growth as an objective was seldom refuted. The supporters of BG theory would not find it difficult to accept that the differences in demand and supply of goods could be partially adjusted by the differences in elasticities in demand with respect to prices and producers do respond in some cases to relative output and input prices. As regards the desirability of creating social overheads, it is interesting to point out that both Streeten and Nurkse have emphasized the need to build up supply in excess of demand and, here again, the difference between the two schools is negligible.

Notes

1. Note that the traditional theory may incorporate *some* time dimension.
2. The implication here is that maximizing the capital/labour ratio is the same as adopting capital goods industries. This need not be the case. It has been argued that capital goods industries could be relatively more labour-intensive than some other forms of industries (see Pack and Todaro, 1969).
3. In an open economy it is not necessarily a question of allocating resources for the *production* of consumer and investment goods: rather, it could be a problem of allocating *expenditure* on such goods.
4. However, in both China and Taiwan, there are important links between the agricultural sector and rural industry.

Appendix

The dichotomy between savings and output maximization and its solution

The conflict between savings and output maximization can be shown with the help of the following equations.
Let the production function be:

$$Q = \alpha N - \beta N^2 \qquad [4.1]$$

Let the investible surplus be given by:

$$S = \alpha N - \beta N^2 - wN \qquad [4.2]$$

Where Q = output
S = investible surplus
N = Labour employed
w = rate of wage per unit of labour employed.

To maximize surplus, we differentiate equation [4.2] with respect to N and set it equal to zero:

$$\text{i.e.} \quad \frac{dS}{dN} = \alpha - 2\beta N - w = 0 \qquad [4.3]$$

$$\text{or} \quad \alpha - 2\beta N = w$$

$$\text{or} \quad N = \frac{\alpha - w}{2\beta} \qquad [4.4]$$

To obtain the highest level of output, we differentiate [4.1] with respect to N. Thus

$$\frac{dQ}{dN} = \alpha - 2\beta N = 0 \tag{4.5}$$

$$\text{therefore} \quad N = \frac{\alpha}{2\beta} \tag{4.6}$$

Note that the difference between [4.4] and [4.6] will tend to disappear as w falls to zero. Models which emphasize the dichotomy between employment and output maximization usually assume wages as given (see Thirlwall 1976b). It is easy to show that this dichotomy also disappears if we have a Cobb–Douglas production function; i.e. $Q = AN^{\alpha}K^{\beta}$ where K = capital.

5

Domestic resources for development

5.1 Introduction

Most LDCs mainly depend upon domestic resources for their development. Foreign resources and trade also play some part in financing the economic development of the LDCs, but a more comprehensive discussion of their role will follow later (see Chs. 8 and 9). At the outset, it is necessary to emphasize the importance of shifting funds from low to high productivity users and also the need for small farms, and other businesses to have working balances and funds for new (and replacement) investment in LDCs. Here we shall chiefly examine the roles of: (*a*) monetary; (*b*) inflationary; and (*c*) fiscal policies in financing growth. We shall first analyse some features of the money markets of the LDCs.

5.2 The nature of money markets in LDCs

It is important to stress at the outset the nature of money markets in LDCs. Such a money market is distinguished by its *duality*, with its *organized* and *unorganized* sectors, with different business practices and interest rates (Wai, 1957, Myint, 1971, Ghatak, 1976). The *organized* sector usually comprises the commercial and cooperative banks, the central bank, and other governmental agencies like the agricultural finance corporations. The *unorganized* sector mainly comprises the money lenders, indigenous bankers, landlords, traders and merchants. The organized money market tends to be highly sophisticated and specialized with its developed bill-market. However, funds sometimes flow between the *organized* and *unorganized* sectors but their links with one another seems to be very weak. Note that the unorganized markets are far from homogeneous in the LDCs and this implies the presence of many interest rates within the rural money markets. The main features that distinguish the unorganized sector from the organized sector are as follows:

1. Informality in dealings with customers and personal contact with the borrowers.

2. Flexibility of loan operations and simple systems of maintaining accounts.
3. Absence of specialization, i.e. blending money-lending with other economic activities.
4. Secrecy in financial dealings.

The role of a money market in LDCs

A money market usually caters for the demand and supply of *short-run* loanable funds. In this context, several useful functions of a money market can be mentioned. First, by allocating saving to investment, it tends to allocate resources more efficiently. Second, it tends to establish an equilibrium between demand for and supply of funds. Third, by promoting liquidity and ensuring the safety of financial assets, it promotes saving and investment. This is important in LDCs where savings and investment habits leave much room for improvement. In the rural sector, very frequently, savings consist of bullion-hoarding and land-holding rather than the holding of financial assets. Thus, even if there is ability to save, in the absence of a developed money market, the economy is deprived of an array of financial assets which could lead saving into productive investment (Gurley and Shaw, 1960, p. 49; also, 1967). Fourth, a money market ensures the flow of funds from one sector to another and thus encourages financial mobility. Fifth, a developed money market is essential for implementing the monetary policies (e.g., the Bank Rate and open market operations) of the central bank. Also, a developed money market is crucial for providing elasticity in the flow of funds.

The dualism in the money markets in the LDCs has had certain effects. First it has led to restricted use of cheques. Second, to supplement the credit needs of the economy, especially of the rural sector it has led to the growth of different types of instruments of credit. This, again, has reduced the use of bank credit. Third, it has restricted the volume of monetary transactions and perpetuated non-monetized transactions. Fourth, the absence of a well-developed money market has deprived the economy of necessary financial assets with which savings could have been more efficiently tapped and converted into investment for raising the rate of development. Last, but not least, the presence of the "financial dualism" has perpetuated some age-old customs, like gold-hoarding, which have restricted the use of available resources for productive investment.

5.3 Money and economic growth

It is now easy to see how a process of monetary expansion can aid the growth of LDCs. First, money replaces barter transactions which are frequently wasteful and time-consuming to strike the right balance between demand and supply. Notice that the relative cost of printing money is small. Second, money as a medium of exchange induces specialization and increases productivity. Specialization in the production of specific crops in a peasant economy would increase the interdependence and exchange among the various sectors and increasing monetization (i.e. increase in the ratio of monetary (M) to total transactions (T) or an increase in M/T) could only facilitate this process of increasing productivity. Third, in a developing country, to match increasing output and the demand for money, it is necessary to increase money supply. Fourth, if barter transactions are replaced by monetary transactions, then real resources will be released to promote growth. In fact, increasing monetization would require the promotion of banking and credit institutions which could help considerably the promotion of saving, investment and growth (Kaldor and Mirrlees, 1972; Wai, 1972; Wallich, 1969). Fifth, money can also act as a store of value, and the government by incurring public debt can provide alternative channels to mobilize enough saving to achieve equality between the natural rate and the warranted growth-rate of capital (Tobin, 1965).

It has been argued that empirical evidence for some Latin American and Asian countries suggests positive and significant correlation between money supply and real output growth between 1959 and 1966 (Fan, 1970). However, a high rate of inflation tends to exert a negative influence on real income growth. This analysis is plausible; but, here again, it is important to point out that the low value of R^2 (i.e. the proportion of explained variation to total variation of real output growth) reduces the predictive power of the model. For the Latin American countries, Fan calculates the critical *rate of increase of money supply as 16.5 per cent p.a.* beyond which monetary expansion would be inflationary. However, these figures should be treated with due caution because the models on which they are based may be wrongly specified and the predictive power of these models is limited.

For the LDCs, evidence suggests a positive and significant relationship between the ratio of investment to income and the growth of *per capita* income (Thirlwall, 1974). A similar relationship, between investment ratio and the growth of real income, is observed by others (Hill, 1964; Modigliani, 1970). However, evidence from some Asian countries suggests that if saving is treated as a function of income, then it is also possible to find a positive and significant relationship (Williamson, 1968). This is indicated in the following equation:

$$\frac{S}{N} = -9.45 + 2.03\left(\frac{Y}{N}\right)$$

$$(1.31)(0.010) \qquad r^2 = 0.829$$

(Figures in parentheses are the standard error.)
Source: Williamson (1968)

S = total saving

N = population

Y = total income.

Notice that about 83 per cent of the total variation in saving per head is explained by income per head and the value of the income per head coefficient is statistically highly significant. Notice also that at a very high level of income this strong and positive relationship could weaken.

The above discussion shows the relationship between monetary expansion, saving, investment and economic growth. It has been mentioned that an expansionary monetary programme in an LDC could be inflationary beyond a certain level, given the supply inelasticities. The effects of such inflationary finance on growth will now be analysed.

5.4 Inflation and economic growth

It is tempting for the LDCs to resort to inflation as a major "tax" to finance their public expenditure to promote economic development, particularly when the tax revenue as a proportion of the gross national product is low and tax elasticity with respect to income is not always greater than unity. Given certain demand for money assumptions, inflation can raise revenues. Second, by increasing profitability of industries, inflation can provide incentives to investment. Third, the government will be less obliged to depend upon foreign resources if it can raise more revenue at home. Fourth, it has been argued that inflationary financing could promote the growth of banks and other financial institutions. These agencies may induce the public to hold financial rather than physical assets and thus release real resources for economic growth (Thirlwall, 1974). This, however, is a rather dubious argument because at times of high inflation, people may be induced to hold more physical rather than financial assets.

On the debit side, inflation could easily distort the efficient allocation of resources and reduce real growth. Second, a high level of inflation will reduce a country's competitive power in the export market and it may eventually price itself out. The LDCs which suffer from a chronic balance of payments deficit, therefore, should exercise greater caution in the use of inflationary policies. Third, inflation may make the distribution of income more unequal. Many LDCs experience significant inequalities in the distribution of income and, as such, inflationary financing, which often tends to redistribute income in favour of profits rather than wages, may arouse public hostility. However, it may be argued that even if inflation promotes more inequality, it tends to raise profit share and thereby the saving ratio in national income and this could have a beneficial effect on growth. Critics argue that consumption could also have a favourable effect on growth in the LDCs (Mirrlees, 1975; Foxley, 1976; Bliss and Stern, 1976). Fourth, a high level of inflation could easily shake people's confidence in the currency and this could induce greater holding of physical rather than financial assets with detrimental effects on growth. Finally, hyperinflation could only have disastrous consequences on the currency and financial system without conferring much significant benefit on the real growth of a country.

On balance, the weight of the arguments seem to be in favour of a mild degree of inflation for promoting growth. The mechanism has been illustrated by Mundell (1965) and his model will be analysed next.

Mundell's model of inflation and growth

Mundell starts off with the basic quantity theory equation to show the relationship between inflation and economic growth (Mundell, 1965). Thus, we have

$$MV = PQ \qquad [5.1]$$

where M = money supply
P = price level
V = velocity
Q = total output

If we differentiate [5.1] with respect to time (t), we have

$$\frac{1}{V}\frac{dV}{dt} = p + g - m \qquad [5.2]$$

where p = rate of growth of prices $\left(\text{i.e. } \frac{1}{p}\frac{dP}{dt}\right)$

g = rate of growth of quantity $\left(\text{i.e. } \frac{1}{Q}\frac{dQ}{dt}\right)$

m = rate of growth of money supply $\left(\text{i.e. } \frac{1}{M}\frac{dM}{dt}\right)$

Let us assume that

$$Q = \beta K \qquad [5.3]$$

where β = output–capital ratio or productivity of capital
K = total stock of capital

It is implicitly assumed that labour is in "surplus" because output (Q) simply depends on capital (K).

Differentiating [5.3] with respect to t, we obtain

$$\frac{dQ}{dt} = \beta\frac{dK}{dt} \qquad [5.4]$$

Let us assume that all public investments are financed by the banks and the true value of public investment is

$$\frac{G}{P} = \frac{1}{P}\frac{dB}{dt} = \frac{dK}{dt} \qquad [5.5]$$

where G = public investment
B = Bank reserves

The association between B and M is given by

$$B = rM \qquad [5.6]$$

where r = fractional reserve ratio.

Differentiating [5.6] with respect to time, we have

$$\frac{dB}{dt} = r\frac{dM}{dt} \qquad [5.7]$$

Substituting into [5.5], we have

$$\frac{dK}{dt} = r\frac{1}{P}\frac{dM}{dt} \qquad [5.8]$$

Making necessary substitution between [5.8] and [5.4], we obtain

$$\frac{dQ}{dt} = r\beta\frac{1}{P}\frac{dM}{dt} \qquad [5.9]$$

Dividing [5.9] by Q, we have

$$\frac{1}{Q}\frac{dQ}{dt} = r\beta\frac{1}{PQ}\frac{dM}{dt}$$

$$= r\beta\left(\frac{1}{M}\frac{dM}{dt}\right)\frac{M}{PQ} \qquad [5.10]$$

Equation [5.10] tells the relationship between the rate of output growth and the growth of money supply. Recalling [5.2], we can now write:

$$g = \frac{r\beta}{V}m \qquad [5.11]$$

If V is constant, we can rewrite [5.2] as

$$p = m - g \qquad [5.12]$$

Substituting into [5.11], we have

$$p = \left(1 - \frac{r\beta}{V}\right)m \qquad [5.13]$$

or $$p = \left(\frac{V}{r\beta} - 1\right)g \qquad [5.14]$$

Equations (5.13–5.14) show the relationship between p, m and g which could be promoted by deficit financing.

Note that $\frac{1}{V}$ is the *planned* money–income ratio. If the government decides to spend r units on investment goods and if prices are stable, then such spending would raise output by $r\beta$. However, should output rise by one unit and money demand rises by 1/V, a rise in output of $r\beta$ would raise money demand by $r\beta/V$ units, while money supply rises by one unit. Thus whether or not deficit financing is inflationary or deflationary will depend upon

$$V \gtrless r\beta$$

Deficit financing could be inflationary since in general both r and $\beta < 1$ but $V > 1$.

To find out more about the actual working of the model, let us assume that $V = 4$, $\beta = 0.33$ and $r = 0.4$. Solving the equation [5.14], we find that

$$p = 29.303\ g$$

Thus a 29 per cent inflation is necessary to increase growth-rate by 1 per cent only. Note that given the capital–output ratio, i.e. $1/\beta$, or 3.03, a rise of about 10 per cent (i.e. 29.303/3.03) in prices is necessary to raise savings by 1 per cent.

It may be argued that V would not remain constant if inflation tends to be excessive; rather it should rise with inflation. More formally,

$$V = V(P) \quad [5.15]$$

and $$\frac{dV}{dP} > 0$$

Imagine the relationship between V and P is linear. Thus,

$$V = Vo + \alpha p \quad [5.16]$$

where Vo = rate of velocity with no inflation.

This equation coupled with equation

$$p = \left(\frac{V}{r\beta} - 1\right)g \quad [5.17]$$

we obtain,

$$p = \frac{Vo - r\beta}{r\beta - \alpha g}\ g \quad [5.18]$$

It is clear from equation [5.18] that p/g rises with a rise in g. At the limit inflation would be infinite and the growth-rate can no longer be promoted by inflation. The optimal credit-financed rate of growth (g^*) is then

$$g^* = \frac{r\beta}{\alpha} \quad [5.19]$$

Using equation [5.14] and assuming with Mundell that $Vo = 3$, $\beta = 0.5$ and $r = 0.3$, $p = \dfrac{57}{3 - 20\alpha g}$ g and if $\alpha = 0$, p = 19 g or prices should rise by 19 per cent p.a. to increase growth by 1 per cent p.a. If $\alpha = 10$, then

$p = \dfrac{57g}{3 - 200g}$ or 1.5 per cent growth p.a. would be related to infinite inflation.

Notice that to raise growth-rate, g, by 1 per cent p.a. the necessary rate of price increase would be 57 per cent p.a.

Some of the limitations of the Mundell model may now be mentioned. First, Mundell's assumption that the output–capital ratio, or β, would remain fixed during the process of economic development is questionable when the whole structure of the economy could undergo important changes. Indeed, if credit-financing can increase capacity utilization, output–capital ratio will rise.

Second, should the credit-financed public investment displace private investment rather than consumption, the rate of growth may be adversely affected.

Third, the model is closed; but if the role of foreign trade is included, then output–capital ratios could be raised by importing capital by credit-financed government investment (Thirlwall, 1974).

Fourth, if inflation is high, velocity is likely to change. This would imply that for achieving a certain growth-rate, a much higher rate of inflation will be needed. From the standpoint of policy formulation, it is almost preposterous to assume that a government would allow prices to rise by 57 per cent p.a. to increase the growth-rate by 1 per cent p.a.

Fifth, it is argued that the value of r should depend upon the proportion of money holdings supported by government securities rather than the ratio of bank reserves to money supply, as implied by Mundell, since a proportion of the expansion of bank deposits will reflect the purchase of government securities, and to this extent the need for borrowing from the central bank for any given expenditure requirement is reduced (Thirlwall, 1974, p. 139). Notice that the former is generally higher than the latter (0.5 as against 0.3 in LDCs).

Sixth, to the extent that growth in the LDCs is constrained by a lack of demand (Bottomley, 1971), credit-financed investment, particularly in projects where the fruition lags are small, could have favourable impact on growth without seriously disturbing price stability.

Empirical evidence in LDCs shows that although inflation has a positive effect on saving, such impact, in most cases, is statistically insignificant. However, the relationship between inflation and investment appears to be positive and significant. This could partly be explained by the impact of inflation on a higher level of imports of investment goods. However, inflation beyond a certain rate (an "optimal rate") is bound to affect adversely not only investment, but also the rate of exchange, balance of payments and the level of unemployment. Existing information also supports this intuitive judgement (Thirlwall, 1974).

Further evidence suggests that an inflation tax is feasible in the case of many LDCs. However, inflation may have an important adverse impact on allocation of resources in LDCs in particular with fixed foreign exchange and interest rates (Newlyn, 1977). However, whether inflation as a deliberate policy is desirable or not depends on whether the effect of inflation on resource mobilization is greater than its impact on efficiency. "A full assessment would require one to compare the costs involved with the costs associated with distortions introduced by other taxes which would be needed to replace the revenue lost from the inflation tax." (Ayre, 1977) Among other costs of inflation note that it distorts the real rates of return between the different sectors and between the different types of financial assets since in many LDCs, while inflation goes on, nominal interest and exchange rates are kept constant and "*financial repression*" occurs (McKinnon, 1973; Shaw, 1973), resulting in reduction in the demand for real balances. A change in the financial structure in the LDCs is thus regarded as an important factor in promoting economic growth (Galbis, 1977; McKinnon, 1973; Shaw, 1973). The development policies in many LDCs are supposed to have resulted in "*shallow finance*" rather than "deepening" finance or financial "liberalization" which, *inter alia*, "matters" in promoting economic growth (Shaw, 1973). If inflation takes place, although nominal finance rises, real finance does not rise by the same proportion since it is taxed away by inflation and this state is considered as shallow finance. If finance is shallow as a proportion of income, the real rates of return tend to be very low or even negative. When finance is deepening (one index of which is an increase of liquidity reserves; other indices include an increase in the accumulation of average balances of liquid assets – which would prevent waste of resources in barter transactions – in all markets; an increase in the proportion of financial assets in income or wealth; and greater diversification of financial assets), government tends to be less dependent on taxes and foreign savings, capital flight is reversed, velocity falls, real savings grow in financial rather than physical assets and pave the way for a greater integration between the organized and unorganized money market. As the real size of the monetary system grows, the differences between the interest rates in the organized and unorganized money markets tend to diminish and real rates of interest tend to rise, reflecting more accurately the opportunity cost of capital (as capital is generally the more scarce input in relation to labour in LDCs). Higher real rates are likely to raise real savings and real growth. An increase in real rates would also help to choose a more appropriate technology (usually labour-intensive in this case) with a higher level of employment and a more egalitarian system of income distribution. It is argued that as long as an interventionist policy keeps the nominal interest rates and foreign exchange rates fixed and a state of "financial repression" prevails, "the costs in both inefficiency and corruption are high" (Shaw, 1973, p. 12).

Evidence suggests that between 1963 and 1968, while Uruguay experienced a rise in nominal money supply (which included the time and savings deposits) of 710 per cent its real value actually fell by 55 per cent. During the same period in Ghana, the index of nominal money supply (as defined above) rose from 1.00 to 1.63 while the index of real value remained almost constant. Real output and real consumption fell sharply in Uruguay with severe repercussions upon its financial system and exchange rates. The economy of Ghana also received a considerable setback. On the other hand, in Iran and Thailand where a process of financial deepening took place, i.e. growth in nominal money supply almost matched the increase in real finance, in the same period a rise in both real income and consumption was observed (Shaw, 1973, p. 5).

The complexity of this discussion is now clear. A realistic policy of financial reform is called for to promote real saving and growth and employment in the LDCs. Rates of interest should be raised to reflect more correctly the relative scarcity of capital and this would have beneficial effects upon the choice of technology, employment and income distribution. Although the attraction of an inflation tax is obvious in situations where the real values of revenues from other taxes are falling with rising prices (see Bird, 1977, who shows how the real revenue from land tax in Japan was much less than its nominal value in the late nineteenth century) and when "inflation is a taxation *without representation*", which even the weakest government could enforce upon its people (Keynes, 1930) it could be used only in moderate amounts to mobilize resources (say, not more than 10–15 per cent depending upon the country) and great caution is needed to handle it before it gets out of hand.

5.5 Objectives of fiscal policy in LDCs

The major objectives of fiscal policy in the LDCs are as follows:

1. To raise revenue for the government.
2. To stabilize prices by changing aggregate demand.
3. To promote economic growth by mobilizing "surplus".
4. To promote foreign investment should it be considered desirable.
5. To change the pattern of income distribution according to some social objectives, e.g., more equal distribution of income.
6. To minimize the adverse effects on resource allocation.

Most governments in the LDCs try to achieve a combination of some of these major objectives. The main instruments to attain the targets are usually taxation, expenditure, and deficit finance. Each one of these will be examined in turn, but first it is necessary to discuss briefly the role of fiscal policy in promoting growth.

5.6 Fiscal policy and growth

The role of fiscal policy in promoting economic growth is fairly well known. In the classical period it was, however, believed that the very best of all principles of government finance was to tax little and spend little. With the development of what is known as the "balanced budget multiplier" (BBM) this attitude has altered. The BBM states that if the tax (ΔT) and expenditure (ΔG) by the government rise by, say, £100 million, national income (ΔY) will also rise by £100 million.

More formally, let

$$Y = C + I + G \qquad [5.20]$$

and assume that

$I = Io$ or fixed

where I = autonomous investment

C = consumption

Y = income

G = government expenditure

then $\Delta Y = \Delta C + \Delta G$ [5.21]

The effect of a change in public expenditure is then

$$\Delta Y = \frac{1}{1-b}\Delta G \qquad [5.22]$$

where b = marginal propensity to consume (MPC)

and $\frac{1}{1-b}$ = multiplier

Then $$\frac{\Delta Y}{\Delta G} = \frac{1}{1-b} \qquad [5.23]$$

Next, to find out the effect of changes in taxes (ΔT) on income (Y), note that when taxes are raised, consumption is likely to fall, *but not by the full amount of the change in tax* (ΔT). In fact, consumption will fall by the product of MPC and ΔT.

Thus $\Delta C = -b\Delta T$ [5.24]

Using the multiplier theory, we have

$$\Delta Y = \frac{1}{1-b}\Delta C \qquad [5.25]$$

By substitution $$\Delta Y = -\frac{b\Delta T}{1-b} \qquad [5.26]$$

or

$$\frac{\Delta Y}{\Delta T} = -\frac{b}{1-b} \qquad [5.27]$$

Combining the effects of public expenditure and taxes on income, we have

$$\frac{\Delta Y}{\Delta G} + \frac{\Delta Y}{\Delta T} = \frac{1}{1-b} - \frac{b}{1-b} = \frac{1-b}{1-b} = 1 \qquad [5.28]$$

The result indicates that the effects of a, say, positive change in government tax and expenditure will have an equal and positive effect on national income (for a detailed discussion, see, e.g. Dernburg and McDougall, 1976).

The BBM theory, as described above, does not include the role of foreign trade. It assumes a constant MPC which may not be valid particularly when the economy of a LDC is developing rapidly. Nor is there enough empirical reason to believe that there would always be a one-to-one correspondence between changes in taxes and expenditure and changes in income, particularly if the economy experiences serious bottlenecks on the supply side, a common problem for many LDCs. However, the general prediction of the theory about the expansionary role of fiscal policy has been of special interest to the LDCs. Here more empirical research is necessary to draw firm conclusions. The BBM theory, within it limitations, has the very interesting implication that *without a budget deficit*, income could be expanded only if the budget size is large enough. In the next section we relax the assumption regarding the closed economy and introduce trade in our model.

Fiscal policy in an open economy

In an open economy, for one country, the basic Keynesian income equation could be written as follows: (see Morss and Peacock (1969) for details).

$$Y = C + I + G + (X - M) \quad [5.29]$$

where X = exports

M = Imports

Let $C = a + b(Y_d)$ [5.30]

$$M = c + dY \quad [5.31]$$

$$Y_d = Y - eY - T \quad [5.32]$$

$T = fY$, e = fraction of income which goes to the corporate sector [5.33]

Assuming fixed Io, Go and Xo, and by substitution we have

$$Y = \frac{a - c + Io + Go + Xo}{1 - b + d + be + bf} \quad [5.34]$$

where the multiplier

$$k = \frac{1}{1 - b + d + be + bf} \quad [5.35]$$

For another country similar multipliers could be observed. If we allow the government expenditure to vary, then its effect could now be predicted on the level of income. It is, however, possible to modify some other assumptions. For instance, X_1 can be regarded as a function of income in country 2 (Y_2) net of taxes in country 2 (T_2). More formally

$$X_1 = g_2 Y_2(1 - T_2) \quad [5.36]$$

Similarly, the import equation could also be related to disposable rather than nominal income. In such cases, an autonomous rise in marginal propensity to import in country 2 will tend to raise income in country 1. In the same way, income expansion in country 1 will tend to raise exports from country 2. The determination of income in country 1 will now depend upon income, marginal propensity to import and taxes in country 2. It seems that a more comprehensive discussion could only be made in terms of fiscal, monetary and exchange rate policies (for details, see Peacock and Shaw, 1974). This may require a complicated exercise in the estimation of the actual parameters to predict the effects of changes in taxes and expenditure on national income. Presently the relationship between fiscal policy and growth will be discussed.

Peacock and Shaw model

The relationship between fiscal policy and growth can best be analysed within a Harrod–Domar (HD) framework rather than a neo-classical framework. Recalling the HD equation for growth (see Ch. 2) we have

$$y = s/v$$

where y = growth rate of output

s = saving ratio

v = capital–output ratio

It is easily observed that fiscal policy, by raising s, can raise growth. But no such role could be played by fiscal policy within a neo-classical theory as the population growth-rate (n) will determine the growth-rate. A change in taxation or public expenditure could change saving, but this would also change the capital–output ratio (v) with no change in growth-*rates* (Sato, 1963, 1967). The present discussion within the HD model is based on the analysis of Peacock and Shaw (1974).

Let us assume that on the supply side output capacity (Y_t^c) in the period t is given by private investment and government expenditure in the past period (i.e. I_{t-1} and G_{t-1} respectively). Thus we have

$$\Delta Y_t^c = \beta(I_{t-1} + \rho G_{t-1}) \qquad [5.37]$$

where β = output–capital ratio

ρ = proportion of government expenditure that consists of investment.

Let the equation for the demand side be

$$Y_t = C_t + I_t + G_t \qquad [5.38]$$

Let $C_t = bY_t(1 - T_y)$ [5.39]

and $I_t = I_{t-1} = I_{0t}$ or fixed [5.40]

where T_y = given rate of income tax

Let $G_t = gY_t$ [5.41]

Then the level of income equilibrium is given by

$$Y_t = \frac{I_{0t}}{1 - b + bT_y - g} \qquad [5.42]$$

A variation in investment will be reflected in income changes via changes in demand. Thus

$$\Delta Y_t = \frac{\Delta I_t}{(1 - b + bT_y - g)} \qquad [5.43]$$

To maintain the equilibrium in the economy, the supply side or capacity output must be equal to money demand. That is

$$\Delta Y_t^c = \Delta Y_t \tag{5.44}$$

$$\text{or,}\quad \beta(I_{t-1} + \rho G_{t-1}) = \frac{\Delta I_t}{(1 - b + bT_y - g)} \tag{5.45}$$

Dividing by Y_{t-1},

$$\frac{\Delta Y_t}{Y_{t-1}} = \frac{\beta I_{t-1}}{Y_{t-1}} + \frac{\beta\rho G_{t-1}}{Y_{t-1}} = \frac{\Delta I_t/(1 - b + bT_y - g)}{I_{t-1}/(1 - b + bT_y - g)} \tag{5.46}$$

Note that

$$\frac{G_{t-1}}{Y_{t-1}} = g \quad \text{and} \quad \frac{I_{t-1}}{Y_{t-1}} = (1 - b + bT_y - g) \tag{5.47}$$

so that we have,

$$\frac{\Delta Y_t}{Y_{t-1}} = \beta(1 - b + bT_y - g + \rho g) = \frac{\Delta I_t}{I_{t-1}} \tag{5.48}$$

In other words, in order to utilize capital stock fully, the necessary growth of demand must be equal to the required investment growth which in itself is functionally related to both changes in taxes and public expenditure. Should the actual growth be less than desired growth, actual growth could be raised by inducements to invest or to lower the desired growth by altering fiscal policies. Thus changes in taxes or public expenditure would considerably influence the equality between desired and actual growth-rate. Notice that for the LDCs, it is of prime importance to utilize fully both capital and *labour*. In this sense, the HD model loses some of its appeal for devising fiscal policies for the LDCs, though the advocates of "prior-saving" theory may find it useful.

5.7 Deficit financing (DF) and LDCs

Deficit financing (DF) has played an important role in many LDCs. Given the inability of their governments to mobilize enough resources to achieve a desired rate of growth, unreliability of foreign investment and lack of tax elasticity, the temptation to adopt DF is understandable. The impact of money supply on prices, saving and growth has already been discussed. It remains to be pointed out that for DF to be effective in the LDCs, the supply of output must be elastic with respect to demand. Otherwise, inflation is inevitable. To count the net benefit of DF, it is necessary to examine the costs of inflation against the possible gains in resource mobilization. Among these costs, most important are: (a) distortions of real rates of return; (b) inefficiency in allocation; (c) inequalities in income distribution; and (d) an increase in imports and unemployment. Among the possible benefits are the stimulus to profitability and investment, greater utilization of capacity because of increased demand and consequent lowering of the costs of production should there be excess capacity, and a larger investment provided that private investment was not forthcoming in any case. The other points which have been mentioned in its favour are, first, if an increase in money supply can stimulate growth, its presence can be tolerated. Here it is important to find out the "optimal" level of money supply. Second, if income distribution becomes more unequal because of DF, then a rise in profit share will stimulate investment. If, however, profits are not reinvested, then growth is likely to suffer. Also, if private saving is not forthcoming spontaneously, government may resort to DF for generating more savings (Oyejide, 1972).

If the aggregate supply is very inelastic, then the different effects of DF can be shown with the help of Fig. 5.1. In quadrant I, the Keynesian

Fig. 5.1

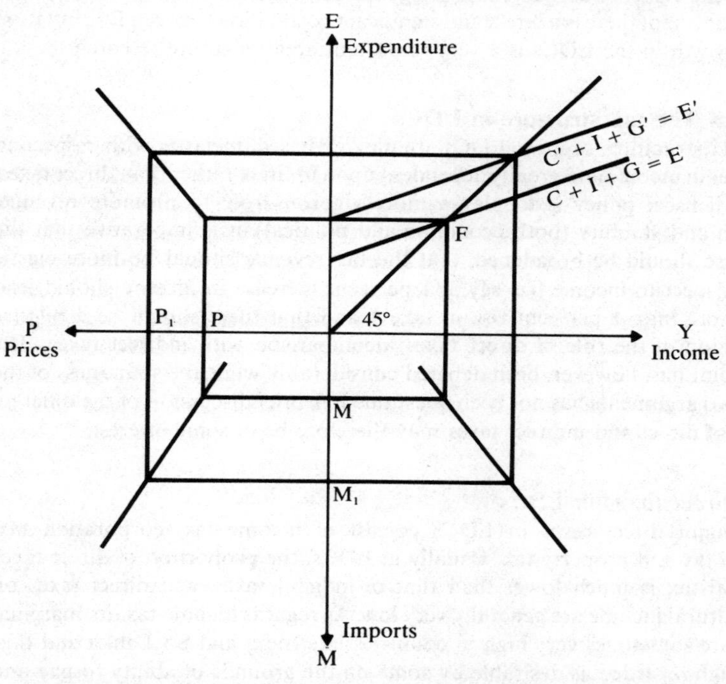

income–expenditure equilibrium is shown at F. A tax cut or a rise in public expenditure or both will stimulate monetary demand and this is shown by the shift of the expenditure line from E to E′. A rise in aggregate demand raises the price level from P to P_1 in quadrant II. In quadrant III, the effect of such a rise in domestic prices is shown on the imports and balance of payments. Thus imports tend to rise from M to M_1. Quadrant IV shows the relationship between a change in money income and imports and this relationship is assumed to be positive. Note that the fall of unemployment is virtually nothing if supply does not respond with changes in demand. Indeed, as the rates of inflation increase with demand stimulation, unemployment may actually rise. This has led some to conclude that in LDCs since a "money" multiplier rather than a "real" multiplier operates, the Keynesian theory has a very limited role to play (Rao, 1952; Hasan, 1960). On the other hand, supporters of the DF theory argue that as long as public expenditure takes place in quick-yielding investment with a short fruition-lag and/or if DF of such investment could reduce the capital–output ratio either through the choice of appropriate technology or by greater utilization of existing excess capacity, then growth-rate could indeed rise. The empirical evidence available so far does not help much to say anything very conclusively. The DF, generating moderate rate of inflation may help to promote growth, but once again, the evidence seems to weigh against the use of a high rate of inflation. To what extent there is a direct and significant correlation between DF, inflation and growth in the LDCs is a very important area for future research.

5.8 The tax structure in LDCs

The tax structures of most LDCs are narrow-based, inelastic with respect to changes in income and greatly dependent upon indirect rather than direct taxes. Thus, if fiscal policy is to play a more vigorous role to promote revenue, growth and stability (both economic and political), it is imperative that the tax-base should be broadened, that the tax revenue should be more elastic with respect to income (i.e. say, a 1 per cent increase in income should lead to a more than 1 per cent rise in taxes), and that there should be a *relative* expansion of the role of direct taxes incomparison with indirect taxes. The last point has, however, been debated considerably while the soundness of the first two arguments has not been questioned. A brief discussion of the different types of direct and indirect taxes may therefore be of some interest.

Direct taxes in LDCs

The major direct taxes in LDCs consist of income tax, corporation tax, wealth tax and property tax. Usually in LDCs, the proportion of direct taxes in total tax is much lower than that of indirect taxes, and direct taxes on agricultural income are generally very low. As regards income tax, its marginal rates are sometimes very high in countries like India and Sri Lanka and this, although regarded as desirable by some on the grounds of ability to pay and social justice, has been criticized by others because of its adverse effects on saving and work-effort. Second, with the growth of agriculture from the late sixties in many Asian countries and the emergence of a "Kulak" or relatively well-off class of peasants who have been the main beneficiaries of the "Green Revolution", it is argued that agricultural income taxation should be made progressive. However, most governments in South Asia as well as in other LDCs did not raise the proportion of agricultural income taxes to total taxes by more than 5 per cent. However, the high marginal tax rates plus administrative corruption have resulted in large scale tax evasion and revenue losses.

In order to widen the tax-base, Kaldor (1956) in his tax-reform proposal for India suggested the imposition of expenditure tax, wealth tax, gift tax and property tax. Out of these, the *expenditure tax* is very novel. It implies a tax on income minus saving, i.e. spending. The main reasons for its favour are: (a) restriction of consumption and increase of saving; (b) avoidance of the difficulty of identifying "income" in the LDCs; and (c) the fulfilment of the canon of ability to pay with social justice without reduction of saving and capital formation.

The Indian government accepted the proposal, imposed the tax but repealed it, reimposed it and repealed it again! Apart from India the only other country which imposed it was Sri Lanka which also withdrew it soon after its imposition. One of the reasons for such loss of enthusiasm about expenditure tax is intuitive. As Prest says ". . . the notion that there is a large amount of luxurious consumption expenditure in these countries which can be curtailed by very simple tax legislation, thereby releasing vast sums of money for domestic capital purposes, is singularly superficial." (Prest, 1972, pp. 80–81) Second, the assessment of expenditure is unlikely to be simple as it is now necessary to measure both income and saving and the administrative costs of expenditure tax are likely to be large. Third, evidence from India and Sri Lanka suggests that the revenue effect was small and given the administrative cost of collection, such small revenue was inadequate to justify the high cost of collection. Fourth, in India, it became very difficult to differentiate between business and personal expenditure and this simply highlights the problem of administration (Chelliah, 1969). However, as a supplement rather than a substitute for income tax, the expenditure tax could still be introduced in the LDCs as long as the tax is simple and economical to operate.

Other forms of direct taxation which could increase the tax-base include wealth tax, gift tax, profits tax and some other forms of company taxation. Although these taxes could increase the tax-base in LDCs, empirically their revenue effect turned out to be smaller than what was expected in some South Asian countries. Marginal rates of corporation and profit taxes were deliberately kept low in some LDCs to reduce their disincentive effect on saving and capital formation. The other reason for keeping business taxes low in LDCs is to attract foreign investment. On the other hand, from the point of view of administration and convenience of collection, a higher revenue could be raised with less difficulty via increases in the rates of company taxes. However, income of the companies is not a large proportion of the national income in the LDCs. Also, high company tax rates could inhibit the development of new enterprises. In addition, few LDCs would take the risk of destroying incentives to invest by raising company tax rates too high. However, given high rates of company taxes in some DCs, the LDCs could effectively raise revenue by raising rates of company taxes as long as there is a positive difference between company tax rates in DCs and LDCs.

Land tax has been considered as one of the major instruments for mobilizing surplus from agriculture. The case of land tax in Japan during the nineteenth century has usually been cited as important evidence in favour of such tax as it contributed a significant proportion of total tax revenue, though its importance might have been exaggerated (Sinha, 1969), and its real impact might have been reduced because of inflation (Bird, 1977). The main reasons in favour of land tax are as follows:

1. In the LDCs, although it is possible to conceal income and its sources, it is difficult to conceal land and hence the task of assessment becomes easier.
2. A tax on land will not make it move from one country to the other; but a tax on some other types of capital might.
3. Land tax could be formulated in such a way as to encourage the farmers to undertake the cultivation of more land or to cultivate land more intensively where land is scarce. The evidence from Chile supports this argument (Furtado, 1970, p. 52).
4. The importance of land in comparison with other forms of capital asset in LDCs implies that a land tax would broaden the tax-base.
5. From the standpoint of equity, if a tax on large land-holdings forces the landowners to sell some parts of their land to the small farmers, then this could be regarded as a more equitable distribution of wealth.
6. From (**5**) it can be argued that if the productivity of land per acre and size-holding are inversely related (a phenomenon which is supposed to have been observed in India), then from the point of view of *efficiency*, a tax on large land-holding is all the more desirable. Also, since small-scale farms tend to be more labour-intensive rather than capital-intensive, employment may increase.
7. In a subsistence economy, a land tax should increase the demand for money. Farmers would thus be induced to raise their marketed surplus and greater "real" surplus could be mobilized to promote economic growth.

The main drawbacks in the land-tax system can now be mentioned.

1. Fragmentation of land and lack of a clear legal idea about land ownership in most LDCs could make the administration of land tax very difficult.
2. There are important problems of assessment of land taxes in the LDCs either with reference to the value of output or the value of capital or potential productivity of land or by some other index.
3. If the tax is a fixed proportion of per hectare land-holding without due regard to its productivity, then total revenue might not be high.
4. The information about land-holding and title deeds in most LDCs is rather poor and sometimes out of date. This makes the task of land tax administration very difficult.
5. Given the political importance of the well-off class among the landowners, many LDCs have found the introduction of land taxation to be very difficult.

On balance, the strength of the arguments in favour of land tax seem to outweigh those against it. Where political will exists, the case for a land tax in one form or other, deserves serious consideration. If its imposition requires some institutional reforms, then such reforms also merit urgent attention. Different types of land taxation could also be introduced. For instance, in Nicaragua, such a tax is related to the fertility of land. Also, in Honduras and Guatemala, the tax rates on land tend to rise should the land be kept unused (Bird and Oldman, 1975). The principle of self-assessment has also gained attention. The main point to emphasize is that wherever there is an appreciation in the capital value of land, such gains, like any other capital gains, should be taxed. The spread of the "Green Revolution" in many LDCs has enhanced the capital values of land. Given a rise in farm income and profit and the narrow base of direct taxes, it is both necessary and desirable to tax the main beneficiaries of such "revolution" not only from the standpoint of mobilizing surplus for capital formation but also to promote social justice.

Indirect taxes in LDCs

Indirect taxes in LDCs usually consist of sales taxes, excise taxes and customs duties. Sometimes, marketing boards offer less than international price to the domestic producers, the differential being the tax. Tariffs on imports are also recognized as an important type of indirect tax. Value-added tax and payroll taxes are now increasingly regarded as important types of indirect taxation for LDCs. The indirect taxes are generally borne by the consumers and as such they are sometimes regarded as consumption-based taxes.

The overwhelming importance of indirect taxes as a proportion of total tax revenue is clearly shown in Table 5.1. Countries earning less than $100 *per capita* collect 68 per cent of total tax revenue in indirect taxes whereas DCs usually collect about 32 per cent of their total tax revenues by such taxes. The main reasons for such heavy dependence can easily be pointed out:

Table 5.1 Reliance on indirect taxes by *per capita* GNP class

Estimated per capita *GNP* (*US dollars*)	*No. of countries included*	*Indirect taxes as % of total tax revenue (average)*
Developing countries:		
100 or less	20	68
101–200	11	64
201–500	19	64
501–850	9	50
Highly developed countries:		
Over 850	15	32

Source: Due, John F. (1970).

First, the revenue that could be raised by indirect taxes is likely to be greater in comparison with revenue that could be obtained by imposing direct taxes. This is clear given the narrow tax-base and low income of most people in LDCs.

Second, since the indirect taxes are less difficult to collect and relatively easier to administer than direct taxes, this form of taxation has wide appeal in LDCs.

Third, it is argued that compared with, say, income taxes, indirect taxes as they are related to spending rather than earning, should have less adverse effect on saving and investment. Since indirect taxes are based on consumption, they can directly affect demand.

Fourth, in most LDCs, the proportion of wages and salaries in national income is quite low. This would obviously limit any potential expansion of the direct tax base. However, in theory, the elasticity of tax revenue from indirect taxes is unlikely to be greater than one in LDCs as consumption does not grow as fast as income. In practice, revenue elasticities of sales tax and excise duties in LDCs are estimated to be 2.4 per cent, as against 1.5 per cent in the case of income taxes (Chelliah, 1971).

Fifth, indirect taxes could be made "progressive" to the extent that "luxury goods", home-produced or imported, are subjected to a higher level of excise or import duties. When these taxes are levied on luxury imports, the foreign exchange constraint is eased.

Criticisms of indirect taxes in LDCs are generally made on the following grounds:

1. Indirect taxes are usually regarded as regressive. If the objective of the LDCs is to minimize the inequalities in the distribution of income and wealth, then such taxes are unlikely to be very effective policy instruments, despite steep taxes on "luxuries".
2. Indirect taxes do not direct investment and production in the socially most desirable channels as they distort optimal choice.
3. Consumers' choice is always distorted because of indirect taxes and a loss of consumer surplus and social welfare is indicated.
4. Customs duties, which sometimes form a significant source of tax revenue in the LDCs become increasingly inadequate as a means of raising sufficient revenue over time as domestic production rises. In an advanced stage of economic development, imports of investment goods form the bigger share of the total imports in comparison with imports of luxury products. When customs duties are increased, the undesirable aspects of high level protection may well emerge. For example, the production of "luxury" goods would be profitable and investment may well take place in luxury industries rather than in other socially more desirable channels.
5. In many LDCs, several exportables are subject to taxes. Although these taxes are simple to administer, this form of taxation has adverse effects on exports as it raises prices in the international market.

6. Sales tax – single or multi-stage – and excise duties are often regarded as important types of indirect taxes which are quite productive and easy to operate in the LDCs. But, here also, the point could be made that once a large variety of goods is produced with a general increase in production, sales tax and excise duties become very complicated and difficult to administer.

Given these arguments, it seems that although the indirect taxes in general do not always satisfy the principle of equity or ability, most LDCs would continue to bank upon them heavily in the near future, given their tax elasticity, revenue effect, administrative simplicity and broad-base. Recently, the introduction of *Value Added Tax* (VAT) has been advocated and this is discussed in the next section.

The case for and against VAT in the LDCs

While under a system of single-stage sales taxation, total tax revenue is obtained at only one point in the channels of production or distribution, under VAT a tax could be imposed on different stages in such channels, but only to the amount of value added. The service sector may be exempted from the purview of VAT. The very poor farmers in LDCs need not pay VAT. It is argued that VAT is superior to other forms of sales tax because it is neutral among different types of organization of production and distribution whereas the sales tax could increase vertical integration among firms since it applies to every stage of sale of the product – from the point of its initial production to the point of its ultimate consumption. It is clear that under such circumstances a firm would avoid paying taxes if it were the producer of the intermediate goods (Due, 1976). Thus, the inducement to the growth of monopoly is strengthened which could result in lower output, higher prices, and inefficiency in resource allocation. Evidence from Chile seems to support this argument.

Second, the adverse effects of indirect taxes on exports would be avoided if the amount of VAT could be worked out at the export points and given back to the exporters. Similarly, if the aim is import substitution, VAT may be formulated in such a way as to exclude the imports of capital goods.

Third, within a trading block, or common market, fiscal policy needs a certain degree of harmonization of tax instruments and very often VAT plays a more useful role than the different types of sales tax in different countries. This is witnessed in the case of the EEC countries.

Fourth, the sales taxes discriminate in favour of imports compared with home produced goods because the latter go via a greater number of sales within an economy than do imports. Again, the imposition of VAT will have neutral effects on imports and home production because at every transaction of importable goods which adds to the value, the goods would be subject to VAT.

Lastly, VAT makes cross-checking possible. Indeed, VAT has the merit of providing incentive to firms to report non-payment of taxes by other firms if they are allowed some tax credit.

However, the differences between sales tax and VAT are not large. The final choice between VAT and sales tax would depend upon the following factors:

1. The relative importance of retail as against wholesale trade. If the latter is more significant and the large firms operate, the case for VAT will be strengthened.
2. If the size of revenue needed from tax is small, then a sales tax might be preferred to VAT.
3. If a LDC strongly desires an import substitution via large-scale import of capital goods, then the greater will be the pressure to exempt such goods from taxes and the stronger will be the case for VAT.

The arguments against VAT can now be summarized:

1. VAT can make the tax structure very complicated. Given the lack of skilled manpower in many LDCs, its actual implications may be misinterpreted.
2. VAT could be difficult to administer given large-scale illiteracy in the LDCs.
3. Under VAT, a certain degree of "tax morality" is assumed on the part of the tax-paying firms and this could be lacking in many parts of the underdeveloped world.

In the light of the above arguments, it seems fair to conclude that where administrative machinery permits, the case for VAT rests chiefly on its neutral effect on production and distribution. Extended to the retail level, it would be broad-based to raise a significant amount of revenue. From the standpoint of equity and ability to pay, several modifications could be introduced to the VAT for a more egalitarian distribution of income and wealth. For example, exemptions from paying VAT might include the small farmer, primary education and rural health services, particularly for the poorer class of peasant who could be wholly excluded from the scope of VAT. If the great reliance on indirect taxes in the LDCs is likely to continue both as an instrument of earning revenue as well as an instrument for stabilization, then VAT for the LDCs merits serious consideration.

6

Sectoral allocation of resources: agriculture

6.1 Introduction

Agriculture in most LDCs is the dominant sector of the whole economy. Indeed, it accounts for 40 to 90 per cent of the total output in LDCs and offers employment to 40 to 80 per cent of their working population. Given its overwhelming importance, the case for its improvement to promote economic growth can hardly be overemphasized. In this chapter, first, we will discuss the role of agriculture in economic development. Next, we will examine the merit of the policies generally advocated for "squeezing" agriculture for industrialization. An alternative model would then be formulated to analyse the problems of mobilizing surplus from agriculture. Finally, empirical evidence of farmers' response to economic incentives in LDCs will be provided.

6.2 The role of agriculture in economic development

Agriculture plays a crucial role in the economic growth of LDCs. We can summarize its role as follows:

1. Agriculture provides *labour* to the non-agricultural sector. It has been shown before (see Ch. 3) that many LDCs experience the existence of "surplus" labour. Thus, availability of labour at a very low social opportunity cost could be an important factor to promote growth.

2. Food and raw materials are supplied by agriculture. Indeed, the cost of industrialization depends substantially upon low food and raw material prices. Since the industrial real wages would depend upon food prices, a steady food price is supposed to be imperative for achieving economic development. Further, in most LDCs the demand for food is high and is not expected to fall significantly partly because of "population explosion" (i.e. high birth-rate coupled with low death-rate) and partly because of subsistence livelihood. In fact, the income elasticity of the demand for food is estimated to be much higher in LDCs in comparison with the DCs. In most cases, it is 0.6 higher in LDCs while the comparative figure for the DCs is about 0.2. (Johnston and Mellor, 1961). The estimation of change in demand for food per annum could easily be made by using the following formula:

$$AD = l + \varepsilon y$$

where AD = changes in demand for food p.a.

l = population growth-rate

ε = elasticity of income (y) with respect to demand for agricultural products

It must be borne in mind that since in LDCs, consumption of food accounts for a high proportion of income, a rise in food prices, given as inelastic supply, could have an adverse impact on the whole economy.

3. Exports of agricultural products can help a country to earn valuable foreign exchange. When a country supplies only a small percentage of total exports chiefly in primary goods, it is likely to face an inelastic demand curve. However, if many LDCs try to export the same goods at the same time, prices may fall, given low income and price elasticities of demand of these goods. The answer to this problem lies in not putting "all the eggs in the same basket". Diversification of export crops will help to reduce the risks.

4. The rate of capital formation in LDCs can be considerably improved by the agricultural sector. The process of capital accumulation and the role of agriculture in that process has already been discussed in the Lewis, Ranis and Fei, and the Jorgenson models. It is enough to recall here that the process of accumulation depends upon the elasticity of food supply because given the bottlenecks on the supply side, wages and costs will rise, profit margins are supposed to fall, leading to an overall decline in surplus and growth.

The process of capital formation will also depend upon fiscal and monetary policies to siphon off surplus from agriculture. Tax on agriculture in Japan accounted for about 80 per cent of total tax revenue during 1893–97 and 50 per cent between 1913–17 (Johnston and Mellor, 1961).

However, political factors often stood in the way of imposing agricultural tax in many LDCs, including India, Pakistan and Burma. Frequently, simple inertia and weaknesses in the tax system have been major factors. (Johnston and Mellor, 1961). The Russian economic development illustrates vividly the price the agricultural sector had to pay for capital formation even when "the birth pangs were sharp and the attendant midwifery was rough" (Dobb, 1948). Whether the price was worth paying or not is another matter.

5. Agriculture in LDCs may play a crucial role in expanding the size of the home market. This can be achieved by enlarging the money and real income of the cultivators which will increase the demand for industrial products and thus will act as a stimulus to industrialization (e.g. Gold Coast, see Lewis, 1953, for details; see also Nurkse, 1959).

It is clear from the above analysis that agriculture can help or hinder the pace of economic growth and industrialization, given the considerable linkages between them in many LDCs. The next important issue is how to raise agricultural productivity to achieve a higher rate of growth. Here the main concern is how to raise "surplus" (difference between food production and food consumption) from agriculture to achieve higher rate of capital formation. The problem is not new but very important. In the following section we shall examine the nature of the debate between different schools about the ways of mobilizing surplus for reinvestment.

6.3 The concept of "marketed surplus"

The concept and role of marketed surplus is hardly new in development economics. Smith (1967), for example, observed: "When by the improvement and cultivation of land . . . the labour of half the society becomes sufficient to provide food for the whole, the other half . . . can be employed . . . in satisfying the other wants and fancies of mankind." Unfortunately, many economics. Smith (1776), for example, observed: "When by the improvement complains: ". . . Western economists have tended to ignore or seriously underestimate the importance of an agricultural surplus both in the earlier economic history of today's developed countries and in those countries which still remain at or near the bare subsistence level of food consumption." (Nicholls, 1963, p. 1.) However, recently, some have recognized its importance (Nicholls, 1963; Owen, 1966; Khusro, 1967), and it is now argued that the size of surplus is crucially related to the size of capital formation.

Marketed surplus and capital formation

It is generally stated that in a labour-surplus economy, without any loss of agricultural production, surplus population from agriculture can be transferred to other projects so long as consumption of agricultural output of agricultural and newly transferred non-agricultural labour remains constant. Defining marketed surplus as the difference between total food production and total food consumption, it may be argued that if *per capita* consumption remains fixed, surplus could be mobilized for real capital formation (Lewis, 1954; Nurkse, 1953, 1959). Obviously, the process involves leakages and the smaller the leakages, the greater is the marketed surplus. It is also important that: (1) those who still work in agriculture, will refrain from consuming more agricultural goods; (2) the agricultural population, with expansion of marketed surplus and thus with rising capacity to consume more manufactured goods should be prevented from consuming more agricultural goods at constant terms of trade.

The objectives are: (a) to transfer marketed surplus; and (b) to enforce savings on the agricultural population. To achieve these objectives, government may: (i) impose taxes or levies; or (ii) try to persuade peasants to save more. The first policy *may* be successful in a command economy; the success of the second policy is questionable. It may require a man like Mao who may persuade the masses to swim, sometimes against the tide; or it may require a certain ideology and value-judgement (e.g. everybody would be better off by giving up something). In any case, it is difficult to see the application *and* success of such a policy in all the LDCs. Alternatively, the terms of trade, i.e. the ratio of agricultural price to industrial price could be changed against agriculture. This policy gained considerable favour in Russia in the twenties. Originally advocated by Preobrazhensky (1965) and blessed by some key political leaders of the USSR at that time, the implications of this policy are interesting and deserve attention.

Marketed surplus and terms of trade

The method of turning the terms of trade against agriculture is supposed to be similar to that of a country's use of its favourable terms of trade with other countries for its capital formation. The terms of trade may be changed against agriculture in different ways (Narain, 1957). For example:

1. The prices of agricultural goods may be prevented from rising in proportion to the prices of manufactured goods through price control.
2. Industrial goods entering into villagers' consumption could be taxed.
3. The prices of domestic manufactured goods may be allowed to rise by granting protection to the industries holding agricultural prices constant.
4. Through state trading in manufactured goods.

By adopting policies (1) and (3) the margins of profits of the private industry could be raised and fiscal policy may be used to mop up the surplus. Adoption of methods (2) and (4) should directly raise the resources for financing development.

It should be noted that the higher the percentage of surplus agricultural population to be transferred, *cet. par.*, the more will the terms of trade have to be moved against agriculture to absorb the potential savings. It is assumed that the required increase in marketed surplus is forthcoming.

However, the policy has limitations. It is plausible to think that when the surplus agricultural labour will be transferred to the non-agricultural sector, those who would be left behind in the agricultural sector may consume more of their own produce than they did previously because they might be feeling better off. This may be regarded as the direct income effect and this may reduce marketed surplus. When the terms of trade are moved against agriculture, there would be two other effects. These are "derived" income and substitution effects. When the terms of trade move against agriculture, the demand of agriculturists for everything including their own goods is thereby reduced by reducing this real income. This may raise the marketed surplus, but since agricultural goods become cheaper relative to industrial goods, it induces the agriculturists to substitute their own goods instead of industrial goods. If the direct income and substitution effects are more powerful than the derived income effect, then total marketed surplus *declines.*

There is an additional problem related to savings. The strength of the policy depends upon the compulsion under which the peasant should sell part of his production. Such compulsion exists in a command economy. But in a democratic society there is nothing to prevent a "spite-effect", i.e., as the terms of trade go against agriculture, a farmer might decide not to sell as much

Fig. 6.1

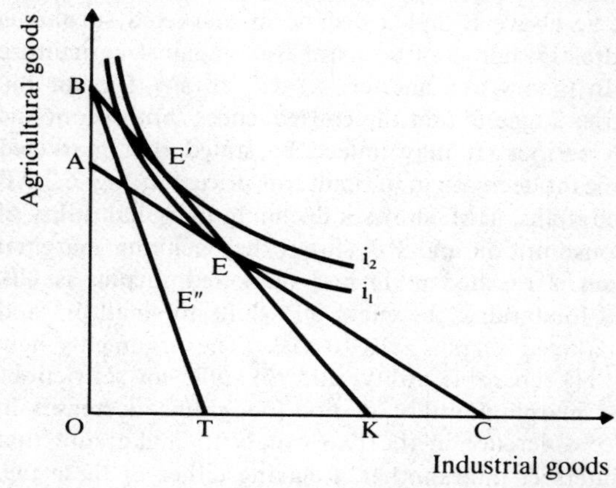

as he might have sold before any worsening of the terms of trade. In the extreme case, farmers may refuse to sell anything. These points are illustrated in Figs. 6.1 and 6.2.

In Fig. 6.1, the reactions of a farmer are described with changing terms of trade. The farmer's income in rural goods is given by OA and OB respectively, prior to and after the transference of surplus population. Since the diagram depicts every quantity as per head of agricultural population AB shows the addition per head of rural population after the transfer of surplus labour. The initial equilibrium is reached at E where AC – the slope showing the initial terms of trade – is tangent to the indifference curve i_1. The slope of BK passing through E shows the terms of trade that are required to absorb total potential savings (assuming that the appropriate rise in marketed surplus is

Fig. 6.2

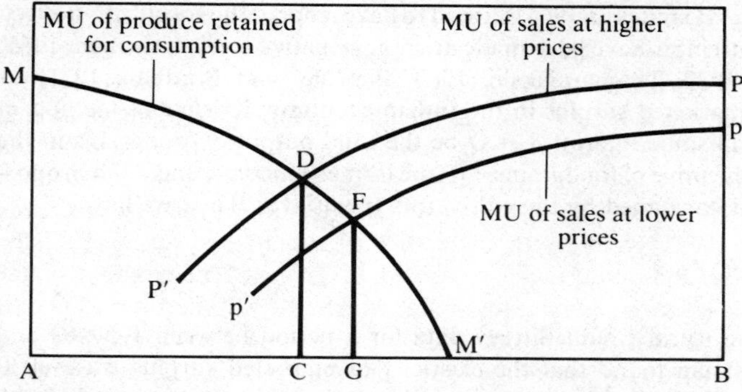

forthcoming). As the slope of BK is greater than the slope of AC, and since indifference curves cannot intersect each other, it follows that E′, the point of new equilibrium, must lie above E and a decline in marketed surplus is observed. Could a more drastic change of terms of trade against agriculture raise marketed surplus? In theory, the answer is “yes” at, say E″, but the experience of some countries suggests that the consequences (both economic and social) could be very serious. It may indeed be stated that marketed surplus will fall with significant decrease in agricultural prices. In Fig. 6.2 AB is the given amount of foodgrains, MM′ shows a declining marginal utility of foodgrains retained for consumption and PP′ shows the declining marginal utility of sales. Equilibrium is reached at D and marketed surplus is CB. With a fall in the price of foodgrains, the curve PP′ shifts to small pp′ and at new equilibrium F, marketed surplus falls to GB. (The arguments here rest on two assumptions: (1) separable utility; and (2) sufficient restrictions on the rate at which the marginal utility of non-foodgrains decreases in comparison with the price difference in the two events to make sure that PP′ and pp′ would not intersect one another. Relaxing either of these two assumptions might allow for the reappearance of negative price elasticity (Bhagwati and Chakravarty, 1969).) As long as production is positively elastic with respect to price changes, then even when consumption rises, marketed surplus must rise so long as positive price elasticity of foodgrains is greater than the price elasticity of consumption (Bhagwati and Chakravarty, 1969, p. 33).

The point is, however, made that if price falls, marketed surplus may rise (see, Ghatak, 1975, for a summary) for several reasons. Thus, it is argued that farmers wish to maintain the same level of money income because their demand for cash is fixed (Mathur and Ezekiel, 1961). Such an assumption would imply very low income elasticity of the demand for non-foodgrains of the farmers as well as a zero substitution effect – an assumption which is hardly valid logically or empirically. Further, this model applies to only very short-run and does not show what happens when the initial equilibrium is disturbed. Indeed in their model, price movements could be explosive once the equilibrium is disturbed. (Bhagwati and Chakravarty, 1969, p. 33). Similarly, other advocates (Dandekar, 1964) seemed to have ignored the substitution effect.

Several attempts have been made at an aggregative level (Krishnan, 1965; Bardhan, K. 1970, Thamarajakshi, 1969; Bardhan and Bardhan, 1971) to estimate the marketed surplus in the Indian economy. Krishnan's method of estimation is of some interest. Let $\overline{Q}$ be the total output of foodgrains in the short-run, P the price of foodgrains, $\overline{Q}P$ the farmer's income, and r the proportion of output consumed by the cultivators themselves. Then we have:

$$r\overline{Q} = AP^{-\alpha}(P\overline{Q})^{\beta}$$

Using the Rural Credit Survey data for a period between 1959–60 and 1962–63, Krishnan found that the elasticity of marketed surplus was -·3030 in India. But this finding is based upon the assumption that output is fixed.

If that assumption is relaxed one might get positive elasticity (Bhagwati and Chakravarty, 1969, p. 35). Second, in the equation the effects of factors affecting supply (e.g. input costs, land tenure, etc.), but not demand, are ignored (Macrae, 1971, p. 404). Further, it may be argued that the parameter in the demand function of Krishnan is not the price elasticity of demand of farmers. In fact, such elasticity is given by $(\beta - \alpha)$. Note that

$$r\overline{Q} = AP^{-\alpha}(p\overline{Q})^{\beta}$$

$$\text{or} \quad r\overline{Q} = AP^{\beta-\alpha}\overline{Q}^{\beta}$$

$$\text{therefore} \quad \frac{\delta r\overline{Q}}{\delta P}\frac{P}{r\overline{Q}} = (\beta - \alpha)$$

Redefined in this way, and using Krishnan's own estimation, price elasticity of marketed surplus becomes positive (MaCrae, 1971).

But several criticisms can be made about almost all these empirical studies. First, no attempt has been made to look at the problem from the standpoint of the utility function of an individual farmer. Second, the data used in some of these studies are too aggregative (see Krishnan, 1965, Thamarajakshi, 1969). Third, the inverse relationship between price, terms of trade and marketed surplus observed at the national level may not be valid at the state level. Fourth, the variations of different crop prices are not usually considered. For example, the effects of changes in the price of one crop may be neutralized by changes in price of other crops. In view of these criticisms, a formal model is set out in Section 6.4 to examine the response of the marketed surplus to changes in terms of trade; empirical estimates are also given. Section 6.8 draws some conclusions.

6.4 The model to mobilize agricultural surplus

Contrary to previous analysis, the problem of mobilizing surplus from agriculture is analysed in the following model, from the point of view of farmer's utility. Let the farmer's utility function be

$$U_a = U_a(a, i, L) \qquad [6.1]$$

Where U_a = utility of the farmer

a = consumption of agricultural goods

i = consumption of industrial goods

L = leisure.

It is assumed that in a traditional society, the farmer's demand for agricultural goods is given: i.e. $a = \bar{a}$. Hence rewriting the equation [6.1], we have

$$U_a = U_a(\bar{a}, i, L) \qquad [6.2]$$

The income of the farmer is given by the revenue from agricultural goods that could be sold in the market:

$$Y_a = p_a M \qquad [6.3]$$

where Y_a = income from the sale of agricultural goods,

p_a = price of agricultural goods,

M = marketed surplus.

Marketed surplus is, in turn, regarded as a function of leisure; this simple assumption can be relaxed later. At the moment, we are abstracting away from the product relationship not because it is unimportant, but because it is another vast field of enquiry and because it facilitates diagrammatic exposition. Thus, we have

$$M = f(L) \qquad [6.4]$$

$$p_a M = p_i i + T + R \qquad [6.5]$$

P_i = Price of industrial goods

T = Taxes

R = Rents

Equation [6.5] states that the income of the farmer is spent on industrial goods, as well as on taxes and rent that he pays in cash.

Substituting equation [6.4] into [6.5], we obtain equation [6.6]:

$$p_a \cdot f(L) = p_i \cdot i + T + R \qquad [6.6]$$

or $$p_a \cdot f(L) - p_i \cdot i - T - R = 0 \qquad [6.7]$$

Expressing the Lagrangian for the maximization of the farmer's utility function subject to his income, equations [6.8] and [6.9] are obtained:

$$V = [p_a \cdot f(L) - p_i \cdot i - T - R] = 0 \qquad [6.8]$$

$$\max \quad V = U_a^* (\bar{a}, i, L) + \lambda[p_a \cdot f(L) - p_i \cdot i - T - R] \qquad [6.9]$$

Setting the partial derivatives equal to zero, we obtain:

$$\frac{\partial v}{\partial i} = \frac{\partial U_a^*}{\partial i} - \lambda p_i = 0 \qquad [6.10]$$

$$\frac{\partial v}{\partial L} = \frac{\partial U_a^*}{\partial L} + \lambda p_a \cdot f'(L) = 0 \qquad [6.11]$$

$$\frac{\partial v}{\partial \lambda} = p_a \cdot f(L) - p_i \cdot i - T - R = 0 \qquad [6.12]$$

Dividing [6.10] by [6.11] and eliminating λ we have:

$$\frac{\partial U_a^*/\partial i}{\partial U_a^*/\partial L} = \frac{-P_i}{P_a \cdot f'(L)} \qquad [6.13]$$

Note that since

$$M = f(L) \qquad [6.4]$$

Therefore

$$\frac{dM}{dL} = f'(L)\ 0 \qquad [6.4a]$$

Thus, $-p_a \cdot f'(L)$ may be regarded as the unit price of leisure since $-f'(L) = \frac{dM}{dL}$ = change in M resulting from a unit change of leisure, and the sign of the derivative is negative. Hence, equation [6.13] may be rewritten as:

$$\frac{\text{Marginal Utility of i}}{\text{Marginal Utility of L}} = \frac{\text{Unit price of industrial goods}}{\text{Unit price of leisure}} \qquad [6.14]$$

The points are illustrated in Fig. 6.3. In the north-east quadrant, the relationship between leisure and industrial goods is described by a family of indifference curves. Similarly, the relationship between consumption of industrial goods and terms of trade, i.e. p_a/p_i is shown in the north-west quadrant.

Fig. 6.3

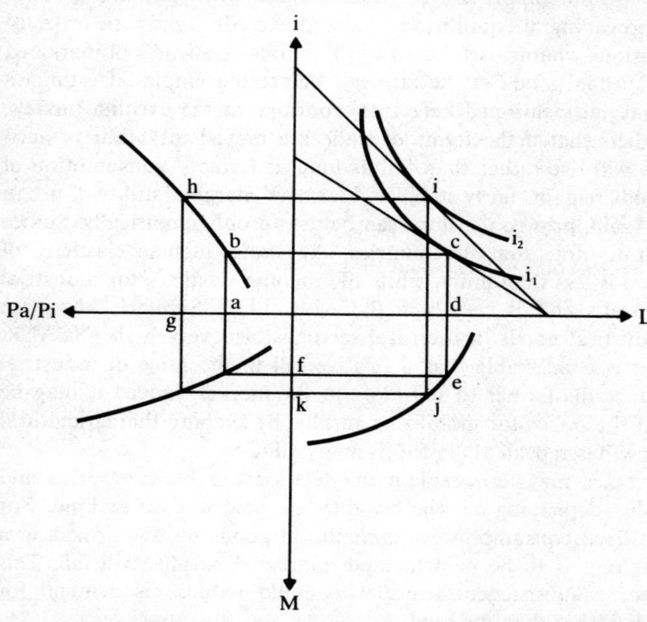

The curve indicates that as the price of industrial goods will fall relative to agricultural goods, demand for industrial goods will rise. In the south-west quadrant, it is shown that when the terms of trade move in favour of agriculture, marketed surplus will *rise*, though the rate of rise will decrease gradually. This is partly because the limited role that terms of trade could play at a more developed stage, and also because there is an absolute limit after which peasants will be unwilling to sacrifice leisure, which also explains the nature of the relationship between leisure and marketed surplus in the south-east part of the diagram. It is implied that an indefinite increase in the relative prices of agricultural goods may not increase surplus because after a point farmers may wish to consume more of leisure and the supply curve of labour may turn backwards. However, the case of the backward-bending supply curve of labour has never been well proved for agricultural systems in poor countries (Blake, 1962). Similar doubts have been voiced about price responsiveness of peasants in poor countries. But almost all the empirical studies show that farmers are responsive to economic incentives (Bauer and Yamey, 1959; Krishna, 1963; Behrman, 1968). It may indeed be said that before branding the farmers as unresponsive, they must be given the opportunities to respond.

In our model, price movements need not be divergent so long as the elasticity of the marketed surplus curve, i.e. "the offer curve", is less than the elasticity of the urban demand curve. The stability of equilibrium in the Walrasian sense would be maintained when it could be shown that at prices above the equilibrium, supply exceeds demand and when prices are lower than the level prevailing at equilibrium, demand exceeds supply. In order to evaluate conclusions what is useful is to test the price elasticities of marketed surplus and of urban goods of the farmers. Before the empirical estimates are made, it may be mentioned here that, contrary to the existing models, our model predicts that if the terms of trade are moved in favour of agriculture, surplus will rise rather than fall as long as farmers' consumption of agricultural goods remains fairly stable and farmers' marginal utility of urban goods is high. Again, firm conclusions can be drawn only empirically. Suffice for the present to note that in countries like India, income elasticity of demand for food is less than unity, while the income elasticity for industrial goods in the rural sector is very high (NCAER, 1972). Similarly, the price elasticity of industrial goods in the rural sector is also very high (NCAER, 1972). Hence, it is conceivable that a relative fall in the price of industrial goods may induce the farmer to sell more in the market. Indeed it may be noted here that the policy for mobilizing surplus by keeping the agricultural prices rather low has repeatedly failed in many LDCs.

Rent and taxes may also explain the relationship between price and marketed surplus, depending on whether they are paid in cash or kind. For example, given fixed consumption of agricultural goods by the farmers in a bad year, if the rent is to be paid in kind, marketed surplus will fall. This may be true for a subsistence farmer who could reduce his demand for industrial goods rather than for food.

Empirical estimates

Empirical estimates of the relationship between terms of trade and marketed surplus do not yield any conclusive answer. While Krishnan (1965), Thamarajakshi (1969), Bardhan, K. (1970) have found negative elasticity with respect to agricultural prices, Krishna (1965) found positive elasticity for a single crop. Using the data for wheat production and supply in Punjab–Haryana, Ghatak (1975) also found positive elasticity with respect to both barter and income terms of trade (see also, Bardhan and Bardhan, 1971). Similarly, the long-run price elasticity is estimated as positive in Thailand (Behrman, 1968). Also, both long- and short-run elasticities are shown as positive in Africa (Helleiner, 1975).

6.5 Acreage response to prices

An alternative way that has been used by many economists to test the "rational" behaviour of the peasants in LDCs was to examine the change in the distribution of acreage of land under cultivation because of price changes. It was sometimes held that the peasants in LDCs do not respond "rationally", i.e. they do not respond to economic incentives. However, almost all the numerous studies which have been conducted so far confirm the hypothesis that the peasants in LDCs do respond to changes in economic incentives. This is shown in Table 6.1. In only *one* case, (sorghum in undivided Punjab), the price elasticity is negative and significant. But this was due to the fact that it was an inferior feed crop (Krishna, 1968). Similarly, considerable evidence from African smallholders supply elasticities suggests the responsiveness of the African farmers to economic incentives (Helleiner, 1975). This is shown in Table 6.2.

6.6 Marketed surplus, size-holdings and output

It has been suggested that size-holdings could affect the size of the surplus (Narain, 1961, Krishna, 1965). Empirical evidence suggests that the supply of marketed surplus is not a feature if only the *proportions* of output marketed are considered. Thus, the land-holdings in the size-class of less than 5 acres supplied about 20.7 per cent of the value of their output as marketed surplus. This conclusion can, however, be questioned when the sale of individual crop is concerned. The following reasons can be offered to account for such inconsistencies:

(*a*) different definitions of marketed surplus;
(*b*) differences in the times and places covered;
(*c*) while some have considered all the crops, others have considered only one crop.

It is worth noting that according to one survey of Indian agriculture (Narain, 1962), the proportion of marketed surplus declines until size-holdings of 10–15 acres are reached but rises after that. If this is true, then the implication is that the break-up of the large holdings may *increase* rather than diminish the marketed surplus, assuming away any negative effect of any

Table 6.1 Estimated price elasticities of acreage of specified crops, less-developed countries and regions

Crop and country or region	Period	Elasticity Short-run	Long-run	Source
Rice				
Punjab (India–Pakistan)	1914–45	0.31	0.59	Krishna, 1963
Pakistan	1948–63	0.05[a]		Hussain, 1964
Indonesia (Java and Madura)	1951–62	0.30		Mubyarto, 1965
Philippines	1947–63	[b]	[b]	Mangahas *et al.*, 1965
Ilocos	1954–64	0.22	0.51	
C. Luzon	1954–64	0.13	0.62	
S. Tagalog	1954–64	0.24	0.42	
E. Visayas	1954–64	0.13	0.15	
Cagayan	1954–64	[b]	[b]	
Wheat				
Punjab (India–Pakistan)	1914–43	0.08	0.14	Krishna, 1963
Pakistan	1944–59	0.20		Falcon, 1964
Maize				
India–Pakistan	1914–43	0.23	0.56	Krishna, 1963
Philippines	1911–41	0.02	0.04	Mangahas *et al.*, 1965
Philippines	1947–64	0.07	0.42	Mangahas *et al.*, 1965
Ilocos	1953–63	0.07	0.11	
C. Luzon	1953–63	[b]	[b]	
S. Tagalog	1953–63	0.42	0.47	
E. Visayas	1947–63	0.40[c]	0.57[c]	
W. Visayas	1947–63	0.03	0.04	
Cagayan	1953–63	[b]	[b]	
Bicol	1953–63	0.16	0.26	
Mindanao				
S. & W.	1953–63	[b]	[b]	
N. & E.	1947–63	[b]	[b]	
Barley				
Punjab (India–Pakistan)	1914–45	0.39[c]	0.50	Krishna, 1963
Millets				
India–Pakistan	1914–45	0.09	0.36	Krishna, 1963
Gram				
Punjab (India–Pakistan)	1914–45	−0.33[c]		Krishna, 1963

Table 6.1 (continued)

Crop and country or region	*Period*	*Elasticity*		*Source*
		Short-run	*Long-run*	
Sorghum				
Punjab (India–Pakistan)	1914–43	−0.58		Krishna, 1963
Sugarcane				
Punjab (India–Pakistan)	1915–43	0.34	0.60	Krishna, 1963
Cotton				
India–Pakistan	1922–43	0.59	1.08	Krishna, 1963
India	1948–61	0.64	1.33	Krishna, 1965
Pakistan (8 districts)	1933–58	0.41		Falcon, 1964
Pakistan	1935–62	0.50[d]		Mohammad, 1963
Egypt	1900–38	0.4–0.6[e]		Stern, 1959
Egypt	1913–37	0.40		Stern, 1962
Jute				
India–Pakistan	1911–38	0.46	0.73	Venkatamaranan, 1958
Bengal (India–Pakistan)	1911–38	0.68	1.03	Stern, 1962
India–Pakistan (Bengal, Bihar, Orissa)	1893–1938	0.57–0.65		Stern, 1962
Pakistan	1931–53	0.60		Clark, 1957
Pakistan	1948–63	0.40		Hussain, 1964
Rubber				
Malaysia				
Estates	1953–60	0		Stern, 1965
Smallholders	1953–60	0.20		Stern, 1965
Estates	1951–61	−0.02[c,f]		Chan[g]
Smallholders	1948–61	0.12[f]		Chan[g]
Estates	1954–61	0.03[c,h]		Chan[g]
Smallholders	1953–60	0.34[h]		Chan[g]

[a] For summer and winter crops combined; elasticity for summer crop alone, 0.12.
[b] Negative coefficient indicated.
[c] Not significant at 10 per cent level.
[d] Based on simple calculations from yearly variations.
[e] Based on year-to-year arc elasticities.
[f] Based on annual data.
[g] Reported in Wharton, 1964, Tables 6.2, 6.3, 6.4. Wharton also reports (1963, 7) estimates of less than 0.21 for some other countries of South-East Asia.
[h] Based on monthly data.

Source: R. Krishna (1968).

Table 6.2 Evidence on African smallholder supply elasticities[a]

Product and country	*Period*	*Short-run elasticity*	*Long-run elasticity*	*Positive response but no elasticity data*[b]	*Source*[c]
Cocoa					
Ghana	1930–40		0.43		Ady, 1949
	1920–39	0.17			Stern, 1965
	1920–46	0.15			Ibid.
	1946–62		0.32–0.87		Bateman, 1965
	1946–62		0.77–1.28		Ibid.
	1947–64		0.71		Behrman, 1968
Nigeria	1920–45		1.29		Stern, 1965
	1947–64		0.45		Behrman, 1968
	1948–67		0.20		Olayide, 1972
Ivory Coast	1947–64		0.80		Behrman, 1968
Cameroun	1947–64		1.81		Ibid.
Ghana	1947–64			*	Ady, 1968
Nigeria	1947–65			*	Ibid.
Sierra Leone				*	Saylor, 1967
Coffee					
Kenya, estates acreage	1946–64	0.16	0.47		Maitha, 1969; Ford, 1971
Kenya, smallholder acreage	1946–64	0.20	0.56		Ibid.
Kenya, estates yield	1946–64	0.66	0.71		Maitha, 1970; Ford, 1971
Kenya, smallholder yield	1946–64	0.64	1.01		Ibid.
Ethiopia	1964–70				
					Goering *et al.*
Uganda	1950–64			*	Ady, 1968
Palm oil					
Nigeria	1950–64	0.81			Diejomaoh, 197
	1949–63	0.41			Helleiner, 1966
	1948–67		0.22–0.26		Olayide, 1972
Eastern Nigeria	1949–66	0.41–0.70			Oni, 1969a

Table 6.2 (continued)

Product and country	*Period*	*Short-run elasticity*	*Long-run elasticity*	*Positive response but no elasticity data*[b]	*Source*[c]
Palm kernels					
Nigeria	1950–64	0.25			Diejomaoh, 1972
	1949–66	0.22–0.28			Oni, 1969a
Sierra Leone				*	Saylor, 1967
Cotton					
Nigeria	1950–64	0.67			Diejomaoh, 1972
	1948–67	0.21–0.38			Oni, 1969b
	1948–67	0.3			Olayide, 1972
Tanzania	1953–69		2.44		Malima, 1971
Tobacco					
Malawi	1926–60	0.48			Dean, 1966
Rubber					
Nigeria	1948–67	0.21	0.17–0.24		Olayide, 1972
Haricot beans					
Ethiopia	1953–70	1.60			Goering *et al.*
Civet					
Ethiopia	1957–70	3.16			Ibid.
Pulses					
Ethiopia	1952–70	0.72			Ibid.
Lentils					
Ethiopia	1953–70	1.30			Ibid
Sesame					
Ethiopia	1957–70	0.61			Ibid

It is difficult to summarize results in a number or two. A complete assessment of the meaning and value of these various estimates requires reference to the original source.

Asterisk indicates statistically significant response.

Full references are given below in source notes.

Source: Helleiner (1975), pp. 40–41.

consequent change in output. But another study of Indian agriculture has shown that in the absence of any change in the number of land-holdings, changing output among different sized groups of land will not influence the amount of marketed surplus (Krishna, 1965). However, this result could occur in the case of a single crop and not with the total agricultural output. On balance, it must be stated that in the absence of the availability of *time-series* data for most LDCs, no firm conclusion can be drawn.

The other important issue in agriculture in many LDCs is the relationship between farm size and output per acre of land. It has been observed on the basis of the Farm Management Surveys for some provinces of India between 1955 and 1957–58 that as farm size increases, output per acre diminishes. In other words, smaller farms are more efficient than larger farms. Again from the point of view of policies, this finding has very important implications. Several explanations have been offered (see, for details, Bhagwati and Chakravarty, 1969). We will summarize here the major points.

1. While the larger farms are based on the capitalistic system of cultivation, the smaller farms are run on the principle of family farming. Hence on the larger farms, output is produced at a point where marginal productivity (MP) is equal to the wages whereas on smaller farms, cultivation is carried out beyond this point as output could be extended up to the point where $MP = 0$. Small farms are, thus, regarded as more efficient on the basis of per acre productivity. But this explanation is not adequate.
2. Larger farms are less fertile than the smaller farms because poorer peasants sell, frequently in distress, the inferior quality land to rich peasants.
3. Larger farms may be scattered over a wide area particularly if the "distress sale" hypothesis is true, and this could account for inefficiency emanating from fragmentation and distance. Also, since the smaller farms are in distress and may be operating close to the level of their survival, they would be more induced to use the inputs more efficiently, whereas the larger farms are not under compulsion to do so because of the higher marginal disutility from labour that they would now associate with marginal changes in income. Note that the point about the trade-off between leisure and income is not new, as Chayanov (1966) has demonstrated (see Fig. 6.4). The horizontal axis measures farm income. The curve CD shows the declining marginal utility of farm income whereas the curve AB depicts the marginal disutility of work associated with longer hours and higher income. The slope of the curve AB clearly shows that as income rises, the marginal disutility after a point, say x, rises at a very high rate. Equilibrium is reached at a point like x (see Chayanov, 1966 for details).

However, Chayanov's argument that an increase in prices of crops will increase leisure preferences is open to question.
4. *Tenurial disincentives* in large farms may account for inefficiency. Nevertheless, empirical evidence to test this hypothesis has yielded conflicting results.
5. The poor managerial and innovative capacities are very frequently witnessed in many large farms which are often characterized by *absentee landlords*.

Fig. 6.4

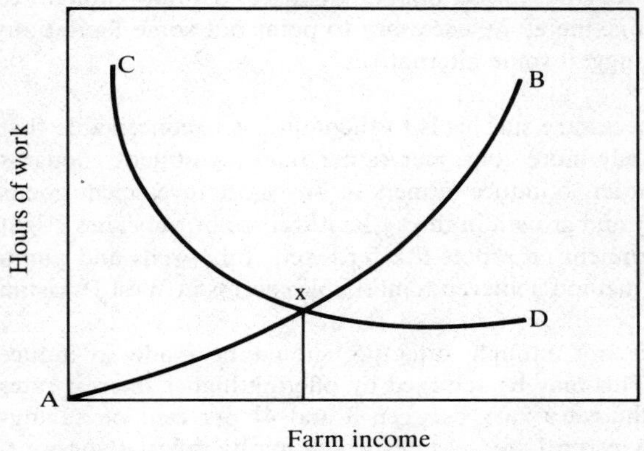

6. While large farms may wish to maximize profits, small farms may wish to maximize output or income. Figure 6.5 illustrates this point. The revenues (R) and costs (C) of the peasant farms are measured on the vertical axis whereas output of crops is measured along the horizontal axis. The large farm produces at a point like P where its marginal revenue is equal to marginal cost whereas a small farm would produce at a point to the right of the point P (say, M) as it is trying to maximize output. Thus, a small farm produces a larger output (Oq_2) than a large farm (Oq_1).

Fig. 6.5

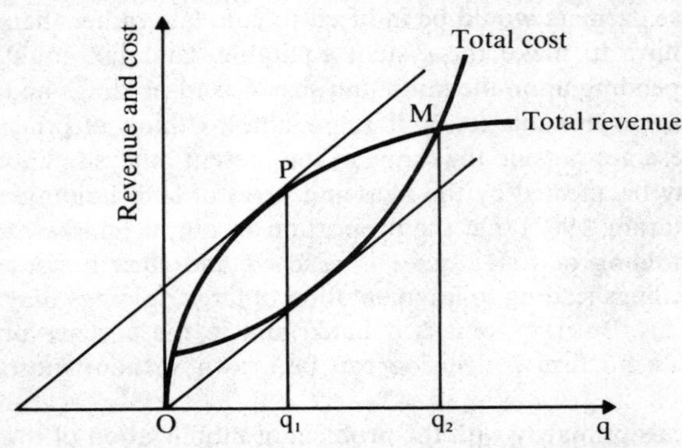

6.7 Limitations of price policy and some alternatives

It is not difficult to see that price policy, by itself, is not enough to mobilize the surplus. It is, therefore, necessary to point out some limitations of price policy and to suggest some alternatives.

1. Assuming that the necessary surplus is forthcoming, it is conceivable that farmers would like to buy more consumer rather than investment goods as their income rises. In order to induce farmers to buy more investment goods to promote productivity and growth in the agricultural sector, subsidies might be offered by the government on inputs like fertilizers, tube wells and pump sets for irrigation. This method achieved remarkable success in West Pakistan (Nulty, 1972).

2. Since price policy is not enough, attempts should be made to induce farmers to save more. This may be achieved by offering higher interest rates on savings. In LDCs the rates vary between 3 and $4\frac{1}{2}$ per cent on savings (e.g. in the Post Office) in rural areas – rates which hardly reflect the opportunity cost of capital. Although savings are generally not regarded as very sensitive to changes in interest rates in poor countries (Williamson, 1968), in India, the interest elasticity is found to be positive and highly significant (Gupta, K., 1970; Gupta, S., 1971).

3. Fiscal policies may be required to supplement monetary policies to mobilize the surplus. Agricultural income is hardly taxed in LDCs, and land tax is almost non-existent. Indeed, direct taxes on land or on agricultural income form less than 1 per cent of total tax revenue. Thus there is scope to raise taxes on agricultural income. Since a very high level of taxes might impair the incentives of farmers to produce and sell, it may be necessary to introduce a differential system of taxation. That part of agricultural produce which is marketed may be taxed at a very low rate, or even be exempted for small farmers, whereas the part that is retained may be taxed at a higher rate.

In view of the difficulties in estimating agricultural income, it may be necessary to introduce land taxes. The advantage here is that while income sources could be concealed, it is difficult to conceal land. Second, if the tax has to be paid in any case, farmers would be induced to cultivate rather than to leave land fallow. Third, to make the system equitable, land tax could be made progressive, depending upon the minimum size of land-holdings and on the proportion of the surplus marketed. It is possible to think of other methods as well, but these are outside the scope of the present analysis.

4. Marketed surplus may be affected by the sizes and types of land-holdings. In India, it is argued (Narain, 1962) that the proportion of output marketed declines until the size-holding of 10–15 acres is reached and then it rises. This implies that land ceilings leading to fragmentation of large holdings may raise the marketed surplus. But the point is debated and in the absence of necessary time-series data no firm conclusion can be drawn without more research.

5. The present model deals primarily with the problem of mobilization of the surplus from the point of the farmer's utility. The model could be extended to accommodate the factors affecting production, for example, land, capital, rainfall and temperature.

6.8 Conclusions

Given the role of agriculture in the economic development of the LDCs it is imperative to invest considerable resources for their agricultural development. Unfortunately, in many countries agriculture is synonymous with backwardness and planners too often equate development with urban industrialization. Lipton has noticed the presence of "urban bias" in the Indian planning, (Lipton, 1968a). It is doubtful whether the large-scale investment for urban industrialization would actually raise the living standard of the impoverished teeming millions among the peasantry, particularly when in terms of employment generation and income distribution, the results in many countries have fallen short of expectations. The recent change in agricultural production in some parts of South and South-East Asia, a phenomenon often characterized by the "Green Revolution", has demonstrated that the farmers in the LDCs are quite willing to try new methods to raise their income and they are not unresponsive to economic incentives.[1] However, the gains from the "Green Revolution" have not been distributed very equally (Bardhan, 1970a,b, 1973; Dandekar and Rath, 1971). But this is more a problem of distribution and public policy may be used to rectify the situation. The crucial point to realize is that the role of agriculture in the economic development of LDCs can hardly be overemphasized. "Whereas in the past, agriculture was often viewed as the passive partner in the development process, it is now typically regarded as an active and co-equal partner with the industrial sector." (Thorbecke, 1969) Also, the existing evidence conclusively shows that farmers do respond to economic incentives and changes in technology, though perhaps in a cautious way, in most LDCs and given the necessary inputs to introduce technical change, they are not averse to adopting new technology. The analysis of the relationship between farm size and productivity shows that larger farms are not necessarily more "efficient" than the smaller farms when efficiency is measured by productivity per acre. The Japanese experience also suggests the prospects of increasing output within small-scale farming (Okhawa and Johnston, 1969). Radical land reforms involving the promotion of small-scale farming need not be ruled out, given the inefficiency of the larger farms, preponderance of landless peasants and absentee landlords in many LDCs.[2]

Notes:

1. The literature on the "Green Revolution" is huge. For a "feel" of the subject, see, for example, Brown, D. (1971); Brown, L. (1970); Byres, T. (1972), includes an excellent bibliography; Griffin, K. (1974, 1976); Harris, B., (1971); Johnston and Cownie, (1969); Sen, S. (1974, 1975).
2. On the economic theory of share-cropping, tenancy and some related issues, see Cheung (1969); Bardhan and Srinivasan (1971); and Bardhan (1977).

7

Development planning

7.1 Concept of economic planning

Economic planning has become one of the main instruments of achieving a higher growth-rate and better standard of living in many LDCs. Planning can be defined as a conscious effort on the part of any government to follow a definite pattern of economic development in order to promote rapid and fundamental change in the economy *and* society. Such a concept of planning is fairly broad as it seeks to promote not only a fast growth-rate but also significant structural socio-economic changes via public intervention. However, the degree of state intervention defines the nature of different types of planning.

7.2 Types of planning

Planning could be of various types. For example, it could be *totalitarian* when all the means of production are usually owned and manipulated by the state. In the Soviet Union or China, all the "commanding heights" of the economy are governed by the state. Here the degree of state intervention is the highest. At the other extreme planning could be democratic. In France, for example, the state does not own all the means of production. But it sets out some guidelines for the private sector to follow. Thus, planning here takes place through *inducement* rather than through *control*. This kind of democratic planning is sometimes known as *indicative* planning. In between these two extremes there are cases of mixed planning. Here both the public and the private sector operate side by side. Some means of production (usually the basic and strategic industries) are owned by the state while the free private sector is expected to attain the targets laid down by the government in the plan document. Social welfare takes precedence over private welfare although the private sector is free to operate on the basis of the principle of profit maximization. The price mechanism is far less constrained in the mixed systems and does have a real resource allocation role to play (see Turner and Collis, 1977).

Planning horizons can vary considerably. Thus, *short-term* planning can be undertaken which would last up to, say, one to two years. Similarly, medium-term planning would last for three to five years. The duration of long-term planning could be ten, fifteen or even twenty years. These are generally regarded as *perspective plans* which set out the long-term targets and the likely instruments to achieve these targets. *Emergency planning* is usually drawn up for a short period to deal with specific problems arising from, say, famine, flood, drought, civil war and earthquakes. Many countries adopt *cyclical planning* mainly to tackle the cyclical problems emanating from fluctuations in growth-rate, prices and unemployment. Here the main objective is to achieve stability in the movements of the major economic variables. These planning measures require a degree of state intervention in the market economy and the degree of intervention is generally determined by public policies.

7.3 Economic models and economic planning

Economic models are frequently used to construct economic planning. These economic models are useful to set out: (a) the objective function or the targets that should be achieved; (b) the interrelationships among the different economic variables which would indicate the general structure of the economy; and (c) the constraints (e.g. capital, labour, foreign exchange) which should be overcome to realize the objective function. Note that sometimes the models set out the objectives; sometimes these objectives are derived from some political process.

Economic models should have the dual characteristics of *clarity* and *consistency*. Some other properties of the model can also be stated. For instance, models must be *selective* so that only the behaviour of the major variables is analysed. Minor factors may account for some disturbances in the economic system, but they are not regarded as very significant. It may be contended that the best way to describe an economic system would be to set out a general equilibrium model, but such models could be unmanageable and their testing very difficult, given the data constraint and the statistical problem of identification. Further, models should be *closed*, i.e. given the assumptions, the conclusions must follow logically. Finally, models should be *quantifiable* as far as possible (Streeten, 1966).

The limitations of such models clearly follow from the above analysis. First, models may not be wholly comprehensive. Second, the validity of the models could be questioned if they rest on very dubious assumptions. Third, within the economic system, there may be many non-quantifiable variables. For example, it is not easy to evaluate in money terms the worth of a life or the cost of pain or suffering. Thus it is easy to realize that any particular economic model in the context of over-all planning cannot provide all the answers. Hence the practical economist tries to isolate some variables for developing a model which are regarded as important. Such a model may rest on some simplifying assumptions but they should be based upon the economic realities. Models thus developed should be operational, i.e. they should be tested, accepted, modified or rejected. However, a model based on sound logic need not be castigated if it runs counter to the available evidence because, very frequently, in the LDCs, information about the relevant variables is not always available, and even if it is available, it is not very reliable. Indeed, the need to improve the data-base of most LDCs can hardly be overemphasized. Economic planning based on economic models would not be very effective as long as wide gaps remain between the required and available information. In brief, economic models provide systematic and logical frameworks for economic planning to obtain feasible and optimal solutions in the light of the available information.

7.4 The case for and against planning

Planning in different forms has been accepted as an important policy instrument to attain specific targets in most LDCs. It is thus necessary to examine carefully the arguments for planning.

First, since the product and the factor markets in most LDCs are usually imperfect, market forces fail to attain efficient allocation of resources. Hence, state intervention in the form of planning is necessary to obtain an efficient allocation of resources, since prices give "wrong" signals to the decision makers.

Second, private investors usually do not pay much attention to the dynamic externalities (see note 1, p. 178) which could be generated in the process of development and which would account for the differences between marginal net social benefit (MNSB) and marginal net private benefit (MNPB). To obtain optimal allocation of resources, planning is necessary to remove the difference between MNSB and MNPB.

Third, private investors are usually interested in maximizing short- and not long-term profits and this again may lead to a resource allocation which is less than socially optimal in the long-run.

Fourth, the path to economic progress via reliance upon market forces is considered very long and, given the present differences between rich and poor countries, the task of achieving a high rate of growth in the shortest possible time is considered to be of paramount importance. It is believed that planning would accelerate the rates of growth in LDCs.

Fifth, rapid economic growth would be retarded if necessary institutional and structural reforms were not carried out simultaneously. Planning is supposed to achieve the necessary institutional reforms to allow for more rapid growth. Also, planning may exert some such psychological impact upon the nation as a whole which is conducive to the attainment of a higher standard of living (Todaro, 1971a).

Finally, since many LDCs have very limited resources, it is necessary to utilize such resources (e.g. capital, skilled manpower, foreign exchange etc.) in the most productive way and this can only be achieved if the whole economy, including the different sectors and subsectors, is brought under an over-all planning mechanism.

The arguments against planning can now be analysed.

First, it is argued that if planning is necessary to avoid the imperfections of the market mechanism, then what is necessary is to make the market more perfect, not planning.

Second, when there are differences between MNSB and MNPB because of externalities, the best way to solve the problem would be to tax or to provide subsidies and information to the producers so that the differences could be removed (Johnson, 1962). "Imperfect operation of the market in an underdeveloped country can be attributable to ignorance in the sense of lack of familiarity with market mechanisms and of awareness of relevant information, or to the prevalence of other modes of behaviour other than rational maximization of returns from effort." (Johnson, 1962)

Third, it is argued that many LDCs have lacked the skilled manpower necessary to tackle the problem of preparing and executing an efficient planning mechanism. Given wide intervention by the state in the decision-making process, an inefficient and corrupt bureaucracy may easily increase the waste of resources that would otherwise have resulted in the operation of the imperfect market. Also, planning requires a large amount of information about many branches of the economy. The availability and reliability of such information is doubtful. Further, once power is concentrated within the hands of a few bureaucrats, vested interest could inhibit further growth and technical change.

Fourth, the costs of planning are quite large for the LDCs. Apart from the costs of running the planning administration, government intervention and planning for promoting industrialization via protection, industrial licensing and quotas have increased the real cost (in terms of net value added at world prices) enormously for the LDCs (Little *et al.*, 1970; Bhagwati and Desai, 1970).

Most LDCs have shown the tendency to adopt planning as an important policy to achieve a higher rate of growth. However, apart from China, in very few LDCs have all the means of production been owned by the state. Few LDCs have resorted to totalitarian forms of planning and the private sector is allowed to operate alongside the growing public sector. It is interesting to observe that in most cases the price mechanism is not suppressed and market prices are sometimes relied upon by the planners for allocating resources. Perhaps the desire to accelerate the economic growth-rates, promotion of self-reliance, the inadequacy of the imperfect market mechanism, the inefficiency of the existing private sector and the need for structural reforms, are the main reasons for the adoption of planning in most LDCs.

7.5 Development planning models

Development planning models can be *aggregative*. Here the entire economy is taken into account and the behaviour of some of the major variables such as output, income, saving and capital are taken into consideration. These are also regarded as macro-models and as an example, the use of the Harrod–Domar model can be cited. Sometimes macro-econometric models are constructed for the whole economy to achieve some specific targets. The applications of these models will be shown later.

In many LDCs, relevant data for the entire economy may not be available although enough information could be obtained for a single project. In such cases *sectoral* models are developed and different sectoral plans are combined together to form an over-all sectoral-project plan (e.g. Ghana 1958–64; Kenya 1964–69/70; Pakistan 1956; Nigeria 1963–68). The main defect of the sectoral plans lies in the lack of co-ordination among them. Thus the heterogeneous collection of plans for different projects may neither be consistent with each other nor feasible when they are taken together. Also, in the absence of a unified contour of analysis, different rules could be applied to assess different sectors.

As aggregative models do not provide a detailed description of the inter-industry relationships between supply and demand, to achieve greater balance or consistency between various sectors, inter-industry models are now being used to determine the demand for intermediate goods plus imports. Relationships among different sectors are described by *linear* equations between output produced by a sector and its input requirement, and the model can only be applied where some industrialization has taken place, and the information about the linkages between input needed to produce output is known and available. These models are useful:

(*a*) to achieve consistency between demand and supply in different sectors;
(*b*) to know whether investment demand would be enough to produce a target output;
(*c*) to determine intermediate demand for inputs including capital and labour;
(*d*) to provide the basis for the use of programming models in which, apart from achieving consistency, the planner can test the feasibility and optimality of different projects within a plan.

Aggregate models: the Harrod–Domar model

In the aggregative models only a few crucial variables are taken into consideration. The model which is most used is the one developed by Harrod–Domar (HD) in the context of growth theory. In a simple form, the model could be set out as follows:

$$S_t = I_t \qquad [7.1]$$

$$I_t = K_{t+1} - K_t \qquad [7.2]$$

$$S_t = sY_{t-1} \qquad [7.3]$$

$$K_t = vY_{t-1} \qquad [7.4]$$

where S = savings
I = investment
K = capital stock
Y = income
v = capital–output ratio or capital coefficient
s = propensity to save.

After making the necessary substitutions from [7.1], [7.2] and [7.3] we get

$$sY_{t-1} = vY_t - vY_{t-1} \quad [7.5]$$

or $$sY_{t-1} = v(Y_t - Y_{t-1}) \quad [7.6]$$

or $$\frac{Y_t - Y_{t-1}}{Y_{t-1}} = s/v \quad [7.7]$$

Since growth of income (g) is defined as

$$g = \frac{Y_t - Y_{t-1}}{Y_{t-1}}$$

we get the familiar HD equation:

$$g = s/v \quad [7.8]$$

The model helps the planner to predict the required savings rate once the target growth-rate and the capital–output ratio (v) are given. In any economy, if the actual growth-rate is 3 per cent p.a., given $s = 9$ per cent and $v = 3:1$, then in order to achieve a target g of 5 per cent, the planner will have to recommend a rise of s to 15 per cent with given v $(= 3:1)$. Thus, fiscal (e.g. high taxation) and/or monetary policies have to be used to acquire the desired rate of saving. The model is also helpful to find out the extent of foreign resources that would be necessary to realize the target growth-rate should domestic savings be inadequate. For example, if the use of fiscal and monetary policies yields only 12 per cent rather than 15 per cent savings, then the difference between planned savings and actual savings would be 3 per cent (i.e. 15 per cent − 12 per cent) and this amount of resources could represent the amount of foreign resources necessary to realize the target.

7.6 Application of the Harrod–Domar model in development planning: India's First Five Year Plan

The HD model has been applied as a basis to develop more comprehensive plans for some LDCs. In India, for example, the HD model has been used to formulate the First Five Year Plan (1950–51 to 1955–56). The following equations illustrate the use of the HD model and most of the notation has already been explained in the previous section.

$$I_t = S_t \quad [7.9]$$

$$S_t = aY_t - c \quad [7.10]$$

$$Y_t = vK_t \quad [7.11]$$

$$I_t = \dot{K}_t \quad [7.12]$$

where $\dot{K}_t$ = incremental capital stock $\left(\text{i.e. } \frac{dK}{dt}\right)$.

Substituting we get

$$\dot{K}_t = avK_t - c \quad [7.13]$$

The time-path of capital accumulation is thus

$$K_t = \left(K_0 - \frac{c}{av}\right)e^{avt} + \frac{c}{av} \qquad [7.14]$$

Unlike the HD model, the growth-rate in this model can be increased from period to period if $a > \frac{S_0}{Y_0}$, i.e. if the marginal rate of savings is higher than the average rate of savings. The asymptotic relative growth-rate is given by the expression av.

The use of the HD model has its advantages. Its clarity and simplicity deserve attention. Also, the model is complete in the sense that it covers the entire economy; it is selective and fairly realistic. Moreover, the model does not suffer from any internal inconsistencies. However, it is highly aggregated and does not provide any idea about the internal relationships between different sectors. Thus it fails to give us any idea about the consistency between different sectors. The use of the concept of capital–output ratio has its limitations. For one thing, it is necessary to distinguish between *marginal* and average capital–output ratios (v). For another, planned v and realized v may not be the same and global v may be different from local (i.e. regional) v. The estimation of capital in LDCs is always a rather difficult task. However, the HD model has been disaggregated into two sectors for planning purposes in Kenya and this is shown in the next section.

7.7 A two-sector HD model for planning: the Kenyan case

Let the total output (Y) be divided into two forms: consumer goods (Y_1), capital goods (Y_2). Thus we have

$$Y = Y_1 + Y_2 \qquad [7.15]$$

Let $Y_1 = m(Y_1 + Y_2)$ [7.16]

where m = marginal propensity to consume. The ratio of output of the two sectors would then be given by

$$\frac{Y_1}{Y_2} = \frac{m}{1 - m} \qquad [7.17]$$

If m = 0.80 the ratio of consumer goods output (Y_1) to capital goods output is fixed at 4 : 1. If m falls because of a rise in savings, output of Y_2 will tend to grow at a higher rate. However, more of Y_2 (capital goods) would have to be used in order to release the bottleneck in the production of more consumer goods, and the production of capital goods is then given by the following relationship:

$$Y_2 = v_1\,\Delta Y_1 + v_2\,\Delta Y_2 \qquad [7.18]$$

where v_1 = capital–output ratio in Y_1

v_2 = capital–output ratio in Y_2

Then the overall growth would be given by*

$$g = \frac{\Delta Y_1 + \Delta Y_2}{Y_1 + Y_2} = \frac{1 - m}{mv_1 + (1 - m)v_2} \quad [7.19]$$

Given the values of m, v_1, v_2 and the productive capacity of Y_1 and Y_2 sectors at the base level, it is possible to work out the rate of economic growth for the whole economy.

The type of disaggregation described above is not sufficient for planning for LDCs. More comprehensive sectoral planning has been attempted in some other countries. Such a case of sectoral planning is described in the next section.

7.8 The Feldman–Mahalanobis (FM) sectoral planning and the Indian Second Five Year Plan

In India's Second Five Year Plan (1955–56 to 1960–61), an interesting attempt has been made to develop sectoral planning as a basis for more comprehensive planning. The model developed by Feldman (1928) and Mahalanobis (1953) (FM) deserves special attention as it provides a picture of contrast to the HD model. The main difference between the two types of model lies in the fact that whereas a Keynesian flow analysis is accepted in the HD model which emphasizes the desirability of raising savings that could be channelled into higher investment, a "structuralist" view is adopted in the FM model. Here it is emphasized that important bottlenecks can appear in the process of this type of transformation of savings into investment and as such the only way in which such constraints can be released is to alter the structure of the economy in such a way as to allow the economic system to produce more capital goods to maintain a higher rate of investment. In the FM model, it is assumed that there are real bottlenecks in the channelling of savings into investments which are ignored in the HD model, since the structural rigidities and the inter-temporal choice between present and future consumption benefits are assumed away in the HD model. The argument is important, since in the HD model it is indeed assumed that the marginal propensity to consume or save remains unchanged.

The following assumptions are usually made in the FM model:

1. The economy is divided into two sectors – one produces consumer goods, C and the other produces capital goods, K;
2. Once a machine is installed in one sector it cannot be transferred to the other sector, i.e. capital is not shiftable;
3. The technological coefficients in both sectors are fixed;
4. Capital is the only scarce factor;
5. Depreciation of capital stock is ruled out and thus incremental capital stock is equal to total investment. However, such an assumption is not strictly necessary for the analysis of the FM model (Bose, 1968);

* Since $s = 1 - m$, $v = mv_1 + (1 - m)v_2$ and $g = \frac{s}{v}$.

6. Trade is assumed away in the model and as such capital goods cannot be imported from abroad;
7. Production of capital goods is independent of the production of consumer goods.

Given these assumptions the FM model can be shown with the following equations. Let λ_k be the proportion of investment in capital goods, λ_c be the proportion of investment in consumer goods, β_k the output–capital ratio in the capital goods sector and β_c the output–capital ratio in the consumer goods sector. Then

$$1 = \lambda_k + \lambda_c \qquad [7.20]$$

and $$\beta = \lambda_k \beta_k + \lambda_c \beta_c \qquad [7.21]$$

Let K_t = capital stock at time t

We have $$K_{t+1} - K_t = \lambda_k \beta_k K_t \qquad [7.22]$$

$$C_{t+1} - C_t = \lambda_c \beta_c K_t \qquad [7.23]$$

$$K_t = (1 + \lambda_k \beta_k)^t K_0 \qquad [7.24]$$

Then $$Y_t = \left[1 + \alpha_0 \frac{\lambda_c \beta_c + \lambda_c \beta_k}{\lambda_k \beta_k}\right] [(1 + \lambda_k \beta_k)^t - 1] \qquad [7.25]$$

where $\alpha_0 = \dfrac{I_0}{Y_0}$ i.e. initial investment–income ratio. Note that given α_0, β_k and β_c, λ_k is the instrumental variable and since the asymptotic growth-rate is given by $\lambda_k \beta_k$, a choice of higher value of λ_k will produce a higher growth-rate and a higher level of consumption eventually. This is because by allocating more investible resources to the production of capital goods, a higher marginal savings rate and a higher output or consumption growth-rate would be obtained. The greater emphasis on the production of capital goods for industrialization in the early Soviet and in the Second Five Year Plan of India is not difficult to understand in the light of the above analysis. However, the precise amount of investment in the production of capital goods has not been stated and the optimal choice would depend upon both domestic and foreign transformation constraints.

Evaluation of the FM model

Despite the ingenuity of the FM model, the following criticisms are usually made against it.

1. The absence of the role of foreign trade is regarded as a very unsatisfactory part of the FM model since capital goods can be imported instead of being produced at home at a high cost, chiefly behind the protectionist wall which could sometimes lead to a welfare loss to the economy (Bhagwati and Desai, 1970). The limited role that exports usually played in India's economy might have prompted Mahalanobis to neglect foreign trade, but it is doubtful to what extent such a neglect of the export sector is justified for many LDCs today.

2. The FM model is aggregative. Though Mahalanobis disaggregated the model later into four sectors, Komiya (1959) has shown that the value which Mahalanobis chose for λ_k yielded inefficient resource allocation as it lay within the feasibility locus between an increase in employment and a rise in output. In other words, reallocation of the investment among the three sectors apart from the capital goods sector would have resulted in higher output and employment.
3. In the FM model, the problem of unemployment has not received due emphasis. The choice of more capital-intensive methods of production usually increases the problem of unemployment, particularly in a labour-surplus economy. Brahmananda and Vakil (BV), (1956), in their planning model, have tried to focus attention on wage-goods rather than fixed capital and have pointed out the need to promote employment. However, in the BV model, the basic problem of capital accumulation that FM encountered has not been solved satisfactorily as the supply of abundant labour alone is not enough to achieve a higher level of capital formation. It is, of course, true that the problem of employment creation in labour-surplus countries can hardly be exaggerated, and such a problem has not really been solved in the FM model.
4. Given the predominant role of agriculture in the LDCs, the planner is generally expected to consider the dynamic development of agriculture within the model. Unfortunately the FM model does not take into account the role of agriculture and public policies based on such models have led to the growth of "urban bias" (Lipton, 1968a) in the planning of many LDCs. It is argued that a policy of industrialization on the basis of the recommendation of the FM model has resulted in the neglect of the rural sector and has widened the development gap between the modern, urban industrial sector and the backward, rural agricultural sector within the LDCs.

In view of the aggregative nature of the HD and the FM models, methods have been devised to include sectoral details within the macro-models to obtain greater information for the whole economy. Some of these methods are described in the next section.

7.9 Macro-econometric models in development planning

The use of macro-econometric models is now popular in the planning exercises for the LDCs. One way to demonstrate the application of such models is to use a simple Keynesian framework of analysis as described by Hicks and Lange. More formally,

let C_t = consumer expenditure
I_t = capital formation
Y_t = national income
r_t = interest rate
M_t = money supply (exogenous or determined outside the system)
t = time
u_t, v_t, z_t = error terms.

We can write,

$$C_t = a_0 + a_1 Y_t + a_2 r_t + u_t \quad [7.26]$$

$$I_t = b_0 + b_1 Y_t + b_2 r_t + v_t \quad [7.27]$$

$$Y_t = C_t + I_t \quad [7.28]$$

$$M_t = c_0 + c_1 Y_t + c_2 r_t + z_t \quad [7.29]$$

However, such a model is not dynamic; it does not determine prices; it ignores foreign trade; also, public policy (i.e. changes in government taxes and spending) is not allowed to play any role. A more sophisticated model has been set out by Klein and this is illustrated below (see Klein, 1965):

$$C_t = a_0 + a_1 \frac{Y_t - T_t}{p_t} + a_2 C_{t-1} + u_{1t} \quad [7.30]$$

$$I_t = b_0 + b_1 \frac{Y_{t-1}}{p_{t-1}} + b_2 K_{t-1} + b_3 r_{t-1} + u_{2t} \quad [7.31]$$

$$F_t = c_0 + c_1 \frac{Y_t - Y_{t-1}}{p_t} + c_2 F_{t-1} + c_3 \frac{p_{ft}}{p_t} + u_{3t} \quad [7.32]$$

$$E_t = d_0 + d_1 T_{wt} + d_2 \frac{p_{et}}{p_t} + u_{4t} \quad [7.33]$$

$$\frac{Y_t}{p_t} = C_t + I_t - F_t + E_t + G_t \quad [7.34]$$

$$T_t = e_0 + e_1 Y_t + u_{5t} \quad [7.35]$$

$$I_t = K_t - K_{t-1} \quad [7.36]$$

$$\frac{Y_t}{p_t} = g_0 + g_1 L_t + g_2 K_t + u_{6t} \quad [7.37]$$

$$p_t = h_0 + h_1 \frac{w_t L_t}{Y_t/p_t} + h_2 \frac{p_{ft}}{p_t} + u_{7t} \quad [7.38]$$

$$\frac{w_t - w_{t-1}}{w_{t-1}} = j_0 + j_1 \frac{N_t - L_t}{N_t} + j_2 \frac{p_t - p_{t-1}}{p_{t-1}} + u_{8t} \quad [7.39]$$

$$N_t = k_0 + k_1(N_t - L_t) + k_2 w_t/p_t + u_{9t} \quad [7.40]$$

$$\frac{M_t}{p_t} = l_0 + l_1 \frac{Y_t}{p_t} + l_2 r_t + u_{10t} \quad [7.41]$$

$$p_e = m_0 + m_1 p_t + u_{11t} \quad [7.42]$$

The endogenous variables (i.e. variables which are determined within the system) in the Klein model are as follows:

C = real consumer expenditures
Y = national income (in current prices)
T = taxes less transfer payments
p = index of general price level
I = net real investment
K = real capital stock
r = interest-rate
F = real imports
E = real exports
p_e = export prices
L = employment
w = wage-rate
N = labour supply.

The exogenous variables may be stated as follows:

p_f = import prices
T_w = volume of world trade
G = real government expenditures
M = money supply.

Notice that the above model describes a set of *linear* relationships among the variables and it now determines both absolute and relative price levels. Foreign trade has now been included. The role of taxes and expenditures by the government has been described and lags are introduced to make the model dynamic. However, the practical economist will have to determine different types of interest rates, consumption, investment, taxes, expenditures and trade to render such a model applicable to the special problems of LDCs. The actual econometric techniques to be used will depend upon initial specifications of the equations and the subjective judgement of the planner in the light of the actual state of information. (For a discussion of different types of econometric models and their applications to LDCs, see Ghosh, 1968; Ghosh *et al.*, 1974; Agarwala, 1970; Chenery, *et al.*, 1971.)

It is important to remember some of the difficulties that the planners are likely to encounter in their attempts to build up the econometric models. First, the testing of the model will usually depend upon the *availability* of *reliable* data. It is generally accepted that such data are not always available. Second, it is assumed in the application of linear least square regression analysis that the explanatory variables should be independent of one another to avoid the problem of multicollinearity and the disturbance terms should not be serially correlated with one another to avoid the problem of autocorrelation (Johnston, 1972). However, many macro-models for LDCs suffer from the difficulties involved in what is called "misplaced aggregation and illegitimate isolation" (Streeten, 1966). Misplaced aggregation occurs in the economic models for LDCs mainly because of market imperfection. "If there is excess demand in one sector and excess supply in another, but the supply in one cannot be used to meet the demand in the other, there is no sense in talking of aggregate demand or aggregate supply." (Streeten, 1966) Illegitimate isolation occurs in the opposite case; i.e. when the explanatory variables are not independent of one another or what is known as the problem of multicollinearity in econometrics. "Violins, however fine, cannot produce a melody without skilled violinists, nor can violinists without violins. The appropriate unit is violin plus violinist, and to talk of a violin/melody ratio is to commit both the fallacies, misplaced aggregation and illegitimate isolation." (Streeten, 1966) Thus the case for the proper specification of equations to test the econometric models for planning can hardly be overemphasized. Third, relationships between the variables could be non-linear. Finally, it must be borne in mind that the results of regression analysis by themselves do not establish causation. Causality comes from economic theory. Here it is important to remember that in choosing an "appropriate" model for a less developed country, the realities should dominate the technique instead of the converse.

Given the need for analysing many important sectors of the economy and their interrelationships to provide greater consistency between aggregate supply and aggregate demand, development planners have increasingly turned their attention to the application of the input–output (IO) technique originally invented by Leontief (1951). Such a technique is described in the next section.

7.10 Input–output (IO) analysis in development planning

Usually the input–output technique (IO) delineates the general equilibrium analysis and the empirical side of the economic system of production of any country. Its use in development planning has become quite noticeable and in the following paragraphs, its salient features will be described.

The assumptions of the IO analysis

It is important to note the basic assumptions of the IO analysis:

(*a*) no substitution takes place between the inputs to produce a given unit of output and the *input-coefficients are constant*. The linear input functions imply that the marginal input coefficients are equal to the average;

(*b*) joint products are ruled out, i.e. each industry produces only one commodity and each commodity is produced by only one industry;

(*c*) external economies are ruled out and production is subject to the operation of the *constant* returns to scale.

These assumptions require that to produce one unit of the jth good, the required i^{th} input would be constant and let us call it a_{ij}. Thus, the production of each unit of the jth good would need, say, a_{1j} of the first commodity, a_{2j} of the second, and a_{nj} of the nth input. Note that the first subscript refers to the input and the second subscript refers to the output. Hence, if $a_{ij} = 0.20$ pence, it means that 20 pence worth of the first commodity is necessary as an input to produce a £1 worth of the jth good. The symbol a_{ij} is regarded as the input coefficient.

Let there be n number of industries in the economy. The input–output table in the form of the matrix $A = [a_{ij}]$ would state the input coefficients. The availability of the input–output table is thus an important condition for any calculation. Actually, the table shows the inter-industry flows where each column shows the necessary input for producing one unit of the output of a certain industry. If any element in the matrix is zero, it shows that the input demand is zero. The input coefficients can be written as:

$$a_{ij} = \frac{x_{ij}}{X_j} \qquad \begin{array}{l} i = 1, 2, \ldots n \\ j = 1, 2, \ldots n \end{array}$$

where X_j = total output of the jth industry

x_{ij} = number of units of ith good used by the jth industry.

The IO table is usually given in the following matrix:

$$\begin{array}{cc} & \text{Output} \\ \text{Input} & \begin{array}{cccc} \text{I} & \text{II} & \text{——} & \text{N} \end{array} \end{array}$$

$$A = \begin{array}{c} \text{I} \\ \text{II} \\ \\ \\ \text{N} \end{array} \begin{bmatrix} a_{11} & a_{12} & \text{——} & a_{1n} \\ a_{21} & a_{22} & \text{——} & a_{2n} \\ \text{—} & \text{—} & & \text{—} \\ \text{—} & \text{—} & & \text{—} \\ a_{n1} & a_{n2} & & a_{nn} \end{bmatrix}$$

However, the IO table in the above form considers only inter-industry flows and ignores final demand. An "open" IO table can be easily constructed where a final demand for the product of each industry is included. Note that corresponding to the *demand* for the products, the IO table should now be expanded to include *supplies* of primary inputs. For example, if the household sector's final demand for output is now included it is also necessary to include the labour supplied by the households as inputs. It is now obvious that because of the supply of labour inputs, the sum of the elements in each column of the matrix A would be less than one because in the absence of primary input costs (e.g. labour supply) the sum of each element in any column would be exactly equal to one. Thus:

$$\sum_{i=1}^{n} a_{ij} < 1 \qquad (j = 1, 2, \ldots n)$$

It follows that the value of primary input required to produce one unit of the jth good is given by:

$$1 - \sum_{i=1}^{n} a_{ij}$$

Now for the industry 1, to produce enough output to cater for the final demand plus the input demand of n industries, the equation below must hold:

$$x_1 = a_{11}x_1 + a_{12}x_2 + \cdots + a_{1n}x_n + D_1$$

or $\quad (1 - a_{11})x_1 - a_{12}x_2 \cdots - a_{1n}x_n = D_1$

where $\quad D_1$ = final demand for the output of industry 1

Similarly, for the second industry, the equation can be set out as below:

$$-a_{21}x_1 + (1 - a_{22})x_2 - \cdots - a_{2n}x_n = D_2$$

Thus $\quad -a_{n1}x_1 - a_{n2}x_2 - \cdots + (1 - a_{nn})x_n = D_n$

The system of equations can be written in the following matrix form:

$$(I - A)x = D \begin{pmatrix} (1 - a_{11}) & -a_{12} & -a_{1n} \\ -a_{21} & (1 - a_{22}) & -a_{2n} \\ \vdots & \vdots & \vdots \\ -a_{n1} & -a_{n2} & (1 - a_{nn}) \end{pmatrix} \begin{pmatrix} x_1 \\ x_2 \\ \vdots \\ x_n \end{pmatrix} = \begin{pmatrix} D_1 \\ D_2 \\ \vdots \\ D_n \end{pmatrix}$$

where the identity matrix I is given by

$$I = \begin{pmatrix} 1 & 0 & 0 & \text{———} & 0 \\ 0 & 1 & 0 & \text{———} & 0 \\ 0 & 0 & 1 & \text{———} & 0 \\ \cdot & \cdot & \cdot & \text{———} & \cdot \\ 0 & 0 & 0 & \text{———} & 1 \end{pmatrix}$$

that is, all the elements in the principal diagonal are 1 and elsewhere zero.

Now solving for x, we have:

$$x = [1 - A]^{-1}D$$

The rule for matrix inversion, i.e. $[A]^{-1}$ can be given as

$$A^{-1} = \frac{1}{|A|} A^*$$

The following example can be given:

Let $\quad A = \begin{pmatrix} a_{11} & a_{12} \\ a_{21} & a_{22} \end{pmatrix}$

Then $\quad |A| = a_{11}a_{22} - a_{12}a_{21}$

and $\quad A^* = \begin{pmatrix} a_{22} & -a_{12} \\ -a_{21} & a_{11} \end{pmatrix}$

$$A^{-1} = \frac{1}{|A|}\begin{pmatrix} a_{22} & -a_{12} \\ -a_{21} & a_{11} \end{pmatrix}$$

$$= \begin{pmatrix} \dfrac{a_{22}}{|A|} & -\dfrac{a_{12}}{|A|} \\ -\dfrac{a_{21}}{|A|} & \dfrac{a_{11}}{|A|} \end{pmatrix}$$

A numerical example can help one to understand the solution more clearly. To simplify the analysis we are concerned with only two sectors, Agriculture (X_1) and textiles (X_2). Let the IO table be given as

	Agriculture	Textiles
Agriculture	0.6	0.2
Textiles	0.4	0.3

Then $A \quad = \begin{pmatrix} 0.6 & 0.2 \\ 0.4 & 0.3 \end{pmatrix}$

Now $I - A \quad = \begin{pmatrix} 1 & 0 \\ 0 & 1 \end{pmatrix} - \begin{pmatrix} 0.6 & 0.2 \\ 0.4 & 0.3 \end{pmatrix} = \begin{pmatrix} 0.4 & -0.2 \\ -0.4 & 0.7 \end{pmatrix}$

$$[I - A]^{-1} = \begin{pmatrix} 0.7/0.2 & 0.2/0.2 \\ 0.4/0.2 & 0.4/0.2 \end{pmatrix} = \begin{pmatrix} 3\frac{1}{2} & 1 \\ 2 & 2 \end{pmatrix}$$

Let the final demand be given by

$$D = \begin{pmatrix} 10 \\ 5 \end{pmatrix}$$

Recall that $x = [I - A]^{-1}D$

Thus we have $x = \begin{pmatrix} 3\frac{1}{2} & 1 \\ 2 & 2 \end{pmatrix}\begin{pmatrix} 10 \\ 5 \end{pmatrix}$

$$= \begin{pmatrix} 40 \\ 30 \end{pmatrix}$$

Thus the agricultural sector (X_1) would produce 40 units and the textile sector (X_2) would produce 30 units. Note that the effects of change in final demand on the production of X_1 and X_2 can easily be found. Further, given the employment coefficient, the effect on employment can be traced out. The IO analysis can be extended to include many other sectors like foreign trade and the balance of payments. (For simple illustrations, see for example, Todaro, 1971a). It is now easy to see how the IO tables are used for comprehensive development planning in many sectors, to find out total output in different sectors, to obtain certain demand targets, the size and direction of inter-industry flows, the amount of imports and the level of use of different inputs like capital and labour.

The limitations of the use of the IO model

The assumptions set out at the outset of the discussion of the IO analysis help us to understand the major limitations of this analysis.

First, it is assumed in the IO analysis that the input coefficients would remain unchanged. However, these coefficients may not remain constant when growth is taking place. In the long-run the validity of the assumption of a constant coefficient is all the more questionable as technical progress gains momentum, substitution possibilities arise and returns to scale might be rising instead of being constant. Thus marginal input coefficients might no longer be equal to the average.

Second, if the linkages among the different sectors are rather weak or non-existent, then the IO table will give us only very limited information.

Third, the IO analysis assumes that the composition of demand is constant. In the long-run this is unlikely to be valid and any change in demand composition is likely to change input coefficients.

However, it should be pointed out that some of these limitations in the application of the IO analysis can be removed by continuously up-dating the IO tables to incorporate any effects of changes in technical progress and/or demand pattern on sectoral input coefficients. Also, if the IO analysis is used to make short-, rather than long-run, predictions, and if the data are reliable, then the margin of errors is unlikely to be large.

Finally, the IO analysis further assumes that each industry has only one way of producing a given product. But it is conceivable that there could be more than one process or activity to produce a commodity. IO analysis cannot help to find out which process among two or more activities would use the minimum amount of resources. In short, IO analysis cannot help to solve the choice of optimal technique of production. This would necessitate the use of linear programming analysis to which we now turn.

7.11 Linear programming and development planning

Linear programming (LP) is really a mathematical tool which is now being increasingly used in economic analysis. Its use in the field of development planning is of much interest chiefly because it helps the planner to allocate resources optimally among alternative uses within the specific constraints. At the micro-level, programming technique could be used to find out optimal and efficient (least expensive) methods of production. Actually, LP can be regarded as a powerful and complementary tool which can be used to analyse the IO tables in order to solve the problems of choice of techniques on the supply side as well as the problem of choice of final demand. It is important to emphasize that the LP technique helps to tackle the major problems of investment planning: (a) *consistency* between sectors; (b) *feasibility* of plans; and (c) *optimality* in resource allocation. However, it should be pointed out that the important assumption that is made in the LP analysis is that variables are interrelated in a *linear* way. This assumption may not be very realistic in all cases. But if they are, then the LP is indeed very useful for planning. On the other hand, if the relationships among the variables are non-linear, then the non-linear programming can be used to solve the problems.

General formulation of LP problems

In a LP exercise, usually the objective is to *maximize* or *minimize* some linear function of the variables given, say, r variables. The programmer seeks to obtain non-negative values of these variables subject to the constraints and maximize (or minimize) the objective function. More formally

$$\text{Max } V = c_1 x_1 + \cdots + c_r x_r$$

with m inequalities or equalities in r variables, i.e.

$$a_{i1} x_1 + \cdots + a_{ir} x_r \{\geq, =, \leq\} b_i, \; i = 1, \ldots m$$

$$\text{and} \quad x_j \geq 0, j = 1, \ldots r$$

where a_{ij}, b_i and c_j are given constants.

The problem is sometimes written in a more compact way, e.g.

$$\text{Maximize} \quad Z = \sum_{j=1}^{n} c_{ij} x_j$$

$$\text{subject to} \quad \sum_{j=1}^{n} a_{ij} x_j \leq r_i \; (i = 1, 2, \ldots m)$$

$$\text{and} \quad x_j \geq 0, \; (j = 1, 2, \ldots n)$$

where c_j and a_{ij} are the given coefficients and r_i symbols show the constraints. Note that in a matrix form, a_{ij} helps us to find out the exact location of each coefficient.

Let us assume a simple case of two variables to illustrate diagrammatically the LP solution. Let the objective function be to maximize

$$\begin{aligned} \text{Max} \quad & V = 5X_1 + 3X_2 \\ \text{Subject to} \quad & 3X_1 + 5X_2 \leq 15 \\ & 5X_1 + 2X_2 \leq 10 \\ & X_1, X_2 \geq 0 \end{aligned}$$

The graphical solution of this LP problem will be shown first and then the numerical solutions will follow. (The examples are taken from Hadley, 1962.)

The graphical solution:

Let us, first, convert the inequalities into equalities, i.e.:

$$3X_1 + 5X_2 = 15 \qquad [7.43]$$

$$\text{and} \quad 5X_1 + 2X_2 = 10 \qquad [7.44]$$

Fig. 7.1

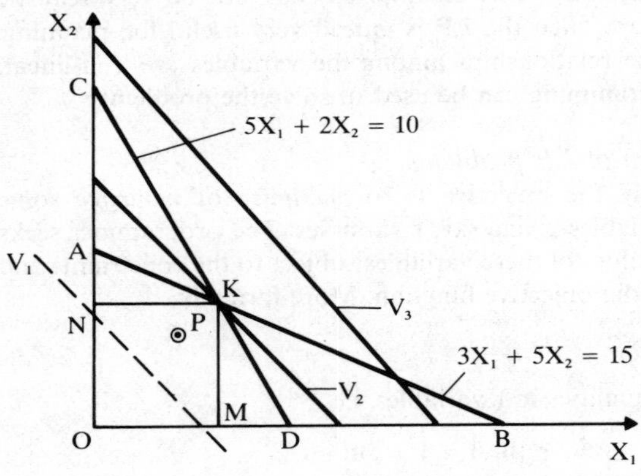

Accordingly, we get lines like AB for equation [7.43] and CD for [7.44] (see Fig. 7.1).

Note that any point *on* or *below* AB satisfies the inequality $3X_1 + 5X_2 \leq 15$, just as any point *on* or *below* CD satisfies the inequality, $5X_1 + 2X_2 \leq 10$. Also, there is no point above, say, AB (or CD) which satisfies the above inequalities. The points which will satisfy both the non-negativity restrictions are given by the area OAKD. This area is then regarded as a feasible region. Any point such as P is regarded as feasible because production of X_1 and X_2 at point P does not violate the constraints. Note that a *feasible* solution could lie at a point like O (at the origin). But such a feasible solution should imply that *no* production of X_1 and X_2 would take place! In order to obtain the *optimum* feasible solution it is necessary to find out the point at which the iso-profit curve is tangent to any point lying on AKD. Any iso-profit line such as V_1 which lies *inside* the area OAKD does not yield the optimum profit because profit could always be increased by moving further away to a higher iso-profit line like V_2 which just touches the area AKD at K. Similarly, the iso-profit line V_3, although indicating higher profit, is not attainable. Thus, the optimum profit is given at the point K where OM of X_1 and ON of X_2 will be produced. Thus at K the objective function $V = 5X_1 + 3X_2$ is at a maximum. It is necessary to point out here that given the above profit equations, iso-profit lines are straight lines. Since constant returns to scale operate, the further we move away from the origin along the iso-profit line, the greater is the level of profit. The iso-profit lines, i.e. V_1, V_2 etc. are parallel to one another because the slope of V_1, V_2 etc. is $-5/3$ and is independent of V_1, V_2. To obtain the optimal values of X_1 and X_2, it is necessary to solve the two equations for lines AB and CD at K. Thus, we have:

$$3X_1 + 5X_2 = 15$$
$$5X_1 + 2X_2 = 10$$

Solving for X_1 we have $X_1 = 1.053$, for $X_2 = 2.368$. The maximum profit now is $V = 12.37$.

Note that the line V could lie along one edge of the polygon AKD. In such a case, no unique values of X_1 and X_2 would maximize V. Indeed, there will be more than one optimal solution which would imply that there exists more than a single way to juxtapose resources to obtain highest profit.

The above example of solving the LP problem is highly simplified. In reality, it is generally found that an optimum solution has to be found subject to some inequalities in the constraints. These inequalities are usually converted into equalities by adding extra or "slack" variables for solving the equations. Optimum solutions are then derived by using the "simplex" method. In the simplex method, the optimum solution is reached via an iterative procedure. According to the rules of LP, any corner solution such as O, A, K, D, in the figure is a basic solution. In the simplex method, starting from any basic solution (e.g. O), we move to the adjacent corner solution (e.g. either A or K) to improve upon the value of the objective function until the optimum is reached (i.e. any further move will worsen the situation). At each corner the simplex procedure states whether the corner point is optimal, and if not, what the next corner point will be.

To show the use of the slack variables, we first state the system of inequalities, i.e.

$$\text{Max } V = 5X_1 + 3X_2$$
$$3X_1 + 5X_2 \leq 15$$
$$5X_1 + 2X_2 \leq 10$$
$$X_1, X_2 \geq 0$$

With the slack variables, we can now write:

$$3X_1 + 5X_2 + X_3 = 15$$
$$5X_1 + 2X_2 + X_4 = 10$$

where X_3 and X_4 are the slack variables.

After the choice of a "pivot", the optimum solution is found in successive steps. (For the choice of "pivot" and solution, see Hadley, 1962; Baumol, 1977; Panne, 1976.)

Duality

LP problems are also solved by the application of the principle of "*duality*". Previously we have observed how to maximize an objective function, e.g. profit. Corresponding to every maximization of profit problem, which is regarded as a "*primal*", a "*dual*" involves minimization, say, of cost. Note that if the constrained equations are given by $\leq$ signs, the dual would imply $\geq$ signs. The profit constants r_i will be replaced by the capacity constraints C_j and a different set of variables appears in the dual. More formally, we can write:

The primal

Max $V = r_1X_1 + r_2X_2 + \cdots + r_nX_n$

Subject to $b_{11}X_1 + b_{12}X_2 + \cdots + b_{1n}X_n \leq L_1$

$b_{m1}X_1 + b_{m2}X_2 + \cdots + b_{mn}X_n \leq L_m$

and $X_1 \geq 0, \ldots X_n \geq 0$

The dual can be written as

Minimize $\gamma = L_1C_1 + L_2C_2 + \cdots + L_mC_m$

Subject to $a_{11}C_1 + a_{21}C_2 + \cdots + a_{m1}C_m \geq r_1$

$a_{1n}C_n + a_{2n}C_n + \cdots + a_{mn}C_m \geq r_n$

and $C_1 \geq 0, C_2 \geq 0, \ldots C_m \geq 0$

Note that in the constrained inequalities, while the coefficients appear in the *rows* in the primal, they are observed in the *columns* in the dual. Also a new set of variables, $C_1, C_2, \ldots C_m$, appears in the dual.

If the slack variables are introduced, the system of *equations* can be written as follows:

Primal:

Max $V = r_1X_1 + \cdots + r_nX_n$

Subject to $b_{11}X_1 + \cdots + b_{1n}X_n + S_1 = L_1$

$b_{m1}X_1 + \cdots + b_{mn}X_n + S_m = L_m$

$X_1 \geq 0, \ldots X_n \geq 0, S_1 \geq 0, \ldots, S_m \geq 0$

Dual:

Min $\gamma = L_1C_1 + \cdots + L_mC_m$

Subject to $a_{11}C_1 + \cdots + a_{m1}C_m - K_1 = r_1$

$a_{1n}C_1 + \cdots + a_{mn}C_m - K_n = r_n$

and $C_1 \geq 0, \ldots C_m \geq 0, K_1 \geq 0, \ldots K_n \geq 0$

The economic interpretation of the dual is not difficult. The structural variables, $C_1, C_2, \ldots$ etc. of the dual are really the "shadow prices" assigned to each input or resource. They represent the marginal product of each resource included in the optimal solution. The link between the shadow price of an input as its marginal yield to profit could be seen through changes in profit resulting from the subtraction of a single unit of an input from its use. Also, in the dual, the objective function, i.e. minimization of cost, shows the total value of the inputs as it is the product of shadow prices of the inputs $(C_1, C_2, \ldots)$ and their respective input capacities. The constrained inequalities in the dual suggest that profits made from the production of goods must be wholly imputed to the resources used in their production. At the point of optimal solution, all inputs would be valued according to their marginal product and the total profit will be exhausted. Note that should the value of an input used in the production of an additional unit of any output be greater than the unit profit of that output, a loss will be indicated and the size of this loss is given by the slack variable in the constrained equations of the dual. It is now easy to see the main argument in one of the major theorems of the duality in relation to the primal solution. First, at the optimal point of the feasible solution, the shadow prices of each unit of resources should be such that there would not be any profit which could be made from anywhere and hence at the optimal point, the highest profit, V is equal to the minimum cost of resources, i.e. γ, in the dual. The other duality theorem states that should the "shadow" cost of inputs to produce a unit of output exceed the unit profit that could be made from that output, then at the optimal point, such a product should not be produced as its production means a loss. At the optimal point, those goods should be produced whose loss is nil. It is now clear that wherever the values of the slack variable, $K_1, K_2, \ldots, K_n$ are positive (which would mean loss), such activities should be excluded from the optimal solution. Thus, LP shows the utility of the use of shadow prices for inputs for efficient allocation within the context of planning.

It should, however, be mentioned that in a LP solution, prices are regarded as the indicators of the marginal worth to the society. But in LDCs, where the market is mostly imperfect, prices will be usually higher than the marginal cost. Second, the relationships in the LP analysis are assumed to be linear. On the other hand, many constraints in the LDCs are non-linear functions of the structural variables. However, here the problem is not insuperable as non-linear programming methods could be used. Finally, if the society attaches considerable weight to the growth objective and if the market price of labour is overestimated (because wages are artificially high despite the abundance of labour) and/or that of capital is underestimated (since interest rate is kept low despite capital scarcity), then some necessary corrections ought to be made by using some "accounting" prices for a more efficient allocation of resources. In practice, some such corrections are attempted using cost–benefit analysis (CBA) and this will be examined in the next section.

7.12 Micro-planning: aims of cost–benefit analysis (CBA)

The reasons for undertaking *social* CBA could be stated at the outset. Whereas a private producer is generally interested in the maximization of private profit, a project evaluator of, say, a fertilizer plant, or of an underground railway system, would like to maximize the *social* net benefits of the project. The distinction between private profit and social benefit is usually made because of the presence of externalities. Thus while the firm producing cigarettes would only be interested in the pure economic gains, the project evaluator would have to know about the possible costs to the society arising out of the danger of lung cancer. Further, while the private owner of the fertilizer plant would be interested in maximizing his private profit, the economist in charge of evaluating such projects for the public should also calculate the costs to the society because of effluent discharges and water pollution. Thus the problem of choosing appropriate prices (or shadow prices) to reflect social gains or losses becomes important. Further, since the project may last for several years, it is necessary to discount the benefits and costs. Here again, while the commercial firm would be inclined to use the existing market interest rate (at which it can borrow) to discount the future benefits and costs, the project planner would have to choose a *social* rate of discount or opportunity cost of capital to the society as a whole. The task of the project planner is not easy as he will have to decide about the relative valuation of the *social* preference between consumption today or consumption at some future point in time. In short, "The main reason for doing social cost–benefit analysis in project choice is to subject project choice to a consistent set of general objectives of national policy." (UNIDO, 1972, p. 11) In order to realize such an objective, the project planner tries to choose some "shadow" prices (which could be different from market prices) which would be relevant for measuring net *social* benefits. Such a measurement is supposed to be more useful for taking decisions regarding project choice as it is not based upon some purely subjective judgements on which decisions could sometimes be made.

Some basic principles of CBA

Some of the basic principles of CBA are generally derived from welfare economics (for general discussion, see, for example, Dasgupta and Pearce, 1972; Mishan, 1975; Layard, 1974). The objective is to choose the project which yields positive Net *Social* Benefit (NSB) where the NSB is defined as

NSB = Benefits (willingness to pay) – Costs (compensation needed).

All benefits and costs are expressed in monetary units. The *willingness* to pay is given by the area under the demand curve, but the actual total price paid is given by the price times the quantity. In other words, the amount of consumer surplus reflects the size of gains. Thus in Fig. 7.2, although the consumers are willing to pay ODSM for OM quantity, they actually pay OPSM and hence the area DPS measures consumers' surplus. Now suppose that a cost-saving device is used in a project (e.g. time saved because of the construction of a new highway), prices fall to OP_1 from OP, *cet. par.*, and an increase in the goods provided is shown by MM_1. Now the total willingness to pay is given by ODS_1M_1 which is greater than ODSM by MSS_1M_1 out of which MM_1S_1E accounts for actual payments and as such, the change in consumer surplus is given by the shaded area ESS_1. This is equivalent to the NSB for the society. However, its actual estimation is beset with many problems. For example, the demand curve is assumed to be linear; marginal utility of income is supposed to remain fixed; utility is supposed to be measurable cardinally; prices of all other goods are expected to remain unchanged; there are some intangibles which cannot be measured (e.g. scenic beauty). However, Hicks tried to tackle some of these problems by allowing changes in the marginal utility of income and by using the indifference curve analysis. Also, Kaldor and Hicks pointed out that to increase social welfare, it is only necessary to show that the gainers should be able to compensate

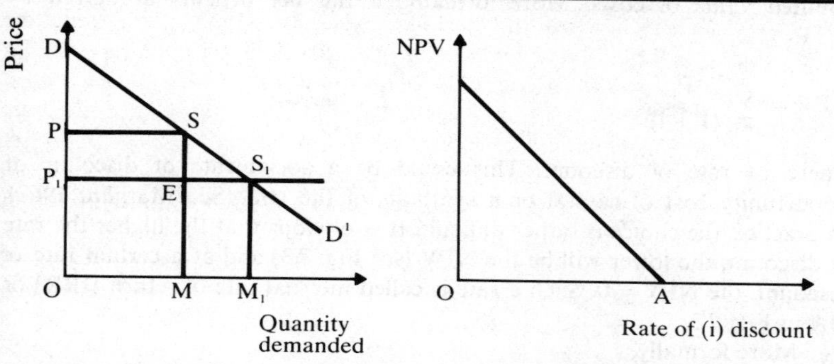

the losers and still remain gainers. However, difficulties arise if these compensations are potential, rather than actual. Moreover, as Scitovsky points out, if the gainers can compensate the losers in accepting a change and the losers can "bribe" the gainers back to the "*status quo*", then a clear contradiction emerges as there is no way to tell whether social welfare has increased or decreased (Arrow and Scitovsky, 1969). Critics of CBA further argue that market preferences shown in the demand curve are not equivalent to voting preferences; it is thus undemocratic. Since projects affect not only the present but also future generations, it is therefore regarded as ethically immoral to pass judgement today on behalf of the future generations, (for details, see Dasgupta and Pearce, 1972; Mishan, 1975). However, despite these criticisms, some of which are tackled in subsequent literature, CBA analysis retains its appeal as an important analytical and rational framework for the formulation of public policies.

The decision rules in CBA

To take decisions regarding project choice, the project planner confronts the following sets of problems:

(*a*) the problem of identification of the benefits and costs;
(*b*) the problem of valuation of these benefits and costs at prices which would be relevant to society;
(*c*) the problem of choosing an appropriate rate of discount for evaluating such benefits and costs;
(*d*) the problem of identifying the actual constraints;
(*e*) the problem of uncertainty.

After carefully solving these problems, the planner tries to find out the Net Present Value (NPV) discounted by a certain rate of discount and if the NPV > 0, then the project should be accepted. If the projects are mutually exclusive, then the one which yields the highest NPV should be accepted.

Note that NPV means present discounted value of benefits less present discounted value of costs. More formally, if the net benefits are given by $P_1, P_2, \ldots,$

$$NPV = \sum_{t=0}^{n} \frac{P_t}{(1+i)^t}$$

where i = rate of discount. This could be a social rate of discount or opportunity cost of capital or a synthesis of the two (See Marglin, 1967). In practice, the choice is rather difficult. It is obvious that the higher the rate of discount, the lower will be the NPV (see Fig. 7.3) and at a certain rate of discount, the NPV = 0. Such a rate is called internal rate of return (IRR) or OA in Fig. 7.3.

More formally,

$$\sum_{t=0}^{n} \frac{P_t}{(1+\lambda)^t} = 0$$

where λ = internal rate of return. If $\lambda > i$, then the project should be accepted; if not, the project should be rejected.

In practice, the use of the NPV criterion rather than the IRR rule has gained preference (for an exception, see Mishan, 1967) for a number of reasons. First, the IRR rule simply provides a rate rather than the size of total gains to the project planner. In many cases, it would be important to know the total size of gains rather than a single rate. Second, the use of the IRR rule can yield multiple-roots without any unique solution. The number of roots will be given by the number of times the benefits change signs. For example, there are projects which could incur losses in the first year, yield benefits in the next two years and show losses again for the subsequent year followed by benefits in the next year, then we would find three values of λ. Third, IRR tends to favour short-life projects in comparison with those with longer lives. Fourth, projects which have long fruition lags or gestation periods will be discriminated against under the IRR rule. Similarly, projects which involve larger capital costs would be discriminated against under the IRR rule (for a reconciliation between the two, see the normalization criterion, proposed by Mishan, 1975).

After briefly explaining the major principles of CBA, the special reasons for undertaking CBA for LDCs in particular will be discussed in the next section.

Reasons for undertaking CBA in LDCs

Several reasons are given for undertaking CBA for the LDCs to make a realistic estimate of the net social benefits (NSB) (see Little and Mirrlees, 1968, 1974).

1. Inflation Inflation in many LDCs, emanating chiefly from the supply inelasticities, alters the relative prices and government's intervention in the form of price controls results in the distortion of NSB.

2. Overvaluation of currency In most LDCs, exchange rates of the domestic currencies are kept artificially high. This again leads to an excess demand for foreign exchange and when the government imposes import restrictions, market prices of goods exceed their world price and such market prices tend to overestimate the NSB within the country.

3. Wages and unemployment Given the imperfections of the labour market in the LDCs, different modes of production (e.g. use of family labour rather than wage labour and the absence of a unique relationship between marginal productivity of labour and wages) and the presence of large-scale unemployment, it is argued that wages paid to labourers in LDCs tend to overestimate their true social opportunity costs, and hence a "shadow" wage rate should be calculated to work out the true cost of labour to society.

4. Capital market and interest rate Given the imperfections of the capital market in most LDCs, the interest rate is kept artificially low, particularly when capital is very scarce in supply, and here again, a "shadow" rate of interest should be calculated to remove the underestimation of the cost of capital to society.

5. Large projects Since large projects are likely to yield significant *secondary* benefits to the economy, it is not enough to count only the primary benefits of a project.

6. Protection: tariffs, quotas, etc Since many LDCs have decided to industrialize their economies behind protectionist walls by using tariffs, quotas, exchange controls, etc., market prices within the economy would fail to reflect the NSB.

7. Saving deficiency and public income Given the dearth of savings in LDCs, the government can value an extra unit of saving more than the extra unit of consumption and impose appropriate taxes (which of course imposes some costs) to raise such savings. It is assumed that money at the disposal of the government of any country is worth more than private consumption because while money in the hands of the government could be invested to produce future consumption, it would be wasteful if left in the hands of private individuals who have very high propensity to consume.

8. Wealth distribution The problem of inequalities in the distribution of income and wealth is very much present in the LDCs. Such a problem would be lessened if public savings could substitute for private savings by the rich in LDCs.

9. Externalities It is argued that whenever externalities are present (say, in the presence of diminishing costs in certain industries with a large investment project), such externalities should be fully taken into account in the project appraisal for the LDCs.

7.13 The Little and Mirrlees (LM) method of project evaluation in LDCs

Given the nature of distortions in the product and factor markets in LDCs, Little and Mirrlees (LM) have suggested a novel way to measure the costs and benefits of projects in LDCs. Fundamental to the understanding of the LM method for project appraisal are two points.

1. Foreign exchange, rather than domestic price, measures the true costs and benefits of commodities produced. Therefore, the net value of all the goods produced should be converted into its foreign exchange equivalent, i.e. foreign exchange is used as the numéraire. As LM say: "It is present uncommitted social income measured in terms of convertible foreign exchange of constant purchasing power." (Little and Mirrlees, 1974) In practice, the rate of conversion is equal to convertible foreign exchange at the official rate of exchange.
2. Since total saving is less than socially optimal in LDCs, one additional unit of investment is more valuable than an extra unit of consumption at the margin. Note that on the basis of these principles, LM have altered the usual procedure of revaluing foreign resources in terms of domestic ones; on the contrary, they convert all domestic costs into "border" prices. The choice of the numéraire and the nature of its measurement has enabled LM to derive the special rate of discount which they have called the accounting rate of interest (ARI) and the cost of labour which they have tried to measure with the shadow wage rate (SWR). The arguments for using the foreign exchange rate rather than market prices to evaluate net benefits are supposed to be as follows:

1. Every domestic demand and supply has a balance of payment effect.
2. The rate of free foreign exchange is the true yardstick of the costs and benefits to society.
3. Foreign exchange is a reasonable unit of account.
4. Foreign exchange could be used to satisfy domestic demand and supply.

These reasons are not without criticisms. But before we state these criticisms, we will describe the actual methods of estimation as suggested by LM.

LM methods of estimation

Let the income of the public project be given by Y, V the value added, c the consumption per worker and N the number of labourers employed in the project. Then we have

$$Y = V - cN \qquad [7.45]$$

But Y is not the only benefit as additional consumption would not be without any social value. Hence the whole of extra consumption should not be regarded as a cost. Also there are externalities which should be included within the concept of benefits.

Additional consumption is accounted for by the excess of industrial wages over the marginal product of rural labour (m). If the industrial worker consumes all his wage and if c denotes the consumption of the labour employed in the new industrial project, then the total effect *in terms of consumption* for employing N number of labourers in a project, would be (c – m)N. As mentioned before, the whole of this extra consumption should *not* be treated as a cost. Accordingly, it has to be evaluated in terms of public income or the numéraire. Here, LM have argued in favour of weighting government income with reference to consumption arising out of new employment. This is the parameter s. Since LDCs are likely to suffer from a savings constraint, an extra unit of government income is regarded as more valuable than an extra unit of private consumption. Thus, £1 of current savings or investment is worth s (say £10) of present consumption. Hence, consumption has $\frac{1}{s}$ or $\frac{1}{10}$ the value had the same resources been saved and invested. In principle, s would depend upon the following factors:

(*a*) social returns earned on marginal investment;
(*b*) the time horizon within which savings are regarded as less than socially optional;
(*c*) rate of decline of extra consumption over time or what LM consider as the "consumption rate of discount". This is usually known as the social rate of discount.

Given the above concepts, the net social benefit (NSB) is given by the following:

$$NSB = (V - cN) + (c - m)\frac{N}{s} \qquad [7.46]$$

Note that (V – cN) is the net benefit which arises because of a rise in government's income. Next, $(c - m)\frac{N}{s}$ shows the value of extra consumption measured in terms of income by the government. Alternatively, we have

$$NSB = V - \left\{c - \frac{1}{s}(c - m)\right\}N \qquad [7.47]$$

and the shadow wage rate (W) is given by

$$W = c - \frac{1}{s}(c - m) \qquad [7.48]$$

This is exactly the term within the second bracket of equation [7.47]. Equation [7.48] could also be written as:

$$W = m + (c - m)\left(1 - \frac{1}{s}\right) \qquad [7.49]$$

It is clear that W is given by m (the marginal product of rural labour or the opportunity cost of labour measured in terms of additional output foregone) plus (c – m) or the cost of providing extra consumption because of employment of a new worker *net* of the *benefit* of such additional consumption given in terms of government income, i.e. $(c - m)\frac{1}{s}$. Note that if there is no difference in the value of public income and private consumption, the value of s = 1 and W = m [check equation [7.49]]. If no value is attached to additional consumption, the value of s would be equal to ∞ and the market wage would be equal to W.

The accounting rate of interest (ARI)

The accounting rate of interest (ARI) or i is the rate at which the value of government income falls over time. In principle, it can be determined by the social rate of return on the marginal public investment (r), the fraction of it that is saved (λ) and s. In practice, r could be determined by the weighted average of "social" rates of profit earned from present investments. The value of λ could be derived from the information of saving propensities and tax rates. The ARI can now be defined as

$$i = r[\lambda + (1 - \lambda)/s] \qquad [7.50]$$

where $s = [1 + \frac{1}{2}(i - k)]^T$ [7.51]

k = social rate of discount

T = the time when savings and consumption are regarded as equally valuable.

$$k = (1 + v_t)^e - 1 \qquad [7.52]$$

v_t = *per capita* consumption growth-rate

e = elasticity of marginal social utility with respect to consumption

Note that since the social rate of discount describes the social time preference between present and future consumption and since in the growth process, future consumption is expected to be greater than at present leading to a decline in marginal utility of future consumption, therefore we require information of consumption growth-rate (v_t) and e as defined above (for the derivation of equation [7.52], see, for example, Dasgupta and Pearce (1972).

After making substitution of [7.50] for [7.51], we get:

$$s = \{1 + \tfrac{1}{2}[r(\lambda + (1 - \lambda)/s] - k]\}^T$$

Given the values of λ, r, k and T, s could be determined. Of these T is difficult to estimate and projections of income and savings growth-rates are necessary to arrive at the most likely year when savings would be enough for achieving sufficient long-run growth-rate and that year will determine the value of T.

For the evaluation of output and input, LM classify all the items as *traded* and *non-traded* goods. However, they acknowledge that there could be *partially traded goods*. According to LM, *traded goods* are:

"(*a*) goods which are actually imported or exported;

(*b*) goods which would be exported or imported if the country had followed policies which resulted in an *optimum industrial development*." (author's italics)

Note that definition (*b*) would take account of tax and subsidy policies and hence departures from free trade policies to accommodate the external effects arising from domestic industries.

The non-traded goods are defined as those goods which would not enter world trade even if there was no tariff or quota, simply because of high costs of transport and lack of physical mobility (e.g. unskilled labour, transport, power etc.).

The concept of "*partially traded goods*" is introduced by LM in the second edition of their manual (1974) and the definition is as follows:

"Only if domestic production (if there is any) and consumption are unaffected can one strictly say that the commodity is wholly traded; and similarly a good is wholly non-traded only if imports and exports, (if any) are unaffected. All other commodities can be said to be partially traded."

The exact classification of any item depends very much upon the nature of the commodity concerned and the judgement of the project planner.

After classifying the different goods in different ways, all traded goods should be evaluated at their world (or "border") prices. All exportables should be valued at f.o.b. prices; likewise, all importables should be valued at c.i.f. prices. All domestic (e.g. distribution and transport) costs should be converted into world prices. Here the fundamental principle in the LM analysis remains the same. In an open economy, the actual value of a commodity produced in a public project is equal to the foreign exchange earned in the case of the exportables or foreign exchange saved in the case of the importables.

For evaluating non-traded goods, it is necessary to break down such items into their different components: i.e. traded items, other non-tradeables, unskilled labour. Since the aim is to evaluate the non-tradeables at their marginal social costs, these items should be split further into traded items and unskilled labour; finally, all tradeables should be valued at their "border" prices while shadow wage rates should be used to calculate the costs of unskilled labour. In practice, difficulties may arise in the estimation procedures in the above-mentioned way. A standard conversion factor (SCF) can then be used to transform domestic costs of non-tradeables into their world prices where the SCF is the mean of the proportions by which home prices of all home-produced commodities are in excess of their world prices. However, excise taxes should be excluded from the domestic prices. Actually, the SCF is a rough guide to show the excess of domestic price over world price.

Several criticisms are made against the LM method.

1. The principle of using the world price as the shadow price is only valid in an economy which is open, fairly competitive in the context of world markets and not suffering from excess capacity. If, for example, a commodity has a restricted access to the world market, then it would be improper to use world prices for its evaluation. Similarly, in the presence of excess capacity within the economy, a rise in demand for its product because of the setting up of a project is unlikely to influence the trade balance (Joshi, H., 1972). LM here argue that it is very hard to predict the occurrence of excess capacity and hence it is reasonable to assume full capacity working.

2. The determination of world price is not easy, given the large number of heterogeneous goods, different forms of transactions, different supplies, bilateral agreements and the monopolistic structure of the market. Further, world prices may be influenced by the project's supply or demand of a commodity if less than perfect elasticities in supply of, and demand for, the product are assumed away. LM here advocate the use of marginal export revenue and marginal import cost. But in practice, such revenues and costs are not easy to estimate.

3. LM have not paid much attention to the linkages and externalities because of the problems involved in the measurement of such external economies. Note that the LM assumption that public projects would affect trade only and not domestic economic activities is valid only when the linkages and externalities are completely assumed away – an assumption which to some would be regarded as very restrictive (see, for example, Stewart and Streeten, 1972).

4. LM have assumed governments will follow "sensible" or "optimal" economic policies, but this would be incongruous with "the assumption – and the fact – that governments lack the full powers assumed in classical welfare economies" (LM, 1972).

5. The problems of inequalities in income distribution are not highlighted in the LM analysis. This argument is not compelling as attempts have been made by LM (1974) and others (Squire and Tak, 1975) to deal with the problems of income distribution within the LM framework of analysis.

6. The evaluation of non-tradeables in terms of world prices poses both conceptual and practical difficulties. However, in the second edition of the manual (1974) LM have recognized this difficulty and suggest the use of willingness to pay principle to evaluate social benefits.

In the light of some of these criticisms it is now possible to set out the alternative method of project appraisal which has been set out by the UNIDO (Sen *et al.*, 1972).

7.14 The United Nations Industrial Development Organization (UNIDO) (1972) guidelines

The basic differences between the LM and UNIDO guidelines stem from the facts that while LM have tried to convert all benefits and costs to an index of government income, UNIDO translates all such benefits and costs to an index of present consumption. The difference in the choice of numéraire accounts for the divergences in the two methods in the estimations of discount rate, shadow wage rates and the social value of investment. Like LM, UNIDO recognizes that in LDCs the social value of a marginal unit of consumption is *less* than that of a marginal unit of investment. But instead of converting all the consumption benefits into government income as in the LM procedure, the UNIDO recommends the conversion of all investment into present consumption since the UNIDO report uses the present consumption rather than public income as the numéraire. Thus UNIDO tries to find out the NPV of all the consumption flows because of an additional unit of investment. The concept of accounting the price of investment (API) is introduced by the UNIDO to imply the worth of the present value of the discounted consumption emanating from an additional unit of investment. Thus, there will be no difference between social rate of discount and the opportunity cost of capital where the API = 1 and at the margin, present consumption will be as valuable as investment. There is no reason why the API cannot change over time with changes in social productivity of investment, different weights given to consumption at different periods and different rates of reinvestment from profits.

The shadow wage rate (W*) in the UNIDO is defined in a way which is similar to the one observed in the LM procedure. Thus,

$$W^* = m + \alpha(\beta - 1)W$$

where m = marginal product of labour in rural areas, estimated in terms of consumption (i.e. the direct opportunity cost of labour).

α = the marginal propensity to save from the income of the project

β = API (as defined above)

Note that the second term on the right-hand side of the above equation is derived from the following relationship (see UNIDO, 1972, Ch. 15 for details):

$$[(1 - \alpha) + \beta\alpha]W - W = \alpha(\beta - 1)W$$

where $(1 - \alpha)W$ is equal to the present fall in aggregate consumption and $\beta\alpha W$ shows the aggregate consumption value of the fall in investment. However, this loss would be offset by increased consumption and extra labour and therefore W is subtracted. It is possible to make adjustments for the problems of income distribution in W* by choosing appropriate weights for the extra consumption of industrial labourers.

UNIDO uses the social rate of discount for calculating the NPV and this is different from the API used by LM. Further, since UNIDO recognizes that the stated foreign exchange rates in many LDCs do not estimate the actual benefits to society, it therefore derives "shadow exchange rates" (SER) given by the value to consumers of the commodities which one extra unit of foreign exchange makes available to them. Thus, if an additional unit of a domestic currency (pesos or rupees) buys foreign exchange (pounds or dollars) which will provide a commodity to the consumer whose domestic value (i.e. the price at which it is sold domestically) is equal to 5 pesos or rupees, then the SER = 5. According to UNIDO, the SER is equal to the weighted average (where weights are the proportions in which foreign exchange is expected to be distributed at the margin to different types of imports) of the ratio of domestic prices at which markets are cleared and the world prices (c.i.f.) at the government stated rates of foreign exchange. Note that unlike the LM method where the world price is used to revalue the domestic costs and benefits, in UNIDO the domestic currency is used to evaluate the costs and benefits of foreign resources by using the SER.

However, the use of LM and UNIDO methods is likely to achieve the same result. In the LM analysis, given the lower level of shadow prices, production of non-tradeables would be disfavoured (although their domestic use would be favoured); similarly, the use of SER under UNIDO would promote exports or those projects which would save imports. In the estimation of SWR, the differences between the two approaches are also minimum. This can be shown easily. Let ρ_t be equal to the shadow price of savings and let the total wage for unskilled labour be equal to W_t under the UNIDO principle. Under the LM rule this wage bill would be W_t/ρ_t simply because $\frac{1}{\rho_t}$ is the shadow price of consumption in terms of investment at period t (Dasgupta, 1972).

In working out the NPV under the LM and UNIDO rules, the difference could arise in $\rho > 1$ because of the choice of different numéraires in the two methods – present consumption under UNIDO and present investment under LM. However, as long as the decision rule is to accept the projects whose NPV > 0, the choice of different numéraires will not lead to difference in the prediction of final results. But there could be difference in the estimation of shadow prices as well as in the classification of the different outputs and inputs of the project. The scope of UNIDO is larger as it emphasizes the objectives rather than maximization of the sum of total consumption. Also, it seeks to incorporate the importance of the principle of income distribution in project selection. However, in the second edition of the LM manual (1974), some principles have been discussed to adjust for differences in income distribution and more recently, Squire and Tak (1975) have tried to highlight the adjustment principles to account for changes in income distribution in project appraisal within the framework of LM analysis. It is necessary to point out that while UNIDO distinguishes between consumption and investment, LM have distinguished between private and public funds. The latter is regarded as superior by LM since public investment is considered as more valuable than private investment and a "rational" government should try to equate the social value of public consumption and investment. Further, the SER as defined by UNIDO is regarded as a "very slippery concept and treacherous parameter" (Lal, 1974). The formula for calculating the SER under UNIDO is as follows:

$$\text{SER} = \sum_{i=1}^{n} \text{fi} \frac{P_i^D}{P_{ic}} + \sum_{i=n+1}^{n+h} \text{xi} \frac{P_i^D}{P_{if}}$$

where fi = "the fraction of foreign exchange allocated to imports of the ith of n commodities at the margin",

P_i^D = domestic market clearing prices of imports and exports (inclusive of taxes and subsidies),

xi = "rupee amount by which each of h exports falls in response to earnings of foreign exchange",

P_{ic} = world prices of imports

P_{if} = world prices of exports.

(See Lal, 1974; for details see also UNIDO, 1972).

It is argued that the proper values of the weights that should be attached to the ratio of domestic prices to world prices are not easy to define in principle and sometimes very hard to determine in practice. Also, it is not easy to classify the commodities over which the averaging should be carried out. Because of these difficulties, different SER can be observed for the same country. Here the use of multiple conversion factors as recommended by the LM method can solve the problem of obtaining a unique SER. The use of LM method is thus regarded as less difficult to apply; it is also supposed to yield more accurate estimates. Further, since many governments do not like the idea of working out the SER for their countries, it is claimed that there are "diplomatic advantages" in not finding out the SER for any LDC.

On the other hand, it may be argued that the use of SCF as prescribed by the LM to evaluate the non-traded inputs in terms of world prices would raise the familiar problems of averaging over a large number of goods as well as the problems of using a system of proper weighting. Further, when the commercial policy of the government of any LDC renders the project output as a non-tradeable item, then the production of such a commodity would alter domestic supply. Here, the proper method to evaluate the social value of such a non-tradeable commodity would be to use the principle of willingness to pay as recommended by UNIDO. Also, it is worth remembering that the concept of world price is not always very clear. The practical project planner should thus be guided by the realities of the situation before choosing one technique or the other.

The application of the two methods could lead to significant divergencies in the ranking of projects because of the differences in the rules as to when the domestic or world price should be applied to evaluate the costs and benefits and also because of differences in the methods for translating domestic values and world prices into domestic currencies. In practice, the use of these two methods is unlikely to alter substantially the ranking of projects. Both approaches emphasize the need to use shadow prices to correct for market distortions. Both recognize the importance of savings and foreign exchange bottlenecks in the process of economic development. Both stress the need for using different weights to adjust for income distribution, given massive unemployment and poverty in the LDCs.

8

Industrialisation, protection and trade policies

8.1 Major reasons for industrialization in LDCs

Industrialization has been regarded as a major strategy for achieving a faster rate of economic growth and a higher standard of living in many LDCs. Several reasons are advanced to justify such a strategy. First, it is contended that economically advanced countries are usually more industrialized than the economically poor countries. The strength of this argument is derived from the lessons of economic history of developed countries. Second, industrialization is sometimes regarded as the major way to solve the problem of unemployment and underemployment in LDCs, many of which suffer from problems of highly adverse man–land ratio. Third, the nature of trade of many LDCs prompts them to choose industrialization as an avenue to solve the problem of instabilities in the earnings from exports which chiefly consist of primary products. The demand for primary products in the international market is usually price and income inelastic. The LDCs also suffer from a chronic balance of payments deficit. Fourth, it is argued that industrialization alone can alter the present economic and social structure of many LDCs which is not conducive to achieving a higher level of economic development since dynamic externalities[1] concomitant with industrialization are necessary conditions for attaining a high level of growth. Some of the advocates of the "big-push" theory have actually emphasized the need for industrialization on the strength of dynamic externalities. Fifth, given the low level of productivity in most LDCs, particularly in agriculture, industrialization is supposed to improve productivity by increasing efficiency. Sixth, the desire to attain self-sufficiency has prompted many LDCs to choose the path of industrialization. Finally, industrialization is regarded as important policy to affect fundamental economic *and* social changes in LDCs which are considered as necessary conditions to raise their growth potentials.

8.2 The role of tariffs in economic development

In economic history tariffs as an instrument of protection have played some part in the economic growth of industrially advanced countries though the exact extent of such a role has been debated considerably. Classical economists like Smith, Ricardo and Mill advocated the doctrine of free trade based on the theory of comparative advantage. Such a doctrine is an offshoot of the principles of *laissez-faire*, although it was soon realized that the principles of *laissez-faire* may not be the best for a country to follow, as some of the basic assumptions such as perfect competition and optimal income distribution may not hold. Several qualifications of the doctrine of free trade were made, and indeed Mill has suggested the use of tariffs to protect the infant industries. Some others (e.g. Bickerdike) have shown the case for tariffs to improve upon a country's terms of trade through trade restriction. This has now been regarded as the *optimum tariff* argument.

8.3 The optimum tariff argument

The point about optimum tariffs could be illustrated by a diagram. In Fig. 8.1 let OV_1 be the offer curve of country No. 1 and OV_2 the offer curve of country No. 2. (For the derivation of offer curves, see Meade, 1952.) In a free-trade situation OT is the terms of trade between the two countries. An imposition of tariff by country 1 (assuming away any retaliation by country 2) will shift the offer curve to OV_1' and the terms of trade move in favour of country 1 as OT shifts to OT_1. Here country 1 acts like a monopolist, and tries to realize higher gains through trade contraction. Such gains could not be made when the elasticity of foreign demand for imports is very high. Since this would imply a straight-line offer curve, the terms of trade would remain

Fig. 8.1

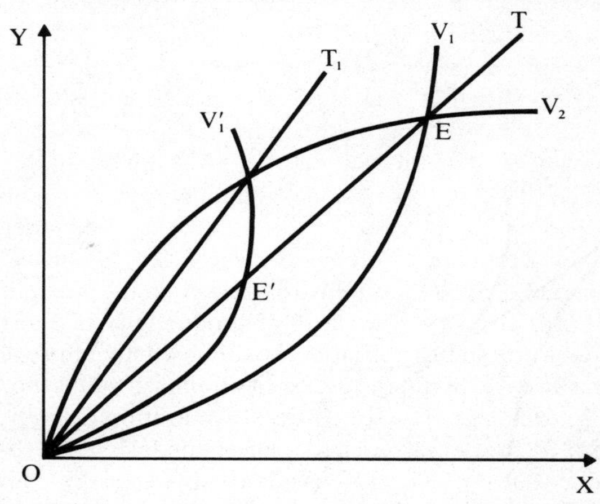

the same. In Fig. 8.1 it will be the same on E′ as on E. It can be shown easily how country 2 can gain by imposing a tariff on the offer curve V_1' of country 1. But this could lead to further retaliation by country 1 and the final outcome is not easy to say. It is only when the equilibrium is reached, (i.e. no country gains via imposition of more tariffs) that it could be shown that either country 1 or 2 is actually better off. It is also hard to determine the exact significance of optimum tariff in commercial policies. Similarly, no positive conclusion has been drawn about the impact of commercial policy on Europe's terms of trade (Kindleberger, 1956).

Johnson (1964), Bhagwati and Ramaswami (1963) argue that as far as protection in the LDCs is concerned, only the optimum tariff argument is the valid one, and all others are really arguments for subsidies. The theory is derived from the principles of Paretian welfare maximization which requires that optimum welfare would be reached at that point where the domestic marginal rate of substitution in consumption (DRS, i.e. the slope of the "social" indifference curve) is equal to the domestic marginal social rate of transformation in production (DRT, i.e. the slope of the transformation function at home production between any two goods) which is also equal to the foreign marginal rate of transformation (FRT, i.e. the slope of the price line which indicates the fixed world price ratio). This could be easily shown in the Fig. 8.2.

Let TT′ be the domestic transformation curve for two goods X and Y. In the absence of any distortion a country can produce at Z and consume at C, and since this would make DRS = DRT = FRT, welfare is maximized. Let us assume a domestic distortion (e.g. in the labour market of a LDC because, say, the social opportunity cost of labour is less than private cost

Fig. 8.2

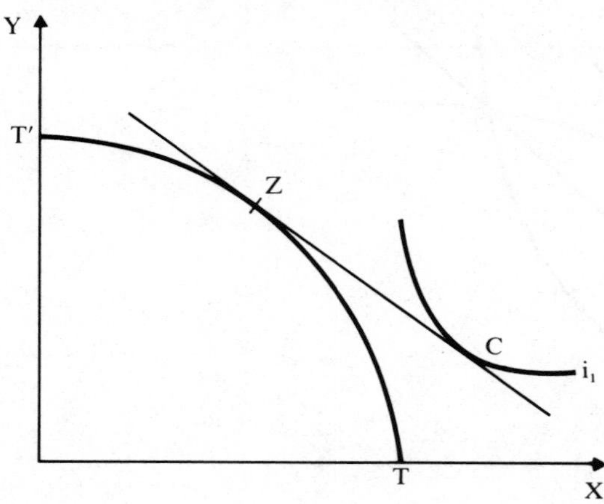

because of disguised unemployment. See Chs. 3 and 7.). This would lead to a divergence between DRT and the ratio of marginal private costs of X to Y. These points are shown in Fig. 8.3. The equilibrium for the producers is shown at Z and consumers will maximize their satisfaction at C because producers will produce according to the ratio of world prices (FRT) and the marginal private costs whereas consumers will equate the DRS to the FRT. But note that optimum welfare in the Paretian sense is not obtained because FRT = DRS ≠ DRT. Here it is necessary to impose a tax on Y and subsidize the production of X which would lower the production of Y and raise the production of X until the point of optimum welfare is reached at Z_2 where DRT = DRS = FRT. On the other hand a tariff on X raises its domestic production.

This policy raises the production of X to Z_1. Equilibrium for production and consumption would now be given by the price line P_t–P'_t which is steeper than the world price line since a tariff is now being included. Consumers attain a higher level of indifference cuve at C_1 and they are better off in comparison with their previous point of equilibrium at C. (This need not always happen. Indeed, they may be worse off. See Bhagwati and Ramaswami, 1963, for details.)

Note that at C_1 optimum welfare is not obtained as the Paretian conditions are not fulfilled, i.e., DRT ≠ FRT ≠ DRS. Thus, the use of tariffs to correct domestic distortions is not an optimal policy. On the other hand, the use of domestic tax-cum-subsidy policy (in this case a tax on Y or a subsidy on X or both) clearly maximizes welfare since DRT = FRT = DRS when consumption takes place at C_2 and production takes place at Z_2.

As Johnson concludes, "Only the optimum tariff provides an economic justification for tariffs. All other arguments for protection are arguments for subsidies." (Johnson, 1968, p. 353)

Fig. 8.3

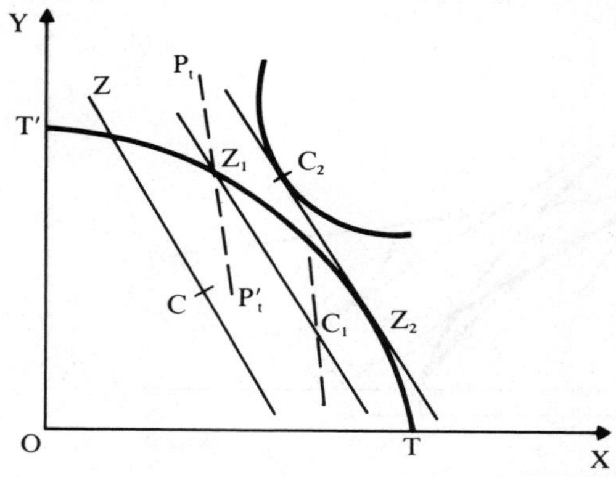

For most LDCs, the relevance of the optimum tariff is not much because few can exercise sufficient monopoly or monopsony power to cause an international income transfer by improving their terms of trade. The LDCs are actually the price takers, so their optimum tariffs are low or even zero, because alternative suppliers of foodstuffs generally exist, and the economically rich nations are developing substitutes for natural raw materials, and the size of a less developed country's domestic market for a particular import is not large and its adaptability of demand and supply is not great.

8.4 The infant industry argument

It is contended that if free trade will not allow a country's true comparative advantage situation to develop, due to a difference between marginal social and marginal private costs, then trade should be temporarily protected during its initial high cost period, until the correct pattern of international specialization is established. The incurring of costs for a limited initial period in return for future benefits is the normal investment procedure. To increase social welfare the infant industry must grow up, and be able to compete on equal terms with foreign producers in domestic and world markets (Mill's Test). It is a dynamic argument involving the lowering of production costs through learning by doing. The infant industry must be able to cover the costs of subsidizing its infancy by lowering production costs (Bastable's test).

As illustrated in Fig. 8.4, under free trade, the country produces at P on the transformation curve TT′ and consumes at C, given the terms of trade are P_w–P_w. A tariff on industry will shift production and consumption to P′ with domestic prices, P_h–P_h. Social welfare has fallen since P′ is on a lower indifference curve (i.e. i_2) in comparison with C which is on i_1.

Fig. 8.4

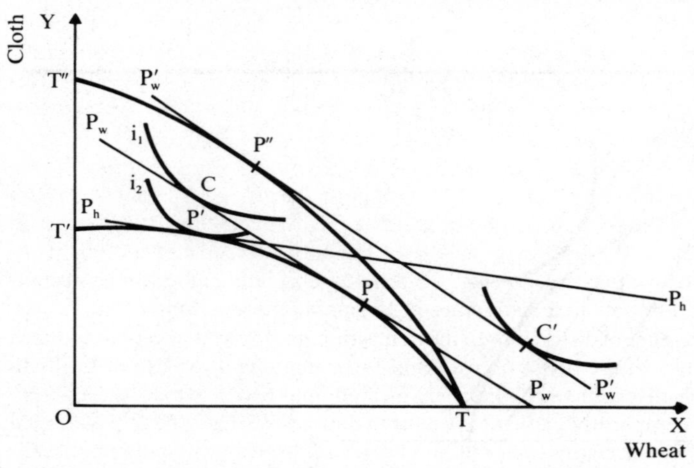

Protection could increase the output of cloth and shift the transformation curve outwards to TT″ where the country again operates under free trade, with the same terms of trade as before protection P'_w–P'_w. It will produce at P″ and consume at C′, which is Pareto better than T, so there is a higher level of welfare than before protection.

To provide an argument for government intervention, free traders require that the following two rules be satisfied:

1. The social rate must be greater than the private rate of return on an investment.
2. The private return necessary to induce the investment must exceed the private and social returns available on alternative investments sufficiently to make socially profitable investments privately unprofitable. Here, two points should be made:
   (*a*) Producers may be pessimistic about future returns or unwilling to take risks in an unprotected market. Here the government should provide expert information on investment prospects in each sector.
   (*b*) Lack of perfection in the capital markets in LDCs make investment expensive, especially if an initial large scale is necessary for economic efficiency. The optimal policy is to subsidize the provision of capital.

To justify the infant industry argument, the whole society must gain from the knowledge generated as the industry grows. Then it is reasonable for the society to bear the costs of helping the industry mature. However, a tariff is not the optimal policy instrument, because the situation needs an alteration of loss in production, and not of consumption, and a tariff involves a loss in consumption which would not be the impact of the right subsidy. The existence of infant industries leads to FRT = DRS = DRT. A tariff would make FRT = DRT but ≠DRS. Note that only a policy of taxes and/or subsidies to the learning process can make FRT = DRS = DRT.

Advocates of free trade argue that protection is a selective method of granting differential price or cost advantage to particular industries, relative to other domestic industries. Protection to all industries means special protection to none. A policy of deflation or devaluation is generally preferred to tariffs or subsidies.

On the other hand, protectionists contend that it should apply to the whole infant economy, but the LDCs manufacturing sector usually covers several import-substitute consumer goods industries matching the pattern of domestic demand, whereas the idea is to lower future costs of the infant industries by the educative process. So their case is rather one for protection where there are potential economies of large-scale production.

The presence of distortions in the domestic commodity market has induced the supporters of the protectionist school to recommend the use of tariffs to correct such divergences. If the price of a commodity in which the country has a true comparative advantage is above its social cost, then it is argued that a tariff could rectify such a difference. Also, protection would enable the home market to expand and the industries could enjoy the external economies

(Scitovsky, 1954). However, there could be external diseconomies as well. In such cases, private costs would be lower than social costs. Cultivators in LDCs, for example, do not take into account the (social) costs of soil erosion in their private profit calculation. Here a tariff may raise welfare as the production of agricultural goods would be discouraged, and allocation of resources would be more efficient because of a reduction in soil erosion. Thus, factor market divergences are sought to be rectified by the use of tariffs. However, gains in production via tariffs must be viewed against the loss of consumption to draw any conclusion about the over-all impact of tariffs. Figure 8.5 illustrates this. A partial equilibrium analysis is used for simplification.

Fig. 8.5

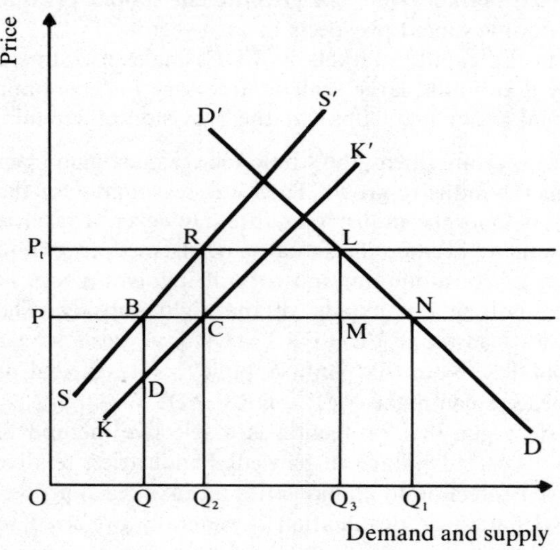

Let DD′ be the domestic demand curve and SS′ the domestic supply curve of an importable product. Under free trade, QQ_1 would be the level of imports (because domestic demand = OQ_1 and domestic supply = OQ and $OQ_1 - OQ = QQ_1$).

Recalling the case for external economies, it may be argued that marginal social cost is less than the marginal private costs. Since external economies represent social benefits, their value should be deducted from cost from the viewpoint of the community. We then obtain KK′. (Note that should there be external diseconomies, KK′ would lie above SS′.) Should producers be given a subsidy of P_tP per unit of the commodity (i.e., P_tP/OP rate), then domestic production rises to OQ_2. The price remains at OP. Imports fall by QQ_2. The value of imports replaced ($QBCQ_2$) minus the social cost ($QDCQ_2$) is the gain for the society which is shown by BCD. Note that a rate of subsidy higher than $P_t P/OP$ will reduce the gains as prices will be lower than their social costs. Similarly, a rate lower than this would be inadequate to take full advantage of the economies of scale.

A tariff at the same rate (i.e., $P_t P/OP$) could increase the *production* by the same amount, i.e. QQ_2, but *consumption* will now suffer by Q_1Q_3. The loss of consumer's surplus is the area LMN. A subsidy does not inflict on the society any such loss. Now the gain, i.e. area BCD must be set against the loss, i.e. area MNL. (See Corden, 1974, for detailed analysis.) The ultimate gain in terms of welfare will depend upon the relative sizes of the production gains and consumption losses. Here the weight of opinion seems to be in favour of the argument that domestic distortions should be corrected by domestic tax subsidy policies rather than by tariffs to achieve Paretian optimum welfare (i.e. DRS = DRT = FRT). Whenever there are domestic distortions, they should be dealt with directly (Ramaswami, 1971).

8.5 Distortions in the factor markets

In many LDCs, distortions exist in the factor markets. For instance, in the presence of large-scale unemployed labour, particularly in agriculture, low wages in agriculture and high wages in industry, a tariff on importable industry is sometimes advocated as an offset against high cost of labour. The differences in wages between agriculture and industry overestimate the private cost of labour in industry since industrial wages exceed the social opportunity cost of labour. Such a situation shows inefficiency in resource allocation and underestimation of the benefits of industrial transformation. The aim is to increase real income over and above the level of sub-optimal free trade by raising the relative price of industrial output via tariff on industries and a better allocation of resources (here, labour) is attempted by transferring labour from agriculture to industry (Myrdal, 1956, Hagen, 1958).

It is said that given the imperfections of the labour market in the LDCs, a tariff can never be the optimal policy and a subsidy is better than the policy of imposing tariffs. Figure 8.6 illustrates this. Let TAT_1 be the transformation curve in the presence of distortions and TBT_1 the transformation curve in the absence of distortions. Actually, TBT_1 is derived if the country were producing along its contract curve in the Edgeworth box diagram. (For the derivation of such a contract curve, see for example, Staley, 1970.)

TAT_1 is inside TBT_1 because production is sub-optimal, given the distortions and the inefficiency in resource allocation (except at the extreme points of specialization).

Under free trade, the country operates on the TAT_1 curve (given the distortions in the labour market), produces at P and consumes at C. The line WW_1 indicates the terms of trade. A tariff on industrial output will take production to P_1 and this is a better situation (in terms of Paretian principles) than P. But such a tariff is not an optimal policy because DRT $\neq$ FRT.

Fig. 8.6

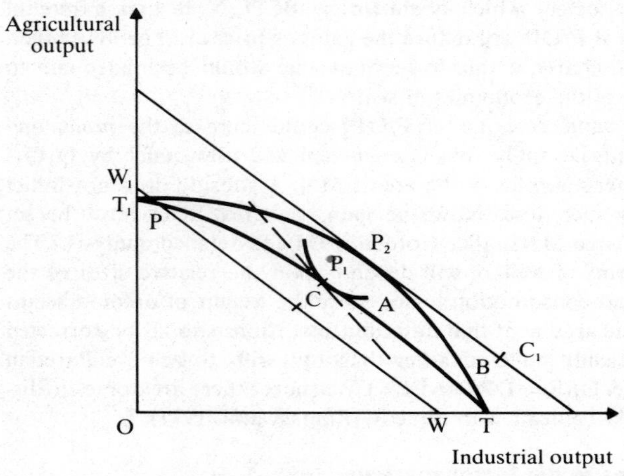

Hagen's case for protection is derived from increased real income at P_1. But the policy is not the best. A subsidy, on the other hand, can take the economy to a point like C_1 which is better than P_1 or C. Again, a policy of subsidizing the use of labour input in industry is required for a more efficient resource allocation.

8.6 The balance of payments argument

Tariffs have been regarded as an effective weapon to reduce the balance of payments deficit. Both DCs and LDCs have taken resort to tariffs to reduce their trade deficits from time to time. The method is regarded as a simple one by some (Galbraith, 1964). This is obvious if we consider Fig. 8.5. The imposition of tariffs by the amount of PP_t reduces the deficit from QQ_1 to Q_2Q_3. However, such a policy is not regarded as optimal by others (Johnsòn, 1962) and a policy of a cut in domestic expenditure or devaluation is preferred to tariffs.

8.7 The employment argument

The use of tariffs to protect employment at home is advocated from time to time. In the LDCs, employment in more productive manufacturing industries is usually protected by tariffs in preference to the labour utilization in low-productivity sectors like agriculture. But this argument is not regarded as very convincing. Although a tariff may protect employment for some time, it creates distortions in both production (by favouring import substitution rather than export promotion) and consumption (by reducing consumer surplus)

It is possible to envisage an *optimal* tariff in the event of a trade-off between distortion costs and unemployment, but this will be a second-best solution since the best solution is to allow devaluation of the currency which would avoid the costs of distortions introduced by tariffs (Corden, 1974). However, in the past, many countries, both developed and less developed, have shown great reluctance to adopt devaluation as a policy variable and used tariffs chiefly for protecting the balance of payments, employment and capital flows. But in the middle-seventies, in an era of flexible exchange rates, such arguments for tariffs have lost ground.

Despite the theoretical criticisms of the use of tariffs for import substitution and industrialization, their appeal still remains strong in many LDCs. However, it was soon realized that in the process of stimulating domestic production, it is not only necessary to consider the impact of tariffs on domestic prices, but also it is equally important to consider the effects of tariffs on *inputs* which are used in domestic production. (Note that a tariff on intermediate inputs does not alter the decision of the consumers.) This is the essence of the distinction between "nominal" and "effective" tariffs to which we now turn.

8.8 "Nominal" and "effective" rates of protection

Import controls protect the domestic firms from foreign competition, and the extent of protection can be measured by the degree to which import controls cause domestic prices of imports to exceed what their prices would be in the absence of such controls. When import control refers to an imported product and its price, it is known as the *nominal rate* of protection (NRP). When it refers to a stage of production and relates to the value added of the product at that stage of production it is known as the *effective rate* of protection (ERP). The NRP shows in percentage terms the extent to which the domestic prices of imported goods exceed what their domestic prices would be in the absence of protection. Thus, NRP is equal to the rate of tariff (*ad valorem*) over the domestic price. The ERP shows the percentage by which the value added at a stage of production in a domestic industry can exceed what this would be in the absence of protection. The NRP does not permit the analysis of the effects of a number of separate trade barriers upon a complex process of production. Thus, the concept of ERP is the more useful one, since it analyses the net effects on a plant or industry of controls on the imports of both its inputs and outputs.

There are some difficulties in the measurement of the rate of protection because of the use of non-traded inputs and methods used differ from each other. This point will be discussed later and for the present, a more rigorous analysis of ERP is given.

Let us assume that cloth and yarn are imported and will continue to be imported after the imposition of tariffs; that there are two factors of production: i.e. yarn, (a finished product) and a value-added product, which is the value added by the cloth industry. This product is produced by, say, labour, capital and natural resources. It is also assumed that:

(*a*) The input coefficients for domestic production are fixed for transforming yarn into cloth; this coefficient is equal for all firms.
(*b*) The elasticities of foreign supply of imports of cloth and yarn are both equal to infinity (Corden, 1971).

The effective rate of protection in a partial equilibrium model is shown in Fig. 8.7, the assumption of fixed input coefficient is retained and both cloth and yarn are measured on the horizontal axis, so that, one unit of yarn is required to make one unit of cloth.

Fig. 8.7

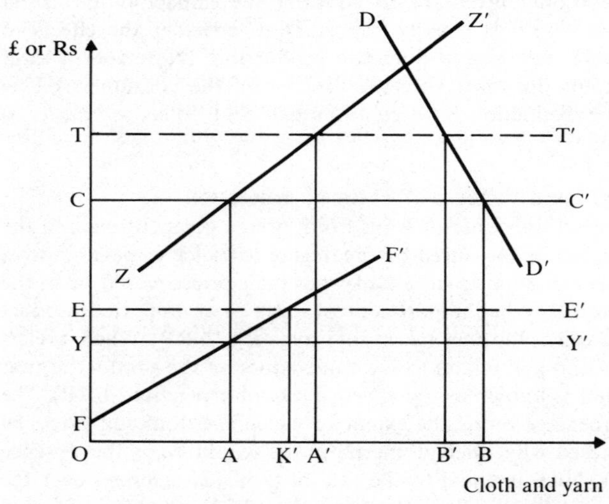

The perfectly elastic foreign supply curves for yarn and for cloth are YY′ and CC′ respectively and OY and OC are free trade import prices of yarn and cloth respectively. The price for a unit of value added by the cloth industry – for the value added product – is YC. This is the "effective price" of cloth, as distinct from OC which is the "nominal price" of cloth. If a nominal tariff of CT/OC is imposed on cloth, with no tariff on yarn, then the "effective price" of cloth increases from YC to YT. This yields the "effective rate of protection" or ERP for cloth CT/YC – the proportional increase in the effective price because of the imposition of the nominal tariff.

In the case of a tariff imposed on yarn by the extent of YE/OY, instead of the nominal tariff on cloth, the ERP of cloth would have decreased from YC to EC. The ERP for cloth would be negative, $-\frac{EY}{CY}$.

Had a normal tariff on cloth of CT/OC been combined with a nominal tariff on yarn of EY/OY, the "effective" price of cloth would have altered from CY to ET, and the ERP would be equal to (CT – EY)/CY. Thus the proportion of CT to EY determines whether the effective price increases or decreases and whether the ERP is positive or negative.

Let DD′ be the domestic demand for cloth and ZZ′ be the domestic supply curve of cloth. Under free trade, consumption of cloth is OB. The domestic supply of yarn is FF′ and under free trade the domestic production of yarn is OA. A tariff on cloth raises domestic supply by AA′, cuts domestic demand by BB′ and reduces the deficits in the balance of payments to A′B′. Similarly, a tariff on yarn raises domestic supply of yarn by AK′.

The algebraic formulations of ERP and NRP could be stated as follows:

Z_v = value-added per unit of k in activity k in the absence of tariffs (i.e. free trade price)
Z_{v1} = value-added per unit of k in activity k made possible by the tariff structure ("effective price" after the imposition of tariffs)
E_k = the proportional increase in the effective price of k because of the imposition of tariffs
P_k = nominal price of a unit of k in free trade
a_{ik} = share of i in the cost of k at free trade prices
t_k = nominal tariff rate on k
t_i = nominal tariff rate on i

The formula for calculating the ERP for the activity producing k – for the k value-added product – would be given by the following equations:

$$Z_v = P_k(1 - a_{ik}) \quad [8.1]$$

$$Z_{v1} = P_k[(1 + t_k) - a_{ik}(1 + t_i)] \quad [8.2]$$

$$E_k = \frac{Z_{v1} - Z_v}{Z_v} \quad [8.3]$$

From [8.1], [8.2] and [8.3], we obtain,

$$E_k = \frac{t_k - \sum_{i=1}^{n} a_{ik} t_i}{1 - \sum a_{ik}} \quad [8.4]$$

Equation [8.4] shows that the ERP (E_k) depends on t_k (nominal cloth tariff), t_i (nominal yarn tariff), and a_{ik} (free trade input share).

It is clear that the ERP is a better index to measure protection than the rate of nominal tariffs because it takes account of the amount by which the prices of inputs are raised by tariffs, as well as the amount by which the price of the output is increased. However, there are some difficulties with this useful index of ERP (Helleiner, 1972).

1. It was assumed at the outset that the input–output coefficients (a_{ik}'s) are constant and not influenced by the tariff. If they were not, and indeed, it is unlikely that they would be in reality, the measurement of ERP becomes very complicated. Variations from these assumed constant points could take place between intermediate and factor inputs as their relative prices change or because of economies of scale as production rises.
2. The other difficulty lies in one of the basic drawbacks of the index itself. The measurement of the ERP aims to estimate the impact of the tariff upon particular industries without including the indirect effects on other industries. This is a major limitation. But despite these difficulties it is a better index compared to the alternatives usually suggested.

There are other difficulties. Should tariffs be used to measure ERP rather than the difference between world prices and domestic prices, it is necessary to assume that tariffs are the only forms of trade controls, and also that the domestic price of an imported commodity is equal to the world price plus the tariff. Similarly, it will be assumed that the domestic price of an export good is the world price net of the export tax. This is only true if the country faces an infinitely elastic world demand for that product (Helleiner, 1972, p. 127). Needless to say, such an assumption may not always be valid. Also, the value of capital–output ratio may be different in different industries and capital can depreciate at different rates in different industries and as such in any two industries with the same ERP, the net returns to capital could be different. Thus, the cost of depreciation should be deducted from the value-added.

Non-traded goods

As regards the non-traded goods, three different ways are suggested to tackle this problem:

(*a*) the Corden method (1966);
(*b*) the method proposed by Balassa *et al.* (1971);
(*c*) the "ideal" method of Scott (Little *et al.* 1970).

Each one of these methods will be discussed in turn.

1. The *Corden* method redefines value added to include non-traded inputs. Thus, what is measured is the percentage by which value added plus the payments for non-traded goods can be increased. The percentage ERP, then, is given by the following (Corden, 1966):

$$\text{ERP} = 100\left(\frac{h_k - \sum a_{ik} h_i}{f_k - \sum a_{ik} f_i} - 1\right)$$

Where h_k are home prices, f_k foreign prices and a_{ik} is the input of the ith commodity for every unit of output k, the i's being limited to traded commodities. Note that whenever the ERP is high, the method underestimates the percentage by which value-added alone is increased.

2. An alternative is to assume that there is no effect on the prices of non-traded inputs. Indeed, Balassa assumes that non-traded inputs are in infinitely elastic supply so that they can be treated the same as traded inputs. This method is not without criticisms since if the index of the ERP is too high, it overestimates the amount by which the value-added is increased because the negative effects of tariff on export subsidies to indirectly traded inputs are ignored and none of the non-traded inputs is taken into consideration.
3. Scott measures the percentage by which domestic value-added (DVA), given in domestic currency, is raised by protection above what it would be if the same process were operated at world prices (WVA) (Little *et al.*, 1970). Thus,

$$\text{ERP} = \left(\frac{\text{DVA}}{\text{WVA}} - 1\right) 100$$

Alternatively,

$$\text{ERP} = \left(1 - \frac{\text{WVA}}{\text{DVA}}\right) 100$$

which gives the proportion of value-added at domestic prices because of protection.

The rate of protection can, however, be negative (Little *et al.*, 1970). This can occur when the inputs of an activity are protected, but not the final output. Note that even when $\text{DVA} > 0$ and $\text{WVA} > 0$, $\text{ERP} < 0$ if $\text{DVA} < \text{WVA}$. Also, WVA could be negative which implies that after considering only traded inputs and outputs, production costs foreign exchange for the economy.

In Table 8.1, it is shown that the treatment of non-traded inputs differs according to the method used. Corden method includes non-traded inputs in the value-added. Where protection is high this is likely to give a lower estimate than the Scott method. In the Balassa method, it is assumed that non-traded inputs in free trade would have the dollar or pound value given by their existing market value in domestic currency transformed at the official rate of exchange. Should the currencies be overvalued, it is likely to give a too high dollar or pound value. It is a better index if it is possible to estimate the value-added at world prices to find out what the value-added would be under free trade. Thus, dollar or pound prices of non-traded inputs are used. In the "ideal" method of Scott, it is assumed that the proportionate difference between the actual and free-trade values of non-traded inputs is given by a weighted average of protection for manufacturing as well as agriculture. Reflection suggests that the Scott method is not exactly ideal but it is really a cross between the Balassa and the Corden methods minus their basic disadvantages (i.e. over- and underestimation).

It can be seen from Table 8.1 that in all cases, except Brazil and Pakistan, the "ideal" method gives results between the other two methods, and closer to the Corden method. It is also easy to check from the table how the ERP differed between different countries.

Table 8.1 Effect of different treatment of non-traded inputs on the measurement of effective protection for manufacturing (percentages)

Country	*Year*	*"Balassa" method*	*"Ideal" method*	*"Corden" method*
Z				
Argentina	1958	247	174	162
Brazil	1966	155	98	118
Mexico	1960	28	27	27
India	1961	733	n.a.	313
Pakistan	1963/4	00	2,000	271
Philippines	1965	52	50	49
Taiwan	1965	50	38	33
U				
Argentina	1958	71	64	62
Brazil	1966	61	50	54
Mexico	1960	22	21	21
India	1961	88	n.a.	76
Pakistan	1963/4	100	95	73
Philippines	1965	34	33	33
Taiwan	1965	33	28	25

Source: Little, Scitovsky and Scott (1970) p. 431.

$$Z = \left(\frac{\text{value-added manufactures at domestic prices expressed in terms of domestic currency}}{\text{rate of exchange x value-added in manufactures at world prices expressed in dollars or pounds}} \right) - 1$$

$$U = 1 - \left(\frac{\text{rate of exchange x value-added in manufactures at world prices expressed in dollars or pounds}}{\text{value-added manufactures at domestic prices expressed in terms of domestic currency}} \right)$$

The effects of protection on exports

High rates of protection for industrialization could create a bias against the export sector of the economy. Discouragement of exports is conceivable under protectionist policy for the following basic reasons:

1. Import control raises the exchange rate above its free trade level, therefore, the exporter receives less domestic currency than he would under free trade.

Thus if the exchange rate is Rs.10 = £1 under import control rather Rs.20 = £1 under free trade, the Indian exporters would be receiving Rs.10 rather than Rs.20 under a system of import restrictions. This implies that the size of an industry is likely to be smaller than it might be in the absence of such disincentives to exports.

2. The costs of production of export industries using inputs which come under import restriction is likely to rise. This has the effect of making exports less competitive in the international market.

In the post-Second World War period, the unfavourable treatment of primary exports might have contributed to the fall in their share in the world market of major exports of countries such as Brazil, Chile and Pakistan. Brazil's major primary commodity export, coffee, is a special case; while African producers increased plantings, Brazil reduced output to cushion against the drastic fall in prices. But she also experienced a decline in her market share for cocoa and lumber (Bergsman, 1970).

There has been little rise for minor agricultural commodities such as bananas, tobacco, wool, processed oil and nuts. The policies adopted have not been very conductive to the development of new exports. In fact, in Pakistan, both volume and value of major exports declined in absolute terms between 1950 and 1967 (Balassa *et al.*, 1971, p. 226) and Pakistan's share in the world exports of cotton and jute fell considerably. The import substitution of cotton and jute textiles by domestic production did not compensate for this loss.

In Malaya, the imposition of export taxes seems to have caused a similar fall in her share in the world exports of rubber. However, she has enjoyed substantial rises in the exports of some other primary products such as tin and tropical timber that are not subject to any discrimination (Balassa *et al.*, 1971, p. 207).

Thus where protection imparts a bias against exports, a fall in the shares of exports of many LDCs has been observed. Discrimination against exports has also prevented the development of new types of exports. The limit to imports is usually set by exports and this has engendered the severe and chronic balance of payments deficit in many LDCs. Export industries are not usually protected but many inputs which are used by such export industries are subject to tariffs. This results in the inelasticity of the supply of primary goods in many LDCs following policies for import substitution. Thus the policy of imposing high tariffs for industrialization could easily dampen export promotion by taxing the primary sector.

8.9 The "cost" of protection

An attempt has been made by Balassa to measure the cost of protection in some LDCs. Table 8.2 provides a comparison of the cost of protection in LDCs.

In Table 8.3 different ERP on different types of industries in some selected LDCs are shown. Once again, the differences as in the ERP for different types of industries in different countries are quite clear. Such differences

Table 8.2 The "cost" of protection in individual countries (per cent of GNP)

	Brazil 1966	*Chile 1961*	*Malaya 1965*	*Pakistan 1963/64*	*Mexico 1960*	*Norway 1954*	*Philippine 1965*
Static (allocative cost of protection of import substitutes[a]	0.6	1.4	0.6	1.5	0.6	0.5	2.0
Dynamic cost of protection of import substitutes[b]	9.5	9.6	0.4	5.4	2.2	2.0	2.6
Consumption effect[c]	0.1	0.6	0.1	0.2	0.1	0.1	0.4
Terms of trade effect[d]	−0.5	3.5	−1.4	0.6	−0.3	−0.7	−0.6
Cost of increased exports under free trade[e]	−0.2	1.9	−0.1	0.3	−0.1	−0.1	−0.7
Net cost of protection	9.5	6.2	−0.4	6.2	2.5	1.8	3.7

[a] Excess cost plus above-normal profits and wages in industries that would not surviv under free-trade.
[b] Excess costs plus above-normal profits and wages in industries that would becom competitive under free trade.
[c] Consumer surplus on the increased consumption of imports.
[d] Reductions in export prices in the event of free trade.
[e] The rise of the cost of exports under free trade under the assumption that expor industries are subject to increasing costs.

Source: Balassa (1971), p. 82.

The figures suggest that, except for Malaya, the net cost of protection as a percentag of Gross National Product was quite significant. For Malaya, the negative cost i regarded as a reflection of the absence of discriminatory policies towards a larg number of primary export products.

Table 8.3 Average effective protection for manufacturing in relation to official exchange rates[a]

Country	*Year*	*Consumption goods*	*Intermediates*	*Capital goods*	*All manufactures*
Argentina	1958	164	167	133	162
Brazil	1966	230	68	31	118
Mexico	1960	22	34	55	27
India	1961	n.a.	n.a.	n.a.	313[b]
Pakistan	1963/4	883	88	155	271
Philippines	1965	94	65	80	49[c]
Taiwan	1965	n.a.	n.a.	n.a.	33[d]

[a] For Brazil, the basic import rate of 2,220 cruzeiros. For Argentina, it is assumed that the average export exchange rate was used.
[b] For one-sixth of large-scale manufacturing industry only.
[c] Eighty-five for home market only. Other columns, home market only.
[d] Very approximate.

Source: Little, Scitovsky & Scott (1971).

partly reflect the different types of trade and industrial policies as well as different forms of idiologies. The lessons of the depression of the thirties, the Second World War and the economic history of many rich countries have prompted a significant number of LDCs to build up a "seige" economy by imposing tariffs, controls and quotas. Thus, it is not difficult to understand the desire for autarky in many LDCs. Further, given the pattern of trade between DCs and LDCs (i.e. LDCs chiefly being the exporters of primary products and the importers of finished goods from the developed countries), the nature of foreign trade in the LDCs which too often suggests concentration in the production of too few goods (i.e. commodity concentration of trade) and their exports to too few markets (i.e. geographic or market concentration), very low price and income elasticities of world demand for their product, many LDCs have deliberately chosen protection for the industrialization and diversification of their economies. Although restrictive trade and tariff policies in the developed countries have been liberalized since the Second World War, the LDCs complain that they do not go far enough to give large access to their exports in the markets of the developed countries. The system of tariffs used by some of the regional trading blocks within the developed countries, e.g. EEC which imposes a flat 30 per cent rate of tariff against the imports from the "rest of the world" hits the LDCs particularly hard. Also, the LDCs complain about the existing international economic system in general which does not help much to stabilize fluctuations in the income from exports by LDCs. It is in the light of these considerations that we shall now proceed to discuss the reasons for advocating trade, growth and a new international economic order.

8.10 Economic growth and trade

The Ricardian and the Hecksher–Ohlin models are modified in the current theories of trade to take into account the effects of growth. Since these developments are well covered in the literature (Johnson, 1962, 1967), I shall mainly concentrate here on some of the major issues.

The effects of the growth of factor supplies can first be mentioned in the light of the Rybczynski theorems (Rybczynski, 1955). Let us assume a rise in the supply of labour. If the terms of trade are given, then the Rybczynski theorem says that with the increase in the supply of labour relative to capital, the production of a labour-intensive commodity will rise and that of a capital-intensive good will fall. This may be labelled as the "*pro-trade*" bias at a given terms of trade (TT). On the other hand, capital accumulation will imply an increase in the production of capital-intensive goods and a fall in the production of labour-intensive good at a given TT, and this impact on production has been labelled as "*anti-trade*" bias. The impact on consumption can be measured by noting that at a given TT and fixed factor properties and marginal products, an increase in labour with fixed stock of capital will transfer income to labour. If the marginal propensity to consume by the labourers is high for the labour-intensive good, then a larger proportion of society's income would be spent on the labour-intensive good in comparison with the capital-intensive commodity. This is "anti-trade" bias because of consumption. However, the over-all effect depends on the nature of assumptions made and the actual values chosen. Similarly, the reverse conclusion will follow in the face of capital accumulation. (For a detailed discussion, see, for example, Johnson, 1964. For a rigorous analysis of growth, trade and accumulation, see Bardhan, 1970c.)

Welfare loss in trade through growth

A special case of *net* welfare loss through trade can be demonstrated with the help of Fig. 8.8. This is sometimes known as 'immiserizing growth" (Bhagwati, 1958). Let P_1P_1 be the transformation curve between two goods X and Y. Let X be an exportable whose improved production is shown by the new curve P_2P_2. Trade results in a decline of the TT and the ultimate point of equilibrium V_1 is on a lower indifference curve in comparison with V_0. Increased production results in welfare gains but this is more than offset by a loss of welfare because of the fall in TT so that there is a net welfare loss. Note that this result depends on the premises that the foreign demand curve for the exportables is inelastic and/or a very high marginal propensity to import or an ultra-pro-trade bias exists in LDCs. Such a model also presumes mobility of resources in between different industries. In many LDCs, this is the case in some sectors, but not in others as suggested by Kindleberger. Empirically, it is hard to say whether "immiserizing growth" has actually taken place. In the United Nations Conference on Trade and Development (UNCTAD) in 1964, it was suggested that the TT has declined by 17 per cent between 1950 and 1961 against the LDCs (leaving out the oil

Fig. 8.8

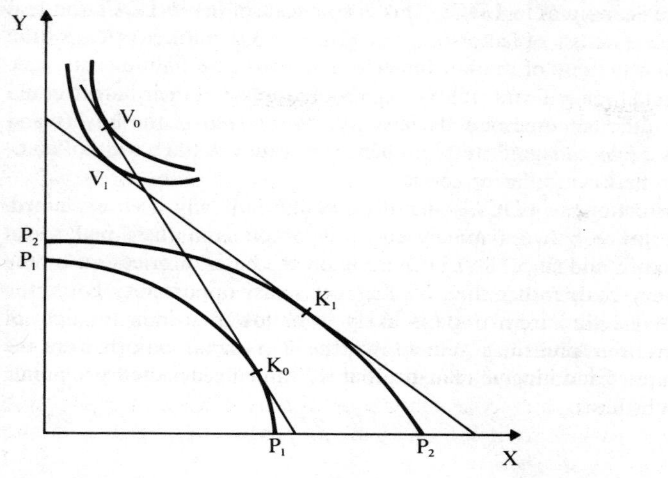

producers) *vis-à-vis* the DCs. But a fall in TT is not a sufficient condition to maintain the hypothesis about the net loss of welfare because such a fall should be viewed against the gains from production.

8.11 Terms of trade between developed countries and LDCs

The terms of trade (TT) between the developed countries and the LDCs have recently been a major arena of debate and investigation in trade theory and policy (Prebisch, 1959, 1964; MacBean, 1966). The TT are generally defined as the ratio of export to import price paid by the LDCs in their trade with developed countries (DCs). If the TT moves against the LDCs for some time, it would imply that the LDCs are losing out in their trade with the DCs. During the sixties it was suggested that such an index of TT had actually moved against the LDCs, *vis-à-vis* the DCs for a long time and hence, existing trade theory is inadequate to help the LDCs and a new economic order is called for both internationally (to help the LDCs) and nationally, chiefly via protection and industrialization.

The applicability of the trade theory to the problems of LDCs has already been questioned during the fifties (Myrdal, 1956). Indeed, it has been suggested that the strict adherence to the doctrine of Ricardian comparative cost theory would imply specialization in the production of primary goods by the LDCs, and this would eventually lead to a transfer of the gains of technical progress from the LDCs to the DCs (Prebisch, 1959). Chenery (1961) points out that growth theories in LDCs do not usually accomodate the principles of comparative advantage. Trade is not relied upon as a method to optimize productivity since the premises upon which the traditional trade theory (i.e. Ricardo and Hecksher–Ohlin models) rests have little relevance to the realities of the economics in LDCs. This is so because: (a) in LDCs the real social opportunity costs of factors are not given by the market prices of the different factors in view of market imperfections; (b) externalities and scale economies could be significant; (c) the supply of inputs and their nature could alter between different time periods; and (d) the demand of the buyers and the producers could be significantly influenced because of the nature of complementarities between different goods.

These distortions in LDCs, some of which have already been explained, create a divergence between money costs of factors and their real social opportunity costs, and since the LDCs trade on the basis of prices set by the distorted money costs rather than by the real social opportunity costs, the optimum rate of return from trade is likely to be lower. It is in the light of these considerations, plus the argument that the demand for exports from the LDCs is both price and income-realistic, that we will consider the basic points in the Prebisch thesis.

The Prebisch thesis

Prebisch has envisaged a global model with a developed centre and a backward periphery. Technical progress in the DCs has resulted in improved income for their labourers, an improved standard of living and a high price for their goods, some of which are exported to the periphery, i.e. the LDCs. But such technical progress in the LDCs has not raised wages of their workers. Indeed, prices have gone down and the prices of their exportables *vis-à-vis* their imports from exportables have decreased as the TT have moved against the LDCs. In other words, the fruits of technical progress have been transferred from the LDCs to the DCs. To alter the situation, Prebisch advocates industrialization via protection and import substitution.

Prebisch tries to explain such an adverse movement of the TT against the LDCs with the help of the following reasons. First, the trades unions in the DCs are more capable of raising wages for their workers than the trades unions in the LDCs which are frequently very weak. Second, the increase in population in the LDCs and the consequent rise in the labour supply has been absorbed mainly in those sectors where the labour productivity is quite low and this has also resulted in a lower level of real wages. Next, in the LDCs, given a low income-elasticity of demand for the exports of the LDCs and a high income-elasticity for the exports of DCs in the LDCs, with growth in both the DCs and LDCs, it is likely that the LDCs will run into severe balance of payments deficit as their exports will tend to fall behind their imports. One way that has been suggested to overcome the problem is to reduce export prices, but here the danger is that given price inelasticity of the demand for their exports which consist mainly of primary goods, the total earnings of the LDCs are likely to fall. Prebisch suggests that the "rational" policy for the LDCs would be industrialization and import substitution.

Prebisch adds that the LDCs generally suffer from significant price fluctuations in the export earnings and the impact of such "instabilities" is very damaging to growth and investment of the LDCs. Here again, the proper policy for the LDCs would be to diversify their economies in the line of industrialization.

An evaluation of the Prebisch thesis

The Prebisch thesis has been questioned both on empirical and theoretical grounds. First, it may be argued that although the UNCTAD study between 1950 and 1961 has shown a relative decline of TT for the LDCs, *vis-à-vis* the DCs, the choice of the base period (1950) is questionable as it was the boom year for primary goods because of the Korean war. On the basis of long-term information, Lipsey (1963) has shown that the TT have actually moved in favour of the LDCs *vis-à-vis* the USA and Europe. But during the same period, starting with the last quarter of the nineteenth century, the TT have moved against the LDCs *vis-à-vis* the UK. However, Lipsey's conclusion about the movement of the TT in favour of the LDCs as opposed to Europe has been contradicted in the findings of Kindleberger (1956). Note that the discussions about the TT are inconclusive one way or the other since the results crucially depend upon the base period and the nature of the index.

At the theoretical level, it has been argued that Prebisch's notion that the gains from technical progress should be distributed globally, independent of the countries of their origin, is of doubtful validity because if such distribution of gains means equalization of global real wages, then the realities of the present world (e.g. externalities, monopolies, economic and non-economic trade barriers) which rule out factor–price equalization will also rule out any such global equalization of real wages (June–Flanders, 1964). Also gains from technical progress could emerge from the expenditure on research and development (R & D) and such gains are not for free global distribution. The value judgement about their equal distribution has also been questioned.

8.12 Export instability and economic growth in LDCs

During the fifties and the early sixties, instability in the export earnings of the LDCs has been considerably highlighted. The reasons for such instability are supposed to be:

(*a*) the nature of exports of LDCs;
(*b*) low price and income-elasticity of the demand for their products;
(*c*) specialization in the production of only a few commodities, i.e. commodity concentration of exports;
(*d*) large proportion of exports only to a few markets which usually followed the pattern of colonial trade, i.e. market or geographic concentration. It has been argued that such instabilities have serious adverse effects on growth, investment, balance of payments and planning in the LDCs. Policies were recommended to iron out such instabilities to help the LDCs in attaining higher growth (UN, 1962).

During the sixties, some of the above hypotheses were tested to find out their empirical validity. Most of these empirical studies have cast considerable doubt about the validity of the above hypotheses. Thus, Coppock (1962) by using a log-variance index of instability (which comprises the dispersions from the trend line given by the first and last observations and thus makes it vulnerable to the specific period chosen for research) for exports of eighty-three countries between 1946 and 1958, has found that export instability was mainly correlated with price, terms of trade, volume of exports and imports. However, the statistical significance of these variables has not been mentioned. The interesting aspect in Coppock's findings is that export instability was *negatively* related with *geographic* concentration (as given by the Hirschman index, i.e. square root of the sum of the squares of the percentage shares in given goods), was positive but very poor. However, Michaely's (1962) study of thirty-six countries for the period between 1948 and 1958 shows *positive* and statistically significant association between commodity concentration and export *price* instability. It is noteworthy that Michaely has tried to explain changes in *export prices* rather than *export earnings*. On the other hand, for about the same period for the same number of countries, Massell (1964) has failed to discover a significant relationship between instability and commodity concentration and geographic concentration. Further, by using the data of Coppock and Michaely, MacBean (1966) shows the absence of a significant difference between the levels of instability in export earnings for DCs and LDCs. MacBean then uses the indices of geographic and commodity concentration as well as the proportion of primary exports to total exports to account for the divergences in instability among different countries. His conclusion is: "... such theoretically proposed general factors as specialization in primary products or commodity concentration *per se* may have some slight instability, but their explanatory value in particular cases is very small." (MacBean, 1966, p. 56). This view is also supported by Kingston (1976).

MacBean's study has, however, been questioned by others (e.g. Sundrum, 1967). When differences in time horizons are considered, (i.e. 1946–58 and 1954–66), the divergences in the levels of instability tended to increase (Erb and Schiavo-Campo, 1969). Massell (1970) has found that the different levels of instability have been strongly influenced by the index of commodity concentration. Also, he observes that there is "slight suggestion that LDCs tend to experience greater instability than DCs net of other explanatory variables" (Massell, 1970, p. 628).

As regards the effects of instability on growth and investment, empirical evidence tends to refute the view that such effects are *always* damaging to the LDCs (see e.g. MacBean, 1966; Knudsen and Parnes, 1975). Indeed, MacBean's study suggests that instability has a positive and significant effect on the rate of growth of investment. However, from MacBean's study, it does not follow that instability in export earnings has no detrimental effects on the LDCs. On the other hand, by using the normalized variance of transitory income – à là Friedman – Knudsen and Parnes (1975) have shown that the increased instability reduces the propensity to consume and thus, raises savings, investment and growth of the economy. But the same study has also shown that an increase in commodity concentration results in increased instability with the implication that the decline in such concentration will reduce instability. This is similar to the view (Massell, 1970, p. 629) that product concentration results in instability of exports. The study by Knudsen and Parnes (1975) should, however, be accepted with caution as the predictive power of their model is rather low.

On balance, empirical evidence available so far does not entirely rule out the relationship between instability and commodity concentration. But the adverse impact of such instability on the level of investment and growth of the LDCs has been doubted. Interestingly, despite the empirical findings most writers on the subject went on to suggest the means to stabilize export earnings of the LDCs because it has been gradually acknowledged that a sharp fall in export earnings in some period may produce such a random shock to the economy which it may fail to absorb; thus severe balance of payments problems could mean inability to import not only capital goods but also food items in a period of harvest failure, accentuation of large-scale unemployment, particularly in labour-surplus economies, mass starvation and death, and the failure of planned economic growth. With these observations, it is now possible to turn attention to the different proposals which are put forward by UNCTAD and others to stabilize export earnings in the LDCs

8.13 The role of the United Nations Conference on Trade and Development (UNCTAD) and some of the trade policies to help LDCs

The role of UNCTAD to protect and champion the case for the LDCs as against the trades policies of the DCs has become increasingly prominent. Thus the UNCTAD meeting in 1964 specifically called for ironing out of the commodity price oscillations via commodity agreements, to reduce the non-tariff barriers such as quotas by the DCs, to castigate the "most favoured nation" clause and to give general preference to imports, particularly of manufactured goods from the LDCs. It is clear from this list of demands that UNCTAD is chiefly interested to protect the "infant" industries in the LDCs and to promote their exports.

As regards the commodity agreement scheme, it has been observed that in theory the scheme is not likely to be effective because, should prices be raised, supply usually overtakes demand and it is very difficult to avoid a decline in prices. Also, the type of income transfer that it involves from the consumers of the DCs to the LDCs does not imply an optimal distribution of the burden of higher prices (Staley, 1970).

It can be pointed out that a more efficient transfer of income from the DCs to the LDCs could be achieved by imposing direct taxes in the DCs rather than by increasing commodity prices.

However, one of the important factors to account for a low world demand for the primary goods from the LDCs is the high level of protection given to agriculture in some DCs. For example, the United States has offered considerable protection to her agriculture via a system of import quotas. The European Economic Community (EEC), by following a Common Agricultural Policy (CAP) keeps the prices of agricultural goods artificially high (despite the rise of butter or beef mountains from time to time) within the Community by imposing "variable levies" on imports. Such policies obviously discriminate against the exports of agricultural goods from the LDCs. Nor are these the best policies to help agriculture of the DCs (Colman and McInerney, 1975) chiefly because an artificially higher level of prices (compared with the world market prices) will involve considerable loss of consumers' surplus. Also, if the high prices are paid for running the *buffer-stock* scheme, there is no guarantee that such costs would be recovered from future sales. Further, income subsidies could be offered to the farmers in DCs. However, in the 1975 Lomé Convention, it has been decided that the system of subsidies within the EEC via import levies should be modified.

Several Commodity Agreement Schemes (CAS) have been concluded in the last twenty years, chiefly to guard against the short-run oscillations in commodity prices, e.g. sugar, coffee, tin and wheat. From the consumers' point of view, it was expected that such agreements would help to maintain adequate supply at reasonable prices. However, quite a few of these schemes have failed to work successfully. Thus, the high rise in coffee prices since 1973 to 1977 has caused major concern among the importing countries and the agreement is in danger of falling apart. Again, in the case of International Wheat Agreement (1971), the council has avoided the issues related to prices. Since many LDCs are net importers of wheat, the advantages of this agreement from their point of view is understandable, given the ready availability of wheat. But such a scheme also leads to a loss of incentive for producing wheat in the LDCs because of limits on prices.

In the case of the International Tin Agreement (1971), a buffer-stock has been set up and a maximum and a minimum price is laid down. This scheme has the advantage of smoothing out short-run price changes without altering the effects of long-run demand and supply. On the other hand, as has been argued before, buffer-stock schemes are criticized as inefficient on the grounds of loss of consumers surplus and an increase in the cost of operations.

One of the main changes that the CAS face is the growth of the synthetics in the DCs. Thus, although the price of Tanzanian sisal has been increased through negotiations, the scheme has failed to help Tanzania because synthetic substitutes for sisal are now being supplied in increasing quantities (Singer and Ansari, 1977). One of the reasons why the Organization for Petroleum Exporting Countries (OPEC) has achieved a very significant increase in its export earnings from the huge increases in oil prices since 1973 is that the demand for oil is very inelastic and the substitutes are very few, at least in the short-run. Thus, provided that the agreements reached within the cartels of the oil-producing countries hold, export earnings could be significantly increased. However, for the primary exports of most LDCs, substitutes are available. Nor do all the primary producing countries have the political will to unite together.

The problem of eliminating major changes in the export earnings of the LDCs has once again been highlighted in the UNCTAD Conference of 1976 at Nairobi. More specifically, it calls for: (1) the setting-up of an international buffer-stock of commodities; (2) the creation of a common fund for financing the stock; (3) a method of multilateral assurances on individual goods; (4) an expansion of the transfer of technology from the DCs to the LDCs; (5) promotion of exports from the LDCs; and (6) debt relief.

The points raised in the UNCTAD (1976) Conference are not novel and differences of opinion persist among economists about the effectiveness and desirability of the CAS and the buffer-stock schemes. More attention is now being paid to the Compensatory Financing Schemes (CFS), some of which were proposed in the fifties. In some of these schemes, the exporters are compensated against any divergence from the trend lines of price or output which are mutually accepted between the exporting and the importing countries. The advantage of the CFS over the CAS is that it does not interfere in the activities of the market. In practice, it has been observed that for deriving the gains from the CFS, the exporting country has reduced the volume of production (Singer and Ansari, 1977). Another form of CFS proposed by the IMF (1966) requires that should a country's earnings be less than its mean earning for two years, the country would be entitled to draw up to 25 per cent of its quota with the IMF. This amount of drawing was later raised to 50 per cent. But the scheme did not find much favour with the LDCs since the possibility of ordinary drawings could be adversely affected because of the drawing under CFS. Also, the LDCs have suspected that the IMF would get greater power to meddle with the national economic matters.

In the Lomé Convention (1975), agreements were reached between the forty-six LDCs, mostly from the Caribbean, African and Pacific regions, to include several commodities like cocoa and coffee, bananas, tea, wood products, sisal, palm products, iron ore, etc. and for the importing countries to offer to the producers a fixed sum of earnings subject to the proviso that the individual export forms only a small percentage of the whole export income of the exporting country. It is hoped that the scheme will help to stabilize export earnings of the LDCs. However, LDCs like India, Pakistan, Bangladesh and Sri Lanka are not represented as full members of the Lomé Convention and since these countries account for a very large proportion of the population in LDCs, CFS envisaged in the Convention of Lomé would be inadequate and partial.

Another method to help the LDCs in stabilizing export income is the Supplementary Financing Scheme (SFS) innovated by the International Bank for Reconstruction and Development (IBRD or World Bank) in 1964. Under this scheme, if the actual export earnings are less than the projected earnings of the LDCs then it would be entitled to obtain supplementary finance to bridge the deficit. But the administration of the SFS posed considerable problems. Moreover, doubts were raised about the validity of the projected earnings by the LDCs. However, after the oil-price rise of 1973, some of the LDCs were most seriously affected (MSA) and in 1975–76, the IBRD took special steps to offer SFS to the MSA poor countries.

8.14 Non-tariff barriers, generalized system of preferences (GSP) and trading blocks

Given the nature and level of protection offered to the primary and manufacturing sectors in the DCs through tariff as well as non-tariff barriers like quotas (Balassa, 1972), it has long been pointed out that the LDCs would be able to increase their export earnings by the gradual removal of such restrictions. According to the General Agreement on Tariff and Trade (GATT), such barriers could be removed on a reciprocal basis. In other words, both DCs and LDCs would be required to dismantle the protectionist policies. However, it was increasingly recognized that the removal of such restrictions would be much more harmful to the LDCs in comparison with the DCs and by the beginning of the seventies, non-reciprocal agreement was reached under which DCs should remove or lower the barriers that the LDCs would not be required to reciprocate. Similarly, under GSP, preferences would be given for certain exports such as textiles and leathers from the LDCs which would be subject to a lower level of tariffs. The GSP scheme holds considerable hope for the future as it is flexible and subject to negotiation without significant detrimental effects on the DCs. For an industry like textiles in the DCs, the process of adjustment could be gradual and at the same time allocation could be more efficient by switching resources from the declining to the developing sectors. Further, to tide over the difficulties during the adjustment period, adjustment assistance could be offered. Indeed, in the United States such an act was introduced in 1962 to offer direct financial help to those industries and labourers who were adversely affected. In the UK similar steps were taken by the Act of 1959 in the field of the cotton industry.

The absorption of the resources made abundant in the process of adjustment in the DCs should not pose great difficulties so long as their rate of economic growth is reasonable. However, to tide over the problems of resource mobility within the economy, fiscal and monetary policies (e.g. taxes, grants, subsidies, low interest rates) could be effectively used.[2]

8.15 Regional cooperation among LDCs

The possibility of regional cooperation among the LDCs has been regarded as an alternative method for trade creation. The advocates of this scheme argue that such an integration among the LDCs would:

(*a*) expand the market;
(*b*) enable them to enjoy the benefits of the economies of scale;
(*c*) reduce the dependence of the LDCs on the DCs.

It is known that the creation of such trading blocks is based on the theory and practice of Customs Union among the different developed countries. The benefits of integration usually depend on the fulfilment of certain major conditions. For instance:

(*a*) the member countries should mutually reduce the tariff and non-tariff barriers;

(*b*) there should be greater harmonization of monetary and fiscal policies;
(*c*) the degree of trade between the member countries should be substantial, i.e. integration should increase the pro-trade bias given the complementarity in the production process among the member countries;
(*d*) the countries within the trading block should follow a common external policy against the "rest of the world" particularly with regard to tariffs;
(*e*) the degree of trade dependence of the member countries on the rest of the world should not be very significant;
(*f*) the political will to unite.

Given the above conditions it is easy to see why the regional integration among the LDCs is unlikely to be very successful. It is pointed out that "more than 75 per cent of the LDCs' exports are to the rich countries and imports from the developed world into the LDCs are an even larger proportion of the LDCs' total imports" (Singer and Ansari, 1977). The experience of the Latin American Free Trade Association (LAFTA) since its inception in 1961 has shown that the success of the integration scheme has been limited chiefly because of lack of complementary nature in trade and production as well as defective organization and administration. The gains in industrial production in the LAFTA have been very moderate. Similarly, the East African Community (EAC) consisting of Kenya, Uganda and Tanzania has confronted similar problems since its inception in 1967. Distribution of gains remains a bone of contention and political rivalry among these countries has been the cause of much concern despite some progress towards achieving a higher level of inter-regional trade. By 1977, trading blocks like the Association of South-East Asian Nations (ASEAN), the Asian and Pacific Council (ASPAC), and Central American Common Market (CACM) have come into existence. None of these trading blocks proved to be a great success given the low and oscillating level of trade among them. However, one of the major reasons for setting up such trading blocks is political. Regional co-ordination among the LDCs is supposed to provide them with a greater bargaining power in their economic and political relationships with the DCs.

8.16 Conclusion

Trade policies in the LDCs, despite making some gains in industrialization and import substitution, have also caused some of their welfare-loss in terms of negative value-added at world prices in some of their industries. The ERP has remained quite high in many cases and the policy has promoted monopoly rather than competition and inefficiency in many sectors. Exports of agricultural goods suffered and the policy of export promotion, until very recently, has generally been neglected. The trade policies used to correct domestic distortions are open to question. The problem of instability in export earnings and its effect on growth and investment is also doubted on empirical grounds though the relationship between commodity concentration and export instability cannot be ruled out. However, such instability could stem from both world demand and domestic supply (for climatic and other reasons). Policies to stabilize export earnings such as regional integration or CAS do not hold much hope for the future of the LDCs. However, in schemes like the GSP, multilateral agreements, inter-governmental negotiations, expansion of domestic production, particularly of agriculture, and export promotion lie the best hope for the LDCs. The policy of protection needs to be followed selectively in those cases where the benefits outweigh the losses.

Notes

1. Dynamic externalities refer to the creation of some capital assets over time, for the use of which, firms in future will not be required to pay. Instances like the establishment of educational institutions or the development of transport facilities can easily be cited.
2. Some writers have recently argued that significant "most favoured nation" (MFN) tariff cuts would provide the LDCs with more favourable access to world markets for unlimited trade volumes, as they cover more commodities and countries in comparison with the GSP, and hence MFN tariff cuts should be referred to the GSP (see Baldwin and Murray, 1977; see also Grubel, 1977).

Appendix

Indices of instability of exports

The index of instability in the exports of LDCs can be constructed in different ways and this could account for the differences in the results obtained. The main indices constructed so far can be summarized as follows:

(a) *Index used by the International Monetary Fund* (IMF)

IMF_I seeks to measure the divergences from a three-year weighted average of last year's income from exports, the distribution of weights being given as

$$X_t^* = 0.5\,X_t + 0.25\,X_{t-1} + 0.25\,X_{t-2}$$

where X_t = actual income from exports at period t

and X_t^* = expected income from exports

(b) *Index used by the United Nations* (*1952*) (UN_I)

UN_I measures the sum of absolute divergences of income from exports per annum as a proportion of the higher of the two yearly incomes from exports. Notice that UN_I fails to isolate the trends.

(c) *Index constructed on the basis of moving average method* (MA_I)

MA_I seeks to measure fluctuations as the sum of the absolute divergences of yearly income from exports from the moving average for n number of years where the value of n is subjectively chosen by the researcher. The value of n should be given by the theory that is applied as it influences the removal of fluctuations and difficulties could easily arise here, particularly in a cross-country analysis.

(d) *Percentage divergences of the average from the trend line observed by fitting the least square method* (A_I)

A_I consists of the derivation of the trend line first by fitting the least square method and then to observe the average percentage divergences from such a trend line.

(e) *Index of divergences from the linear least square line* (LLS_I)

LLS_I comprises the additions of the squared divergences from a trend line which is linear and obtained by minimizing the additions of squared residual elements.

(f) *Index of divergences from the exponential least square line* (ELS_I)

ELS_I comprises the additions of the squared divergences from a trend line which is exponential and obtained as in (e).

(g) *Log-variance index of Coppock* (LVC_I)

LVC_I comprises the divergences from a trend line given by the first and last period of the sample. Note that LVC_I would be susceptible to the base period (Knudsen and Parnes, 1975). Thus,

$$LVC_I = \text{antilog}\left[\frac{1}{n-1}\sum_{t=1}^{n-1}\left(\log\frac{V_{t+1}}{V_t} - r\right)^2\right]^{1/2}$$

$$\text{and} \quad r = \frac{1}{n-1}\sum_{t=1}^{n-1}\log\frac{V_{t+1}}{V_t}$$

$$\text{or} \quad r = \frac{1}{n-1}(\log V_n - \log V_1)$$

(h) *Transitory income index of Knudsen and Parnes (1975)* (TKP_I)

TKP_I consists of the normalized variance of the transitory part of income. Notice the Friedmanian approach and its attendant comments.

Let $C_t^* = K_y Y_t^* + K_x X_t^*$

where C_t^* = permanent consumption

Y_t = actual domestic income

Y_t^* = permanent domestic income

X_t = actual income from exports

X_t^* = permanent income from exports

K_y = propensity to consume out of Y_t^*

K_x = propensity to consume out of X_t^*

Let the index of export instability in transitory income be (I_x)

where $I_X = \sum_{t=1}^{T} \frac{(X_t - X_t^*)^2}{(X_t^*)^2}$

Let the index of domestic instability in transitory income (I_Y) be

$$I_Y = \sum_{t=1}^{T} \frac{(Y_t - Y_t^*)^2}{(Y_t^*)^2}$$

9

Foreign resources and economic development

9.1 Introduction

Foreign resources have played an important role in the economic development of many economically advanced countries of today. For example, between 1870 and 1914 the ratio of capital inflow to gross domestic capital formation was about 40 per cent in Canada. The same ratio for Australia was about 37 per cent between 1861 and 1900, and for Norway it was 29 per cent between 1885 and 1914, and 31 per cent between 1920 and 1929 (Hagen, 1975). Even in countries like Japan and the USA, where such ratios were lower during their early stages of economic development, foreign capital played a significant role. The LDCs of today are more or less in the same stage of economic development as the DCs used to occupy in the eighteenth and nineteenth centuries. It is generally contended that foreign resources could play a vital role in promoting economic development in the LDCs. This is explained in terms of concepts such as "the savings gap" and "the foreign exchange gap". But at the outset it is necessary to clarify certain key terms in the definition of foreign resources.

9.2 The concept of foreign resources (FR)

The flow of foreign resources (FR) can be of many types and it is important to know the different elements. First, there are institutions (e.g. OXFAM, War on Want, etc.) which provide *grants* to many countries to alleviate the after-effects of a natural disaster such as famine, flood or earthquakes. Such grants need not be repaid by the recipient countries, nor do they carry any interest charges. Indeed, grants are genuine "aids" but they usually form a tiny fraction of the total inflow of FR. Second, some *loans* are given, chiefly by the international lending agencies (e.g. the World Bank) at interest rates which are lower than those in the market. Here the foreign resources are provided on "soft" terms which reflect a desire to "aid" the receiving countries. Where the loans are granted to the LDCs at a concessionary rate for very long periods (say, forty to fifty years), the inflow of FR takes the character of genuine foreign aid as the net present value of FR provided at a concessionary rate and to be repaid fifty years hence would be almost the same as the value of grants.

However, *foreign private investments* in the LDCs are not exactly "foreign aid" as they are made on commercial terms. Foreign private investment usually carries commercial interest rates and does not stem from altruistic motives. Foreign private investment usually forms a significant proportion of the total inflow of FR. *Government lending* could be carried out on a bilateral or multilateral basis. Sometimes, several governments could set up a consortium to provide FR to a country or countries (e.g. Aid-India or Aid-Pakistan Consortium). Such lending could carry commercial terms; but frequently these loans are provided at concessionary rates and they have to be repaid after a long period. Sometimes, grace periods are offered to relieve the burden of debt repayments. It seems clear that *all* FR are not "aid" or charities, some parts of them being international lending on a commercial basis.

9.3 Criteria for distribution FR

Several criteria for allocating FR are discussed in the literature. Some of them could be highlighted here.

First, FR are usually given for *political* reasons. It is generally the case that FR will not be given to one's enemies (Little and Clifford, 1965). A large part of American aid to the LDCs is allocated on the grounds of keeping intact America's political interest as far as possible. Usually it takes the form of giving aid to "friendly" countries. The "friendly" countries are usually those which would help the United States to protect itself against the danger of the spread of Communism. Similarly, a large part of the flow of Soviet FR is motivated by political factors.

Second, FR are supposed to replenish the dearth of domestic saving in the LDCs. Generally, the difference between planned investment (I_p) and planned saving (S_p) is taken as an indication of the FR(F) that are necessary to attain a target rate of economic growth. In other words,

$$F = I_p - S_p$$

Indeed, in many development planning models, a target level of investment is specified to achieve a certain rate of growth of income and then an estimate of planned savings is made. When the planned investment exceeds planned savings the gap is sought to be made up by FR.

In this "savings gap" type of analysis, notice the implicit assumption that all FR would be used for domestic investments. This need not always be true and the point has been made that it is possible to see the coexistence of both a "savings gap" and a "foreign-exchange" or "trade" or "bottleneck" gap where such a gap (say T_g) is given by the difference between imports (M) and exports (X). Thus,

$$T_g = M - X$$

The equilibrium relationship between the "savings gap" and the "trade gap" can be expressed as

$$I_p - S_p = M - X$$

Notice that these two gaps need not be equal *ex-ante*, though *ex-post* they must be equal because of the method of national accounting. Any excess of investment over savings could only be financed by an excess of imports over exports *ex-post*. It is contended that where the trade gap predominates over the savings gap, a supply of FR could have a positive effect on growth and as such FR should be provided after careful estimation of these two gaps (McKinnon, 1964; Chenery and Strout, 1966). A more detailed discussion will be made later.

Third, the other criterion which is sometimes advocated is known as "absorptive capacity" (Rosenstein–Rodan, 1961). There are some difficulties in the actual estimation of "absorptive capacity" as the concept is not usually regarded as very clear. Basically, it means a country's ability to absorb capital and to use it in a productive way. Such "productive" use of capital is measured by positive "reasonable" rates of return on total investment. Obviously, "absorptive capacity" would depend upon the level of income and its growth-rate, supply of skill and the level of average and marginal rates of savings. If the principle of providing FR is to step up the process of capital formation in the LDCs, then such a principle is more likely to be met in those LDCs where the *marginal* rates of savings are much higher than the average. It may be pointed out that the absorptive capacity of an economy depends, *inter alia*, upon the nature of the infrastructure of an economy. An economy with a poor system of transport and communication, managerial skill handicapped further by lack of proper training and educational facilities is likely to have a low absorptive capacity.

Some rough indices to measure absorptive capacity have been proposed (Rosenstein–Rodan, 1961). None of them is free of subjective bias in its construction. One such index is the *rise in the volume of investment* in the last five or more years. The second index consists of the measurement of *increases in savings* in the past few years. It is of particular interest to note here the difference between marginal and average rates of savings. The third index is to examine the structure of development and administration of a country. Here the judgement is likely to be subjective. The method of finding out the necessary FR can then be stated as follows (see Rosenstein–Rodan, 1961, for details):

$$FR = (ky - s)\sum Y + 5Y_0(s - S_0|Y_0) \qquad [9.1]$$

where FR = required foreign resources
k = capital–output ratio
Y = national income
y = growth rate of Y
s = marginal rate of savings
$S_0|Y_0$ = average rate of savings
S = total savings
S_0 = Initial total savings.

To examine the degree of responsiveness of FR to the parameters mentioned above we differentiate to obtain the following:

$$\frac{\partial FR}{\partial k} = y \sum Y \qquad [9.2]$$

$$\frac{\partial FR}{\partial s} = -\sum Y + 5\, Y_0 \qquad [9.3]$$

$$\frac{\partial FR}{\partial (S_0/Y_0)} = -5\, Y_0 \qquad [9.4]$$

Now the increase in national income, Y, is given by

$$\sum_0^4 Y_t = Y_0\left(\frac{(1+y)^5 - 1}{y}\right) \qquad [9.5]$$

For a fixed y with given k, ky proportion of Y is needed for investment (I) in each year. Hence we have

$$\sum I_t = ky \sum Y \qquad [9.6]$$

$$\text{Let} \quad S_t = sY_t - c \qquad [9.7]$$

$$\sum S_t = s \sum Y_t - \sum c \qquad [9.8]$$

$$\text{Now} \quad FR = \sum I - \sum S \qquad \text{(and ignoring time or t)} \qquad [9.9]$$

$$= ky \sum Y - s \sum Y + \sum c$$

$$= (ky - s) \sum Y + \sum c \qquad [9.10]$$

Notice that since

$$c = \left(s - \frac{S_0}{Y_0}\right) Y_0,$$

equation [9.10] could be used to obtain equation [9.1]. Notice that this criterion emphasizes that the major aim for allocating FR is to promote "self-sustaining growth" without cross-country comparisons.

Several criticisms have been levelled at the criterion of granting FR according to absorptive capacity. First, if the FR are to be allocated on the basis of past productivity of investment, then the poorest LDCs, who are in greatest need because of population pressure, are likely to get very little as the application of this principle is tantamount to backing the winners. Second, past returns on investment are not always the most reliable indicators of the productivity of investment in future. Third, savings and output–capital ratios are likely to alter during the process of development. Fourth, the application of the principle of absorptive capacity does not make proper allowance for the different pattern of distribution of economic resources in different countries. Finally, if it is argued that the principle of distribution of FR is to raise the absorptive capacity of the LDCs rather than to accept it as given, then again there arises a case to devise certain other principles.

Next, the flow of FR is sometimes guided by historical factors. Much of the FR flowing from France and Britain go to their former colonies. The provision of FR in such cases is sometimes regarded as imperialistic or neo-imperialistic (Hayter, 1971).

The other criterion which is said to have been applied in distributing the FR is the maintenance and promotion of the private sector of the economy. Japan, Germany and the United States have sometimes maintained that resources would be provided in certain LDCs so long as the private sector could be allowed to operate freely. This criterion is really derived from the political and ideological reasons for providing FR.

The "efficiency" criterion for allocating FR has received considerable attention. The system seems to be strikingly simple and important as it upholds the pragmatic view that FR should be distributed on the basis of their most efficient use. In practice, its application is not so simple. First, it is necessary to construct a sound index of efficiency. Second, the principle of achieving maximum efficiency may run counter to the achievement of some other objectives, e.g., maximization of employment or more equality in the distribution of income. Further, as Eckaus contends: "Within any one country one could determine whether resources were being allocated and used efficiently if prices did accurately reflect relative scarcities and goals. The 'if' is a big one, however." (Eckaus, 1970, p. 158) Here, one solution of the problem lies in the application of cost–benefit analysis after making due corrections for distortions in the product and the factor markets. An index of measuring the productivity of FR has been made (Adelman and Morris, 1968). But here the major problem lies in its application to different countries as factor efficiencies are likely to be different in different LDCs.

Sometimes, the principle of *stability*, chiefly in prices and in trade balances, has been regarded as the appropriate condition for allocating FR. Such principle usually finds favour with the international organizations such as the International Monetary Fund (IMF). But this principle is really the application of the doctrine of efficiency at the national level. Notice that the application of this principle implicitly assumes that stability should be given high priority in national development policy.

The above discussion suggests the difficulties which are inherent in finding out an appropriate value-free index to measure the performance of FR on growth and development of the LDCs not only at a point in time, but also over time. Any decision regarding the most desirable direction of development is likely to be subjective. However, these subjective judgements could be stated clearly. A more composite index for measuring the effects of FR on not only saving, investment, capital–output ratios, but also on development in general, could be built. Any conflict between objectives like efficiency and self-help could be minimized if some of the criteria are treated as *constraints* (e.g. maximization of growth-rate subject to a minimum level of consumption and more equal distribution). Also, a clearer picture of the different types of growth paths with FR and their implications regarding inter-temporal saving and consumption for different generations could help to identify the "appropriate" criteria within a country and among different countries. However, the provision of FR without any political or ideological consideration is unlikely to occur in practice.

9.4 Different types of FR: tied and untied; bilateral (BL) and multilateral (ML); project and programme

The allocation of FR can assume different forms. They can be *tied* to the imports from donor countries (i.e. tying by sources); alternatively, their use could be linked to a specific project (i.e. tying by end-use). The reasons for such tying are not difficult to understand from the point of view of the donor country. First, tying helps to increase the exports of the donor countries and protects their income and employment. Notice that such an argument is inconsistent with humanitarian motives for transferring resources. Second, tying of resources by some deficit donor countries may increase pressure in surplus donor countries to similar tying because tying by the deficit countries is supposed to enhance their relative share in the competitive market for exports. Such a phenomenon is regarded as "competitive aid-tying". Third, tying is supposed to result in efficient utilization of resources. Fourth, project tying is supposed to be effective as the projects could be identified easily. Also, such tying is expected to enhance the reputation of the donor countries. Fifth, when resources are tied both by sources and by uses, then it creates a monopolistic situation in favour of the donor country which it can easily exploit.

It is easy to see from the above-mentioned reasons why tying of resources has created so much resentment among the recipient countries. First, tying does not help the recipient countries to obtain resources at the cheapest prices. In many instances, prices paid by the LDCs are much above their world prices (Haq, 1965). Second, tying will not necessarily improve the balance of payments of the donor country if the cause of such deficit is an excess demand for resources. Third, the objective of tying resources will be defeated if a recipient country decides to spend on goods and services of the donor country from its total reserves of foreign earnings, a fraction which is greater than or equal to the value of tied resources (Bhagwati, 1970). Fourth, resources may be tied to the construction of a specific project which does not satisfy the objective of the national plan. Fifth, in the event of a double-tying (i.e. both by source and by end-use), monopolistic position of the lender may result in a situation which could be less than optimal from the point of view of the recipient country. Sixth, costs of tying of resources have been regarded as considerable for some LDCs (Bhagwati, 1970). Seventh, the informal agreements about servicing over the life of the capital projects as well as some indirect costs of tying (e.g. carrying the cargo in the ship of the donor country which charges a higher than international price for freight) may well reduce the true value of the tied FR.

In view of the harmful effects of tying FR, some proposals have been made to untie them. First, all resources should be untied as to their source.

The difficulty in implementing this proposal from the point of view of the country which provides FR to the LDCs and at the same time suffers from a balance of payments deficit is understandable if tying has an important balance of payments effect. Second, should the volume of international liquidity be raised to improve the balance of payments position of a deficit country transferring resources to the LDCs, then the task of untying would be less difficult. Third, greater co-ordination among the donor countries is necessary for untying FR. Fourth, double-tying should be avoided whenever possible as it is likely to maximize monopoly gains of the donor countries. Fifth, the LDCs should try to promote international tendering of projects to find out roughly the competitive or world price. It is observed that the excess costs imposed on some LDCs were about 50 per cent when such costs are measured by the ratio of the difference between the highest bid price and successful bid price (Haq, 1965). Finally, the donor country could treat such excess cost on the recipient country as an export subsidy rather than a transfer of resources. However, in the absence of a concerted effort among the economically advanced countries, the prospect of untying of FR does not seem very bright, particularly after the oil crisis of 1973, when many industrialized countries went into a recession between 1974 and 1976 and faced considerable balance of payments deficits.

9.5 Foreign resources for projects or plans

Sometimes FR are given to a particular project or projects in LDCs. The point has been made that such FR may fail to promote the basic objective of the national plan and hence it is necessary to work at the problem of financing the plan rather than the projects. It is clear that such a problem could only arise if the aim in the national plans is different from the one in the project. But to the extent projects included in the plan are so selected as to achieve some national objectives, the problem of financing the plan or the project disappears and the possibility of switching arises.

Donor countries may reveal their preference for financing the projects rather than the plans if the national plans are likely to be revised suddenly with frequent changes in the government (Singer, 1965). Second, if the resources given by the donor country form a small proportion of planned investment, project financing could be considered as more attractive than the financing of the plan. Third, projects are easily identifiable from the point of view of the donor country. Fourth, financing of marginal projects (e.g. projects which might not have been included in the plan without FR) by FR has some advantages.

Financing of the plan has the advantage of generating greater effort in the recipient country. Second, it could improve the relationship between the lending and the borrowing country which is certainly an important goal of supplying resources. Third, plans are supposed to achieve the overall development of a country and their financing is regarded as preferable by some of the recipient countries. However, since there are now very few countries which would allow projects to be set up without analysing their impact on the national plan, the discussion of project versus plan financing seems rather academic. More important, however, is the discussion of the relative advantages and disadvantages of bilateral (BL) and multilateral (ML) financing to which we now turn.

9.6 Bilateral (BL) and multilateral (ML) financing

The bilateral flow of FR is usually advocated on the following grounds:

1. BL financing could be tied while a large part of ML financing is untied.
2. The donor country can keep "operational control" with less difficulty in the case of BL financing.
3. Effective utilization of FR is more likely to take place if financing is BL rather than ML.
4. Politically, the BL rather than the ML financing is more likely to be acceptable to the electorate.

Notice that the advantages from the standpoint of the donor country are not always so from the point of view of the recipient country. The major criticisms levelled at BL financing can be summarized as follows:

1. BL financing is generally used to extend the political influence over the LDCs; it is regarded as an instrument for "buying" friends.
2. BL financing is not always meant for the economic development of a country because more often than not, "strings" are attached to it.
3. Even without the "strings", BL financing is regarded as morally indefensible since "extended in the wrong way, generosity can be perceived by its intended beneficiary as insulting and contemptuous. The problem of BL financing is psychological and political rather than managerial" (Fulbright, 1966).

Despite these criticisms of BL financing, it is difficult to switch over from BL to ML financing. For one thing, such a switch is likely to reduce the supply of FR simply because many donors, while supplying resources like to exercise some leverage over their use. Such leverage is unlikely to be strong if financing is ML. For another, sometimes BL flows take place on grounds of moral responsibility (e.g. between the donors and their ex-colonies). However, BL and ML financing has the advantage of increasing the total volume of FR. Also, ML financing, properly co-ordinated, could discard the inefficiencies in the use of resources. Further, the problem of debt-servicing, which is worrying many LDCs, particularly after the oil crisis of 1973, can be better tackled if financing is ML rather than BL. It is, however, pointed out that ML financing is unlikely to be optimum because of several reasons (Balogh, 1967). First, there is absence of co-ordination among different donors and between donors and recipient countries. Second, absence of skilled manpower may aggravate the problem. Third, the decentralized and democratic controls of the present institutions are not always exercised. But these arguments are not very compelling in the sense that instead of forming a case against ML financing as such, they could be directed towards rehabilitating the different agencies engaged in ML financing. The formation of a single agency could avoid many of these criticisms. On the other hand, the creation of a single agency has its own problems. For instance, donors may be less willing to contribute to a single international agency and this could reduce the flow of FR. Also, there are many practical difficulties in the operation of a single monolithic agency. One of the compromises could be the BL resource transfer within the ML framework (Rosenstein–Rodan, 1968).

Under this "consortia" approach, an international agency can be set up for consultation and co-ordination of the transfer of FR to LDCs. Donor countries may be allowed to transfer FR bilaterally but according to certain principles which are agreed upon internationally within the "consortia". A group of highly skilled people within the "consortia" could try to overcome the problems of proper evaluation of the projects.

However, multilateralization of BL flows of FR has its drawbacks. The major point to note is that if donor countries agree upon certain international principles for transfer of FR, then they are no longer willing to exercise their own controls over the flow of resources. But this is the real point in sticking to BL transfers. If, on the contrary, the international agency fails to discard the "strings" attached to BL flows, then one could easily raise doubts about having such an agency in the first place.

The ML agencies have gained considerable support because of their activities in the field of debt-servicing, granting of long-term loans with low interest rates and easy terms of repayments (Pearson, 1969). It is argued that they try to apply rational economic criteria as far as possible in effecting the flow of FR. All this is commendable. However, it must be mentioned that the voting power within the international ML agencies is closely related to the contributions of the rich nations to the ML agencies. Some of the practices of the World Bank in Latin America have greatly reduced its credibility as a neutral agency (Hayter, 1971). Here is a case to apply the principles of some agencies of the United Nations who try to maintain a more neutral character.

The above discussion is carried out under the implicit assumption that FR play an important role in the process of economic development. Such a role will now be examined in detail within the framework of the "dual-gap" analysis.

9.7 Dual-gap analysis and its evaluation

The "dual-gap" consists of two parts: (a) the savings gap: investment – savings (i.e. I – S); and (b) the trade gap or the difference between imports (M) and exports (X), (i.e. M – X). In national income accounting, *ex-post*, the two gaps must be identical though *ex-ante* they need not be so. Notice that the two gaps cannot be added together. The algebraic representation of the dual-gap analysis could be described following the analysis of Chenery and Strout (1966) and Maizels (1968).

$$C + I + X \equiv Y + M \qquad [9.11]$$

$$C + S \equiv Y \qquad [9.12]$$

$$S + F \equiv I \qquad [9.13]$$

$$M \equiv X + FR \qquad [9.14]$$

where

C = consumption
I = investment
X = exports
Y = gross domestic product
M = imports
S = savings
FR = current account balance of payments or net inflow of foreign resources

Notice that the first three are independent identities and the fourth equation can be determined when the three others are given. Since there are seven variables, four more equations should be added to three independent identities to make the system determinate. Thus, the following five structural equations are suggested of which only four work at any particular period of economic growth.

So we have

$$Y'_t = Y_0(1 + g')^t \qquad [9.15]$$

where Y'_t = target gross domestic product at the target year t
Y_0 = gross domestic product at the initial year 0
g' = target growth-rate

Planned investment (I'_t) is given by

$$I'_t = kg'Y'_t \qquad [9.16]$$

where k = incremental capital–output ratio.

Exports in the year t are given by

$$X_t = X_0(1 + x)^t \qquad [9.17]$$

where x = growth rate of exports which is regarded as exogenous or given.

Planned savings (S'_t) would be equal to

$$S'_t = s_0 + s'_1 Y'_t \qquad [9.18]$$

where s'_1 = planned marginal propensity to save.

Similarly, planned minimum imports (M'_t) to sustain Y'_t would be given

by $$M'_t = m_0 + m'_1 Y'_t \qquad [9.19]$$

where m'_1 = marginal "necessity" to import.

When planned investment is greater than planned savings, i.e. $I' - S'$, the savings gap exists; when planned imports are greater than planned exports, i.e. $M' - X$, a trade gap exists. The two gaps need not be equal *ex-ante* except by chance. Usually, one of the gaps would be greater than the other. Notice that when the trade gap exceeds the savings gap the last equation, i.e. [9.19], operates, but not equation [9.18]; contrariwise, when the savings gap exceeds the trade gap, equation [9.18] works, but not the last equation [9.19].

The basic solution of the Chenery and Strout model in the absence of any skill constraint has been well summarized in Maizels (1968) and this is illustrated in Table 9.1.

Table 9.1 Solution of Chenery–Strout model without skill constraint

Variables	*Trade limited growth*	*Savings limited growth*	
Y'_t	$Y_0(1+g')^t$	$Y_0(1+g')^t$	[9.20]
I'_t	$kg'Y'_t$	$kg'Y'_t$	[9.21]
S'_t	$(kg'-m'_1)Y'_t+X_t-m_0$	$s_0+s'_1Y'_t$	[9.22]
X_t	$X_0(1+x)^t$	$X_0(1+x)^t$	[9.23]
$M_t \mid M'_t$	$m_0+m'_1Y_t$	$(kg'-s'_1)Y'_t+X_t-s_0$	[9.24]
C_t	$(k-kg'+m'_1)Y'_t-X_t+m_0$	$(1-s'_1)Y'_t-s_0$	[9.25]
FR_t	$m'_1Y'_t+m_0-X_t$	$(kg'-s'_1)Y'_t-s_0$	[9.26]

Source: Maizels, A. (1968).

To find out the relationship between the target growth-rate g′ and foreign resources (FR) the following approximations could be used.

$$(1+g')^t = 1+g't \qquad [9.27]$$

$$(1+x)^t = 1+xt \qquad [9.28]$$

To find out the net inflow of foreign resources in the savings-limited growth path (FR^s_t) we obtain the following equation:

$$FR^s_t = (ktY_0)g'^2 + Y_0(k-s'_1t)g' - (s'_1Y_0+s_0) \qquad [9.29]$$

Differentiating with respect to g′ we obtain:

$$\frac{dFR^s_t}{dg'} = Y_0[k+t(2p-s'_1)] \qquad [9.30]$$

given $p = k'g$ or the necessary ratio of investment to Y. Notice that the model predicts a rise in FR^s_t even when planned propensity to save is equal to the necessary ratio of investment to income, if $s'g < 2p + k|t$.

In the trade-limited phase of growth the net inflow of $FR(FR^T_t)$ is given by the following equation:

$$FR^T_t = (m'_1tY_0)g' + (m_0 + m'_1Y_0 - X_0(1+xt)) \qquad [9.31]$$

Notice that with a fixed x, FR_t^S rises at a rising rate while FR_t^T rises at a fixed rate as g′ rises, given the quadratic form of the equation of FR_t^S.

With given FR_t^T, g′ depends on x

$$\text{or} \quad g' = \left(\frac{X_0}{m_1' Y_0}\right) x + \frac{1}{t}\left(\frac{X_0 + F_t - m_0}{m_1' Y} - 1\right) \qquad [9.32]$$

Some extensions of this basic model have been made. Maizels (1968), for example, tried to use the model by relating savings to exports. The model can be altered if some variables are converted into parameters and vice versa. Further, modification of some of the behaviouristic equations could change the model. Notice that the basic model suggests that when exports grow faster than national income, the trade gap will be smaller with given parameters even when FR get smaller because such FR form only a small fraction of exports. Further, should there be import substitution, minimum import requirement will be smaller over time, and thus in the path of economic growth, savings gap is likely to be the dominant one, although at the outset the trade gap might have been the dominant one.

Evaluation of the dual-gap model

Dual-gap models have been criticized on two grounds. The model is criticized either because of its assumed adjustment mechanism or because of its assumptions which have engendered the idea of two separate types of constraints, or both. It is attempted to meet the first criticism by relaxing the assumption regarding saving and the work of Maizels has been mentioned in this connection. But such modifications do not destroy the existence of the two gaps.

More serious criticism of the dual-gap analysis could be made on the grounds that such a model is based on the assumption that FR cannot be regarded as a substitute for domestic savings (Joshi, V., 1970). Note that to the extent FR are substitutes for domestic savings, only one gap exists. Next, some of the assumptions about fixed savings and capital–output ratios in the dual-gap analysis cease to be valid if FR can alter the composition of output of the recipient country in a manner which would reduce the capital–output ratios. But if the rate of transformation of FR into domestic capital is zero or takes a long time, then, two gaps exist. Figure 9.1 illustrates the problem.

In Fig. 9.1 let TT_1 be the domestic transformation curve – or the "availability envelope" à la Baldwin in an open economy; let the X axis measure consumer goods and let the Y axis denote the capital goods. Let us assume that OC_1 and C_1K_1 are the initial levels of consumption and investment respectively. To increase the rate of growth, suppose the planner has managed to reduce the consumption (and increased saving) to OC_2, but finds it difficult to squeeze the consumption (or raise the savings) any more. This, then, is the "savings constraint" which may be lower than the planned level of investment to achieve a target growth-rate. Optimum welfare in the Paretian

Fig. 9.1

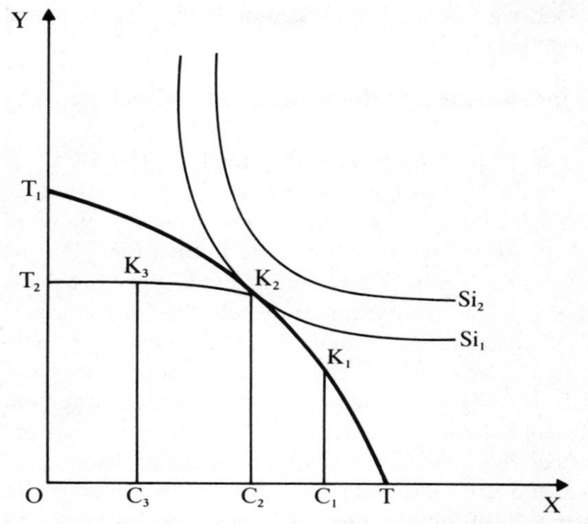

sense will be obtained where the TT_1 is tangent to the highest possible social indifference curve (Si_1), say, at K_2. Here consumption does not enter into the social welfare function of the planner; it only acts as a constraint. Note that the savings constraint exists given the nature of the transformation function and given the fact that the planner fails to raise investment by lowering consumption beyond OC_2 (Joshi, V., 1970). Also, notice that in a pure savings constraint, trade is not a constraint and FR will be used for extra consumption. Likewise, in the case of a pure trade constraint, saving is not a constraint. Domestic savings are equal to domestic investment, but a higher growth-rate will be unattainable in the absence of some critical imports which underline the lack of FR. This trade constraint is shown in Fig. 9.1 in the flat $T_2 K_2$ section of the transformation curve TT_2. Clearly, $T_2 K_2$ shows zero substitution possibility between X and Y. The savings constraint operated before at OC_2. Let us assume that this constraint does not hold any longer and consumption could fall to OC_3. But investment fails to rise. If the minimum consumption was OC_2 with the availability envelope TT_1, there is a savings constraint but no trade constraint. Given TT_2, at K_2 both the saving and the trade constraints operate. As long as the transformation curve like TT_1 slopes downwards monotonically, it is not possible to envisage a trade constraint. The advocates of the dual-gap analysis deny the existence of such a transformation curve in the LDCs, given rigidities in their economies (McKinnon, 1964). Such rigidities are no doubt present in many LDCs partly due to economic policies followed in the LDCs themselves, partly due to the policies of the DCs and partly because of the present international economic order. As long as the substitution possibilities between foreign and domestic resources are limited, the empirical estimates of the sizes of the two gaps are not without their merits (see, e.g., Chenery and Strout, 1966; Adelman and Chenery, 1966; Maizels, 1968).

9.8 Private foreign investment and the transfer of technology (TOT) to LDCs

One of the crucial factors in promoting economic growth in the LDCs is technology. In one sense, here the LDCs of the present time have an advantage over the LDCs of the past because they can now choose from a "menu" of technology available to them from past inventions and innovations. On the other hand, the availability of the menu of technology could pose problems for the LDCs. At the outset it is very important to decide the "appropriate" technology for different LDCs. According to some economists, such appropriateness has to be judged in the light of the relative factor endowments and factor–price ratios of the LDCs. Others have pointed out that such an argument would simply reinforce the *static* theory of comparative cost. Also, the existing factor–prices may not reflect the true social costs and benefits because of distortions in the product and the factor markets. Next, it is necessary to analyse the effects of such a TOT on the level of wages, employment and balance of payments of the LDCs. Fourth, the impact of TOT on the pattern of income distribution of the LDCs should be examined carefully. Fifth, the TOT may have important socio-political implications which could influence the power structure of the LDCs. (Vernon, 1971; Vaitsos, 1974). Sixth, the TOT has to be analysed along with the transfer of the product. It has been suggested that the choice of "consumption" technology cannot be discussed in isolation from the problem of choice of product (Stewart, 1974; OECD, 1974; UNCTAD, 1976b). It is true that where the final product is imported, the foreign exchange cost can often be a heavy burden on LDCs. Where the technology is imported there may often be fears that technology "dependence" is fostered and this could only be explained by the theory of imperialism (Radice, 1975).

Thus, considerable debate has recently been observed about the transfer of technology and the role of multinationals regarding the net social benefits of such transfers to the LDCs. It should be remembered that the TOT and the role of the multinational corporations (MNCs) are two very complex issues. Notice that all MNCs are not involved in TOT. It is equally noteworthy that since the technology supplying industries, and even the final product supplying industries are so often oligopolistic and multinational in character, technology dependence raises the further issue of the relationship between nation states and the giant corporation (Vernon, 1971).

TOT and alternatives for LDCs

To simplify the analysis of the effects of TOT on the LDCs, let us list at the outset the options open to the LDCs. Thus the LDCs could

1. Import the final product.

2. Import the technology for producing the final product using:
   (*a*) imported raw materials; and
   (*b*) indigenous raw materials; or adopt
   (*c*) some combination of imported and indigenous raw materials.
3. Import intermediate product – using indigenous plant for the final mixing of the product.
4. Develop indigenous technology similar to the imported technology.
5. Develop indigenous alternative technology.

Most LDCs try to meet the gap between domestic demand and supply through imports of products or technology, or some combination of the two. Here the policies of the different governments are generally reflected regarding the import of the final product or technology. A LDC strongly in favour of import substitution would prefer to import technology rather than the final product. The difference in public policies could also reflect the differences in market size, expected economies of scale and the level of skill.

Some general remarks regarding TOT in the LDCs are now in order. First, to the extent the LDCs suffer from the skill constraint to absorb technology, they would have to import either skilled labour or substitute capital for labour. Neither of them is inexpensive given the cost of training a highly skilled labour or the high cost of capital in LDCs. Second, many LDCs suffer from high growth-rates or population and consequent unemployment. If the TOT is to contribute to the alleviation of the problem of unemployment, the burden of adjustment will fall to a substantial extent upon the industrial sector as the absorption of extra labour force will depend upon the growth of industrial output. Third, the market for technology is very imperfect and heterogeneous. It is generally characterized by monopolistic or oligopolistic situations with some MNCs operating on a large scale crossing the national boundaries. Such monopolistic situations are accentuated with the systems of patents and export restrictions. The system of patents has the advantage of attracting FR; on the other hand, it gives rise to quasi-rents. Similarly, the parent firm, sometimes the big MNC, can stipulate many controls over the exports of the products produced by its wholly- or partially-owned subsidiary in a LDC. This, again, may adversely affect the benefits of foreign investment.

Fourth, the policy of import substitution via the imposition of tariff, or other forms of control generally leads to many forms of distortions. In such a situation, the TOT is not the basic reason for such distortions though some of its effects could easily aggravate such distortions within the LDCs.

Types of TOT

The TOT can assume different forms. To summarize the major ones, we have:

1. Initiative where the LDCs construct plants chiefly imitating the technology in the DCs.

2. Contractual where a LDC obtains capital and know-how usually through licensing.

3. Joint ventures where foreign firms collaborate with the home industries and could agree with minority holdings in assets.

4. Subsidiaries where the foreign companies set up wholly- or partly-owned subsidiaries with the host country exercising little or some influence.

5. Turn-key projects where the whole plant is transferred along with all the different stages of production to the point of final consumption through the marketing and distribution of the final products.

Contractual agreements, joint ventures and direct foreign investments are usually the major avenues of technological diffusion. Although direct foreign investment is probably the major route (UN, 1975), contractual agreements also figure prominently as such agreements account for about 85 per cent of total foreign investments in India, 87 per cent in Korea and 66 per cent in Brazil. However, these data could be overestimated as the minority foreign equity participations are also included in the agreements. Joint ventures (with majority or minority participation) are also very common in LDCs as they account for 71 per cent of total foreign investments in Sri Lanka and 48 per cent of such investments in Columbia.

Foreign direct investment (FDI) is probably the most important way to affect TOT and its impact is largely felt in the manufacturing sector. From the point of view of the technology supplying country, FDI is preferable to other methods of TOT if the nature of the product is important and durable, if the resources are available, and if TOT through other methods could give away secret information to potential rivals. The recipient country, usually anxious to be economically independent of the DCs, prefers collaboration or joint ventures usually with minority participation in the equity capital by the foreign companies. However, there are major problems in joint ventures and collaborations regarding division of operations, management and profits. Also, foreign firms apply export restriction clauses more to joint venture firms than to those wholly owned by them (Vernon, 1971, p. 144). Nor do joint ventures rely less heavily on imports relative to their total needs than wholly-owned subsidiaries. Thus, whether the local equity interest gives the recipient country any more effective control is sometimes doubted. Similarly, the technical collaboration agreements do not always offer clear advantages (Balasubramanyam, 1973, p. 35). For instance, foreign companies in the technical collaboration agreements rarely adjusted their production techniques in line with the Indian factor–price ratios. It was only in joint ventures where the foreign firms had an equity interest did they modify technology to some extent. Interestingly enough, the Indian firms did not change the techniques either. From the point of view of the donor country, lack of control in management reduced the incentive to alter technology to the economic conditions of the LDCs. It could be argued that only a few LDCs have the administrative skill to choose "appropriate" technology. But this is not always true (Streeten, 1971). On the other hand, Singer and Campo (1970, p. 12) have advocated the establishment of an International Development Fund to support an agency which will help the LDCs in choosing an "appropriate" technology. These different points of view highlight the necessity to undertake realistic appraisal of the difficult alternatives through a social cost–benefit analysis (Streeten, 1971). Such a study could be facilitated by looking at the following benefits and costs of TOT by the MNC.

Benefits and costs of TOT to the multinational corporations (MNCs)
The benefits of TOT to the MNCs could be summarized as follows (see, in particular, Streeten, 1973a):

1. The TOT by the MNCs could ease the "trade gap" in the LDCs.
2. When the TOT take the form of FDI, the difference between planned investment and planned savings could be reduced and to that extent, the savings gap in the LDCs would also be minimized.
3. By supplying skilled personnel and labour the "skill-constraint" could also be eased.
4. To the extent the MNCs contribute to the equity capital, the difference between planned expenditure for a project and domestic resources mobilized (say, through taxes or borrowing) would also be reduced.
5. The MNCs, through TOT, transfer necessary knowledge, skill and entrepreneurship needed by the LDCs. Even if some of these technologies are highly sophisticated, they could be modified to suit the economic situations of the LDCs. Also, the MNCs help the indigenous firms to establish contacts with the international capital markets.
6. The MNCs could increase competition in the economy of the host country and thereby improve the efficiency in the allocation of resources. In the absence of such competition it is argued that the indigenous firms, sheltered by protection, hardly feel the pressure of reducing cost by introducing technical progress and increase profitability.
7. The MNCs, through TOT, could increase the level of output and employment within the recipient country. There is some evidence to suggest that the MNCs have created about 2 million jobs in the LDCs by 1970 which account for about 0.3 per cent of their labour force (ILO, 1976a). This is not insignificant if newly created jobs by the MNCs are taken as a proportion of the 54 million estimated to be in open unemployment in the LDCs. However, unemployment fell chiefly in a few industries and the degree of such reduction varied considerably. In some industries, technology was very capital-intensive and the choice of alternative technology was rather small. In fact, in some extracting industries in Gabon employment actually fell from 14,800 to 8,400 between 1960 and 1970.

The major costs of the operations of the MNCs can now be summarized as follows:

1. The MNCs usually transfer technology which tends to be capital- rather than labour-intensive and such a technology is regarded as generally "inappropriate" for the labour-surplus LDCs.

2. Since technology is related to final product, it is contended that the TOT from the DCs has led to the growth of "Western" type "elitist" consumption within a very small sector of the total market of the LDCs. A pattern of consumption which is related to the average standard of living of the DCs is not appropriate to similar standards in the LDCs because of the vast difference in their level of income.
3. The effects of the operations of the MCNs are not spread very evenly in the different sectors in the LDCs (e.g. between industry and agriculture or urban and rural areas). Further, the MNCs in the process of TOT have introduced or aggravated the distortions in the market of the LDCs. For instance, payment of high wages in the LDCs are a very good way for "buying" industrial peace in the LDCs; on the other hand, such wages hardly reflect the social opportunity cost of labour in poor countries. They aggravate further the process of rural–urban migration as they accentuate the existing dichotomy between urban and rural wages. This, coupled with a higher capital-intensity in the choice of technology, could lead to the aggravation of the inequalities in the distribution of income (Vaitsos, 1974; Bardhan, 1975).
4. The MNCs with their vast resources could easily destroy their indigenous rivals. Far from promoting competition, the MNCs may actually make the market more imperfect by creating barriers to entry to their potential rivals.
5. If the MNCs supply inappropriate technology and/or product on the basis of resources partly obtained from the indigenous sources, then the diversion of such resources from socially desirable projects must be counted as a cost.
6. It is contended that the MNCs wield such strength with some host governments that they get away with large tax concessions, remittance facilities and royalties. Such governments in LDCs grant input subsidies (e.g. low interest rate on capital) or output taxes or both. Coupled with the policy of protection pursued in many LDCs, profits extracted by the MNCs in such markets in LDCs are regarded as exploitative.
7. The existence of the MNCs in the LDCs could easily be the focus of political conflict between the DCs and the LDCs.

It is necessary to clarify certain major points regarding the "exploitative" mechanism in the workings of the MNCs. Usually, such exploitative elements could be identified by looking at the difference between the price charged by the MNCs (P_m) and the world price (P_w) expressed as a proportion of world price. More formally, the degree of "over-pricing" (P_0) will be given by the following formula:

$$P_0 = \frac{P_m - P_w}{P_w}$$

Evidence suggests that the degree of over-pricing is considerable in many LDCs. For example, in Chile, from fifty products for which the data for world prices were available, corresponding to the imports of thirty-nine firms, the figures shown in Table 9.2 were obtained (Vaitsos, 1974).

Table 9.2

Number of products	*Extent of over-pricing (per cent)*
11	0
9	1 – 30
14	31 – 100
12	101 – 500
2	> 500

Source: Vaitsos, C. (1974).

In Columbia, in the field of pharmaceutical industries, the *average* rate of over-pricing is an alarming 150 per cent. Such over-pricing was found to be more among foreign-owned subsidiaries than local firms in Peru (Vaitsos, 1974). Had all this over-pricing been declared as profits, then the host country could have taxed away a part of these profits. Since such profits were not declared by the subsidiaries, both the loss in revenue as well as in balance of payments must be considerable. Such losses would be higher if the crucial "tie-in" clause in TOT is also taken into account whereby the "host" country is required to buy all the inputs from the same single source. If export restrictions operate, then the balance of payments losses would rise further.

The other element in the "exploitative" mechanism is supposed to be the patents. In theory, a patent reflects relative scarcity; its operation is supposed to ensure high price and profit and an inducement towards further innovation. However, patents in LDCs are almost entirely of foreign origin. Also, a large proportion of these patents are now usually owned by the MNCs rather than by individuals. It should be noted that the ability of the local firms in the LDCs to exploit the patents of the MNCs are severely restrained partly because of the huge size of the MNCs. Thus, in Peru, only 1 per cent of the total patents granted in all sectors were exploited between 1964–70 (UNCTAD, 1972).

Next, the operation of the "transfer-pricing" system has raised considerable criticism about the role of the MNCs in the LDCs. The concept is devised to avoid true tax liabilities by understatement of the "real" profit level. Such understatement would take place because of "transfer-pricing" or the system within which prices for goods (say, output of one subsidiary flowing as an input to the other) passing between affiliated companies in different countries can be adjusted in a manner which enables the shift of financial resources from one country to another. Thus should the rate of taxes be higher in B than A, it pays the MNCs to over-price these transactions in B and shift profits to A and should tariffs be higher in country B, then instead of over-pricing these exports from B, it is more lucrative to under-price the imports from the subsidiary into country B.

Notice that transfer-pricing is clearly a useful instrument to manipulate in those LDCs which impose restrictions on the remittances of profits and royalties. Similarly, the transfer-pricing mechanism could be used for the purpose of exchange-rate speculation. For example, in an economy facing serious and chronic balance of payments benefits, the MNCs could easily use the transfer-pricing mechanism to shift out profits from such a country. Clearly, the implications of the transfer-pricing mechanism are quite serious from the viewpoint of the LDCs.

Some policies to deal with the problems of TOT and MNCs

In an ideal world, if all the governments could get together and tax the MNCs jointly, then the dangers of transfer-pricing or over-pricing would be considerably reduced. Unfortunately, such a solution is hardly applicable in the real world. Hence, in an imperfect world, it is possible to suggest only some second-best remedies as follows:

1. Since evidence suggests, that the LDCs are unlikely to alter the nature of technology developed mainly in the DCs simply by altering the factor–price ratios, it is necessary to introduce a package of measures for increasing the competitive environment within the economy. Most empirical studies suggest that the MNCs are likely to choose the more appropriate technology for the LDCs whenever they face a more price-elastic demand curve for their product (UN, 1974). This clearly implies the necessity to develop a more competitive economy.

2. Since the indigenous entrepreneurs are likely to be weak rivals for the MNCs, the governments in the LDCs could take necessary measures to increase the countervailing power of the indigenous firms, through appropriate fiscal and monetary policies.

3. Within LDCs, inconsistencies could easily be observed in the policies pursued by the different ministries. For instance, the Department of Employment may be interested to maximize job opportunities while the Department of Industry could be anxious to import the most sophisticated and highly capital-intensive technology without due regard to the employment implications. The removal of such inconsistencies should be helpful to induce the MNCs to choose more appropriate technology for the economy.

4. Trade in selective second-hand capital goods could be encouraged by choosing suitable policies of tax subsidies. Here due care must be taken with regard to the availability of the spare parts, servicing facilities and the period within which such machinery could be obsolete. It must be emphasized that here the choice may not be too great.

5. Governments facing a surplus-labour but capital-scarce situation should try to alter the existing factor–price ratios between wages and interest rates in a manner which would reflect the real social opportunity costs of inputs. Since in most LDCs capital is generally under-priced as evidenced in low interest rates and wages are over-priced (given high unemployment, open or disguised), there is an important case for increasing interest rates and providing wage-subsidies.

6. More resources should be spent on Research and Development (R & D) to promote appropriate indigenous technology or to adapt imported technology to suit the local conditions. In most LDCs, the expenditure on R & D for developing indigenous technology is a very small proportion of the national income.

7. The host country should try to obtain different items of technology separately rather than in a "package". Such "unpackaging" will tend to reduce the exploitation element in the transfer-price mechanism.

8. Protectionist policies in many LDCs provide a "safe" market for the MNCs as well as domestic monopolies. Such tariff structure ought to be reviewed to foster greater competition. Notice that although a tariff inflates the profits of the subsidiaries of the MNCs it is not always a necessary condition for the establishment of such subsidiaries partly because they could be set up to take some special advantages of the economic conditions of the LDCs, e.g. low wages, and the gap between wages in the DCs and the LDCs (Posner, 1961), or partly because of the nature of innovation, adaptation and export of a successful product in its different stages (i.e. "the product-cycle" hypothesis, see Vernon, 1966). At a more mature stage of the product which could be successfully imitated in the DCs, subsidiaries could be set up in the LDCs to take advantage of low average costs because of low wages and low cost of raw materials and the finished product could be exported from the subsidiary back to the country of origin or to other export markets. However, the "product cycle" or the "wage-gap" theory does not explain why some vertically integrated MNCs are set up in LDCs with low skill often using labour-intensive techniques (Helleiner, 1973).

9. The MNCs should be induced to participate in training local people in co-ordination with the government. Also, local participation in management could remove some of the suspicions regarding the operations of the MNCs.

10. Greater information should be spread regarding the availability of technology. Here the international agencies (e.g. UNIDO, UNCTAD) could provide valuable guidelines to the LDCs.

11. Major criticisms of the different types of mechanisms used by the MNCs in the TOT emanate because of the utmost secrecy observed in their financial and technical operations. One of the best ways to tackle the many criticisms and suspicions with regard to the workings of the MNCs would be to remove much of the secrecy, provide more relevant information and enable others to carry out more objective social cost–benefit analysis regarding the role of the MNCs in the TOT in LDCs.

9.9 Special drawing rights (SDRs) and the "Link"

Special Drawing Rights (SDRs) were created by the International Monetary Fund (IMF) in July 1969, chiefly to meet the international liquidity crisis. This event could also be looked at as an important element of the "New International Economic Order". SDRs are "paper" gold and they augment the volume of international liquid reserves. Originally an SDRs account worth US $3.5 billion was set up. By 1972, its value rose to about $9.5 billion.

Since 1 July 1974 the value of the SDRs account is given every day by a basket of sixteen major currencies. The functions of the SDRs units are the same as those under gold and stable dollar standards. The SDRs are *liquid*; they are *convertible* in any other currency; their value is *stable*; they can be used as a *medium of exchange* to *settle international transactions*. It is easily seen that the SDRs can be regarded as a type of international currency which Keynes had in mind when he advocated the idea of issuing BANCOR through an international clearing bank. The basic features of such a currency would be to promote international *liquidity*, *stability* and *confidence* in the international monetary system. The creation of SDRs has helped to achieve some of these objectives. Indeed, in some ways, the SDRs as reserve assets could be regarded as superior to gold holdings. For instance, the supply of SDRs could be suggested to meet an increased demand for international liquidity while the supply of gold is inelastic. Since the value of the SDRs is linked to an international basket of major currencies, the degree of fluctuations in their value is likely to be much less than any other single currency. Just like gold, SDRs could be held as a store of value or spent to settle net deficits in international trade. The action of an individual country would not diminish the value of SDRs though this could easily happen with gold. As an international asset, SDRs are durable because unlike, say, dollar or pound, they would not disappear if one country spent them, say, in USA or UK. Indeed, if India spends SDRs to acquire goods from UK the SDR *earnings* by UK will *rise*. The SDRs are practically permanent assets because they will disappear only under the extreme assumption of their collective cancellation.

The principle of distribution of the SDRs

Given the importance of SDRs creation as an international reserve asset, their distribution has attracted considerable attention, particularly in the LDCs. The existing principle allows the DCs (twenty-five) to obtain about $7.5 billion while ninety-three or more LDCs (with a huge population) could obtain only about $2.5 billion. This is because the SDRs are allocated on the basis of a country's quota with the IMF. Since the quota of the DCs is much greater than that of the LDCs, it is understandable that the DCs get a much larger proportion of the SDRs. This principle of distribution has caused resentment in the LDCs. Although the original quota with the IMF was fixed in line with a country's economic strength, it is undeniable that such quotas hardly reflect the needs of the poor countries. This apart, several other criticisms could be levelled at the present criterion for distributing the SDRs (Haan, 1971).

First, the existing principle fails to economize the amount of reserves to be set up. SDRs could be accumulated indefinitely and eventually "dehoarded" by a single country without any effective collective supervision.

Second, although the adjustment costs incurred by the LDCs (e.g. deflation and unemployment) in general are higher than those incurred by the DCs, the present system of SDR distribution does not take into account the distribution of adjustment costs in *proportion* to their disequilibria (Cohen, 1966).

Third, since the global distribution of income and wealth is far from being equal, it may be argued that the collective saving in the form of SDRs should accrue to the LDCs in proportion to their needs (say, on a *per capita* basis) rather than on the basis of existing quota.

Fourth, to distribute the SDRs on the basis of quota is to accept the static arguments for initial quota allocation among different countries with total disregard to the dynamic changes that have taken place so far in the world economy. This is considered as unacceptable.

Fifth, Triffin argues that "internationally agreed SDRs should serve internationally agreed purposes" and thus SDRs' distribution on the ground of quotas is regarded as "morally repugnant, economically wasteful and politically unviable" (Triffin, 1971).

From these criticisms, it is clear that the existing principle of SDRs' distribution should be changed considerably from the standpoint of global redistribution of income and the needs of the LDCs. However, global redistribution of income is a noble principle which is rather difficult to achieve in practice, given the nature of present international relations. But if one of the major objectives of the international institutions is to establish a fairer system of existing international assets, then the present principle of SDRs' distribution on the basis of quota is rendered very weak.

The link between SDRs and foreign resources

The idea of linking the SDRs to assist the development plans and projects in the LDCs has received considerable attention (for an early proposal see Stamp, 1958; see also Scitovsky, 1966; Kahn, 1973; Helleiner, 1974; Maynard, 1973; Machlup, 1968; Triffin, 1971; UNCTAD, 1965; Johnson, 1972, 1977; Bauer, 1973; Thirlwall, 1976a; Williamson, 1973; Bird, 1976). The main arguments for and against the "link" could be summarized as follows (see in particular, Maynard, 1973).

Arguments in favour of the "link"

1. Linking of the SDRs to aid development projects at a minimum cost would enable the LDCs not to resort to the painful adjustment procedures (e.g. deflation, unemployment) to rectify persistent difficulties in their balance of payments.

2. The "link" will ensure a smooth *long-term* flow of development finance along with global growth of output and trade.

3. When the "link" would operate through an international agency, the delays in bilateral negotiations would be avoided.

4. The volume of *untied multilateral* flow of foreign resources is likely to rise in the event of a "link" in such a way as to reduce the balance of payments and reserve costs of the donor countries substantially.

Arguments against the "link"

1. Development finance and creation of international liquidity are regarded as two separate issues which are designed to realize separate objectives. But this criticism is not very compelling because the development within the LDCs could be achieved by the use of SDRs and no serious damage is likely to be inflicted on the international monetary system if one instrument (SDRs' creation) attains two objectives (meeting the shortage of international liquidity and aiding the development of the LDCs).

2. It is argued that since the SDRs are reserve monetary assets, they should not be used for the transfer of real resources from the DCs, nor to finance spending within the LDCs. To the extent deficits are historically financed by the creation of new money this argument loses some force. However, it is important to control the money supply firmly, particularly because in the LDCs, supply tends to be rather inelastic.

3. The "link" is supposed to be inflationary. This is a more serious criticism to the extent that the claims of the LDCs on the real resources of DCs could not be met without paying a high cost. Critics argue that most DCs try to acquire international reserve assets via export surpluses which does involve transfer of real resources. To the extent the DCs have the capacity to meet demand, inflation is unlikely to occur. Further, the amount of SDR creation is so negligible as a proportion of total foreign resources flow to LDCs that its additional impact is likely to be small – although it is sometimes maintained by the critics of the link scheme that the present global inflation is partly the result of too much international liquidity rather than too little (Johnson, 1977). Here, it should be pointed out that the major reason for global inflation is the high rise in oil price in 1973–74, not the creation of SDRs. Notice that the LDCs do not obtain SDRs simply to raise their demand and transfer of resources depends upon the net *use* rather than the allocation of SDRs. Some LDCs may decide to *accumulate* SDRs to guard themselves against uncertainties and evidence of SDRs' use by the LDCs up to 1977 seems to support this statement. (See IFS, 1970–1977). Also it has been well argued that

the burden on non-reserve currency countries implied by the transfer of real resource to LDCs through the link would be greater than in the pre-SDRs situation; the transfer would be made to the LDCs rather than to gold producers and reserve currency countries. The need for these countries to pursue appropriate demand management policies to make available the real resources for obtaining an increase in foreign exchange reserve would be no different.

(Maynard, 1973; see also Machlup, 1968.)

4. It is contended that in the presence of the "link" the DCs who offer foreign resources to LDCs will cut their individual or collective offer. This argument is difficult to accept, logically or empirically. To the extent the allocation of SDRs is free of resource cost, some DCs may actually be induced to offer more.

5. The link scheme is sometimes criticized as undemocratic as its burden could be distributed over the taxpayers of the DCs without their assent. This point is also very weak as it could be directed against all forms of untied or even tied aid which are not wholly effective.

6. It is maintained that link would reduce the confidence in SDRs as an asset. Further, the LDCs will be induced to put pressure upon the IMF to create more SDRs than would be indicated by the principles of international monetary policies. Neither of these two objections seems to be sound. The SDRs are safeguarded by the principle of acceptance; also no country is allowed to *accumulate* the SDRs by more than thrice the amount of its initial allocation or *spend* more than 70 per cent of its allocation. Moreover, when 85 per cent of the voting power in the IMF rests with the DCs, it is difficult to see how effective the pressure of LDCs on the IMF could be.

On balance, it seems that the arguments against the link are not very compelling. Indeed, it could be pointed out that if one of the major objectives of the International Monetary Policy is to set up a fairer system of distribution of international assets on the basis of *needs*, then the arguments against the link clearly become rather weak. As regards the inflationary effect of the link, it can be mentioned that such an effect is likely to be smaller in comparison with, say, the dollar standard, because in the case of the link, collective supervision of liquidity will replace the decision made by a single country, say the USA (Johnson, 1972). Further, the link may actually economize on SDRs' creation because once the DCs are under pressure to "earn" the SDRs by increasing their share in the world export market, they would be obliged to hold down the prices (Thirlwall, 1976a).

The link could be developed in different ways. A *direct* link can be established by directly allocating more SDRs to the LDCs which would be greater than their long-run demand for reserves. This would imply, *inter alia*, an increase in LDCs' quotas with the IMF. The link could be *organic* if the SDRs are allocated to the LDCs through, say, an International Development Agency (IDA) for financing development programmes. Any DCs which would export to the LDC will earn SDRs in the credit account of the IDA while the LDCs' account will be debited by the value of such imports from the DC.

The link could be *inorganic* if the DCs decide to contribute voluntarily to any ML agency providing FR to the LDCs with every new allocation of the SDRs. In comparison with other forms of link, this plan has some major defects. For instance, since the scheme is voluntary, some DCs may decide not to provide anything. Also, if a DC, say the USA, suffers from a balance of payments deficit, it may decide not to contribute to the ML fund. It appears that either a *direct* or an *organic* link would be superior to an *inorganic* link.

Empirical evidence about the SDRs' allocation, use and resource transfer

Empirical evidence available so far provides some idea about the SDRs' allocation, use and resource transfer. On the basis of net acquisition of SDRs by the DCs and net use by the LDCs, Helleiner has argued that real resources have been transferred from the DCs to the LDCs between 1970 and 1973. Out of the total allocation of $2,348 million SDRs by July 1973, the LDCs taken together have used \$835 million. By this time, the allocation to the DCs was \$6,967 million and their net use was \$308 million (Helleiner, 1974). It is true that the system of SDRs allocation and use has resulted in an informal link between SDRs and aid, but the use of net acquisition data of the LDCs could be quite misleading to show accurately the extent of such a link (Bird, 1976). The permanent *potential* real resource gain over a period (G_p) should be equivalent to 70 per cent of the initial allocation of SDRs (A) minus interest charges for full *potential* SDRs net use (I). Thus,

$$G_p = \frac{70}{100} Q(A) - I$$

where Q = value of quota

Notice that in the above equation G varies directly with Q and A and inversely with I. If r is the interest rate charged to *actual* net users of SDRs then I and r would vary directly. However, the *actual* real resource gain (G_a) should be equivalent to quota allocation of the SDRs, Q(A), minus transfer to the general account of the IMF (T_g) to pay some charges or for repurchases and the proportion of SDRs which is to be added to reserves (Z). More formally,

$$G_a = Q(A) - T_g - Z$$

Helleiner has assumed unrealistically that T_g or Z or both are equal to zero so that $G_a = G_p$. In practice, it turned out that T_g = \$527.5 million and Z = \$1,512.8 million by the end of July 1973, and therefore, recalculating Helleiner's figure, we obtain, G_a = \$307.7 million. Thus, the overestimation of the actual resource transfer by Helleiner is wholly accounted for by the transfer to the general account by the LDCs (Bird, 1976).

The use of the SDRs could be explained by both demand and supply factors. Assuming that the supply of SDRs is exogenous and given by the allocation of SDRs, the demand use of SDRs (S) could be stated in a simple form as follows (Leipziger, 1975):

$$S = S(B_{t-1}, DR, G, A)$$

where B_{t-1} = Net deficit in balance of payment with one year lag since delays are involved in actual payments following trade flows.
DR = The reserve variable expressed as the change in non-SDRs reserves over the past year.
G = The foreign exchange to gold ratio in a country's portfolio.
A = The SDRs allocation to a country in millions of US dollars.

In theory, if it is expected that

$$\partial S/\partial B_{t-1} > 0, \quad \partial S/\partial DR < 0, \quad \partial S/\partial G \gtrless 0$$

(to test whether the SDRs are substitutes for either gold or foreign exchange) and $\partial S/\partial A > 0$. The linear least square regression for forty-three LDCs in 1971 yielded the following equation:

$$S = 4.57 + 0.44\,A + 0.05\,B_{t-1} - 0.06\,DR + 0.002\,G$$
$$(1.65)\quad (7.97)\quad (3.24)\quad (-3.91)\quad (0.004)$$

$\overline{R}^2 = 0.63$

(The figures in parentheses show the relevant t-values).
(*Source*: Leipziger, D., 1975)

As hypothesized, most of the explanatory variables except for G have the right signs and the estimated coefficients are statistically significant at 99 per cent confidence levels. The proportion of explained variation is 63 per cent and this is not very high. However, when the LDCs are divided between the Latin American and other LDCs, such a model fared well for the Latin American countries though failed to explain very well the SDRs use by the other LDCs. This is illustrated in the following two regression equations.

Latin America:

$$S = 0.58 + 0.06\,B_{t-1} - 0.10\,DR + 0.11\,G$$
$$(11.64)^{**}\quad (4.63)^{**}\quad (-8.71)^{**}\quad (2.45)^{*}$$

$\overline{R}^2 = 0.89 \qquad n = 19$

Other LDCs

$$S = 4.74 + 0.38\,A + 0.04\,B_{t-1} + 0.02\,DR - 0.09\,G$$
$$(1.54)\quad (6.76)^{**}\quad (1.73)^{**}\quad (1.01)\quad (-1.33)$$

$\overline{R}^2 = 0.70 \qquad n = 24$

** significant at 95 per cent confidence level or better
* significant at 90 per cent confidence level
n = number of observations
(*Source*: Leipziger, D., 1975)

The Chow test (Chow, 1960) indicates that the determinants of the use of SDRs by the Latin American and the other LDCs are significantly different (the calculated F value being 9.12). Thus, although the above model has some interesting features, it fails to explain adequately the determinants of the SDRs' use by "other" LDCs. Further, it is not very clear why SDRs' allocation has been dropped as an explanatory variable in the equation for the Latin American countries. Thus, more caution and further research is needed to analyse the pattern of SDRs' use by the LDCs. Since the LDCs are not a homogeneous group, it may be necessary to carry out country- or region-wide (within which LDCs show similar characteristics) study to obtain more unbiased estimates by avoiding the problem of linear aggregation.

The "link" is an important and useful idea for establishing a "new international economic order". Most of the arguments against the link are not very compelling. Internationally supervised, the scheme has considerable promise to assist the LDCs in their efforts to achieve a better standard of living. As Williamson observes

The international community has few instruments to improve the world distribution of income, and therefore it should utilize such opportunities as arise. One of these is the seigniorage resulting from the production of fiduciary reserve assets. There is a long and unfortunate tradition in economics of dismissing this type of argument just because it involves a value judgment additional to that embodied in the Pareto criterion. The degree of egalitariansim needed to justify preference for the link rather than neutrality is minimal, given the existing facts on world income distribution.

(Williamson, 1973, p. 278)

10

Population, poverty and income distribution, employment and migration

10.1 Population and economic development

The relationship between the growth of population and economic development could be regarded as a "challenge" and a "response". Population growth against a given amount of resources at a certain point in time in economic history has posed the challenge of feeding extra mouths; the response has come from more economic growth. Thus, the relationship between population and economic growth can be viewed in two ways. From the standpoint of demand, the growth of population increases the demand for food, services and other resources: from the standpoint of supply, it implies the availability of more labour to produce more goods and services.

In the DCs, the long-run growth of the economy could be constrained by the supply of labour and here an increase in population growth-rate might raise the rate of economic growth. Historically, it is pointed out that the "unprecedented rise in population" led to the emergence of the Industrial Revolution (Hicks, 1957, p. 302). Since necessity is regarded as the mother of invention, the logic of such an argument is not difficult to understand.

Growth of population could have some beneficial effects on economic growth. First, a growing population enlarges the size of the market by raising aggregate demand. Second, a rising population supplies more labour for employment. Third, if the labour supply is a constraint on growth, then an expansion of labour force will raise output and growth.

The major harmful effects of a rapid population growth can be summarized as follows:

1. If the rise in *per capita* income or output growth is regarded as a rough indicator of the improvement of the *average* standard of living in the society, then it is obvious that in an economy with stagnant total income and rising population, the *average* standard of living could only worsen. Similarly, if the population growth-rate is faster than the growth-rate of real income, again the average standard of living will fall. This is the famous "Malthusian" picture of the population problem in the LDCs. A backward economy with limited resources using primitive technology, could only manage to register a slow growth of total output, and if the population growth-rate outstrips the growth-rate of output, *per capita* output is likely to fall. For many people living on the brink of subsistence in many LDCs, this picture may appear to be very real. The poverty, squalor, famine, epidemics, mass starvation and migration that are generally observed in many LDCs, are regarded by many as the major "Malthusian" effects of a rapid rise in population.

2. The positive effects of population growth on output growth could only be obtained if labour could be productively employed with the available resources. For most LDCs, the critical bottleneck in the path of economic development is regarded as the availability of capital, both physical and social. Given the paucity of capital, the availability of more labour does not add much to the output growth. It is argued that in some cases, the contribution of labour in the LDCs, particularly in agriculture, could be very low and even zero (Lewis, 1954, Fei and Ranis, 1964; see also Ch. 3).

3. The rise in population lowers the man–land or the man–resources ratios. This implies that a static, backward economy without any technical progress could only experience greater poverty with growing population pressure on available resources.

4. The lack of enough physical and social capital along with structural and technical rigidities in the LDCs render the supply of output curve rather inelastic and a rise in population coupled with increased supply of labour leads to greater under- and open-unemployment, particularly in the agricultural sector. Where the level of population is very large (e.g. China, India), the population density per acre of land rises. Since the agricultural sector is backward and the industrial sector is generally small, additional labour could not be easily absorbed within the agrarian economy. Migration follows and unemployment in the rural areas turn into unemployment in the urban areas.

5. A high level of population or its rapid growth creates additional demands on social capital like education, housing and health services. Since the supply of such facilities is usually inadequate in the LDCs, a growth in population tends to overstrain the existing limited supply.

6. If the supply of food is inelastic in the LDCs, then a rising population with an increase in demand could lead to inflation. In order to cope with the problem, many LDCs import foodgrains from abroad and this causes an important drain on valuable foreign exchange which could have been used for better purposes. Notice that since many LDCs suffer from serious inflationary and balance of payments problems, the concern about the population problem can easily be understood.

7. The rapid growth of population leads to a high dependency ratio, i.e. the proportion of non-working to working population. Also, the children below, say, 15–16 years tend to form a high proportion of the working population and the existence of such a young age-group within the working population aggravates the problems of food supply and employment creation.

8. High population growth-rates and/or a high level of population could lead to pollution and many environmental problems like the growth of shanty towns or *bustees*, juvenile delinquency, squalor, congestion, etc.

9. A rising population in a fairly static and poor economy could aggravate the problems of inequalities in income distribution. Since, on average, poor families tend to be larger than rich families, as long as there is only one bread-winner in both these income classes, *per capita*, real income and real consumption will be clearly lower in poor income groups in comparison with the richer ones.

The above arguments show that the costs of population growth could be much greater than its benefits for the LDCs. Such costs would rise considerably if they experience what has come to be known as "population explosion" – a topic which will be discussed in Section 10.2.

10.2 Population explosion in LDCs and the theory of demographic transition

Population explosion is a phrase which is commonly used to describe the prevalence of high crude birth-rates with low death-rates in many LDCs. According to the theory of demographic transition, in the pre-industrial, backward society, a high birth-rate (BR) is generally accompanied by a high death-rate (DR) with the result that the net growth-rate of population remains low. Evidence from most countries seems to back up this argument. In the passage of economic growth, it is argued that the BR remains high while the DR falls resulting in a very rapid rise in population growth or "population explosion". In a more mature phase of economic development, the BR tends to decline and the DR falls to its lowest level and remains fairly stationary. Eventually, the BR falls to a low level and the net growth of population becomes low and stable (see Fig. 10.1). The BR and the DR are measured in the

Fig. 10.1

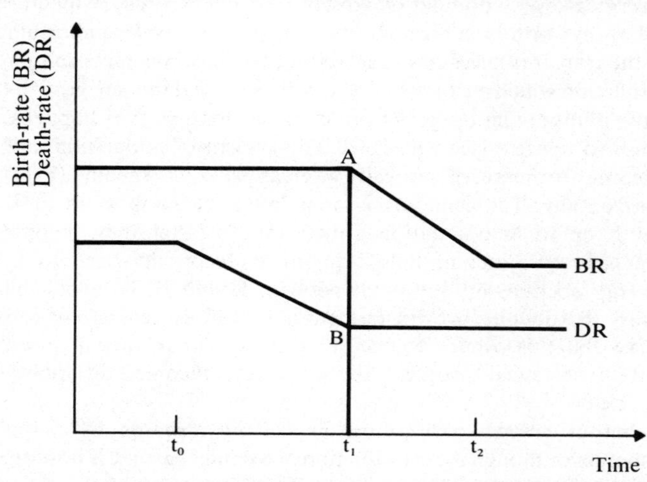

vertical axis and time is measured horizontally. At t_0, both the BR and the DR are high; at t_1, with economic development and say greater and better medical facilities, the DR falls, but the BR remains much the same as before. The difference AB is the "population explosion". In the more mature period of economic growth, say at time t_2, the BR falls and the population grows at a low and stable rate.

Although the *theory* of demographic transition is supposed to be a theory, it is noteworthy that it is not really a theory. Rather, it is a description of facts. Next, although parts of the movements of the BR and the DR in the way described above are observed in the passage of economic growth of the DCs, there is no way to suggest that the institutional conditions of the DCs of today are the same as those of the LDCs of the present time. Also, if the implication of the "theory" of demographic transition is that a higher *per capita* income over time leads to a fall in population growth-rate, then this inference is not always substantiated by the evidence available so far (Cassen, 1976). Indeed Kuznets has found a positive correlation between population growth and economic growth (Kuznets, 1967). Although correlation does not suggest causation, it is interesting to observe that no negative and statistically significant association was observed. Finally, the theory of demographic transition does not say much about the factors which affect the fertility and mortality *behaviour* which would explain some important demographic characteristics.

10.3 Low-level equilibrium trap

The other theory which is advanced to explain the relationship between population and income growth is known as the "low-level equilibrium trap" (Nelson, 1956). Basically, the theory suggests that as long as *per capita* income remains below a critical level, a population growth-rate that exceeds the income growth-rate will always bring the economy back to a "low-level equilibrium trap". To avoid the trap, it is necessary to introduce technical progress so that the production function which accounts for the output or real income growth-rate will lie above the population growth-rate and as long as that happens, the trap will cease to operate (see Fig. 10.2). The growth of population and the growth of income are measured vertically whereas *per capita* income (Y/N) is measured horizontally. The economy is at a low-level equilibrium at L because beyond L up to K population growth-rate is faster than income growth-rate and *per capita* income falls, bringing the economy back to L. Notice that the trap operates on any point between K and L. To avoid the trap it is necessary that income growth-rate curve should exceed population growth-rate curve and this occurs beyond K and *per capita* income rises. In order to attain sustained progress in *per capita* income, the policy implications are clear:

First, the output growth curve must be shifted upwards by better allocation of resources or though the introduction of technical progress or both. Second, population growth-rate must be controlled as far as possible.

Fig. 10.2

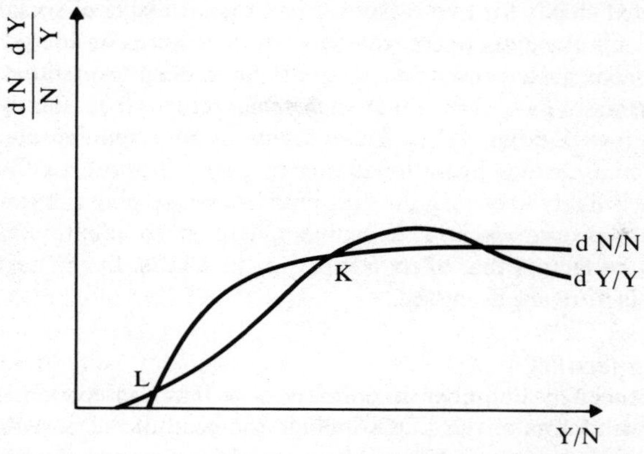

Clearly, the shift of the output growth curve will require massive investments in the LDCs. This may call for greater effort by the government; here the *quality* rather than the quantity of government investment assumes importance. Public expenditure in most LDCs has grown over the last twenty-five years but its effect on output growth has not always proved to be very encouraging. It is imperative to raise productive investment as far as possible and this could call for more technical progress in industry as well as in agriculture.

Evidence to support or reject the low-level equilibrium trap theory is rather scanty. One study indicates the possible existence of such equilibrium in the case of some Asian and Latin American countries (Moreland and Hazeldine, 1974). More research is obviously necessary to draw firm conclusions.

The other important policy to raise *per capita* income is to control population growth-rates. This is a complex issue and here the main problem of controlling fertility has received wide attention.

10.4 Fertility and population growth in LDCs

Most evidence seems to confirm that the majority of LDCs are likely to experience high to moderate growth-rates in population in the near future though for some larger countries like India and China, the phases of highest growth-rates seem to be over (Cassen, 1976). In some LDCs there are now increasing signs of a decline in fertility (e.g. Singapore, Korea, Taiwan, Mauritius). But in general, the fertility rates (as measured by BR per thousand) in the LDCs are considerably higher than those in the DCs. Since the mortality rates in most LDCs are unlikely to be reduced significantly in the future, the population growth-rate could now be controlled mainly by reducing the fertility rates. It has been suggested that the returns from fertility control and family planning in the LDCs could be in excess of one hundred times the returns from other types of investment (Enke, 1967, 1973). These estimates are, perhaps, exaggerated chiefly for two reasons. First, the estimates of social costs were very low as only the costs of contraceptive devices were considered. Second, the benefits from such prevention seem to have been overstated. Nevertheless, other estimates have shown that such social returns from family planning are not very low (Zaidan, 1971). There seems to be a genuine and urgent necessity to increase expenditure for family planning in most LDCs. Since such expenditure is likely to be large, the government has to play a major role in financing these programmes. The problem here is to identify as accurately as possible the factors that affect fertility in the LDCs. In the next section some of these factors are discussed.

Factors affecting fertility

Fertility could be influenced by a number of economic as well as non-economic variables. The economic factors in the LDCs include the need of the parents to have some sort of an insurance against old age while the non-economic factors include biological, psychological and social variables. It is argued that a decline in fertility could be achieved only when the following conditions are satisfied:

1. The parents must be conscious regarding the choice about fertility.
2. The net benefits from the fertility reduction should be considered as considerable by the parents.
3. The supply of effective family planning methods must be assured (Coale, 1973).

The economic choice of the parents for children will no doubt depend on the above conditions. Clearly, it is assumed here that the parents are rational enough to calculate that the net benefits from family planning are significantly positive. In the urban and educated sector of the LDCs it may be possible to apply such a model of economic choice for children. In the vast, rural and illiterate sector, it is difficult to see how the model could be applied. However, many illiterate people living in the rural sector of the LDCs do not always show "economic irrationality". In fact, many parents in the villages consider children as the "investment" rather than the consumption good since they could help the farming and other activities of the families. It is in this context that the relationship between fertility and mortality assumes some significance.

Fertility and mortality

Fertility could be significantly affected by mortality, particularly *infant mortality* (see Table 10.1). In the LDCs, the chances of survival of a child are shown to be much less in comparison with the DCs. From the point of view of a peasant family, if it is assumed that only two out of every three babies born are likely to survive, then the fertility rates are likely to remain high. Note that in most LDCs, social security and old-age assistance programmes are virtually non-existent. Thus the children are naturally regarded as some forms of insurance in old age, and "investment goods". Evidence confirms that in most LDCs, infant mortality and fertility are highly and significantly correlated. The interesting policy implication that follows from this is that in order to reduce fertility, it is imperative to reduce infant mortality. Apart from this, social welfare systems should be extended wherever possible to help the old people.

Fertility and education: importance of female education

Higher education is generally expected to reduce fertility. Evidence available so far indicates a negative and statistically significant correlation between higher education and a decline in fertility in many LDCs. The Indian data strongly suggest such a negative correlation (Parikh, 1976). What is important to emphasize here is that in almost all cases, *female* education had a very strong *negative* impact on fertility. This implies the necessity to educate the female population in the LDCs to reduce population growth, since educated women are likely to see more clearly the logic of fertility control. Education also helps people to get over age-old customs and inhibitions, to change attitudes and motivations and to make a more rational choice. If education should enhance the income of the parents, the arrival of the babies can only diminish it: again, grounds for an "economic choice" for babies can be seen.

An expansion of women's education may be a necessary but not a sufficient condition for reducing fertility. It is important to provide productive employment to the educated women's labour force and to raise their general status in the society to reduce fertility significantly.

Fertility and income

It is sometimes argued that fertility and *per capita* real income are inversely correlated so that a rise in *per capita* real income would tend to reduce fertility. In the "economic choice" model if babies are treated as consumption goods, then their demand will compete against the demand for all other items of consumption, and the benefits from having the babies ("consuming them") have to be viewed against the cost of bearing and rearing them. Such costs would include the allocation of more parental time to mind the babies and the possible loss of income. Thus, the demand for babies should be inversely correlated with income (see, Schultz, 1976; Becker and Lewis, 1973).

It has been mentioned before that the children in the LDCs are also regarded as "investment" goods. Casual observation seems to support this argument as many young children in the LDCs participate and help their families in different activities. It is also true that in the absence of a social security system, parents expect their children to look after them in their old age and if their children (generally their sons) do not, they are regarded as a disgrace to their families. On the other hand, it is doubtful whether children could be classified exactly as "consumption" or "investment" goods; perhaps they are

Table 10.1 Summary of empirical finding for low income countries on the determinants of fertility (After each regression coefficient the absolute value of the t ratio is reported in parentheses and elasticities at regression means in brackets)

	1	*2*	*3*	*4*
Author (year; page)	Schultz (1969; 171)	Schultz (1970; 43)	Nerlove-Schultz (1970; 45)	Harman (1970; 29–30)
Population (time)	Puerto Rico (1951–1957)	Egypt (1960)	Puerto Rico (1950–1960)	Philippines (1968)
Observations (number)	Regions (75*7)	Regions (41)	Regions (78*11)	Individuals (250)
Equation (estimators)[a]	Reduced form (OLS)	Reduced form (OLS)	Structural (TSLS/GLS)	Structural (TSLS)
Dependent variable	Births per 1,000 population	Children (0–9) per women (15–49)	Births per 1,000 population	Children ever born per women aged 35–9
Explanatory variables[b]				
1. Adult education	− 1.58 (5.3) [0.15]	—	− 1.95 (3.2) [0.20]	—
2. Women's education	—	− 65.2 (4.0) [0.087]	—	− 0.092 (1.6) [0.094]
3. Women's wage	—	—	—	—
4. Men's education	—	—	—	—
5. Men's wage	—	—	—	—
6. Death-rate	1.18 (3.5) [0.27][d]	—	0.302 (1.6) [0.082][d]	5.76 (3.9) [1.0] [0.048][e]
R^2 (F; df)[c]	0.46	0.537	(27.3)	(3.5)

[a] Form of estimation equation such as reduced-form equations (only exogenous explanatory variables) which may be estimated by ordinary least squares (OLS), structural equations (including endogenous explanatory variables) estimated perhaps by an instrumental variable technique such as two-stage least squares (TSLS), solved reduced-form equations, derived from the simultaneous equations estimates of the related structural equations (generally without t statistics), and when a time series of cross-sections are pooled for either a reduced form or a structural equation, estimates may be reported using a generalized least-squares procedure (GLS) that assumes a Nerlovian two-component stochastic structure to the disturbances. For instrumental variable estimates asymptotic t statistics are reported.

[b] For definition of explanatory variables, including those not reported in table, see original studies.

[c] Asymptotic significance of entire equation can be evaluated with the F ratio when TSLS estimates are computed. See Dhrymes (1969). For OLS and GLS of reduced-form equations, R^2 can be used to test the equation's overall statistical significance.

Table 10.1 (cont.)

5	*6*	*7*	*8a*	*8b*	
Schultz (1971; 61)	DaVanzo (1972; 80)	Maurer *et al.* (1973; 20–9)	Schultz (1972; 36)	Schultz (1972; 38)	
Taiwan (1964–1968)	Chile (1960)	Thailand (1960)	Taiwan (1964–1969)	Taiwan (1964–1969)	
Regions (361)	Regions (50)	Regions (71)	Regions (361*7)	Regions (361*7)	
Reduced form (OLS)	Structural (TSLS)	Solved reduced form (TSLS)	Reduced form (OLS)	Reduced form (GLS)	
Normalised births per 1,000 women aged 35–9	Children ever born per 1,000 women aged 35–9	Children ever born per women aged 35–9	Births per 1,000 women aged 35–9	Births per 1,000 women aged 35–9	
—	—	—	—	—	1.
0.422 (1.97) [1.8][f]	—	−0.0926 [0.13][h]	98.2 (9.2) [0.37]	−45.4 (2.78) [0.17]	2.
—	−1589 (1.84) [0.35][g]	−22.6 [0.16][h]	—	—	3.
—	—	0.526 [0.55][h]	−274 (16.0) [1.4]	−174 (7.9) [0.98]	4.
—	170 (0.33) [0.054]	—	—	—	5.
5.61 (9.3) [5.5][f] [0.41][e]	7.65 (2.72) [0.28]	—	432 (17.9) [3.9] [0.28][e]	172 (8.2) [1.5] [0.11][e]	6.
0.433[f]	(14.4; 6, 3)	(13.9; 7, 4)	0.461	0.809	

[d] Arithmetic sum of lagged coefficients, and averaged t statistics.

[e] Child death-rate entered regression as the reciprocal of child survival rate. For comparability and ease of interpretation, the second elasticity estimates are with respect to the child death-rate.

[f] Arithmetic average of regression coefficients t statistics, elasticities and R^2 from five annual cross-sectional regressions.

[g] The women's wage was treated as endogenous to this investigation and is therefore estimated as a linear function of exogenous variables such as women's education, etc.

[h] The solved reduced-form equations are reported without asymptotic standard error estimates. The elasticity estimates for education variables incorporate also the effect of an additional variable that is non-linear in male and female education, namely, the relative educational attainment of women to that of men.

Source: Schultz, P. (1976)

regarded as a bit of both in the LDCs and on the basis of available information, it is hard to say whether the parents always calculate very carefully the discounted rates of return at the margin from a "marginal" child! It is rather unlikely that parental decisions for having children would depend always on economic factors with utility or profit maximization being the overriding objective function. Psychological, social and biological factors also play important roles in determining fertility.

The statistical difficulty in assessing the impact of *per capita* real income growth on fertility is that it is not easy to establish the direction of causation. It is possible to argue that fertility decline tends to raise *per capita* real income. Also, it could be argued that parents usually want to provide better opportunities for their offspring, e.g. good health, better education, better nutrition etc. Hence, if *per capita* real income rises, it is possible that parents will be less pessimistic about future costs of increasing the size of the family and the demand for babies will rise. In fact, there is some evidence in the LDCs which suggests a positive correlation between men's wages/earnings and fertility though the coefficients are not always statistically significant. Such results should, however, be accepted with caution because of limited samples and differences between institutions. More research is necessary, perhaps in terms of simultaneous relationship models to draw firm conclusions.

In an interesting micro-economic model of choice, Schultz (1976) has shown that the overall positive or negative change in the demand for babies will depend upon price and income effects. Normally, a rise in the price of a baby should reduce its demand. If prices are given, a sudden rise in parental income could increase the demand for babies. A rise in the husband's income could increase the demand for babies whereas a rise in the wife's income could reduce such demand because of differences in the values assigned to time allocated for work and relative income earned by the parents, even when the same values (but different signs) are assigned to the price and income elasticities of demand for the babies.

Although Schultz's attempt to analyse the demand for children within an economic calculus is interesting, it is not clear whether such a model could be really applied to the LDCs where the vast majority of people are illiterate and unaware of the sophisticated techniques to evaluate at the *margin* the gains and losses from having children. As has been emphasized earlier, fertility is governed by a large number of biological, psychological, social and religious factors and the exclusion of these factors may weaken considerably the predictive power of the models which seek to explain fertility behaviour purely in terms of economic variables.

Fertility and urbanization

The hypothesis is often put forward that fertility should be inversely correlated with urbanization. To the extent, higher *per capita* real income, better education, greater employment opportunities, particularly for women are all associated with greater urbanization in the LDCs, the hypothesis seems to be valid, at least *theoretically*. On the other hand, the *independent* effect of urbanization on fertility is open to question as the statistical problem of multicollinearity among the explanatory variables like *per capita* real income, education, employment and urbanization is obvious. Although it is argued that urbanization could change "attitudes", it is not quite clear how the mere transplantation of the village population into the urban society will lead to immediate changes in age-old customs. The process is thus likely to be slow. In fact, age-specific marital fertility difference between similar income groups in the rural and urban societies may not be significant. Indeed, evidence from Africa suggests that fertility in the urban areas is actually higher in comparison with that in the rural areas. In Latin America and India, it is just the opposite (see UN, 1973, Opinion Research Group, India, 1973). Thus, it is difficult to generalize from the existing evidence the likely impact of urbanization on fertility in the LDCs. However, since the urban areas in the LDCs have more access to education, information and supplies of the family planning devices, it is likely that fertility would be gradually lower in the urban areas in comparison with the rural areas.

Fertility, compulsory sterilization and incentive payments

One of the direct methods to reduce fertility could be compulsory sterilization. But the efficiency of such a method could be very much doubted, particularly in a democratic society. Perhaps in a regimented society (e.g. China), a more direct method to control fertility is likely to succeed. However, the Indian experience of 1975–77 shows how a high-handed compulsory sterilization programme could easily result in not only social unrest but also a dramatic political change. Few would genuinely doubt the necessity to pursue a vigorous family planning programme in India, but a *compulsory* sterilization programme seems to be an extreme and a very unwise policy which could easily defeat the purpose. A more rational scheme should include a system of incentives and disincentives which could be provided to the parents. Economic sanctions (e.g. tax-cum-subsidies) could achieve substantial success as it has been observed in the case of Singapore. Parents with one or two children could be given subsidies in cash or kind whereas families with more than three or four children could be penalized. Legislation may sometimes help to achieve a reduction in fertility. For instance, laws concerning an increase in the marriage age and a more liberal system of abortion may help to diminish fertility.

A rapid growth-rate of population in a poor and a static economy is one of the major reasons for poverty in the LDCs. Such poverty is observed in varying degrees in all the LDCs though where the density of population is high, the existing resources are low, the population growth-rate is high and income distribution is fairly unequal, poverty seems to beggar description. Instances of mass poverty are many in countries like Bangladesh, Ethiopia, Chad, Upper Volta, India, Peru, etc. In Section 10.5 we shall discuss poverty and income distribution.

10.5 Poverty and income distribution

The persistence of absolute poverty (see Appendix) and increase in relative inequality in some developing countries in spite of comparatively rapid economic growth in the last two decades is a subject of increasing concern in recent discussions in development economics. The evidence of the maldistribution of past growth has led some to call in to question the very idea of aggregate growth as a central aim of policy, believing that growth may have to be sacrificed for better distribution. Others, again, see no inevitable conflict between an increase in GNP and distribution, regarding growth as a necessary condition of better distribution, but rather focusing attention on active policies to promote a more equal distribution of the fruits of growth.

In this section we will first deal with the facts as we know them about inequality and absolute poverty in the Third World and their relationship with growth. Then the strategy of *Redistribution with Growth* will be outlined.*

10.6 Income inequality

From sample surveys there is now much more information than formerly on income distribution in a large number of developing countries, however, it is important to bear in mind the limitations of these data. Errors arise from a number of sources. First of all the income concept used is too restrictive. It is usually based on money income alone over a relatively short period such as a month or at most a year, rather than "permanent income" allowing for income in kind and adjusted for tax incidence and transfer payments. Even where the income concept is properly defined it is difficult to measure in practice, particularly at the upper and lower ends of the scale. There is a likelihood that the highest income groups deliberately understate their income for fear of incurring a tax liability. At the other end it is difficult to value own consumption and investment in the rural subsistence sector. Also rural–urban price differentials tend to understate rural real income. The sample surveys used for estimating income distribution are frequently based on samples of insufficient size and representativeness.

Given these familiar weaknesses in the data, the following tentative picture emerges about income inequality. Using the method of measuring inequality by the extent to which the income share of groups of individuals or households differs from their population share and examining the problem in terms of the income shares of the lowest 40 per cent, the middle 40 per cent and the top 20 per cent of households, the following broad patterns emerge from the income share data of the 66 countries in Table 10.2.

The *Socialist* countries have the highest degree of overall equality with average income of the lowest 40 per cent amounting to about 25 per cent of total incomes. Income inequality in these countries derives mainly from inequality in wages and not from the ownership of capital which is largely in public hands.

Developed countries are next in income equality ranging equally between low and moderate inequality with the income share of the lowest 40 per cent

* This section draws heavily on the material in Chenery *et al.*, 1974.

averaging about 16 per cent of total incomes. But the use of pretax data understates the equalizing effect of progressive taxes and transfer payments that are relatively significant in developed compared with underdeveloped countries.

Most *Underdeveloped* countries have more inequality than developed countries with about half falling into the high inequality range and the average share of the lowest 40 per cent amounting to 12.5 per cent of total incomes. But there is a considerable variation around this range with a considerable group in the low inequality range with similar income shares to those of the most egalitarian developed countries.

10.7 Absolute poverty

While the degree of relative inequality is an important element in the problem of poverty in underdeveloped countries, it tells us little about the extent of absolute poverty. Our concern is with absolute standards of living in terms of nutritional levels, health, education, etc. To this extent using a monetary yardstick for measuring "poverty datum lines" is extremely crude, particularly when making international comparisons. Nevertheless, bearing in mind the obvious limitations of using arbitrary money measures of "poverty lines", it is still instructive to see the estimates of absolute poverty that emerge.

In Table 10.3 the 45 countries listed cover about 60 per cent of the population of developing countries excluding China, about one-third of the population falls below a poverty line based on US $50 *per capita* and half falls below US $75 *per capita.*

Most of those living in absolute poverty are to be found in countries with low average levels of *per capita* income rather than in countries with very unequal income distribution patterns. India, Pakistan, Bangladesh and Sri Lanka, with 55 per cent of the total population in the table, alone account for about 75 per cent of the population living below US $50. Yet Pakistan, Bangladesh and Sri Lanka are characterized by low inequality with India displaying only moderate inequality. On the other hand there are some countries like Ecuador which, as in Sri Lanka, have one-third of their population below the US $50 level and yet have an average *per capita* income which is three times that of Sri Lanka. While low levels of *per capita* income may be the predominant cause of absolute poverty, unequal income distribution is also an important factor.

Growth, inequality and poverty

The above discussion only describes existing distributional patterns. Of more interest for assessing performance and guiding policy is the effect of growth on these patterns over time. Again data problems arise particularly with time series on the distribution of income. Based on data for only 18 countries (Chenery *et al.*, 1974, Fig. 1.1, p. 14), comparing rates of growth of GNP with rates of growth of income of the lowest 40 per cent between two points in time, what emerges is a considerable diversity of experience in developing countries in terms of changes in relative equality. Countries like Sri Lanka, Taiwan and Colombia have seen an improvement in equality whereas in Peru, Mexico, Venezuela and Brazil inequality has increased.

Table 10.2(a) Cross-classification of countries by income level and equality (Redistribution with growth)

	High inequality *Share of Lowest 40% less than 12%*					*Moderate inequality* *Share of Lowest 40% between 12% and 17%*					*Low inequality* *Share of Lowest 40%, 17% and above*				
	Country (year)	*Per capita GNP US$*	*Lowest 40%*	*Middle 40%*	*Top 20%*	*Country (year)*	*Per capita GNP US$*	*Lowest 40%*	*Middle 40%*	*Top 20%*	*Country (year)*	*Per capita GNP US$*	*Lowest 40%*	*Middle 40%*	*Top 20%*
Income up to US $300	Kenya (1969)	136	10.0	22.0	68.0	El Salvador (1969)	295	11.2	36.4	52.4	Chad (1958)	78	18.0	39.0	43.0
	Sierra Leone (1968)	159	9.6	22.4	68.0	Turkey (1968)	282	9.3	29.9	60.8	Sri Lanka (1969)	95	17.0	37.0	46.0
	Philippines (1971)	239	11.6	34.6	53.8	Burma (1958)	82	16.5	38.7	44.8	Niger (1960)	97	18.0	40.0	42.0
	Iraq (1956)	200	6.8	25.2	68.0	Dahomey (1959)	87	15.5	34.5	50.0	Pakistan (1964)	100	17.5	37.5	30.0
	Senegal (1960)	245	10.0	26.0	64.0	Tanzania (1967)	89	13.0	26.0	61.0	Uganda (1970)	126	17.1	35.8	47.1
	Ivory Coast (1970)	247	10.8	32.1	57.1	India (1964)	99	16.0	32.0	52.0	Thailand (1970)	180	17.0	37.5	45.5
	Rhodesia (1968)	252	8.2	22.8	69.0	Madagascar (1960)	120	13.5	25.5	61.0	Korea (1970)	235	18.0	37.0	45.0
	Tunisia (1970)	255	11.4	53.6	55.0	Zambia (1959)	230	14.5	28.5	57.0	Taiwan (1964)	241	20.4	39.5	40.1
	Honduras (1968)	265	6.5	28.5	65.0										
	Ecuador (1970)	277	6.5	20.0	73.5										
Income US $300–$750	Malaysia (1970)	330	11.6	32.4	56.0	Dominican Republic (1969)	323	12.2	30.3	57.5	Surinam (1962)	394	21.7	35.7	42.6
	Colombia (1970)	358	9.0	30.0	61.0	Iran (1968)	332	12.5	33.0	54.5	Greece (1957)	500	21.0	29.5	49.5
	Brazil (1970)	390	10.0	28.4	61.5	Guyana (1956)	550	14.0	40.3	45.7	Yugoslavia (1968)	529	18.5	40.0	41.5
	Peru (1971)	480	6.5	33.5	60.0	Lebanon (1960)	508	13.0	26.0	61.0	Bulgaria (1962)	530	26.8	40.0	33.2
	Gabon (1968)	497	8.8	23.7	67.5	Uruguay (1968)	618	16.5	35.5	48.0	Spain (1965)	750	17.6	36.7	45.7
	Jamaica (1958)	510	8.2	30.3	61.5	Chile (1968)	744	13.0	30.2	56.8					
	Costa Rica (1971)	521	11.5	30.0	58.5										
	Mexico (1969)	645	10.5	25.5	64.0										
	South Africa (1965)	669	6.2	35.8	58.0										
	Panama (1969)	692	9.4	31.2	59.4										

Table 10.2(b) Cross classification of countries by income level and equality (Income inequality)

	High inequality Share of Lowest 40% less than 12%					*Moderate inequality* Share of Lowest 40% between 12% and 17%					*Low inequality* Share of Lowest 40%, 17% and above				
	Country (year)	*Per capita GNP US$*	*Lowest 40%*	*Middle 40%*	*Top 20%*	*Country (year)*	*Per capita GNP US$*	*Lowest 40%*	*Middle 40%*	*Top 20%*	*Country (year)*	*Per capita GNP US$*	*Lowest 40%*	*Middle 40%*	*Top 20%*
Income above US $750	Venezuela (1970)	1,004	7.9	27.1	65.0	Argentina (1970)	1,079	16.5	36.1	47.4	Poland (1964)	850	23.4	40.6	36.0
	Finland (1962)	1,599	11.1	39.6	49.3	Puerto Rico (1968)	1,100	13.7	35.7	50.6	Japan (1963)	950	20.7	39.3	40.0
	France (1962)	1,913	9.5	36.8	53.7	Netherlands (1967)	1,990	13.6	37.9	48.5	United Kingdom (1968)	2,015	18.8	42.2	39.0
						Norway (1968)	2,010	16.6	42.9	40.5	Hungary (1969)	1,140	24.0	42.5	33.5
						Germany, Fed. Rep. (1964)	2,144	15.4	31.7	52.9	Czechoslovakia (1964)	1,150	27.6	41.4	31.0
						Denmark (1968)	2,563	13.6	38.8	47.6	Australia (1968)	2,509	20.0	41.2	38.8
						New Zealand (1969)	2,859	15.5	42.5	42.0	Canada (1965)	2,920	20.0	39.8	40.2
						Sweden (1963)	2,949	14.0	42.0	44.0	United States (1970)	4,850	19.7	41.5	38.8

Note: Sources for these data are listed in the Appendix to Chapter 1. The income shares of each percentile group were read off a free-hand Lorenz curve fitted to observed points in the cumulative distribution. The distributions are for pretax income. *Per capita* GNP figures are taken from the World Bank data files and refer to GNP at factor cost for the year indicated in constant 1971 US dollars.

Source: Chenery, H. *et al.* (1974), pp. 8–9.

Table 10.3 Estimates of population below poverty line in 1969

Country	*1969 GNP Per capita*	*1969 population (millions)*	*Population below $50*		*Population below $75*	
			Millions	*% of total population*	*Millions*	*% of total population*
Latin America						
Ecuador	264	5.9	2.2	37.0	3.5	58.5
Honduras	265	2.5	0.7	28.0	1.0	38.0
El Salvador	295	3.4	0.5	13.5	0.6	18.4
Dominican Republic	323	4.2	0.5	11.0	0.7	15.9
Colombia	347	20.6	3.2	15.4	5.6	27.0
Brazil	347	90.8	12.7	14.0	18.2	20.0
Jamaica	640	2.0	0.2	10.0	0.3	15.4
Guyana	390	0.7	0.1	9.0	0.1	15.1
Peru	480	13.1	2.5	18.9	3.3	25.5
Costa Rica	512	1.7	..	2.3	0.1	8.5
Mexico	645	48.9	3.8	7.8	8.7	17.8
Uruguay	649	2.9	0.1	2.5	0.2	5.5
Panama	692	1.4	0.1	3.5	0.2	11.0
Chile	751	9.6	..	..	..	..
Venezuela	974	10.0	..	..	..	..
Argentina	1,054	24.0	..	..	..	..
Puerto Rico	1,600	2.8	..	..	..	..
Total	545	244.5	26.6	10.8	42.5	17.4
Asia						
Burma	72	27.0	14.5	53.6	19.2	71.0
Sri Lanka	95	12.2	4.0	33.0	7.8	63.5
India	100	537.0	239.0	44.5	359.3	66.9
Pakistan (E&W)	100	111.8	36.3	32.5	64.7	57.9
Thailand	173	34.7	9.3	26.8	15.4	44.3
Korea	224	13.3	0.7	5.5	2.3	17.0
Philippines	233	37.2	4.8	13.0	11.2	30.0
Turkey	290	34.5	4.1	12.0	8.2	23.7
Iraq	316	9.4	2.3	24.0	3.1	33.3
Taiwan	317	13.8	1.5	10.7	2.0	14.3
Malaysia	323	10.6	1.2	11.0	1.6	15.5
Iran	350	27.9	2.3	8.5	4.2	15.0
Lebanon	570	2.6	..	1.0	0.1	5.0
Total	132	872.0	320.0	36.7	499.1	57.2
Africa						
Chad	75	3.5	1.5	43.1	2.7	77.5
Dahomey	90	2.6	1.1	41.6	2.3	90.1
Tanzania	92	12.8	7.4	57.9	9.3	72.9
Niger	94	3.9	1.3	33.0	2.3	59.9
Madagascar	119	6.7	3.6	53.8	4.7	69.6
Uganda	128	8.3	1.8	21.3	4.1	49.8

Table 10.3 (continued)

Country	*1969 GNP Per capita*	*1969 population (millions)*	*Population below $50*		*Population below $75*	
			Millions	*% of total population*	*Millions*	*% of total population*
Sierra Leone	165	2.5	1.1	43.5	1.5	61.5
Senegal	229	3.8	0.9	22.3	1.3	35.3
Ivory Coast	237	4.8	0.3	7.0	1.4	28.5
Tunisia	241	4.9	1.1	22.5	1.6	32.1
Rhodesia	274	5.1	0.9	17.4	1.9	37.4
Zambia	340	4.2	0.3	6.3	0.3	7.5
Gabon	547	0.5	0.1	15.7	0.1	23.0
South Africa	729	20.2	2.4	12.0	3.1	15.5
Total	303	83.8	23.8	28.4	36.6	43.6
Grand Total	228	1,200.3	370.4	30.9	578.2	48.2

Note: .. negligible.

Source: Chenery, H. *et al.* (1974), p. 12.

But even in countries like Mexico and Brazil where inequality has increased, the income of the lowest 40 per cent has still grown substantially (averaging about 6 per cent per annum) because of the high overall rate of growth of the economy.

Bearing in mind the weakness of the data, what does emerge is that there is no firm empirical basis for the view that high rates of growth inevitably generate greater inequality. Cases of increases in equality are to be found in both high and low growth countries as are the reverse, but on balance there is a positive correlation between rate of growth of GDP and the share of the lowest 40 per cent suggesting that the objectives of growth and equity may not be in conflict. There is, however, some confirmation for Kuznets' hypothesis based on an historical study of developed countries (Kuznets, 1955). Also in underdeveloped countries there is evidence of some increase in inequality in the early stages of development followed later by a decrease in inequality.

While a theory explaining the causal relationship between different variables and the degree of inequality is still in its infancy, cross-section analysis is suggestive of certain relationships that are of particular interest because of their amenability to policy. For example, education is positively correlated to equality in terms of income shares, with primary school enrolment particularly significant in explaining the share of the lowest income group. Rate of growth of the population, on the other hand, is inversely related to equality. But broad cross country analyses of the determinants of inequality are of limited usefulness in capturing either the complexity of the structural interrelations within a country or guiding policy. There is a need for a more disaggregated approach to the determinants of income distribution and one stage in this process which is emphasized in recent literature (ILO, 1972) is to identify the economic characteristics of poverty groups. It can be argued that the main purpose of studying income distribution is to give us better data on the sectoral distribution of the poor, their occupational characteristics, educational levels, ownership of productive assets and access to resources.

In most countries the poorest would be found among four identifiable economic groups. The rural landless, small farmers, the urban underemployed and urban employed. Although the percentage engaged in agriculture varies considerably between developing countries, it is a general fact that the poor are disproportionately located in the rural areas. It is estimated (Chenery *et al.*, 1974, p. 19) that at least 70 per cent of the poor are to be found in this sector, mostly landless farm workers and self-employed small farmers, but also including small traders and artisans located in the rural areas. The dimensions of this group have obvious implications for policies aimed at reducing poverty. But a mere shift in sectoral emphasis towards allocating resources to rural development is not sufficient if the benefits of policies aimed at this sector are slanted in favour of upper income groups in the rural areas. Policies will have to be designed that specifically favour the target group in question. In general terms this means physical investment, investment in human capital to raise skill levels, increasing access to resources in the form of credit, etc. and in some cases land reform involving a redistribution of land ownership and security of tenure are essential elements in improving the productivity and income of the rural poor.

The next most important poverty group are the urban underemployed. These are the low earning self-employed or wage paid workers in the "informal" urban sector. Until recently this rapidly growing sector comprising petty traders, providers of services, artisans and small scale labour-intensive manufacturers have been given scant attention by investigators or policy makers in government. They share with their rural counterparts a lack of capital assets, limited access to resources and low levels of education and skill. It is a great merit of the Kenya Report (ILO 1972) that it not only identified this sector but recommended specific policies for assisting it.

The urban unemployed, although a much smaller number than the "working poor" in the rural and urban areas, are a poverty group of growing importance in recent years. This group is heavily concentrated among the young and recent migrants to the urban areas. More attention to this group will be given in a later section.

10.8 Redistribution with growth

The strategy of linking the problem of unemployment with that of the working poor with the objective "of bringing every section (and if possible every member) of the population of working age up to a standard of employment productive enough to generate a reasonable minimum income" (ILO 1972, p. 104) was first put forward in a coherent form in the Kenya Report

(ILO 1972, p. 109). It was then generalized in the joint 1BRD/IDS volume *Redistribution with Growth* (Chenery *et al.*, 1974).

Redistribution with Growth describes a set of four basic approaches that can be used individually or in combination to increase the income of low income groups. The exact mix would depend on the economic and social structure of the country and the priority given to improving the welfare of the poorest.

These approaches are:

1. Maximizing GNP growth through raising savings and allocating resources more efficiently, with benefits to all groups in society.
2. Redirecting investment to poverty groups in the form of education, access to credit, public facilities and so on.
3. Redistributing income (or consumption) to poverty groups through the fiscal system or through direct allocation of consumer goods.
4. A transfer of existing assets to poverty groups, as in land reform. (Chenery *et al.*, 1974, p. 48)

1. Maximizing GNP growth may be a necessary but is not a sufficient condition for helping the poorest. Relying on growth alone would take too long to reach minimum income standards even if the poor participate fully in it. But it is more than likely that because of weak income linkages between poverty groups and the rest of the economy that their income will lag behind the general growth. Even though the poor may be better off in this case than with slower GNP growth, the welfare effects of a maximal growth strategy can usually be improved by some forms of redistribution as well.
2. Investing in the human and physical assets of poverty groups is likely to have a high pay-off in welfare terms as it will lead to income growth in groups that have higher welfare weights. But it may require some sacrifice of output in the short-run in so far as returns on investment in human capital take longer to develop. To this extent it may involve a short-run cost to upper income groups but these may also benefit in the long run as the productivity and income of the poor improve.
3. The scope for redistributing *existing* income on any scale in developing countries, while having some positive welfare effects in the short-run, is likely to be severely limited. Many developing countries are too poor for there to be any significant potential gain to the lower income groups from this strategy. There may be a high cost in terms of growth in the long-term from its potentially damaging effect on the incentives, savings and investment of the upper income groups. It is also likely to encounter strong resistance from this group. It is, therefore, a political judgement of the authors of *Redistribution with Growth* that there will be less hostility from the rich if redistribution is confined to the *increment* to their income.
4. The same structure applies to asset redistribution although in "areas such as land ownership and security of tenure, some degree of asset redistribution may be an essential part of any programme to make the rural poor more productive" (Chenery *et al.*, 1974, p. 49). But the preferred strategy is to

divert a proportion of the annual investment resources of the rich towards the poor in this way altering the distribution of the *increment* to the overall capital stock.

Some critics (e.g. Leys, 1975) have criticized RWG for being essentially an incrementalist strategy almost always to be pursued in an evolutionary rather than a revolutionary way. They argue that it offers no theory of political change and underestimates the resistance that the rich would offer to its policies. In its defence Richard Jolly, one of the authors of RWG (Cairncross and Puri, 1976, p. 48), argues that

The four approaches of RWG are generalizations of strategic options each of which if adopted at all might be applied in a more or less incrementalist and less or more radical manner, depending on time and situation, and, no doubt, other factors too. But the essential point is that RWG is neither incrementalist nor radical but a framework for analysing the interconnections between economic growth and redistribution.

It is interesting to note from the case studies included in the 1BRD/1DS volume (Chenery *et al.*, 1974, pp. 253–5), that favourable trends in income distribution have taken place in countries with regimes as different in political ideology and approach as Cuba on the one hand and Taiwan on the other.

10.9 The employment problem

It is now widely held in the literature (see e.g. Cairncross and Puri, 1976, pp. 56–70; Jolly *et al.*, 1973; Robinson and Johnston, 1971; ILO, 1972; Chenery *et al.*, 1974) that open unemployment in the urban areas must be viewed as only one aspect, and not necessarily the most serious one, of the wider problem of underemployment and poverty in developing countries. It is not obvious that the condition of unemployed educated youths (the vast majority of the open unemployed in developing countries), who are supported by the extended family system and pick up casual earnings in the urban informal sector while they seek relatively highly paid jobs in the modern sector, is worse than that of a fully employed peasant who works long hours for a meagre subsistence. Both in the analysis of its causation and the strategy to deal with it, open unemployment must be linked with the general problem of underutilization of resources, poverty and inequalities in income distribution dealt with in the previous section.

Nevertheless, unemployment in the urban areas has become a problem of increasing seriousness in most developing countries in the last two decades. Again, statistics are notoriously inadequate but it is estimated that 15–25 per cent of the urban labour force is openly unemployed in many countries (Jolly *et al.*, 1973, p. 9) and often much higher percentages for persons aged fifteen to twenty-four. The situation is more serious in the developing countries today than it ever was in the advanced countries in the worst period of the depression in the 1930s. The problem is chronic rather than cyclical accompanying relatively high average rates of growth of GDP. Also in developing countries it disproportionately affects the young and better educated whereas in advanced countries it more seriously affects the old and unskilled. This phenomenon of growth without employment has exposed the weakness of conventional development strategies based on the Arthur Lewis type of labour-surplus model with its heavy emphasis on modern sector industrialization and GDP growth. These models seriously overestimated the capacity of the modern sector to absorb the unemployed and underemployed and generate a spread effect to enable the population at large to share the benefits of growth. Worse than that, the form of modern sector development, with its urban bias, capital intensity, high productivity and wages, has exacerbated the situation by acting as a magnet to urban migration while not offering sufficient jobs.

On the supply side a number of factors have contributed to a rapid increase in the labour force. There is first of all high rates of population increase already discussed in Section 10.1. Then there is the "education explosion" which has increased the proportion of the young leaving the rural areas to seek modern sector jobs. The nature of the educational system in developing countries carries a good deal of responsibility for this with its urban-academic bias. The rapid spread of universal primary education, seldom geared to the requirements of rural life, has raised the aspirations of the young to seek modern sector jobs causing widespread unemployment among primary school leavers. In some countries like Sri Lanka (see ILO, 1971), where secondary and higher education have been expanded over a longer period but where the educational system has also not been adapted to job opportunities, the employment problem is even more serious among high school leavers and graduates.

There are also other structural weaknesses on the supply side, particularly in the rural areas, which contribute to the "push" to the towns. Great inequalities in land-holdings in many developing countries result in large numbers of families being unable to provide sufficient work and income for their expanding numbers given their lack of capital and knowledge of techniques. At the same time land-holdings are often underutilized and use capital-intensive techniques employing little labour. Low and unstable prices of agricultural products, poor transport facilities and general infrastructure, turn the terms of trade against the rural sector and the small peasant in particular. The benefits of recent agricultural innovations in the form of the "Green Revolution" have disproportionately favoured large farmers in particular areas and urban dwellers who enjoy lower food prices to the detriment of small peasants who are unable to take advantage of these innovations because of their lack of resources for necessary inputs while having to suffer lower prices as producers.

On the demand side the capital-intensive nature of the modern sector has meant that output has grown faster than employment. Even where earnings in the modern sector are little above those in the rural sector, relatively capital-intensive methods of production are the general rule. There are a number of reasons for this. The importance of multinational corporations in the modern sector means that both the nature of the products and technology are determined by conditions in the advanced countries rather than relative factor prices in developing countries. Even where more labour-intensive methods of production would be justified, these techniques are just not available. Most of the world's research and development takes place in the advanced countries where little attention is paid to intermediate technology. Capital intensity has also been artificially stimulated by policies adopted by governments in LDCs. High rates of protection, excessive tax concessions to foreign enterprises and over-valued exchange rates, all favour the importation of capital-intensive equipment.

In practice, however, earnings in the modern sector are generally well above the differential that may be required to equalize the net costs and benefits of urban modern sector life compared with rural life. A competitive labour market, crucial to the smooth working of the so-called labour surplus model of development where the price of modern sector labour is determined by average earnings in the rural sector, does not often obtain. Government minimum wage legislation is widespread with the minimum usually based on criteria such as "ability to pay" or "requirements of civilized urban existence" rather than rural earnings. Western type trades unions have also interfered with the free market mechanism raising wages above the "minimum price of entry". The new ruling élite in recently independent developing countries have inherited and reinforced an earnings structure based on expatriate Western standards rather than one more relevant to local conditions. Foreign enterprises, in order to avoid the stigma of being regarded as neo-colonialist exploiters, but also because of their superior resources, protected status and capital-intensive methods of production, have frequently set the pace by voluntarily paying wages above the free market level. This in its turn generates a vicious circle as far as employment is concerned by justifying the installation of even more capital-intensive methods of production.

As we will show, this rural–urban differential is a vital factor explaining the continued high rates of rural–urban migration in the face of chronic and growing urban unemployment and underemployment.

10.10 The Todaro model

The fundamental contribution of the Todaro model (Todaro, 1969, 1971b, 1976) to our understanding of the migration process and its links with unemployment is that "migration proceeds primarily in response to differences in 'expected' urban and rural real incomes and that as a result of this the observed accelerated rates of internal migration in developing countries in the context of using urban unemployment are not only a plausible phenomenon but are in fact entirely rational from the private 'expected' income maximization viewpoint of individual migrants" (Todaro, 1976, p. 45).

The two principal economic factors that are involved in the decision to migrate are the existing rural–urban real wage differential and the degree of probability of finding a modern sector urban job. The rural–urban differential alone would not explain the migration given high levels of urban unemployment. The positive stimulus of the differential is likely to be restrained by the negative effect of the risk that a migrant may not find a modern sector job. But even if the probability of finding a highly paid job in the short term is low, it may still be a perfectly rational decision to migrate even though expected urban income in the short period is less than expected rural income. If the migrant takes a longer term view of his permanent income prospects, (which is realistic in view of the fact that the vast majority of migrants are young) and if he expects the probability of finding a job to increase over time as he improves his urban contacts, then as long as the present value of the net stream of expected urban income over his planning horizon exceeds that of expected rural income, the decision to migrate is justified.

The Todaro model can be summarized mathematically as follows (see Todaro, 1976, pp. 32–5):

If V(0) = the discounted present value of the expected "net" urban–rural income stream over the migrants time horizon.

Yu, r(t) = the average real income of individuals employed in the urban and rural economy

n = number of time periods in migrants planning horizon

i = discount rate reflecting migrants time preference

C(0) = the cost of migration

p(t) = the probability that a migrant will have secured an urban job at the average income level in period t.

then the decision to migrate or not depends on whether

$$V(0) = \int_{t=0}^{n} [p(t)Y_u(t) - Y_r(t)]e^{-it}\,dt - C(0) \qquad [10.1]$$

is positive or negative.

In any one time period the probability of being employed in the modern sector, p(t), will be related to the probability Π of having been selected in that or any previous period from a given stock of unemployed job seekers. If it is assumed that for most migrants the selection procedure is random, then the probability of having a job in the modern sector within x periods after migration, p(x) is:

$$p(1) = \Pi(1) \qquad [10.2]$$

and

$$p(2) = \Pi(1) + [1 - \Pi(1)]\Pi(2) \qquad [10.3]$$

so that

$$p(x) = p(x-1) + [1 - p(x-1)]\Pi(x) \qquad [10.4]$$

or

$$p(x) = \Pi(1) + \sum_{t=2}^{x} \Pi(t) \prod_{s=1}^{t-1} [1 - \Pi(S)] \qquad [10.5]$$

where $\Pi(t)$ equals the ratio of new job openings relative to the number of accumulated job seekers in time t.

Expressing the probability variable in this way means that the longer the migrant has been in the urban area the higher is the probability p of his finding a modern sector job and, therefore, his expected income in that period. This is realistic in that migrants improve their contacts and are better informed as time passes. It also avoids having to assume that either the migrant earns nothing at first or the average urban income, and therefore allows for the probability that many migrants will earn some income in the informal urban sector while looking for a modern sector job.

From the above an aggregate dynamic equilibrium model of urban labour demand and supply is developed as follows:

The rural labour force L_R is assumed to grow at a natural rate r less migration m, or

$$\dot{L}_R = (r - m)L_R \qquad [10.6]$$

where $\dot{L}_R$ is the time derivative of LR.

The urban labour force L_U also grows at a rate r plus migration from rural areas.

$$\dot{L}_U = rL_U + mL_R \qquad [10.7]$$

or substituting $M = mL_R$ where M represents the actual amount of rural–urban migration, equation [10.7] can be written as

$$\dot{L}_U = rL_U + M \qquad [10.8]$$

The growth of urban employment opportunities (the demand for urban labour) is assumed to be constant at a rate g, so that

$$\dot{E}_U = gE_U \qquad [10.9]$$

where E_U is the level of urban sector employment.

To this standard model Todaro adds his migration function which assumes that the rate of rural–urban migration m

$$\left(= \frac{M}{L_R}\right) \qquad [10.10]$$

is a function of:

1. The *probability* of finding a modern sector job which can be expressed as some simple positive monotonic function of the urban employment rate

$$\left(\frac{E_U}{L_U}\right) \qquad [10.11]$$

or a negative function of the urban unemployment rate $\dfrac{L_U - E_U}{L_U}$.

2. *The urban–rural real income differential* expressed as a ratio

$$\frac{Y_U}{Y_R} = W \qquad [10.12]$$

where $W > 1$ and is assumed fixed.

3. Other factors, Z, such as personal contacts, travel distance, urban amenities etc. which influence the migrant's view of the worth of migrating.

The basic Todaro migration equation can be stated as

$$m = F\left[\frac{E_U}{L_U}, W, Z\right] \qquad [10.13]$$

where

$$F^1\left[\frac{E_U}{L_U}\right] > 0; \quad F^1(W) > 0; \quad F^1(Z) \gtreqless 0$$

Assuming W and Z as fixed the function F can be stated as

$$F\left[\frac{E_U}{L_U}, W, Z\right] = f\left[\frac{E_U}{L_U}\right] \qquad [10.14]$$

where $f^1 \geq 0$ for all values of $\frac{E_U}{L_U}$ between 0 and 1.

Substituting equations [10.13] and [10.14] in [10.7] yields the basic differential equation for urban labour force growth in the Todaro model, viz

$$\frac{\dot{L}_U}{L_U} = r + \frac{L_R}{L_U} f\left[\frac{E_U}{L_U}\right] \qquad [10.15]$$

Although the Todaro model has been criticized for assuming a "too simple and exclusively economic motivation for migration" (Jolly *et al.*, 1973, p. 13) its virtue lies in the readily quantifiable form it handles the major, even if not the exclusive factors, determining migration.

Among the several modifications of the basic Todaro model that have been suggested so far, the following deserve special consideration.

(*a*) *Harris–Todaro* (*HT*) *model* (*1970*)

An attempt has been made in the HT model (1970) to distinguish between rural and urban sector and to analyse the effects of migration on rural and urban output, income and welfare. The model could be stated algebraically as follows.

Let $E(W_u) = W_u \cdot \frac{E_u}{L_u}$

Where $E(W_u)$ = expected urban income

W_u = urban wages

E_u = amount of urban employment

L_u = current size of urban labour

Assuming that W_R = rural wages

$E(W_R)$ is the expected rural wage

Let $E(W_R) = W_R$

and the rural–urban migration, M, be

$$M = \dot{L}_u$$

Assume that $\dot{L}_u$ is a function of urban–rural expected wage differential, so that we have

$$M = \dot{L}_u = f[E(W_u) - E(W_R)]$$

In the equilibrium,

$$E(W_u) = E(W_R)$$

By substitution, we now have

$$W_u \frac{E_u}{L_u} = W_R$$

An equilibrium unemployment rate is then given by dividing the above equation by W_u and subtracting each side from 1; i.e.

$$1 - \frac{E_u}{L_u} = 1 - \frac{W_R}{W_u}$$

or, the rate of *employment* is given by

$$\frac{E_u}{L_u} = \frac{W_R}{W_u}$$

The final equation illustrates the negative relationship between expected urban–rural wage differences and the rates of equilibrium unemployment.

The modified HT model implies that an increase in the rate of creation of urban employment could raise the unemployment levels. The impact on social welfare is measured by HT in terms of output gains or losses, given the different avenues (e.g. sectoral wage subsidies, demand creation, etc.) to create urban employment. They have also shown the situation where compulsory prohibition of migration could *reduce* the net welfare of the rural sector.

(*b*) *Bhagwati and Srinivasan* (*BS*) *model* (*1974*)

In the model of BS, it has been contended that a second-best solution in the HT model which required control of migration plus an urban wage subsidy to obtain the most efficient production, is unnecessary, because a first-best solution could be obtained via a judicious use of tax/subsidy policies. This would render the physical control of migration of labour irrelevant to the HT argument.

(c) *Fields' model (1975)*

In addition to the quantity adjustment as the major instrument to obtain equilibrium in the urban labour market in the LDCs (a point which has been suggested by HT), Fields has considered some other variables. For example (1) the high probability of an educated person being able to obtain a job in the modern sector; (2) the rate of labour turnover in the urban sector (a point earlier emphasized by Johnson (1971)) and the difference in attitudes towards risks among the migrants; (3) the presence of *under*employed workers in the urban informal sector and the lower probability of their obtaining a job in comparison with those who are wholly occupied in searching for a job; and (4) an urban job search process where people living in rural areas have a reasonable chance of obtaining jobs in the city without first going there. On the basis of these more realistic assumptions in comparison with those made in the HT model (1970), Fields has demonstrated that an urban equilibrium unemployment rate will be lower than the one predicted by the HT model.

Fields has also suggested some policies to tackle the problem of unemployment in the light of his analysis. These include (a) the setting up of an urban/rural job centre to reduce the cost (both private and social) of job search and thus raise output; and (b) "overeducation" of labour, which would appear paradoxical in countries suffering from educated unemployment.

Some other criticisms of the HT model could also be mentioned. For instance, HT ignore the possibility of inter-sectoral capital mobility between the urban and rural areas. Once such possibilities are included, some of the results of the HT model have to be modified (Corden and Findlay, 1975). It could also be argued that HT have unrealistically assumed labour to be homogeneous. Different types of labour respond differently to migration opportunities. Landless workers tend to migrate more frequently than other types of agriculturists in many parts of Asia. Moreover, migrants' income does not wholly accrue to the village sector in many parts of Asia. The HT assumption regarding immobility of capital stock could be doubted. Further, the welfare effect of migration should also include the possibility of transfers of human capital between different sectors. (Corden and Findlay, 1975).

10.11 Employment policy

A number of important implications for employment policy follow from Todaro's analysis of the migration process.

1. An attempt to solve the urban unemployment problem by relying only on increasing the number of modern sector jobs may actually make the situation worse, given a positive rural/urban earnings differential, in so far as the increased demand for urban labour raises the probability of finding a modern sector job and so encourages even higher rates of migration. There is evidence to show that this can occur as in the case of the 1964 and 1970

Tripartite Agreements in Kenya. The agreement between government, industry and the trades unions to tackle unemployment by expanding employment in exchange for wage restraint proved self-defeating.

2. Of crucial importance is narrowing the expected rural–urban income differential. This involves a broad strategy to get at the root causes of the employment problem at both the rural and urban end linking it with the wider problem of underutilization of resources, poverty and inequality discussed earlier. The chief elements in the strategy are:

(*a*) Rural development with all that is involved in improving rural incomes and job opportunities is probably the most important way of reducing the "push" from the countryside.

(*b*) Positive policies to increase productivity and incomes in the informal urban sector. This sector is small scale, labour intensive, competitive and economical in its use of imported inputs and yet not only has it been generally neglected by government but frequently discriminated against by severe licensing restrictions and a range of measures that favour the modern sector. Increasing attention has been given to this sector in the reports of recent ILO employment missions (see e.g. ILO, 1972).

(*c*) An incomes policy to reduce or at least prevent a widening of the gap between earnings in the modern sector and the rest of the economy is widely stressed in the literature (see e.g. Smith, 1967; ILO, 1967; ILO, 1972; ILO, 1972 (Iran)). Governments in a few developing countries like Tanzania and Kenya, have paid serious attention to this problem in their policies and plans (see e.g. Tanzania 1967; Kenya 1973; Kenya 1974). Tanzania has been something of a pioneer in being one of the first to link an incomes policy with a programme for rural development as part of a broad strategy to deal with employment and poverty.

Besides the above, a comprehensive and integrated strategy dealing with the employment problem would also have to include:

1. A population policy to control fertility and labour supply.

2. An education policy which gives less emphasis to the quantitative link between occupation and formal education and more attention to the structure and content of education making it more relevant to the environment in which most of the pupils and students are going to live and work. There is a trend in developing countries away from concentrating expansion on secondary and higher education in favour of improving basic education for the very young and giving a second-chance via informal educational institutions to those who dropped out of the educational system or did not get in to it in the first place.

3. A policy regarding choice of techniques which encourages the use of labour-intensive methods of production and the development of intermediate technology without sacrificing output for employment (see e.g. Morawetz, 1974).

Appendix

The definition of a poverty line

1. An *absolute* index of poverty is a “Head-Count” ratio, or P_h, as Sen (1976) puts it, which shows the *percentage* of people in poverty. Thus

$P_h = q/n$

where q = number of people in poverty with $y_i \leq Z$
n = total population
y = income
Z = poverty line

Note that P_h does not consider the *extent* by which the incomes of the poor fall short of the poverty line.

2. The relative index of poverty (P_g) is the total income necessary to bring all the poor people up to the line of poverty, i.e. Z. Thus, we have

$$P_g = \sum_{i=1}^{q} g_i$$

where $g_i = Z - y_i$
$i = 1, 2, 3, \ldots$ persons

Note that $g = \sum_{i=1}^{q} (Z - y_i) = q(Z - M)$

where M = mean income of the poor.
The *average* gap in poverty = $(Z - M)$

The proportion of shortfall of average income from the line of poverty $= \dfrac{Z - M}{Z}$

Note that the relative index of poverty, P_g, is insensitive to the *number* of people in poverty.
Note also that both P_h and P_g are independent of income transfer *among the poor.*

3. The Sen index or P_s is actually a synthetic yardstick which includes the features of both P_g and P_h and takes into account the distribution of income among the poor. (Sen, 1976). Here the nature of poverty is assumed to be a “normalized weighted sum of the income gaps of the poor”. An income weighting scheme is described and then a method for normalization is suggested by Sen. A rank–order weighting scheme is chosen where the weight in the income difference of a poor is equal to the rank in ordering of income below the line of poverty. Such a method of weighting naturally involves the Gini-coefficient of the distribution of income among the poor. In the normalization axiom of Sen, it is necessary that when every poor man has the same level of income, the value of the index is given by the proportion of persons within poverty times the proportion of average gap between the line of poverty and the income of the poor.

The normalized value of the index of Sen $= \dfrac{q}{n} \cdot \dfrac{Z - M}{Z}$

In the rank–order weighting scheme, a weight $(q + 1 - i)$ on $g_i(= Z - y_i)$ is suggested because we have $(q - i + 1)$ number of people within the poor whose income would be at least equivalent to that of individual i. Now we have the index of Sen or P_s as:

$$P_s = A \sum_{i=1}^{q} (q + 1 - i)(Z - y_i)$$

where A is a parameter which may be defined as:

$$A = \frac{2}{(q + 1)nZ}$$

If $y_i = M$, then the normalized value of the Sen index may be written as:

$$\frac{q}{n} \cdot \frac{Z - M}{Z} = A(Z - M)\frac{q(q + 1)}{2}$$

because

$$\sum_{i=1}^{q} (q + 1 - i) = \frac{q(q + 1)}{2}$$

Now G or the Gini-coefficient of income distribution among the poor may be defined as:

$$G = \frac{q + 1}{q} - \frac{2}{q^2 M} \sum_{i=1}^{q}{}'(q + 1 - i)y_i$$

Hence

$$P_s = \frac{q}{n} \cdot \frac{1}{Z}\left(Z - M + \frac{q}{q + 1} GM\right)$$

For large numbers of the poor, i.e. for large q, $q/(q + 1) \simeq 1$, P_s is simply given by

$$P_s = \frac{q}{n} \cdot \frac{1}{Z}\{Z - M(1 - G)\}.$$

When the index of relative poverty, as defined in (**2**) above, is given by the income–gap ratio, or,

$$I = \sum_{i \in S(Z)} g_i/qZ,$$

then, for large numbers of the poor, we have

$$P_s = P_h\{I + (1 - I)G\}$$

Note that P_s should vary between 0 and 1. When every individual earns an income above Z, $P_s = 0$ as $q = 0$. Similarly, $P_s = 1$, when nobody earns anything so that $M = 0$ and $q = n$. (For a further discussion, see Sen, 1976; see also Anand, 1977, for a comparison between the Sen index and the other indices e.g. Atkinson (1970), and the application of the Sen index to the Malaysian economy.) Anand reports that $P_s = 0.20$ in peninsular Malaysia. Since the estimates for other countries are not available, it is difficult to state its relative significance. Clearly, in absolute terms, the figure is quite substantial. As usual, the use of P_s reveals that the incidence of poverty in Malaysia is the highest among agriculturists and illiterates.

References

Adelman, Irma (1962), *Theories of Economic Growth and Development*, Stanford U.P., Stanford.

Adelman, Irma (1968), "An Ecometric Model of Socio-economic and Political Change in Underdeveloped Countries", *American Economic Review*, **58**, 1184–218.

Adelman, Irma (1975), "Growth, Income Distribution and Equity-Oriented Development Strategies", *World Development*, Feb.–Mar., 67–73.

Adelman, Irma and Chenery, H. (1966), "Foreign Aid and Economic Development: The Case of Greece", *Review of Economics and Statistics*, **48**, 1–19.

Adelman, Irma and Taft Morris, Cynthia (1967), *Society, Politics and Economic Development: A Quantitative Approach*, Johns Hopkins Press, Baltimore.

Adelman, Irma and Taft Morris, Cynthia (1968), "Performance Criteria for Evaluating Economic Development Potential; An Operational Approach", *Quarterly Journal of Economics*, **37**, 2, 260–80.

Adelman, Irma and Taft Morris, Cynthia (1973), *Economic Growth and Social Equity in Developing Countries*, Stanford U.P., Stanford.

Adelman, Irma and Thorbecke, E. (ed) (1966), *The Theory and Design of Economic Development*, Johns Hopkins Press, Baltimore.

Adler, John H. (1969), "Fiscal Policy in a Developing Country", in Agarwala A. N., and Singh, S. P., (eds) (1958).

Agarwala, A. N. and Singh, S. P. (eds) (1958), *The Economics of Underdevelopment*, Oxford U.P., N.J.

Agarwala, Ramgopal (1970), *An Econometric Model of India: 1948–1961*, Frank Cass, London.

Ahluwalia, Montek, S. (1974), "Income Inequality: Some Dimensions of the Problem", in Chenery, Hollis *et al.* (1974).

Ahluwalia, Montek, S. and Chenery, Hollis (1974), "A Model of Distribution and Growth", in Chenery, Hollis *et al.* (1974).

Amin, Samir (1969), "Levels of Renumeration, Factor Proportions and Income Differentials with Special Reference to Developing Countries", in Smith, A. (ed) (1969).

Anand, Sudhir (1977), "Aspects of Poverty in Malaysia", *The Review of Income and Wealth*, **23**, 1, 1–16.

Arrow, K. and Scitovsky, T. (eds) (1969), *Readings in Welfare Economics*, McMillan, London.

Atkinson, A. B. (1970), "On the Measurement of Inequality", *Journal of Economic Theory*, **2**, 244–63.

Ayre, P. C. I. (ed) (1977), *Finance in Developing Countries*, Frank Cass, London.

Bagchi, Amiya (1962), "The Choice of the Optimum Techniques", *Economic Journal*, **72**, 3, 658–76.

Baker, Arnold, B. and Frank, Falero, Jr. (1971), "Money, Exports, Government Spending and Income in Peru, 1951–66", *Journal of Development Studies*, 7, 4, 353–64.

Balassa, Bela (1972), *The Structure of Protection in Industrial Countries*, IBRD, report No: EC–152.

Balassa, Bela and Associates (1971), *The Structure of Protection in Developing Countries*, Johns Hopkins Press, Baltimore.

Balasubramanyam, V. N. (1973), *International Transfer of Technology to India*, Praeger, N.Y.

Balogh, T. (1967), "Multilateral vs. Bilateral Aid", *Oxford Economic Papers*, **19**, 3, 328–44.

Baldwin, Robert E. (1972), *Economic Development and Growth*, Wiley, N.Y.

Baldwin, Robert E. and Murray, T. (1977), "M.F.N. Tariff Reductions and LDC Benefit under the GSP", *Economic Journal*, **87**, 30–46.

Bardhan, Kalpana (1970), "Price Response of Marketed of Foodgrains: A Cross-sectional Study of Some North Indian Villages", *American Journal of Agricultural Economics*, **52**, 51–61.

Bardhan, Kalpana and Bardhan, Pranab (1971), "Price Response of Marketed Surplus of Foodgrains: An Analysis of Indian Time Series Data", *Oxford Economic Papers*, **23**, 255–67.

Bardhan, Pranab Kumar (1970a), "Green Revolution and Agricultural Labourers", *Economic and Political Weekly*, **5**, 29–31, 1239–46.

Bardhan, Pranab Kumar (1970b), "A Correction", *Economic and Political Weekly*, **5**, 46, 1861.

Bardhan, Pranab Kumar (1970c), *Economic Growth, Development and Foreign Trade*, Wiley, N.Y.

Bardhan, Pranab Kumar and Srinivasan, T. N. (1971), "Crop-Sharing Tenancy in Agriculture: A Theoretical and Empirical Analysis", *American Economic Review*, **61**, 48–64.

Bardhan, Pranab Kumar (1973), "On the Incidence of Poverty in Rural India of the Sixties", *Economic and Political Weekly*, **8**.

Bardhan, Pranab Kumar (1975), *Major Issues Arising from the Transfer of*

Technology to Developing Countries: On some Implications of Technology Transfer for Trade, Growth and Distribution in Developing Countries, UNCTAD, TD/B/C:6/5.

Bardhan, Pranab Kumar (1977), "Variations in Forms of Tenancy in a Peasant Economy", *Journal of Development Economics*, **4**, 2, 105–18.

Bardhan, Pranab Kumar and Srinivasan, T. N. (eds) (1975), *Poverty and Income Distribution in India*, Statistical Publishing House, Calcutta.

Bator, F. M. (1957), "On Capital Productivity, Input Allocation and Growth", *Quarterly Journal of Economics*, **71**, 86–106.

Bauer, P. T. (1971), *Dissent on Development: Studies and Debates in Development Economies*, Weidenfeld and Nicolson, London.

Bauer, P. T. (1973), "Inflation, SDRs and Aid", *Lloyds Bank Review*, July, 31–5.

Bauer, P. T. and Yamey, B. S. (1957), *The Economies of Underdeveloped Countries*, University of Chicago Press, Chicago.

Bauer, P. T. and Yamey B. S. (1959), "A Case Study of Response to Price in an Underdeveloped Country", *Economic Journal*, LXIX, 800–5.

Baumol, William J. (1968), *Economic Dynamics* (3rd edn), McMillan, New York.

Baumol, William J. (1977), *Economic Theory and Operations Analysis* (4th edn), Prentice Hall International Inc., London.

Becker, G. S. and Lewis, H. G. (1973), "On the Interaction between the Quantity and Quality of Children", *Journal of Political Economy*, **81**, 2, S 279–88.

Beckerman, Wilfred (1966), *International Comparisons of Real Incomes*, OECD Development Center, Paris.

Beckerman, Wilfred (1974), *In Defence of Economic Growth*, Jonathan Cape, London.

Beckerman, Wilfred and Bacon, Robert (1970), "The International Distribution of Incomes", in Streeten, Paul (ed) (1970).

Behrman, R. L. (1968), *Supply Response in Underdeveloped Agriculture: A Case Study of Four Major Annual Crops in Thailand, 1937–1963*, North-Holland, Amsterdam.

Ben Porath, Y. (1973), "Economic Analysis of Fertility in Israel: Point and Counterpoint", *Journal of Political Economy*, Suppl. 81:2, S. 202–33.

Bergan, Arsbhorn (1967), "Personal Income Distribution and Personal Savings in Pakistan", in Griffin, K. and Khan A. (eds) (1972).

Bergsman, J. (1970), *Brazil: Industrialization and Trade Policies*, OECD and Oxford U.P., Paris and London.

Berill, K. (ed) (1964), *Economic Development with Special Reference to East Asia*, McMillan, London.

Berry, Albert and Soligo, Ronald (1968), "Rural–Urban Migration, Agricultural Output and the Supply Price of Labour in a Labour Surplus Economy", *Oxford Economic Papers*, **20**, 2, 230–49.

Berry, Albert and Soligo, Ronald (1975), "Presumptive Income Tax on Agricultural Land", in Bird, R. and Oldman, O. (eds) (1975).

Bhagwati, Jagdish (1958), "Immiserizing Growth: a Geometrical Note", *Review of Economic Studies*, **25**, 201–5.

Bhagwati, Jagdish (1964), "The Pure Theory of International Trade: A Survey", *Economic Journal*, **74**.

Bhagwati, Jagdish (ed) (1970), *International Trade*, Penguin.

Bhagwati, Jagdish and Chakravarty, S. (1969), "Contributions to Indian Economic Analysis: A Survey", *American Economic Review*, Sept. Suppl., 2–73.

Bhagwati, Jagdish and Desai, Padma (1970), *India: Planning for Industrialization*, OECD, Oxford and Paris.

Bhagwati, Jagdish and Ramaswami, V. K. (1963), "Domestic Distortions, Tariffs and the Theory of Optimum Subsidy", *Journal of Political Economy*, **71**, 44–50.

Bhagwati, Jagdish and Srinivasan, T. N. (1974), "On Re-analysing the Harris–Todaro Model: Policy Ranking in the Case of Sector-Specific sticky wages", *American Economic Review*, **64**, 502–8.

Bhalla, A. S. (1964), "Investment Allocations and Technological Choice – a Case of Cotton-spinning techniques", *Economic Journal*, **74**, 611–22.

Bhalla, A. S. (1965), "Choosing Techniques: Hand-pounding v. Machine-milling of Rice: An Indian Case", *Oxford Economic Papers*, **17**, 147–57.

Bhalla, A. S. (ed) (1975), *Technology and Employment in Industry, a case study approach*, ILO, Geneva.

Bharadwaj, V. P. and Dave, P. K. (1973), "An Empirical Test of Kaldor's Macro-Model of Income Distribution for Indian Economy", *Indian Economic Journal*, XX, **3**, 515–20.

Bird, Graham (1976), "The Informal Link between SDR Allocation and Aid: A Note", *The Journal of Development Studies*, **12**, 3, 268–73.

Bird, Richard, M. (1977), "Land Taxation and Economic Development: The Model of Meiji Japan", in Ayre, P.C.I. (ed) (1977).

Bird, Richard, M. and Oldman, Oliver (1975), *Readings on Taxation in Developing Countries*, (3rd edn) Johns Hopkins Press, Baltimore.

Blake, J. D. (1962), "Labour Shortage and Unemployment in Northeast Sumatra", *Malayan Economic Review*, **7**, 2, 106–18.

Bliss, C. J. and Stern, N. H. (1976), *Economic Aspects of the Connection between Productivity and Consumption*, University of Essex, Discussion Paper No. 67.

Bober, M. M. (1950), *Karl Marx's Interpretation of History*, Harvard U.P., Mass.

Boeke, J. H. (1953), *Economics and Economic Policy of Dual Societies*, Tjeenk Willink and Zoon, Haarlem.

Bolnick, Bruce, R. (1975), "Interpreting Polak: Monetary Analysis in Dependent Economies", *Journal of Development Studies*, **11**, 4, 325–42.

Bose, Arun (1975), *Marxian and Post-Marxian Political Economy*, Penguin.

Bose, Sanjit, K. (1968), "Optimal Growth and Investment Allocation", *Review of Economic Studies*, **35**, 465–80.

Bose, Swadesh, R. (1972), "Trend of Real Income of the Rural Poor in East Pakistan", in Griffin, Keith and Khan, Azizur Rahman, (eds) (1972).

Bottomley, Anthony (1971), *Factor Pricing and Economic Growth in Underdeveloped Rural Areas*, Crosby Lockwood, London.

Brahmananda, P. R. and Vakil, C. N. (1956), *Planning for an Expanding Economy*, Vora & Co., Bombay.

Brown, Doris (1971), *Agricultural Development in India's Districts*, Harvard U.P., Mass.

Brown, Lester, R. (1970), *Seeds of Change: The Green Revolution and Development in the 1970s*, London.

Buchanan, N. S. (1945), *International Investment and Domestic Welfare*, Henry Colt, N.Y.

Byres, T. J. (1972), "The Dialectic of India's Green Revolution", *South Asian Review*, **5**, 2, 99–116.

Cairncross, A. and Puri, Mohinder (eds) (1976), *Employment, Income Distribution and Development Strategy*, McMillan, London.

Cassen, Robert (1976), "Population and Development: A Survey", *World Development*, **4**, 10/11, 785–830.

Chakravarty, Sukhamoy (1959), *The Logic of Investment Planning*, North-Holland, Amsterdam.

Chakravarty, Sukhamoy (1969), *Capital and Development Planning*, M.I.T. Press, Cambridge, Mass.

Chaudhuri, Pramit (ed) (1972), *Readings in Indian Agricultural Development*, George Allen and Unwin, London.

Chayanov, A. V. (1966), in Thorner Daniel *et al.* (eds), *The Theory of Peasant Economy*, Richard Irwin Inc., Homewood, Ill.

Chelliah, Raja J. (1969), *Fiscal Policy and Underdeveloped Countries*, Allen and Unwin, London.

Chelliah, Raja J. (1971), "Trends in Taxation in Developing Countries", *I.M.F. Staff Papers*, **18**, 254–327.

Chenery, Hollis B. (1953), "The Application of Investment Criteria", *Quarterly Journal of Economics*, **67**, 76–96.

Chenery, Hollis, B. (1961), "Comparative Advantage and Development Policy", *American Economic Review*, **51**, 18–51.

Chenery, Hollis, B., et al. (eds) (1971), *Studies in Development Planning*, Harvard.

Chenery, Hollis B., Ahluwalia, Montek S., Bell, C. L. G., Duloy, John H. and Jolly, Richard (1974), *Redistribution With Growth*, Oxford U.P., London.

Chenery, Hollis B. and Bruno, M. (1962), "Development Alternatives in an Open Economy: The Case of Israel", *Economic Journal*, **72**, 79–103.

Chenery, Hollis B. and Strout, A. (1966), "Foreign Assistance and Economic Development", *American Economic Review*, **56**, 680–733.

Chenery, Hollis B. and Taylor, Lance (1968), "Development Patterns Among Countries over Time", *Review of Economics and Statistics*, **50**, 391–416.

Cheung, S. (1969), *The Theory of Share Tenancy*, University of Chicago Press, Chicago.

Chow, G. C. (1960), "Tests of Equality between Sets of Coefficients in Two Linear Regressions", *Econometrica*, **28**, 591–605.

Clark, C. (1967), *Population Growth and Land Use*, McMillan, London.

Coale, A. J. (1973), "The Demographic Transition Reconsidered" in "International Union for the Scientific Study of Population", *International Population Conference*, **1**, Liège.

Coale, A. J. (ed) (1976), *Economic Factors in Population Growth*, McMillan, London.

Coale, A. J. and Hoover, E. M. (1958), *Population Growth and Economic Development in Low Income Countries*, Princeton U.P., Princeton.

Cohen, Benjamin J. (1966), *Adjustment Costs and the Distribution of New Reserves*, Princeton Studies in International Finance No. 18, Princeton.

Colman, David and McInerney, John (1975), "The Economies of Agricultural Policy", in Grant, R. M. and Shaw, G. K. (eds) (1975).

Coppock, Joseph D. (1962), *International Economic Instability*, McGraw Hill, New York.

Corden, W. M. (1966), "The Structure of Two Tariff Systems and the Effective Protective Rate", *Journal of Political Economy*, **74**, 221–37.

Corden, W. M. (1971), *The Theory of Protection*, Clarendon Press, Oxford.

Corden, W. M. (1974), *Trade Policy and Economic Welfare*, Clarendon Press, Oxford.

Corden, W. M. and Findlay, R. (1975), "Urban Unemployment, Intersectoral Capital Mobility and Development Policy", *Economica*, **42**, 37–78.

Dandekar, V. M. (1964), "Prices, Production and Marketed Supply of Foodgrains", *Indian Journal of Agricultural Economics*, **19**, 186–95.

Dandekar, V. M. and Rath, N. (1971), "Poverty in India", *Economic and Political Weekly*, **6**, 1–2, 25–48, 106–46.

Dasgupta, Ajit, K. (1974), *Economic Theory and the Developing Countries*, McMillan, London.

Dasgupta, Ajit, K. and Pearce, D. W. (1972), *Cost-Benefit Analysis: Theory and Practice*, McMillan, London.

Dasgupta, Partha, S. (1972), "A Comparative Analysis of the UNIDO *Guidelines* and the OECD *Manual*", *Bulletin of the Oxford University Institute of Economics and Statistics*, **34**, 1, 33–52.

Dasgupta, Partha, Sen Amartya, K. and Marglin, Stephen (1972), *Guidelines for Project Evaluation*, UNIDO, Vienna.

Dean, E. (1966), *Supply Response of African Farmers*, North-Holland, Amsterdam.

Dernburg, T. F. and Dernburg, J. D. (1969), *Macroeconomic Analysis: An Introduction to Comparative Statics and Dynamics*, Addison-Wesley, Reading, Mass., London.

Dernburg, T. F. and McDougall, Duncan M. (1976), *Macro-economics* (5th edn), McGraw-Hill, New York.

Desai, Meghnad and Mazumdar, Dipak (1970), "A Test of the Hypothesis of Disguised Unemployment", *Economica*, **37**, 39–53.

Dhar, E. N. and Lydall, H. F. (1961), *The Role of Small Enterprises in Indian Economic Growth*, Asia Publishing House, Bombay.

Dixit, Avinash (1968), "The Optimal Development in the Labour Surplus Economy", *Review of Economic Studies*, **35**, 23–34.

Dixit, Avinash (1969), "Theories of the Dual Economy: A Survey", Mimeo, Berkeley, University of California.

Dixit, Avinash, (1971), "Short-run Equilibrium and Shadow Prices in the Dual Economy", *Oxford Economic Papers*, **23**, 3, 384–99.

Dobb, Maurice (1948), *Soviet Economic Development since 1917*, Routledge and Kegan Paul, London.

Dobb, Maurice (1955), *On Economic Theory of Socialism*, McGraw-Hill, New York.

Dobb, Maurice (1960), *Economic Growth and Planning* (1st edn), Routledge & Kegan Paul.

Domar, E. D. (1947), "Expansion and Employment", *American Economic Review*, **37**, 34–55.

Domar, E. D. (1957), *Essays in the Theory of Economic Growth*, Oxford U.P., New York.

Due, John F. (1970), *Indirect Taxation in Developing Countries*, Johns Hopkins Press, Baltimore.

Due, John F. (1976), "Value-Added Taxation in Developing Economies", in Wang, N. T. (ed) (1976).

Duggar, Jan W. (1968), "International Comparisons of Income Levels: An Additional Measure"; *Economic Journal*, **78**, 109–16.

Dunning, John (ed) (1971), *The Multinational Enterprise*, George Allen & Unwin, London.

Eckaus, R. S. (1955), "The Factor Proportions in Underdeveloped Countries", *American Economic Review*, **45**, 4,539–65.

Eckaus, R. S. (1970), "Economic Criteria for Foreign Aid for Economic Development", in Bhagwati, J. (ed) (1970).

Eckaus, R. S. and Parikh, Kirit, S. 1(968), *Planning for Growth*, MIT Press. Mass.

Eckstein, O. (1957), "Investment Criteria for Economic Development and the Theory of Intertemporal Welfare Economics", *Quarterly Journal of Economics*, **71**, 56–85.

Elkan, Walter, (1973), *An Introduction to Development Economics*, Penguin, London.

Emmanuel, A. (1972), *Unequal Exchange*, New Left Books, London.

Enke, Stephen (1963), *Economics for Development*, Prentice Hall, N.Y.

Enke, Stephen (1966), "The Economic Aspect of Slowing Population Growth", *Economic Journal*, **76**, 44–56.

Erb, Guy and Schiavo-Campo, Salvator (1969), "Export Instability, Level of Development and Economic Size of Less Developed Countries", *Bulletin of Oxford Institute of Economics and Statistics*, XXXI, Nov., 263–83.

Fan, L. S. (1970), "Monetary Performance in Developing Economies: A Quantity Theory Approach", *Quarterly Review of Economies and Business*, Summer.

Fei, J. C. and Ranis, G. (1961), "A Theory of Economic Development", *American Economic Review*, **51**, 533–65.

Fei, J. C. and Ranis, G. (1964), *Development of the Labour Surplus Economy: Theory and Policy*, Homewood, Ill., Irwin.

Feldman, G. A. (1928), "On the Theory of Growth Rate of National Income – I, in Spulber, N. (ed) (1964).

Fellner, William (1957), "Marxian Hypotheses and Observable Trends under Capitalism", *Economic Journal*, **67**, 16–25.

Fields, Gary, S. (1975), "Rural–Urban Migration, Urban Unemployment, and Job-Search Activities in LDCs", *Journal of Development Economics*, **2,** 2, 165–87.

Findlay, R. (1966), "Optimal Investment Allocation between Consumer Goods and Capital Goods", *Economic Journal*, **74**, 70–83.

Fleming, Marcus (1955), "External Economies and the doctrine of balanced growth", *Economic Journal*, **65**, 241–56.

Foxley, A. (1976), "Redistribution of Consumption: Effects on Products and Employment", *Journal of Developmental Studies*, **12**, 3, 171–90.

Frank, André Gunder (1969), *Capitalism and Underdevelopment in Latin America*, Monthly Review Press, N.Y. and London.

Frank, André Gunder (1975), *On Capitalist Underdevelopment*, Oxford U.P., Bombay.

Frankel, Francine, R. (1971), *India's Green Revolution: Economic Gains and Political Costs*, Princeton U.P., New Jersey.

Fulbright, W. (1966), *Congressional Record*, 89th Congress, 2nd session, 112, 120, pp. 16020–24, Washington D.C.

Furtado, C. (1970), *The Economic Development of Latin America*, Cambridge U.P., Cambridge.

Galbis, Vicente (1977), "Financial Intermediation and Economic Growth in Less-Developed Countries: a Theoretical Approach", in Ayre, P.C.I. (ed) (1977).

Galbraith, John K. (1964), "The Balance of Payments: A Political and Administrative View", *The Review of Economics and Statistics*, **46**, 2, p. 120.

Galenson, W., and Leibenstein, H. (1955), "Investment Criteria, Productivity and Economic Development", *Quarterly Journal of Economics*, **69**, 343–70.

Geary, R. C. (1951), "A Note on a Constant-Utility Index of the Cost of Living", *Review of Economic Studies*, **18**, 65–6.

Ghatak, Subrata (1975), "Rural Interest Rates in the Indian Economy", *Journal of Development Studies*, **11**, 3, 190–201.

Ghatak, Subrata (1975), "Marketed Surplus in Indian Agriculture: Theory and Practice", *Oxford Bulletin of Economics and Statistics*, **37**, 2, 143–53.

Ghatak, Subrata (1976), *Rural Money Markets in India*, McMillan of India, New Dehli.

Ghosh, Ambika (1968), *Planning, Programming and Input-Output Analysis*, Cambridge U.P., Cambridge.

Ghosh, Ambika, Chakravarty, D. and Sarkar, H. (1974), *Development Planning in South-East Asia*, Rotterdam U.P., Rotterdam.

Grant, R. M. and Shaw, G. K. (eds) (1975), *Current Issues in Economic Policy*, Philip Allan, Oxford.

Gray, Clive, S. (1963), "Credit Creation for Nigeria's Economic Development", *Nigerian Journal of Economic and Social Research*, **5**, 3.

Griffin, Keith (1969), *Underdevelopment in Spanish America*, George Allen & Unwin, London.

Griffin, Keith (1974), *The Political Economy of Agrarian Change*, McMillan, London.

Griffin, Keith (1976), *Land Concentration and Rural Poverty*, McMillan, London.

Griffin, Keith and Khan, Azizur, R. (eds) (1972), *Growth and Inequality in Pakistan.* McMillan, London.

Grubel, Herbert, G. (1977), "The Case Against the New International Economic Order", *Weltwirtschaftliches Archiv.*, **113**, 2, 284–307.

Guha, Ashok (1969), "Accumulation, Innovation and Growth under Conditions of Disguised Unemployment", *Oxford Economic Papers*, **21**, 3, 360–72.

Gupta, K. L. (1970), "Personal Saving in Developing Nations", *Economic Record*, **46**, 243–49.

Gupta, S. G. (1971), "Interest Sensitiveness of Deposits in India", *Economic and Political Weekly*, **20**, 2357–63.

Gurley, J. G. and Shaw, E. S. (1960), *Money in a Theory of Finance*, The Brookings Ins., Washington D.C.

Gurley, J. G. and Shaw E. S. (1967), *Economic Development and Cultural Change*, **15**, 3, 257–68.

Haan, Roelf, L. (1971), *Special Drawing Rights and Development*, H. E. Stenfert Kroese N. V./Leiden.

Hadley, G. (1961), *Linear Algebra*, Addison-Wesley Inc., Reading, Mass.

Hadley, G. (1962), *Linear Programming*, Addison-Wesley, Inc., Reading, Mass.

Hagen, Everett, E. (1958), "An Economic Justification of Protectionism", *Quarterly Journal of Economics*, **72**, 4, 496–514.

Hagen, Everett, E. (1975), *The Economics of Development* (2nd ed), Richard D. Irwin Inc., Homewood, Illinois.

Hahn, F. H. (ed) (1971), *Readings in the theory of Growth*, McMillan, London.

Hahn, F. H. and Matthews, R. C. O. (1964), "The Theory of Economic Growth: A Survey", *Economic Journal*, LXXIV, 779–902.

Hansen, B. (1968), "The Distributive Shares in Egyptian Agriculture, 1897–1961", *International Economic Review*, **9**, 175–94.

Haq. M. Ul. (1965), "Tied Credits: A Quantitative Analysis" in Adler, J. (ed) (1965), *Capital Movements and Economic Development*, McMillan.

Harris, Barbara (1971), "Innovation Adoption in Indian Agriculture – The High Yielding Varieties Programme", *Modern Asian Studies*, **6**, 1, 78–98.

Harris, J. R. and Todaro, M. P. (1970), "Migration, Unemployment and Development: A Two Sector Analysis", *American Economic Review*, **60**, 126–42.

Harrod, Roy, F. (1948), *Towards a Dynamic Economics: Some Recent Developments of and their Applications to Policy*, McMillan, London.

Harrod, Roy, F. (1970), "Harrod after Twenty-one Years: A Comment", *Economic Journal*, **80**, 737–41.

Hasan, P. (1960), "The Investment Multiplier in an Underdeveloped Economy", *Economic Digest*, **3**, Karachi.

Hayami, Yujiro, and Ruttan, Vernon, W. (1971), *Agricultural Development: An International Perspective*, The Johns Hopkins Press, Baltimore and London.

Hayter, Teresa (1971), *Aid as Imperialism*, Penguin.

Heal, G. M., (1973), *The Theory of Economic Planning*, North-Holland, Amsterdam.

Helleiner, G. K. (1972), *International Trade and Economic Development*, Penguin.

Helleiner, G. K. (1973), "Manufactured Exports from Less Developed Countries and Multi-national Firms", *Economic Journal*, **83**, 21–47.

Helleiner, G. K. (1974), "The Less Developed Countries and the International Monetary System", *The Journal of Development Studies*, **10**, 3, 347–71.

Helleiner, G. K. (1975), "Smallholder Decision Making: Tropical African Evidence", in Reynolds, L. (ed) (1975).

Hicks, John, R. (1957), *Value and Capital*, Oxford U.P., London.

Hicks, John, R. (1965), *Capital and Growth*, Clarendon Press, Oxford.

Higgins, B. (1968), *Economic Development* (2nd edn), Constable, London.

Hill, T. P. (1964), "Growth and Investment according to International Comparisons", *Economic Journal*, **74**, 287–304.

Hirschman, Albert, O. (1958a), *The Strategy of Economic Development*, Yale U.P., New Haven.

Hirschman, Albert, O. (1958b), "Investment Criteria and Capital Intensity Once Again", *Quarterly Journal of Economics*, **72**, 469–71.

Ho, Yhi-Min (1972), "Development with Surplus-Labour Population – The Case Study of Taiwan: A Critique of the Classical Two-Sector Model, à la Lewis", *Economic Development and Cultural Change*, **20**, 210–34.

International Bank for Reconstruction and Development (IBRD) (1969), *The Problem of Stabilization of Prices of Primary Products*, Washington D.C.

International Labour Office (ILO) (1967), *Report to the Government of United Republic of Tanzania on Wages, Incomes and Prices Policy*, Government paper No. 3, Government Printer, Dar Es Salaam.

ILO (1971), *Matching Employment Opportunities and Expectations: A Programme of Action for Ceylon*, Geneva.

ILO (1972), *Employment, Incomes and Equality, A Strategy for Increasing Productive Employment in Kenya*, Geneva.

ILO Iran (1972), *Employment and Incomes Policy for Iran*, Geneva.

ILO (1973), *Sharing in Development: A Programme of Development, Equity and Growth for the Philippines*, Vol. 1., Main Report, Geneva.

ILO (1976a), *The Impact of Multi-national Enterprises on Employment and Training*, Geneva.

ILO (1976b), *Wages and Working Conditions in Multi-national Enterprises*, Geneva.

International Monetary Fund (IMF) (1966), *Compensatory Financing of Export Instability*, Washington D.C.

Ishikawa, Shigeru (1967), *Economic Development in Asian Perspective*, Kunokuniya, Hototsubashi, Tokyo.

Jarvis, L. (1973), "The Relationship between Unemployment and Income Distribution in Less Developed Countries", in *Employment Processes in Developing Countries*, Ford Foundation, Bogata.

Johnson, G. E. (1971), "The Structure of Rural–Urban Migration Models", *Eastern Africa Economic Review*, June, 21–8.

Johnson, Harry, G. (1962), *Money, Trade and Economic Growth*, George Allen & Unwin, London.

Johnson, Harry, G. (1964), "Tariffs and Economic Development", *Journal of Development Studies*, **1**, 1, 3–30.

Johnson, Harry, G. (1967), *Economic Policies Towards Less Developed Countries*, George Allen & Unwin, London.

Johnson, Harry, G. (1968), "Tariffs and Economic Development: Some Theoretical Issues", in Theberge, J. D. (ed) (1968).

Johnson, Harry, G. (1969), *Hearing* before the Sub-Committee on International Exchange and Payments of the Joint Economic Committee, Congress of the United States, May 28, p. 16.

Johnson, Harry, G. (1972), "The Link that Chains", *Foreign Policy*, Autumn.

Johnson, Harry, G. (1975), *Technology and Economic Interdependence*, McMillan, London.

Johnson, Harry, G. (1977), "The New International Economic Order", *Boletin International*, Banco de Vizcaya, (Spain), **5**, 4–9.

Johnston, B. F. and Mellor, J. (1961), "The Role of Agriculture in Economic Development", *American Economic Review*, **51**, 566–93.

Johnston, B. F. and Cownie, John (1969), "The Seed-Fertilizer Revolution and Labour Force Absorption", *American Economic Review*, **59**, 569–82.

Johnston, J. (1972), *Econometric Methods* (2nd edn), McGraw-Hill.

Jolly, Richard (1974), "International Dimensions", in Chenery, H., Ahluwalia, Montek, S., Bell, C. L. G., Duloy, John H. and Jolly, Richard (1974).

Jolly, Richard, Emanuel, Kadt, Singer, H. and Wilson, F. (eds) (1973), *Third World Employment*, Penguin.

Jones, Hywel (1975), *An Introduction to Modern Theories of Economic Growth*, Nelson.

Jorgenson, D. W. (1961), "The Development of a Dual Economy", *Economic Journal*, **71**, 309–34.

Jorgenson, D. W. (1966), "Testing Alternative Theories of the Development of a Dual Economy", in Adelman, I. and Thorbecke, E. (eds) (1966).

Jorgenson, D. W. (1967), "Surplus Agricultural Labour and the Development of a Dual Economy", *Oxford Economic Papers*, **19**, 3, 288–312.

Joshi, Heather (1972), "World Prices as Shadow Prices: A Critique", *Bulletin of Oxford University Institute of Economics and Statistics*, **34**, 1, 53–73.

Joshi, Vijay (1970), "Saving and Foreign Exchange Constraints", in Streeten, Paul (ed) (1970).

Joshi, Vijay (1972), "The Rationale and Relevance of the Little–Mirrlees Criterion", *Bulletin of Oxford University Institute of Economics and Statistics*, **34**, 1, 3–32.

June–Flanders, M. (1964), "Prebisch on Protectionism: An Evaluation", *Economic Journal*, **74**, 305–326.

Kahn, A. E. (1951), "Investment Criteria in Development Programs", *Quarterly Journal of Economics*, **65**, 38–61.

Kahn, R. (1973), "SDRs and Aid", *Lloyds Bank Review*, **110**, 1–18.

Kaldor, N. (1955), *An Expenditure Tax*, George Allen & Unwin, London.

Kaldor, N. (1956), Ministry of Finance, Government of India, *Indian Tax Reform*, Delhi.

Kaldor, N. (1956), "Alternative Theories of Distribution", *Review of Economic Studies*, 83–100.

Kaldor, N. (1957), "A Model of Economic Growth", *Economic Journal*, **67**, 591–624.

Kaldor, N. and Mirrlees, James, A. (1962), "A New Model of Economic Growth", *Review of Economic Studies*, 174–192.

Kaldor, N. (1965), "The Role of Taxation in Economic Development" in Robinson, R. (ed) (1965).

Kaldor, N. (1972), "The Irrelevance of Equilibrium Economics", *Economic Journal*, **82**, 1237–55.

Kay, Geoffrey (1975), *Development and Underdevelopment: A Marxist Analysis*, McMillan, London.

Kelly, Allen, C. Williamson, Geoffrey, G., Cheetham, Russel, J. (1972), *Dualistic Economic Development: Theory and History*, The University of Chicago Press, Chicago, London.

Kenya (1973), *Sessional Paper on Employment*, Government of Kenya, 10.

Kenya (1974), *Third Economic Development Plan*, (1974–78), Government of Kenya.

Keynes, John, Maynard (1930), *A Treatise on Money*, McMillan, London.

Keynes, John, Maynard (1936), *The General Theory of Employment, Interest and Money*, McMillan.

Khusro, A. M. (1967), "The Pricing of Food in India", *Quarterly Journal of Economics*, **81**, 271–85.

Kindleberger, Charles, P. (1956), *The Terms of Trade: A European Case Study*, N.Y.

Kindleberger, Charles, P. (1958:1977), *Economic Development* (1st and 3rd edns), McGraw-Hill, New York.

Kindleberger, Charles, P. (ed) (1970), *The International Corporation*, Cambridge, Mass, MIT Press.

Kingston, Jerry, L. (1976), "Export Concentration and Export Performance in Developing Countries, 1954–67", *Journal of Development Studies*, **12**, 4, 311–19.

Klein, L. (1965), "What kind of Macro-econometric model for Developing Economies?", *Indian Economic Journal*, **13**, 3, 313–24.

Knudsen, Odin and Parnes, Andrew (1975), *Trade Instability and Economic Development*, Lexington.

Komiya, R. (1959), "A Note on Professor Mahalanobis' Model of Indian Economic Planning", *Review of Economics and Statistics*, **41**, 29–35.

Krishna, Raj (1962), "A Note on the Elasticity of the Marketable Surplus of a Subsistence Crop", *Indian Journal of Agricultural Economics*, **17**, 79–84.

Krishna, Raj (1963), "Farm Supply Response in India–Pakistan: A Case Study of the Punjab Region", *Economic Journal*, **73**, 477–87.

Krishna, Raj (1965), "The Marketable Surplus Function for a Subsistence Crop: An Analysis with Indian Data", *The Economic Weekly*, **17**, 309–20.

Krishna, Raj (1968), "Agricultural Price Policy and Economic Development", in Southworth, H. and Johnston, B. F. (eds), *Agricultural Development and Economic Growth*, Cornell University Press, Ithaca.

Krishna, Raj (1975), "Measurement of the Direct and Indirect Employment Effects of Agricultural Growth with Technical Change", in Reynolds, L. (ed) (1975).

Krishnan, T. N. (1965), "The Marketed Surplus of Foodgrains: Is it Inversely Related to Price?", *The Economic Weekly*, **17**, 325–28.

Kuznets, Simon (1955), "Economic Growth and Income Inequality", *American Economic Review*, **45**, 1–28.

Kuznets, Simon (1965), "Demographic Aspects of Modern Economic Growth", *World Population Conference*, Belgrade.

Kuznets, Simon (1966), *Modern Economic Growth: Rate, Structure and Speed*, Yale University Press, New Haven.

Kuznets, Simon (1967), "Population and Economic Growth", *Proceedings of the American Philosophical Society*, **3**, 170–93.

Kuznets, Simon (1971), *Economic Growth of Nations: Total Output and Production Structure*, Oxford U.P., London.

Kuznets, Simon (1974), *Population, Capital and Growth: Selected Essays*, Heinemann, London.

Lal, Deepak (1972), *Wells and Welfare*, OECD, Paris.

Lal, Deepak (1974), *Methods of Project Analysis: a Review*, IBRD and The Johns Hopkins University Press, Baltimore and London.

Lal, Deepak (1974), *Appraising Foreign Investment*, Heinemann, London.

Layard, Richard (ed) (1974), *Cost-Benefit Analysis*, Penguin.

Leibenstein, Henry (1957), *Economic Backwardness and Economic Growth*, Wiley.

Leipziger, Danny, M. (1975), "Determinants of Use of Special Drawing Rights by Developing Nations", *The Journal of Development Studies*, **11**, 4, 316–24.

Leontief, W. W. (1951), *The Structure of the American Economy 1919–39* (2nd edn), Oxford University Press, New York.

Lewis, Arthur, W. (1953), *Industrialization and the Gold Coast*, Gold Coast Government, Accra.

Lewis, Arthur, W. (1954), "Economic Development with Unlimited Supplies of Labour", *Manchester School of Economic and Social Studies*, **22**, 139–91.

Lewis, Arthur, W. (1955), *The Theory of Economic Growth*, George Allen & Unwin, London.

Lewis, Arthur, W. (1966), *Development Planning*, George Allen & Unwin, London.

Leys, C. (1975), *Underdevelopment in Kenya: The Political Economy of Neo-Colonialism*, Heinemann.

Leys, C. (1977), "Underdevelopment and Dependency: Critical Notes", *Journal of Contemporary Asia*, **2**, 92–107.

Lipsey, Robert, E. (1963), *Price and Quantity Trends in the Foreign Trade of the United States*, National Bureau of Economic Research, Princeton U.P., New Jersey.

Lipton, Michael (1962), "Balanced and Unbalanced Growth in Underdeveloped Countries", *Economic Journal*, **72**, 641–57.

Lipton, Michael (1968a), "Strategy for Agriculture: Urban Bias and Rural Planning", in Streeten, Paul and Lipton, Michael (eds) (1968a), *The Crisis of Indian Planning*, Oxford U.P., London.

Lipton, Michael (1968b), "The Theory of the Optimizing Peasant", *Journal of Development Studies*, **43**, 327–51.

Lipton, Michael (1969), *Supply Problems Matter Most in the Economy*, Institute of Development Studies, Brighton.

Lipton, Michael (1977), *Why Poor People Stay Poor: A Study of the Urban Bias in World Development*, Temple Smith, London.

Little, I. M. D. and Clifford, J. (1965), *International Aid*, George Allen & Unwin, London.

Little, I. M. D. and Mirrlees, J. A. (1968), *Manual of Industrial Project Analysis for Developing Countries*, Vol. II, *Social Cost-Benefit Analysis*, OECD, Paris.

Little, I. M. D. and Mirrlees, J. A. (1972), "A Reply to Some Criticisms of the OECD Manual", *Bulletin of the Oxford University Institute of Economics and Statistics*, **34**, 1, 153–68.

Little, I. M. D. and Mirrlees, J. A. (1974), *Project Appraisal and Planning for Developing Countries*, Heinemann, London.

Little, I., Scitovsky, T. and Scott, M. (1970), *Industry and Trade in Some Developing Countries: A Comparative Study*, OECD and O.U.P., London.

Mabro, Robert (1967), "Industrial Growth, Agricultural Under-employment and the Lewis Model: The Egyptian Case, 1937–1965", *Journal of Development Studies*, **3**, 4, 322–51.

MacBean, Alasdair, I. (1966), *Export Instability and Economic Development*, George Allen & Unwin, London.

Machlup, Fritz (1968), *Remaking the International Monetary System*, Johns Hopkins Press, Baltimore.

McKinnon, Ronald, I. (1964), "Foreign Exchange Constraints in Economic Development", *Economic Journal*, **74**, 388–409.

McKinnon, Ronald, I. (1973), *Money and Capital in Economic Development*, The Brookings Institution, Washington D.C.

Macrae, John (1971), "The Relationship between Agricultural and Industrial Growth with Special Reference to the Development of the Punjab Economy from 1950–1965", *Journal of Developmental Studies*, **7**, 4, 397–422.

Mahalanobis, P. C. (1953), "Some Observations on the Process of Growth of National Income", *Sankhya* (*Indian Journal of Statistics*), **14**, 307–12.

Mahalanobis, P. C. (1955), "The Approach of Operational Research to Planning in India", *Sankhya* (*The Indian Journal of Statistics*), **16**, 3–13D.

Maizels, Arthur (1968), *Exports and Economic Growth of Developing Countries*, Cambridge U.P., Cambridge.

Marglin, Stephen, A. (1967), *Public Investment Criteria: Studies in the Economic Development of India*, George Allen & Unwin, London.

Marglin, Stephen, A. (1976), *Value and Price in the Labour Surplus Economy*, Oxford U.P., London.

Marx, Karl (1853), "The British Rule in India", *The New York Tribune*, 25 June, reprinted in Burns, A., *A Handbook of Marxism*.

Marx, Karl (1906), *Capital*, Vol. I revised by Untermann, E., Kerr and Co., Chicago.

Massell, Benton, F. (1964), "Export Concentration and Export Earnings", *American Economic Review*, **54**, 47–63.

Massell, Benton, F. (1970), "Export Instability and Economic Structure", *American Economic Review*, **60**, 618–30.

Mathur, Ashok (1964), "The Anatomy of Disguised Unemployment", *Oxford Economic Papers*, **16**, 2, 161–93.

Mathur, Ashok (1966), "Balanced v. Unbalanced Growth – A Reconciliatory View", *Oxford Economic Papers*, **18**, 2, 137–57.

Mathur, P. N. and Ezekiel, H. (1961), "Marketed Surplus of Food and Price Fluctuations in a Developing Economy", *Kyklos*, **14**, 396–408.

Maynard, Geoffrey (1973), "Special Drawing Rights and Development Aid", *The Journal of Development Studies*, **9**, 4, 518–40.

Meade, James, E. (1952), *A Geometry of International Trade*, George Allen & Unwin, London.

Meade, James, E. (1961), *A Neo-Classical Theory of Economic Growth*, George Allen & Unwin, London.

Meade, James, E. (1964), "International Commodity Agreements", *Lloyds Bank Review*, **73**, 28–42.

Mehra, S. (1966), "Surplus Labour in Indian Agriculture", *Indian Economic Review*, **1**, 1, also reprinted in Chaudhuri, Pramit (ed) (1972), *Readings in Indian Agricultural Development*, George Allen & Unwin, London.

Meier, Gerald M. (1976), *Leading Issues in Economic Development* (3rd edn), Oxford U.P., N.Y.

Michaely, Michael (1962), *Concentration in International Trade*, North-Holland, Amsterdam.

Mishan, E. J. (1975), *Cost-Benefit Analysis* (2nd edn), George Allen & Unwin, London.

Mirrlees, James, A. (1975), "A Pure Theory of Underdeveloped Economies", in Reynolds, Lloyd (ed) (1975).

Modigliani, Franco (1970), "The Life Cycle Hypothesis of Saving and Inter-county differences in the Savings Ratio", in Eltis, W. A., Scott, M. F. G. and Wolfe, N. J. (eds) (1970), *Induction, Trade and Growth: Essays in Honour of Sir Roy Harrod*, Oxford U.P.

Morawetz, David (1974), "Employment Implications of Industrialization in Developing Countries: A Survey", *Economic Journal*, **84**, 491–542.

Moreland, R. S. and Hazeldine, A. (1974), *Population, Energy and Growth: A World Cross Section Study*, Paper to European Econometric Society Meeting, Grenoble.

Morss, Elliott, R. and Peacock, Alan, T. (1969), "The Measurement of Fiscal Performance in Developing Countries", in Peacock, Alan, T. (ed) (1969).

Moses, John (1957), "Investment Criteria, Productivity and Economic Development: Comment", *Quarterly Journal of Economics*, **71**, 161–4.

Mundell, Robert (1965), "Growth, Stability and Inflationary Finance", *Journal of Political Economy*, **73**, 2, 97–109.

Myint, Hla (1971), *Economic Theory and the Underdeveloped Country*, Oxford U.P., USA.

Myrdal, Gunnar (1956), *An International Economy*, Harper & Row, N.Y.

Myrdal, Gunnar (1957), *Economic Theory and the Underdeveloped Regions*, Duckworth, London.

Myrdal, Gunnar (1968), *Asian Drama*, Vols. I, II, III, Penguin.

Nakamura, J. I. (1965), "Growth of Japanese Agriculture 1875–1920", in Lockwood, W. W. (ed) (1965), *The State and Economic Enterprise in Japan*, Princeton U.P., N.J.

Narain, D. (1957), "Ratio of Interchange between Agricultural and Manufactured Goods in relation to Capital Formation in Underdeveloped Economies", *Indian Economic Review*, **3**, 46–55.

Narain, D. (1961), *Distribution of the Marketed Surplus of Agricultural Produce by Size-Level of Holding in India 1950–51*, Asia Publishing House.

Narain, D. (1965), *Impact of Price Movements on Areas under Selected Crops in India*, Asia Publishing House.

Nath, S. K. (1962), "The Theory of Balanced Growth", *Oxford Economic Papers*, **14**, 2, 138–53.

National Council of Applied Economic Research (NCAER) (1972), *All-India Household Survey of Income, Saving and Consumer Expenditure*, New Dehli, India.

Nelson, Richard, R. (1956), "A Theory of Low-level Equilibrium Trap in Underdeveloped Economies", *American Economic Review*, **46**, 5, 894–908.

Newberry, David (1974), "The Robustness of Equilibrium Analysis in the Dual Economy", *Oxford Economic Papers*, **26**, 1, 32–44.

Newlyn, W. T. (1967), *Money in an African Context*, Oxford University Press, Nairobi.

Newlyn, W. T. (1969), "Monetary Analysis and Policy in Financially Dependent Economies", in Stewart, I. G. (ed) (1969), *Economic Development and Structural Change*, Edinburgh.

Newlyn, W. T. (1977), "The inflation Tax in Developing Countries", in Ayre, P.C.I. (ed) (1977).

Nicholls, William, H. (1963), "An 'Agricultural Surplus' as a Factor in Economic Development", *Journal of Political Economy*, **71**, 1–29.

Nowshirvani, F. H. (1967), "A Note on the Fixed Cash Requirement Theory of Marketed Surplus in Subsistence Agriculture", *Kyklos*, **20**, 772–3.

Nulty, Leslie (1972), *The Green Revolution in West Pakistan*, Praeger, N.Y.

Nurkse, R. (1953), *Problems of Capital Formation in Underdeveloped Countries*, Basil Blackwell, Oxford.

Nurkse, R. (1959), *Patterns of Trade and Development*, Almqvist and Wiksell, Stockholm.

Okhawa, Kazushi and Johnston, Bruce, F. (1969), "The Transferability of the Japanese Pattern of Modernizing Traditional Agriculture", in Thorbecke, E. (ed) (1969).

Okita, S. (1964), "Choice of Techniques: Japan's Experience and its Implication", in Berill, K. (ed) (1964).

Opinion Research Group (ORG) (1973), *An All-India Survey of Family Planning Practices*, Baroda, India.

Organization of Economic Co-operation and Development (OECD) (1974), *Choice and Adaptations of Technology in Developing Countries: An Overview of Major Policy Issues*, Development Centre, Paris.

Owen, Wyn, F. (1966), "The Double Developmental Squeeze on Agriculture", *American Economic Review*, **56**, 2, 43–70.

Oyejide, Ademda, T. (1972), "Deficit Financing, Inflation and Capital Formation: An Analysis of the Nigerian Experience, 1957–70", *Nigerian Journal of Economic and Social Research*, March.

Pack, Howard and Todaro, Michael (1969), "Technological Transfer, Labour Absorption and Economic Development", *Oxford Economic Papers*, **21**, 3, 395–403.

Panne, van de C. (1976), *Linear Programming and Related Techniques* (2nd edn), North-Holland, Amsterdam.

Parikh, K. S. (1976), "India in 2001", in Coale, A. J. (ed) (1976).

Pasinetti, Luigi (1962), "Rate of Profit and Income Distribution in Relation to the Rate of Economic Growth", *Review of Economic Studies*, **29**, 267–79.

Patinkin, Don (1968), *Money, Interest and Prices* (2nd edn), Harper and Row, New York.

Peacock, Alan, T. (ed) (1969), *Quantitative Analysis in Public Finance*, Praeger, New York.

Peacock, Alan, T. and Shaw, G. K. (1974), *The Economic Theory of Fiscal Policy* (2nd edn), George Allen & Unwin, London.

Pearson, Lester, B. (1969), *Partners in Development*, Report of the Commission on International Development, Praeger, N.Y. and London.

Pen, Jan (1971), *Income Distribution*, Penguin.

Pincus, John (1967), *Trade, Aid and Development*, McGraw-Hill, N.Y.

Polak, J. J. (1943), "Balance of Payment Problems of Countries Reconstructing with the help of Foreign Loans", *Quarterly Journal of Economics*, **57**, 208–40.

Polak, J. J. (1957), "Monetary Analysis of Income Formulation and Payment Problems", IMF *Staff Papers*, **6**, 1–50.

Polak, J. J. and Boissonneult, L. (1959), "Monetary Analysis of Income and Imports and its Statistical Application", IMF *Staff Papers*, **7**, 349–415.

Posner, Michael, V. (1961), "International Trade and Technical Change", *Oxford Economic Papers*, **13**, 3, 323–41.

Prais, S. J. (1961), "Some Mathematical Notes on the Quantity Theory of Money in an Open Economy", IMF *Staff Papers*, **8**, 212–26.

Prebisch, Raul (1959), "Commercial Policy in the Underdeveloped Countries", *American Economic Review, Papers and Proceedings*, XLIX, 2, 251–73.

Prebisch, Raul (1964), *Towards a New Trade Policy for Development*, United Nations, New York.

Preobrazhensky, E. (1965), *The New Communism*, Clarendon Press, Oxford.

Prest, A. R. (1972), *Public Finance in Underdeveloped Countries*, Weidenfeld and Nicolson, London.

Radice, Hugo (ed) (1975), *International Firms and Modern Imperialism*, Penguin.

Ramanathan, R. (1967), "Jorgenson's Model of a Dual Economy. An Extension", *Economic Journal*, **77**, 321–7.

Ramaswami, V. K. (1971), "Optimal Policies to Promote Industrialisation in Less Developed Countries", in Ramaswami, V. K. (1971), *Trade and Development*, George Allen & Unwin, London.

Rao, V. K. R. (1952), "Investment, Income and the Multiplier in an Underdevéloped Economy", in Agarwala, A. N. and Singh, S. P. (ed) (1958).

Reynolds, Lloyd George (ed) (1975), *Agriculture in Development Theory*, Yale University Press, New Haven.

Robinson, Joan (1956), *The Accumulation of Capital*, McMillan, London.

Robinson, R. (ed) (1965), *Industrialization in Developing Countries*, Cambridge U.P., Cambridge.

Robinson, R. and Johnston, P. (eds) (1971), *Prospects for Employment Opportunities in the Nineteen Seventies*, H.M.S.O., London.

Rosenstein-Rodan, Paul, N. (1943), "Problems of Industrialization of Eastern and South-Eastern Europe", *Economic Journal*, **53**, 202–11.

Rosenstein-Rodan, Paul, N. (1961), "International Aid for Underdeveloped Countries", *Review of Economics and Statistics*, **43**, 2, 107–38.

Rosenstein-Rodan, Paul, N. (1968), "The Consortia Technique", in Bhagwati, J. (ed) (1970).

Rybczynski, T. N. (1955), "Factor Endowment and Relative Commodity Prices", *Economica*, **22**, 4, 336–41.

Samuelson, Paul and Modigliani, Franco (1966), "The Pasinetti Paradox in Neo-Classical and more general models", *Review of Economic Studies*, **33**, 269–301.

Samuelson, Paul (1976), *Economics* (10th edn), McGraw Hill, N.Y., London.

Sara, Tejinder Singh (1975), *Cost-Benefit Analysis in Developing Countries: Case Study of a Fertilizer Plant in India*, Unpublished Ph.D. Thesis, University of Massachusetts.

Sato, R. (1963), "Fiscal Policy in a Neo-Classical Growth Model", *Review of Economic Studies*, **30**, 16–23.

Sato, K. (1967), "Taxation and Neo-Classical Growth", *Public Finance*, **22**, 3, 346–70.

Schotta, Charles Jr. (1966), "The Money Supply, Exports and Income in an Open Economy: Mexico, 1939–63", *Economic Development and Cultural Change*, **14**, 458–70.

Scitovsky, Tibor (1954), "Two Concepts of External Economies", *Journal of Political Economy*, **17**, 143–51.

Scitovsky, Tibor (1959), "Growth: Balanced or Unbalanced", in Abramovitz, M. (ed) (1959), *The Allocation of Economic Resources: Essays in Honour of B. F. Haley*, Stanford.

Scitovsky, Tibor (1966), "A New Approach to International Liquidity", *American Economic Review*, **54**.

Schultz, Paul T. (1976), "Determinants of Fertility: a Micro-economic Model of Choice", in Coale, A. J. (ed) (1976).

Schultz, T. W. (1964), *Transforming Traditional Agriculture*, Yale U.P., New Haven.

Sen, Amartya, Kumar (1966), "Peasants and Dualism with or without Surplus Labour", *Journal of Political Economy*, **74**, 425–50.

Sen, Amartya, Kumar (1967), "Surplus Labour in India: A Critique of Schultz's Statistical Test", *Economic Journal*, **77**, 154–61.

Sen, Amartya, Kumar (1968), *Choice of Techniques: An Aspect of the Theory of Planned Economic Development* (3rd edn), Basil Blackwell, Oxford.

Sen, Amartya, Kumar (ed) (1970), *Growth Economics*, Penguin.

Sen, Amartya, Kumar (1972), "Control Areas and Accounting Prices: An Approach to Economic Evaluation", *Economic Journal*, **82**, 486–501.

Sen, Amartya, Kumar, Dasgupta, P. and Marglin, S. (1972), *Guidelines for Project Evaluation*, UNIDO, Vienna.

Sen, Amartya, Kumar, (1973), *On Economic Inequality*, Clarendon Press, Oxford.

Sen, Amartya, Kumar, (1975), *Employment Technology and Development*, Clarendon Press, Oxford.

Sen, Amartya, Kumar, (1976), "Poverty: An Ordinal Approach to Measurement", *Econometrica*, **44**, 2, 219–31.

Sen, Sudhir (1974), *A Richer Harvest: New Horizons for Developing Countries*, Tata, McGraw Hill, New Dehli, N.Y.

Sen, Sudhir (1975), *Reaping the Green Revolution: Food and Jobs for All*, Tata, McGraw Hill, New Dehli, N.Y.

Shaw, Edward, S. (1973), *Financial Deepening in Economic Development*, Oxford U.P., N.Y.

Shetty, M. C. (1963), *Small-Scale and Household Industries in a Developing Economy*, Asia Publishing House, Bombay.

Shukla, Tara (1965), *Capital Formation in Indian Agriculture*, Vora, Bombay.

Singer, Hans, W. (1965), "External Aid: For Plans or Projects?", *Economic Journal*, **75**, 539–45.

Singer, Hans, W. and Schiavo-Campo, S. (1970), *Perspectives of Economic Development*, Houghton Mifflin, New York.

Singer, Hans, W. and Ansari, Javed (1977), *Rich and Poor Countries*, George Allen & Unwin, London.

Sinha, Radha, P. (1969), "Unresolved Issues in Japan's Early Economic Development", *Scottish Journal of Political Economy*, **16**, 109–51.

Smith, A. D. (ed) (1967), *Wage Policy Issues in Economic Development*, McMillan.

Solow, R. M. (1956), "A Contribution to the Theory of Economic Growth", *Quarterly Journal of Economics*, LXX, 65–94.

Solow, R. M. (1957), "Technical Change and the Aggregate Production Function", *Review of Economics and Statistics*, 312–20.

Solow, R. M. (1960), "Investment and Technical Progress", in Arrow K. *et al.* (eds), *Mathematical Methods in Social Sciences*, Stanford, U.P., Stanford.

Southworth, Herman M. and Johnston, Bruce F. (eds) (1967), *Agricultural Development and Economic Growth*, Cornell University Press, Ithaca.

Spulber, N. (ed) (1964), *Foundations of Soviet Strategy for Economic Growth: Selected Soviet Essays, 1924–30*, Indiana U.P., Bloomington.

Squire, Lyn and Tak van der, H. G. (1975), *Economic Analysis of Projects*, The Johns Hopkins Press, London and Baltimore.

Srinivasan, T. N. (1962), *Investment Criteria and Choice of Techniques of Production*, Yale Economic Essays, **2**, 1.

Srinivasan, T. N. and Bardhan, P. K. (eds) (1975), *Poverty, and Income Distribution in India*, Statistical Publishing Society, Calcutta.

Staley, Charles, E. (1970), *International Economics*, Prentice-Hall, New Jersey.

Stamp, Maxwell (1958), "The Fund and the Future", *Lloyds Bank Review*, October.

Stewart, F. (1972), "Choice of Techniques in Developing Countries", *Journal of Development Studies*, **9**, 1, 99–121.

Stewart, F. (1974), "Technology and Employment in LDCs", *World Development*, **2**, 3, 17–46.

Stewart, F. (1975), "Manufacture of Cement Blocks in Kenya", 203–40, in Bhalla, A. S. (ed) (1975).

Stewart, Frances and Streeten, Paul (1971), "Conflicts between Output and Employment Objectives in Developing Countries", *Oxford Economic Papers*, **23**, 2, 145–68.

Stewart, Frances and Streeten, Paul (1972), "Little–Mirrlees Methods and Project Appraisal", *Bulletin of the Oxford University Institute of Economics and Statistics*, **34**, 1, 75–91.

Stone, R. (1964), "Linear Expenditure Systems and Demand Analysis: An Application to the Pattern of British Demand", *Economic Journal*, **74**, 511–27.

Streeten, Paul (1959), "Unbalanced Growth", *Oxford Economic Papers*, **11**, 2.

Streeten, Paul (1966), "Use and Abuse of Planning Models", in Martin, K. and Knapp, J. (eds) (1966), *Teaching of Development Economics*, Frank Cass, London.

Streeten, Paul (1968), in Myrdal, Gunnar (1968).

Streeten, Paul (ed) (1970), *Unfashionable Economics: Essays in Honour of Lord Balogh*, Weidenfeld and Nicolson, London.

Streeten, Paul (1971), "Costs and Benefits of Multinational Enterprises in Less Developed Countries", in Dunning, John H. (ed) (1971).

Streeten, Paul (1973a), "The Multinational Enterprise and the Theory of Development Policy", *World Development*, **1**, 10, 1–14.

Streeten, Paul (ed) (1973b), *Trade Strategies for Development*, McMillan.

Sundrum, R. M. (1967), "The Measurement of Export Instability", Unpublished Mimeo, June, cited in Knudsen, Odin and Parnes, Andrew (1975).

Swan, Trevor (1956), "Economic Growth and Capital Accumulation", *Economic Record*, XXXII, Nov., 334–61.

Sweezy, Paul, M. (1942), *The Theory of Capitalist Development*, Dennis Robson, London.

Tanzania (1967), *Wages, Incomes, Rural Development, Investment and Price Policy*, Government Paper No. 4, Government Printer, Dar es Salaam.

Thamarajakshi, R. (1969), "Intersectoral Terms of Trade and Marketed Surplus of Agricultural Produce, 1951–2 to 1965–6", in Chaudhury, Pramit (ed) (1972).

Theberge, James, D. (ed) (1968), *Economics of Trade and Development*, Wiley, N.Y.

Thirlwall, A. P. (1972), *Growth and Development: with Special Reference to Developing Economies*, McMillan, London.

Thirlwall, A. P. (1974), *Inflation, Saving and Growth in Developing Economies*, McMillan, London.

Thirlwall, A. P. (1976a), *Financing Economic Development*, McMillan, London.

Thirlwall, A. P. (1976b), "Reconciling the Conflict between Employment and Saving and Employment and Output in the Choice of Techniques in Developing Countries", University of Kent Discussion Paper No. 19, Mimeo.

Thorbecke, Erik (1969), *The Role of Agriculture in Economic Development*, National Bureau of Economic Research, New York.

Tobin, James (1965), "Money and Economic Growth", *Econometrica*, **33**, 671–84.

Todaro, Michael P. (1969), "A Model of Labour Migration and Urban Unemployment in Less Developed Countries", *American Economic Review*, **59**, 1, 138–48.

Todaro, Michael P. (1971a), *Development Planning: Models and Methods*, Oxford U.P., London and Nairobi.

Todaro, Michael P. (1971b), "Income Expectations, Rural–Urban Migration and Employment in Africa", *International Labour Review*, **104**, 5, 387–413.

Todaro, Michael P. (1976), *Internal Migration and Economic Development: A Review of Theory, Evidence, Methodology and Research Priorities*, International Labour Organisation, Geneva.

Todaro, Michael P. (1977), *Economics for a Developing World*, Longman, London.

Triffin, R. (1971), "The Use of SDR Finance for Collectively Agreed Purposes", *Banca Nazionale de Lavoro Quarterly Review*.

Turner, R. Kerry and Collis, C. (1977), *Economics of Planning*, McMillan, London.

Turnham, David and Jaegar, Ian (1971), *The Employment Problem in Less Developed Countries*, OECD, Paris.

United Nations (UN) (1952), *Instability in Export Markets of Underdeveloped Countries*, UN Secretariat, N.Y.

UN (1961), Department of Economic and Social Affairs, *International Compensation for Fluctuations in Commodity Prices*, N.Y.

UN (1962), *The Capital Developing Needs of the Less Developed Countries*, N.Y.

UN (1973), *The Determinants and Consequences of Population Change*, N.Y.

UN (1974), *The Acquisition of Technology from Multinational Corporations by Developing Countries*, ST/ESA/12, N.Y.

UN (1975), *Multinational Corporations in World Development*, ST/ECA/190, N.Y.

United Nations Conference on Trade and Development (UNCTAD) (1965), *International Monetary Issues and the Developing Countries*, United Nations, N.Y.

UNCTAD (1968), *Proceedings* of the Conference, New Dehli.

UNCTAD (1972), *Proceedings* of the Conference, Santiago.

UNCTAD (1972), *Merchandise Trade*, N.Y.

UNCTAD (1975), *Major Issues arising from the Transfer of Technology to Developing Countries*, TD/B/AC.11/10/Rev.2, N.Y.

UNCTAD (1976a), *The Role of Transnational Corporations in the Trade in Manufactures and Semi-Manufactures of Developing Countries*, Support Paper, TD/185/Supp.2., Nairobi.

UNCTAD (1976b), *Transfer of Technology: Technological Dependence, its nature, consequences and policy implications*, 12, TD/190, Nairobi.

UNIDO (1972), Dasgupta, P., Sen, A. K., Marglin, S., *Guidelines for Project Evaluation*, Vienna.

Uzawa, H. (1962), "On a Two-sector Model of Economic Growth", *Review of Economic Studies*, **29**, 40–7.

Vaitsos, C. V. (1974), *Inter-country Income Distribution and Transnational Enterprises*, Oxford U.P., London.

Vernon, Raymond (1966), "International Investment and International Trade in the Product Cycle", *Quarterly Journal of Economies*, **80**, 2, 190–207.

Vernon, Raymond (1971), *Sovereignity at Bay: The Multinational Spread of US Enterprise*, Longman, London.

Wai, U. Tun (1957), "Interest Rates Outside the Organized Money Markets in Underdeveloped Countries", IMF *Staff Papers*, V1, 1.

Wai, U. Tun (1972), *Financial Intermediates and National Savings in Developing Countries*, Praeger, New York.

Wald, Haskell, P. (1969), "Taxation of Agriculture in Developing Economies", in Agarwala, A. N. and Singh, S. P. (eds) (1958).

Wallich, H. C. (1969), "Money and Growth: A Country Cross-Section Analysis", *Journal of Money, Credit and Banking*, **1**, 281–302.

Wang, N. T. (ed) (1976), *Taxation and Development*, Praeger, N.Y.

Williamson, Jeffrey, G. (1968), "Personal Savings in Developing Nations", *Economic Record*, **44**, 194–209.

Williamson, John, H. (1972), "SDRs, Interest and the Aid Link", *Banca Nazionale del Lavoro Quarterly Review*, June.

Williamson, John, H. (1973), International Liquidity: A Survey", *Economic Journal*, **83**, 685–746.

Zaidan, George, C. (1971), *The Costs and Benefits of Family Planning Programs*, IBRD and The Johns Hopkins Press, Baltimore and London.

Index

Absolute poverty, 221
absorptive capacity, of foreign resources, 183–5
accounting prices, 137
  of investment (API), 147
accounting rate of interest, 142–3
accumulation,
  Capital, 51, 168
acreage
  estimated price elasticities, 108–9
  response to prices, 107
Africa, 17
African small-holder supply elasticities, 107, 110–11
aggregate models, 120
agricultural
  production cycles, 5
  production seasons, 44
  promoting industrial growth, 44
  sector and Fei–Ranis model, 46
  surplus, 43, 103
agricultural production function, 53
agriculture
  marginal productivity of labour, 51
  predominance in national economy, 7
  role in economic development, 97 ff.
  and surplus labour, 42, 43
aid, 181
Algeria, 55
allocation of resources
  in money-markets, 76
    in traditional static economic theories, 58
"appropriate" technology, 196, 201
Argentina, 164, 167
Asia, 17, 77, 235
  south, 155
  south-east, 109, 155

Backward-bending supply curve of labour, 106
backward sector, in Sen model, 63
balance of payments
  constraints in LDCs, 59
  arguments, 158
balanced budget multiplier, 84
balanced growth,
  arguments against, 70
  between agriculture and industry, 43
  and unbalanced growth, 69
Balassa method, 162, 163
Bangladesh, 2, 56, 175, 219, 221
bank deposits, 82
barter transactions, 76
Bengal, 109
Bhagwati and Srinivasan model, 234
"big push", 69
Bihar, 109
bilateral financing, 188
border prices, 143, 145
bottlenecks, 71
  on demand side, 69
  on supply side, 85
Brazil, 163, 165, 166, 167, 196, 221, 224, 225

Cameroun, 110
capital
  intensive techniques, 66
  labour-ratio, 66
  malleable, 24
  markets in LDCs, 10, 11
  output-ratios, 24, 31, 66
  scarcity in LDCs, 59
capital-turnover criterion, 59–60
capitalism, 29
capitalist behaviour, in urban areas, 56
capitalist surplus, 42, 43
Central American Common Market (CACM), 177
Chad, 219
Chayanov's theory, 112–13
Chenery–Strout model, 189–92
Chile, 165, 166, 198–9
China, 2, 5, 73, 221
choice of capital intensity, 63–8
choice of techniques, 69
choice of technology and LDCs, 33
Chow-test, 207
classical theories of growth, 17
  limitations, 19
Cobb, Douglas, 50
Columbia, 6, 196, 199, 221
commercialisation in Fei–Ranis model, 46
Commodity Agreement Schemes, 174
Commodity-Buffer-Stock Scheme, 8
commodity "concentration" and
  foreign trade, 8
  of exports, 171, 172, 173, 177
commodity market, 11
Compensatory Financing Schemes (CFS), 175
consumer goods, 65
consumption
  marginal utility of, 52
  sacrificed, 65
Coppock's Log-variance index, 172, 179
Corden method, 162, 163, 164
cost-benefit analysis, 137
  basic principles, 138
  decision rules, 139
  Little and Mirrlees method, 140, 142–6
  reasons for undertaking in LDCs, 140–1
  United Nations Industrial Development Organization (UNIDO) guidelines, 146–9
cyclical plans, 117

DCs, comparison with LDCs, 1
deficit financing and LDCs, 88–90
demographic transition theory, 211
dependency theory, 33
development and growth, defined, 12, 13, 14
development planning models, 119 ff.
diminishing returns, 18
  for primary products in DCs, 8
disposable income, 86
distribution of income, uneven in LDCs, 58
Dixit–Marglin model, 52
domestic resources, for development, 75
domestic transformation curve, 152
dual-economy models, 40, 44, 55
  critique, 53–6
"dual-gap" analysis, 189
"dual" societies, 12
dualistic theories, predictions, 56
duality, 135
Durkin–Watson statistic, 39

East African Community (EAC), 177
economic development
  and population, 209–11
  problems of, 1
  strategies, 69
economic growth, 76, 162
  and trade, 168
economic models and economic planning, 117–18
economic planning, 116
economic theory and LDCs, 14
Ecuador, 221
EEC, 174
"effective" rates of protection (ERP), 159–65
Egypt, 2, 43, 44, 56
elasticity, of tax revenue, 94
elites, in LDCs, 13
emergency planning, 117
employment
  agricultural, 17
  coefficients, 131

policy, 235–6
problems, 228–30
Ethiopia, 110–11, 219
excess capacities, 89
in social capital, 71
expenditure tax, 91
exploitation, 10, 11, 33
rate of, 31
export instability
indices of, 178–80
in LDCs, 171
external diseconomies, 71, 156
externalities, 60, 68, 72, 141, 146, 171
dynamic, 118, 178

Factor-cost ratios, 68
factor markets, distortions, 157
factor–price differences between urban and rural areas, 69
farm management surveys, India, 112
farms, large, 112
Fei–Ranis model, 44–9, 54, 56
Feldman–Mahalanobis sectoral planning, 123–5
female education, importance of, 215
fertility
compulsory sterilization, and incentive payments, 219
and education, 215
factors affecting, 214
and income, 215–18
and mortality, 214–15
and population growth in LDCs, 213–19
and urbanization, 218–19
Field's models, 235
finance, 83
"financial dualism" in LDCs, 11, 19, 76
fiscal policies, 62, 114
objectives in LDCs, 67
fiscal policy
and growth, 84
in open economy, 86
foreign exchange gap, 182–3, 189–94
foreign resources (FR) concept, 181–2
criteria for distribution, 182–6
for projects or plans, 187–9
types, 186–7
foreign trade, and LDCs, 8
see also Chs 8 and 9
full employment, growth rate, 23
in Dixit–Morglin model, 52

General equilibrium analysis, 54, 55
generalized system of preferences (GSP), 179
geographic concentration, 171, 172
Ghana, 8, 43, 83, 110, 192
Gini coefficients 6, 15–16, 238
"golden age" economy, 24, 25
"Green Revolution", 6, 7, 49, 90, 93, 155, 229
growth theories, relevance to LDCs, 17 ff.
Guatemala, land tax, 93

Harris–Todaro model, 223
Harrod–Domar model, 22–4, 27, 87
Harrodian "knife-edge" problem, 24
in planning, 120–3
homogeneous labour, 53
Honduras, land tax, 93
hyperinflation, 78

Immiserizing growth, 168
import substitution, 33, 170
income distribution, 6, 83
and poverty, 220
within LDCs, 6, 14
India, 1, 2, 5, 8, 90, 91, 98, 106, 107, 108, 109, 164, 167, 175, 221
First Five Year Plan, 121–2
Second Five Year Plan, 123–5
indicative planning, 116
indirect taxation,
criticisms, 94
in LDCs, 93
Indonesia, 110
industrial sector
and Fei–Ranis model, 46
sluggish expansion in LDCs, 49
industrialization in LDCs, 7, 150
inequalities, 6
in developed countries, 220
income, 220
measurement of, 14, 15
in socialist countries, 220
infant industry argument, 62, 154
inflation, 62, 78, 140
and economic growth, 78–84
tax, 82
"informal" sector, 226
input-output analysis, in development planning, 128–32

inputs, allocation of in LDCs, 59
interest rates, 84
intermediate technology, 230, 236
International Bank for Reconstruction and Development (IBRD), 175
International Labour Organization (ILO), 197, 226, 227, 228, 229, 236
International Monetary Fund (IMF), index to measure instability in exports, 178
International Tin Agreement (1971), 170
investment criteria, *see* Ch. 4
Iran, in LDCs, 58–9
Iraq, 13, 83, 236
Ivory Coast, 110

Japan, 4, 53, 55, 92, 98, 155
joint ventures, 198
Jorgenson model, 49–52
  shortcomings, 54

Kaldor–Mirrlees model, 34–6
Kelly et al. model, 52
Kenya, 110, 177, 236
  and the Harrod–Domar model for planning, 122–3
  Report, 226–7
Keynesian theory, and LDCs, 19–22
Korea, South, 6, 196
"Kulak", in Asia, 90
Kuznets' hypothesis, 225

Labour,
  backward bending supply curve, 47
  in LDCs, 6
  market, 10
  to the non-agricultural sector, 97
  supply, 45
  surplus, 24
land
  fragmentation and distribution, 7, 9
  in LDCs, 9
  reform, 115, 226, 227
  tax, 92–3
Latin America, 17, 77, 219
  free trade association (LAFTA), 177
LDCs
  and agriculture, 7
  characteristics, 1
  and income distribution, 6
  and labour markets, 10
  and "open" growth models, 36
leisure
  and inferior goods, 47
  satiation, 47, 48
Lewis model, 40–4, 54
  limitations, 54
linear programming
  and development planning, 132–5
  and duality, 135–7
"link" and the SDRs, 203–8
Little and Mirrlees, method of project evaluation, 140, 142–6
Lomé convention (1975), 175
"Lorenz Curve", 15
low-level equilibrium trap, 212–13
"lumpy" social capital, 69

Macro-econometric models, in development planning, 125 ff.
Mahalanobis model, 123–5
Malaya, 165, 166
Malaysia, 109, 239
Mao, 99
marginal product, of labour, 6, 40, 42, 45
marginal productivity, of labour, 21
marketed surplus, 99
  and capital formation, 99
  and terms of trade, 100–3
markets
  prices, 58
  types of, in LDCs, 9, 58, 75–6
Malthusian theory of population, 17–19, 28, 210
Marx's theory and LDCs, 28–32
maximization of the rate of creation of investible surplus, principle, 61–2
Mercantilists, 32
Mexico, 164, 166, 167, 221, 224, 225
micro-planning, and cost benefit analysis, 137–49
migration of labour, rural-urban, 230–5
modern sector, in Sen model, 63
Moghuls, 53
money and economic growth, 76–8

money markets
in LDCs, 75–6
role in LDCs, 76
money supply, and Keynesian theory, 20
most favoured nation, tariff, 178
most seriously affected (MSA) countries, 175
multilateral, foreign resources, 186
multinationals, 34
and policies, 200–1
and the transfer of technology, 197–201
multiplier, 85
balanced budget, 84–6
and LDCs, 22
money and real income, 21, 90
Mundell's model, 78–84

Nairobi, UNCTAD Conference (1976), 175
neo-classical theory, of growth and the LDCs, 24–8
neo-Marxist theory of underdevelopment, 32–4
Nicaragua, land tax, 93
Nigeria, 39, 110, 111
nominal income, 86
nominal rates of protection (NRP), 159–65
non-traded
goods, 144, 162
inputs, 149, 163
North-South Dialogue, 8
Norway, 166

Opportunity cost of labour, 61
optimum tariff, 154
optimum technology, 68
organization, 11
Organization for Petroleum Exporting Countries (OPEC), 174
organized money markets, 75
overpricing by the multinationals, 198–9
overvaluation of currency, 141

Pakistan, 56, 108, 109, 163–4, 166, 167, 175, 221
partial equilibrium analysis, 156
partially traded goods, 144
Peacock and Shaw model, 87–8
per capita income, as index for measurement, 12
perspective planning, 117
Peru, 3, 39, 221
Philippines, 108, 164, 166, 167
planning, 71
development, 119 ff.
types of, 116–17
case for and against, 118, 119
Harrod–Domar model, 120
indicative, 116
Polak–Boissonneult model, 37–9
population
and economic development, 209–11
explosion, 211–12
in LDCs, 5
poverty
absolute, 221
definition of, 237–9
evidence from LDCs, 6
and income distribution, 220
indices of, 237–9
Sen index, 237–9
Prebisch thesis, 170
primary products demand, 8
product-cycle hypothesis, 201
production conditions, in LDCs, 9
production functions, Cobb–Douglas type, 50
productivity
and LDCs, 33
low, 5, 33
project appraisal, micro, 137 ff.
protected industries, 62
profit maximisation, 5, 28, 68
protection, 33
cost of, 165
nominal and effective, 159–65
Punjab, 107, 108, 109

Quotas, 119

Real wages, 46
redistribution, with growth, 226–8
regional co-operation, among LDCs, 176–7
reinvestible surplus criterion, 62–9
rent, 106
research and development (R & D), 201

resource-allocation, in LDCs, 58, 59
rural-urban migration, 43, 230–5
Rybczynski theorems, 168

Savings constraint, 192
savings gap, 182, 189–94
Say's Law, 71
Scott's method, 162, 163, 164
seasonalities, 5
sectional allocation, of investments in LDCs, 58
sectoral models, 120
"seige" economy, 167
shadow exchange rates, 147, 148–9
"shadow prices", 11, 51, 136
shadow wages rate, 142, 143
share croppings, economic theory of, 115
Sierra Leone, 110, 111
size-holdings, and size of surplus, 107
social marginal productivity
  criterion, 60
  criticisms, 60, 61
social opportunity cost, of labour, 152
South East Asian Nations, Association of (ASEAN), 177
Spanish America, 56
Special Drawing Rights (SDR), 201
  allocation use and resource transfer, the empirical evidence, 205–8
  distribution of, 202
  and the "link", 201, 203–8
Sri Lanka, 6, 8, 90, 91, 196, 221, 224, 229
stability principle, 185
standard conversion factor (SCF), 145
sterilisation, 219
subsidiaries, of multinationals, 196
subsistence levels, 55
Supplementary Financing Scheme, 175
supply inelasticities in LDCs, 78
"surplus" labour, 40
  and growth of the economy, 41 ff.
  and shadow prices, 51
"Surplus", marketed, 99
  empirical estimates, 107
  from agriculture, 97
  model to mobilize agricultural surplus, 103–6
  size-holdings and output, 107
  and terms of trade, 100

Taiwan, 6, 44, 73, 217, 221
Tanzania, 111, 177, 236
tariffs, 141
  and balance of payments, 158
  in economic development, 151–4
  and employment, 158
  optimum, 151
tax
  on agriculture in Japan, 98
  expenditure, 91
  gift, profit, wealth, 91
  structures in LDCs, 90
taxes
  direct in LDCs, 90–3
  indirect in LDCs, 93–6
  land, 92–3, 114
technical progress, 170, 171
  neutral, 27, 31
technological dualism, in Kelly et al. model, 52
technology
  choice of, 33, 67
  transfer, 194 ff.
techniques of production in LDCs, 59
tenurial disincentives, 112
terms of trade, 70
  between DCs and LDCs, 169
  in Dixit–Marglin model, 52
  in Jorgenson model, 49
  in Kelly et al. model, 53
Thailand, 83, 107
tied, foreign resources, 186
time horizon, in Sen model, 65
Todaro model, 230–3
trade and economic growth, 168
trade gap, 182–3, 189–94
traded goods, 144
transfer-pricing, 199
transfer of savings, 53
transfer of technology, 194
  benefits and costs to the LDCs, 197–200
  and foreign private investment, 194
  policies to deal with the problems of, 200–2
  and types, 195–7
transformation curve, 48

transitory income index, of Knudsen and Parnes, 172–3, 179–80
"Turn-key" projects, 196

Uganda, 110, 177
unbalanced growth, 71–2
  reconciliation with balanced growth, 72–3
UNCTAD, 8, 173
under-employment
  in LDCs, 5, 10
unemployment
  disguised, 5, 10, 21, 44
  in LDCs, 5
unequal exchange, 32
United Nations Index, to measure export instability, 178
United Nations Industrial Development Organization (UNIDO): guidelines in project appraisal, 146–9
unorganized money markets, 75
united foreign resources, 186
Upper Volta, 219
"urban bias", 7
urbanization, and fertility, 218
Uruguay, 83

Value Added Tax, 95–6
variables, slack, 135
Venezuela, 3, 221
"vicious" circle and capital, 11

"Wage-gap" theory, 201
wages
  industrial, in Jorgenson model, 49
  in LDCs, 10
  and unemployment, 141
  urban and rural, in Fei-Ranis model, 47
wealth distribution, 141
welfare loss, in trade, 168
World Bank, 175
world prices, 145, 146, 149
"working" poor in the rural and urban areas, 226